Praise for
I Had the Strangest Dream . . .

"The lines of communication to God are not just open during the day, but are available 24/7. In fact, some of our most profound revelations may be coming to us through our dreams. I'm not sure that there is any such thing as 'the last word' on dream interpretation, but this book is a fascinating tool with which to begin. It opens us to a parcel of intriguing possibilities!"

—Neale Donald Walsch, bestselling author of the
Conversations with God series

"In a world of abundant political, economical, and religious diversity, it is always inspirational to come across a film or book that puts us all on the same page. I HAD THE STRANGEST DREAM is one of those books . . . Use this book not only to interpret your dreams, but as an enlightenment tool and a touchstone to remember who you are and why you came here."

—Steven Simon, producer/director/co-founder
of the Spiritual Cinema Circle

"Kelly integrates her vast knowledge of dream analysis with her wisdom, compassion, and spirituality to create a book that truly gives insight into the place in our minds where we come our deepest thoughts, emotions and fears."

olate
soul series

"If you want to learn about hi ages that are guiding your earthwalk, and are already moving you to a greater sense of self-love, then read this book!"

—Charlene M. Proctor, PhD, author of the bestselling
*Let Your Goddess Grow: 7 Spiritual Lessons on
Female Power and Positive Thinking*

"Finally a resource book that has everything. A masterpiece of information."

—Eric DelaBarre, author of *Why Not: Start Living Your Life Today* and screenwriter of *Conversations with God*

"Kelly Sullivan Walden has an ability to inform, and yet present that information so that it becomes a tool for self-discovery, for inner growth—and that's exactly what she does in I HAD THE STRANGEST DREAM."

—Ruth Light, president, Women's National Book Association, Los Angeles chapter

"Kelly's amazing insights will guide us all to listen deeper to our own inner voice that is attempting to reach us in our dreams . . . This is one of those unique books that is a powerful gift to all that read it!"

—Renee Piane, internationally known love and dating consultant, president of Rapid Dating, and author of *Love Mechanics*

"Kelly has the ability to ignite our truth and clarity through her powerful words of wisdom. In this way and through this book, she brings the understanding of our dreams to a new, enlightening, and uplifting level."

—Robert Silverstone, professional coach and creator of The GROW Principle

"Kelly's phenomenal book is a cutting-edge take on dream analysis, with vary relevant information on issues that we face in our society today. Kelly is both knowledgeable and sensitive with her interpretations, coupled with her obvious spirituality, she has created a dream dictionary with insights for the twenty-first century!"

—Gypsy Racco, musician

I HAD
THE
STRANGEST
DREAM . . .

The Dreamer's Dictionary
for the 21st Century

KELLY SULLIVAN WALDEN

WARNER BOOKS

NEW YORK   BOSTON

Copyright © 2006 by Kelly Sullivan Walden
All rights reserved.

Warner Books
Hachette Book Group USA
1271 Avenue of the Americas, New York, NY 10020

Printed in the United States of America

Warner Books and the "W" logo are trademarks of Time Warner Inc. or an affiliated company. Used under license by Hachette Book Group USA, which is not affiliated with Time Warner, Inc.

ISBN-10: 0-446-69603-X
ISBN-13: 978-0-446-69603-6

Cover design by Brigid Pearson
Cover photo: Ross Anania/GettyImages (RF)
Book design by Stratford Publishing Services, Inc.

To all dreamers everywhere, for your boldness,
courage, passion, and curiosity to journey into the
enchanted and mysterious world of your dreams:
Were it not for you, I never would have been blessed
with the opportunity to create this book.

Acknowledgments

My love and appreciation go out to the following angels:

Dana Walden, for being the best support system, editor, space holder, hero, champion, love of my life, wind beneath my wings, and husband a woman could ever ask for— thank you to the ends of the universe for your meticulous research and for literally living and dreaming every symbol to help me find its authenticity. The Sullivans—Dad, Mom, Shannon, Jeanene, Amber, Tawni, Noel, Granny Sullivan, Andy, Jackie, and the whole Sullivan Stew—you are the family of my dreams, and I love you beyond what words can ever say. Thank you from the bottom of my Sullivan heart for all your love and support. Andie Avila, for your passion and excitement for dreams and for this project, for sharing your dreams with me, as well as coming up with the book's fabulous title. You are a writer's dream come true! Jessica Papin, for being the brilliant goddess that masterminded this project into *wo*manifestation for me. Jim McCarthy, for stepping up to the plate and becoming my agent and for always being a calm voice of wisdom. Jo-e Sutton (Betty), for contributing so many pearls to this book. I am the luckiest cheese-loving goddess on this planet because of your exquisite friendship. Gypsy Racco, for your soul sisterhood and friendship that runs beyond the core of the earth. Tami Walsh, for your prayers, support, friendship, and inspiration. Uncle Rich, for supporting and believing in me. Glenna Walden, for your "Thought for the Day" that always keeps me moving in the direction of my dreams. Esther and Jerry Hicks and Abraham, for your brilliant words of truth that inspire me to create the life of my dreams from a place of pure joy. Byron Katie, for your powerful awakening tools. Carl Jung, for the freedom and permission you gave to dreamers to interpret their dreams based on their own associations. Marianne Williamson, for being one of my spiritual role models and for being a reminder that only love is real. Oprah Winfrey, for doing what you do, and for supporting me in ways you will never know. Alex Power, for your adventurous and inspirational self and for lending me a fantastic laptop. Katherine Newcomer, for your sweet presence, support, and enthusiasm, and for being my MySpace.com champion. The Goddess Queens—Jodi Sutton, Suzanne Rock Sterlie, Jean Molina, Wendy Anton Saez, Helen Djukic, Suzanne Quin Hirabayashi, Firestar, and Ruth de Sosa—for supporting me with your love, strength, power, and vision. Woofie, for lying by my side for the duration of this project, for unconditionally loving me, and giving me the warm and fuzzies to persist when I felt weary. Gini Gentry, for taking me through the Teotihuacan journey and for your invaluable feedback on this book. Reverend Michael Beckwith, my beloved Agape Family, for your spiritual strength and for giving me such fantastic tools for awakening. Jane Dystel and Miriam Godderich, for representing me and being a powerful force in the literary world. I feel so honored to have your support. The prestigious publishing team at Warner Books (Hachette Book Group USA), for your commitment to excellence in the world of publishing, and for allowing me to participate in the collective genius and legacy that you have so powerfully cocreated.

Author's Note

In a real sense, all life is interrelated. All men are caught in an inescapable network of mutuality; tied in a single garment of destiny. Whatever affects one directly affects all indirectly. . . . I can never be what I ought to be until you are what you ought to be. You can never be what you ought to be until I am what I ought to be. . . . This is the interrelated structure of reality.

—Rev. Martin Luther King Jr.

Some say that the world we live in is a collective dream, and that we as global citizens are all dreaming our world together. I believe it is the destiny of every person to awaken. Our destination is fixed, but our timetable is not. Those who sincerely desire to awaken to their magnificence by taking 100 percent responsibility for their lives, and dream heaven into being, are awakening now. Those who'd prefer to put their awakening on the layaway plan, and continue to blame others for their suffering, are welcome to wait. The fact that you are reading this now, during this most important time in our human evolution, indicates that you are one of the pioneers, blazing a trail to awakening.

My intent with this book is to empower and inspire you to become fluent in the language of your dreams so we can fly together through the galaxy of our collective unconscious, bring down to earth the treasures we discover that are beyond measure, make our

"Dreams" come true, and cocreate heaven on earth. As you awaken, you inspire me to awaken, and as I awaken, I will inspire you to awaken . . . and in this way, we will fulfill our individual and collective intentions for incarnating in this dimension. Put your seat belt on and take a deep breath, because understanding your dreams is your rocket fuel to self-realization!

Sweet Dreams,
Kelly

Nothing can be so silly, so impossible, or so unnatural that it cannot happen in a dream.

—CICERO

Your life is a path. Knowingly or unknowingly you have been on a vision quest. It is good to have a vision, a dream.

—AGNES WHISTLING ELK

Dreams are often most profound when they seem the most crazy.

—SIGMUND FREUD

Introduction

"I had the strangest dream!" How many times have you heard that expression fly out of your mouth, and in the telling of the tale found yourself bewildered on that mystical bridge between asleep and awake, scratching your head, asking the question, *"I wonder what it means?"*

As we ponder what it all means, take heart in knowing that it is rare *not* to have a strange dream. In fact, we should be so grateful for our sojourn in the dream world. As scientific evidence demonstrates, depriving a person of his or her dreams for several days encourages psychotic tendencies in the awakened state. We could say that we need to dream more than we need to sleep!

Our nighttime journey begins when our conscious mind takes its bow for the day, exhausted from sixteen hours of appropriate, politically correct behavior, stuffing animal instincts into man-made cubicles of efficiency and order, squelching our desire to make out with the sexy new coworker, resisting the temptation to tell the boss to (bleep) off, dotting i's, crossing t's . . . not to mention minding our p's and q's until we can't see straight. *Whew!* The conscious mind collapses backstage while our subconscious mind, champing at the bit, lunges forth onto center stage for the *Late Show* of our lives where all that was suppressed by day gets expressed by night.

In our fast-paced world of globalization, double half-caf low-cal no-whip soy mochachinos, and turbo-speed Internet access, our dreams are working overtime to keep us sane. Dancing wildly in the gray matter of today's dreamer are such symbols as blog, life coach, laptop, terrorist, eBay, TiVo, and Starbucks, which *I Had the Strangest*

Dream . . . decodes. Instead of a horse and carriage, a modern dreamer might dream of a fuel-efficient hybrid car zipping past gridlock traffic in a HOV lane. Instead of penning a letter with a quill, you might dream of sitting in a cyber café e-mailing a friend. Instead of surfing the ocean blue, you might dream of surfing the Web and meeting Mr. or Ms. Right on Match.com. So, in addition to over three thousand classic dream symbols, *I Had the Strangest Dream . . .* includes such contemporary symbols as BlackBerry, bling bling, blipverts, Botox, buddy list, Curves, Donald Trump, DVD, e-book, frappuccino, Internet, Internet café, key word, Kinko's, liposuction, Match.com, metro-sexual, MLM, MTV, multiplex, Netflix, Oprah Winfrey, rapid dating, retail therapy, ring tone, screen saver, search engine, Viagra, Web site, and World Wide Web. Understanding the symbolism behind these twenty-first-century words will help you keep up with your dreams, which are trying desperately to keep up with you!

Our unedited, unscripted, unrated, uncensored, graphic, high-speed, high-tech, sometimes violent, and XXX dreams toss out the G-rated niceties of our public persona. In our nighttime dream theater our still, small voice of intuition and authenticity gets a bullhorn and runs the show without constraints. We call them "strange dreams" because they act out the metaphors we speak when we are awake. In our waking reality it's common to say *"I'm so hungry I could eat a horse." "That guy is a pain in the neck." "You're pulling my leg." "How many frogs will I have to kiss before I find my prince?" "When pigs fly!"* and *"After he kissed me I felt ten feet tall and I was walking on air!"* We think nothing of it when we hear these figures of speech, but when we recount a dream where we are kissing a frog while pigs are flying overhead, and we are dancing on air as high as a kite, we call it *strange*! So, the mantra to keep in mind as you decode the mystery of your dreams is *"Metaphors be with me!"*

Dreams . . . a Mysterious Wake-up Call

Your vision will become clear only when you can look into your heart. Who looks outside, dreams; who looks inside, awakens.
                                                              —CARL JUNG

Extensive research at Harvard University, the University of Chicago, the Walter Reed Institute of Research, and Mount Sinai Hospital has revealed that we dream between three and nine dreams a night. It's also estimated that we dream for a minimum of two hours every night. If a typical lifespan is seventy years, that means we'll spend 51,100 hours of our lives dreaming! Doesn't it make sense to take an interest in exploring this landscape you visit for 51,100 hours of your life? So, whether you are one of those rare creatures who vividly remember your dreams, or one who has only a single recurring dream, know that your dreams are a great ally. Dreams can indicate the obstacles blocking your greatest expression, and/or illuminate your most direct route to awareness and personal fulfillment. Fortunately, you don't have to understand your dreams or remember them in order to benefit from their power and influence. However, working deeply with your dreams can accelerate and amplify your ability to *grow* through the stresses of modern life and eventually *glow* through them! The following examples demonstrate how dream interpretation can lead to life-altering changes.

David's Dream

I was at work, sitting at my overcrowded desk, I was looking up a number on my BlackBerry . . . business as usual. Suddenly, a man with a gun came in and told us we were all his hostages. I thought to myself, "I KNEW I should have left this job a long time ago . . . had I only listened to my intuition, I wouldn't have to die here at this dreadful job!" Just then the man with the gun wanted to know what time it was, but there were no clocks or watches anywhere in the office. I told the man with the gun I had a clock in my car. The gunman ordered, "OK, go check the time and come right back!" I made sure to sneak my wallet and BlackBerry into my pocket as I dashed out of the building. Once outside, I got into my car, on the driver's side, and drove away.

David's dream brought to his awareness the negative impact his work environment was having on him: the *overcrowded desk* signified an inability to be in control of his life, and that he was *under the gun* to make a drastic change. The *man with the gun* demonstrated his subconscious taking desperate measures, holding David hostage long enough for him to get the message that it was *time* for a reality check. When David saw his opportunity to leave, he took his *wallet* (sense of self-worth) and his *BlackBerry* (organization, order, self-empowerment) and escaped from the *building* (his former identity and belief structure), and got into the *driver's seat of his car* (position of power) and drove away to freedom.

David hated his job of twenty years. Even though he knew in his heart it was time to leave, he was held captive by the security it provided. Soon after he experienced this dream, David quit his job and began working as a freelance writer, his secret passion, and has never been happier and has never looked back.

Joanne's Dream

I was in a wheelchair at a family gathering in my childhood home, sitting alone in a corner. A handsome man, also in a wheelchair, approached me and said that we were supposed to be together, as a couple, because we were soul mates. I asked him why he thought we were soul mates, and he replied, "We're both crippled." I told the man, "I'm so sorry, I'm not really crippled, I just like this chair."

Joanne needed some guidance understanding her dream. She was shocked when I told her this dream was actually a breakthrough: her dream revealed that she was attracting intimate relationships that were based on pain and injury, symbolized by the *wheelchair*. She told me that because of her sensitivity to people's pain, often she would develop similar injuries. Her dream was revealing that her extreme empathy was crippling her. She was at her *childhood home* during a *family gathering*, which symbolized her role as a caretaker in the family as a young girl. Joanne also revealed to me that she was a sickly child, who never felt that she received enough nurturing. This dream uncovered that even though she was now a healthy adult, she was still relating to herself as an injured caretaker. Ultimately this dream was a breakthrough in that it revealed her relationship patterns and demonstrated her willingness to change ("I'm so sorry, I am really not crippled"). With this awareness, Joanne began to drastically alter her relationship patterns and began connecting with people from a place of wholeness, as well as relating to herself as a healthy, vital, and powerful woman.

Good News & Bad News

This book will provide you with the meanings of the symbols you dream about and the tools for interpretation. The good news: there is more than one way to interpret a dream. The bad news: there is more than one way to interpret a dream. The dream symbols interpreted in this book have been inspired by Jungian, Freudian, Hindu, shamanic, and Goddess symbolism, and the miracle of intuition. When these definitions are conjoined with the vastness of your own intuition you are ready to discover the secrets of sleep and the miracles within. Allow this book to be a helpful guide, not a dictator. Remember, this is *your* journey and this book is here to assist, support, and suggest. So, if your instinct about a dream symbol is 180 degrees different from what you read here, by all means, follow your hunches and associations.

The best news about dream interpretation is the opportunity for self-empowerment. I hold nothing against therapy and/or seeking out a special and qualified person to help you through a challenging time. However, I'm of the school of thought that says: *"Feed a man a fish, you feed him for a day; teach a man to fish, you feed him for the rest of his life."* When you learn to interpret your own inner guidance (that is yours for the taking on a daily/nightly basis), you become your own best friend, therapist, and wise counselor. In other words, you become empowered, confident, bold, and a force to be reckoned with. So, until you become your own guide, keep this book on your bedside table, highlight what rings true, cross out what doesn't, write your own hunches in the margins, dog-ear the pages . . . and make this the most worn-out book you've ever owned!

The absolute best news is the possibility of building the life of your dreams via mastery over your nighttime journeys into your sub-conscious mind. Imagine an aspect of your life that you desire to

uplevel, such as your finances, relationships, health, or well-being. If
you listen to a CD, watch affirmative programming, or read inspirational literature right before you slip into the dream state, you will
incorporate these feelings and images into your subconscious mind,
which will in turn begin to express them through your dreams. This
is the fast track to creating a receptive and resonant consciousness
that will quickly prepare you to draw to yourself the fulfillment of
your heart and soul desires.

Dream Classifications

Dreams are therapeutic, cathartic, predictive, cleansing, healing, inspiring, and enable rebuilding and processing. In order to make sense
of these multifaceted, multipurposed, multilayered, and multiplat-
inum gifts that you awaken with each morning, it is helpful to know
how to categorize them. There are telltale signs within each dream
classification to help you discern whether they are helping you to
process information, release negativity, embrace your shadow, break
through limitations, predict the future, receive inspiration from your
higher self, or create a life of your dreams. To simplify this process,
the eight types of dreams can be divided into two major categories:
past and future.

Dreams that deal with your *past* are about clearing the clutter of
your mind by removing negativity, fear, and overwhelm. Dreams dealing with the past include: processing dreams, venting dreams, integration dreams, breakdown/breakthrough dreams, and recurring dreams.

Dreams that deal with your *future* assist you by giving you solutions, preparing you for and inspiring you toward a brighter future
and the creation of your heart's and soul's desires. Dreams dealing
with the future include: precognitive dreams, prophetic dreams, wish
fulfillment dreams, and recurring dreams. (The only type of dream
that deals with both the past and the future is the recurring dream.)

The following descriptions of these eight dream categories and
dreamtime characters will help you organize and make sense of your
dreams.

Processing Dreams (aka "Personal Assistant")

Imagine that you have an after-hours Personal Assistant whose job is to render spotless the messy office of your mind every night while you're asleep. Your Personal Assistant gets out the DustBuster and cleans up the clutter, files important documents, discards irrelevant scraps, and helps find solutions and ideas for questions that were posed throughout the day. Is it any wonder that when people are unsure about a decision they say *"Let me sleep on it . . . I'll let you know in the morning."*

Michelle had just given birth to a beautiful baby girl. When the doctor asked her what the baby's name was, Michelle's mind was a blank. "How can I possibly know my baby's name when I just met her. I have about twenty names on a list, but I was hoping that my baby would somehow let me know what she wanted to be called." That night Michelle went to sleep asking the question "What is your name?"

Michelle's Processing Dream

There was a happy little girl swinging on a swing set. Off in the distance, I heard a woman (the little girl's mother) call out to her, "Noel. It's time to go home, Noel!" The little girl jumped off the swing, smiled at me, and ran off toward her mother.

Michelle awoke the next morning to the sound of her newborn baby crying. As she rocked her in her arms, she whispered, *"Hi, Noel."* The baby quieted down and smiled. Michelle's processing dream helped her to pick the name for her daughter. And you've never met a little girl with a name more perfectly suited to her.

The Personal Assistant looks at your questions and loose ends from the day's events and works the night shift until there is clarity. You may have gone to sleep confused, weary, and overwhelmed, but because of your processing dreams (your Personal Assistant), you awaken the next morning to a mental space that is spick and span, so you are mentally, spiritually, and emotionally prepared to take on the day.

When: Processing dreams usually take place during the first two hours of sleep.

Telltale Signs of a Processing Dream: You dream about unresolved issues in your day-to-day life, and the content is filled with people you are currently interacting with and/or situations you are working on.

Suggestions: Take note of the guidance and clarity you've gleaned and turn it into action (e.g., *"I'll call Bill about helping me with the PowerPoint presentation!"*). If you are irritated with the extensiveness of your processing dreams, try writing an inventory of the day's events before you go to sleep. This will help the Personal Assistant to get you organized and make it easier to transition into a deeper more restful sleep.

Mantra: *"Let me sleep on it."*

Venting Dreams (aka "Pool Man")

Venting dreams are nightmares that, in spite of being traumatic, are extremely helpful and therapeutic. They represent your subconscious mind's attempt to assist you with the process of cleaning out the old in order to make room for the new. They usually occur as nightmares or frightmares; anxiety dreams that leave you shaken up. They are showing you what you are ready to release. Think of venting dreams as the energetic Pool Man whose area of expertise is sweeping the floor of your emotional pool. The Pool Man stirs up your greatest fears, resentments, and unresolved wounds that have been lurking at the bottom of your pool. Once all of this nonsupportive energy surfaces, it can then be skimmed away so that you can have a nice, clean, refreshing emotional pool in which to swim.

Wendy's Venting Dream

I was running for my life down a hill and my boyfriend, with a crazed and controlling look on his face, was chasing me with a knife. He kept screaming for me to get in his car!

Wendy was venting her fear of being controlled and losing her freedom in a monogamous relationship. The *knife* represented her fear that monogamy would not only cut away at her freedom, but that it would take her *downhill* and eventually kill her. Because she had been single for so long, she was a self-professed *control freak*. Though she desperately wanted to be in a committed relationship, she was afraid of giving up being in the driver's seat (*get in his car*) to anyone.

At first when Wendy shared this dream with me, she was afraid it was a premonition that her boyfriend would turn out to be a *Fatal Attraction* type. To me, her dream had the signs of a venting dream written all over it. I shared this with her and she slowly, yet bravely tiptoed in the direction of deeper and deeper love and commitment. Her venting dream (and the many that followed) helped her to release her barriers to love so that she could actually have her heart's desire.

The Pool Man pokes and prods at your limiting beliefs and deepest fears that haunt you and keep you stuck in unworkable patterns. When you awaken from a scary dream and lift your head from your tear-drenched pillow, give thanks for knowing that the dream is helping you to release nonsupportive energy so that, upon waking, you can deal with situations in your life more confidently.

Keep in mind that if you watch the news or a horror movie before going to sleep, you are giving your Pool Man a lot more work to do, and you can bet that your dreams will be scary. You are, however, less likely to have venting dreams if you read, listen to, or watch life-affirming literature, music, or programming before going to sleep.

When: Venting dreams usually take place during the final two to three hours of your sleep cycle.

Telltale Signs of a Venting Dream: There are gradations of intensity. On the low end of the scale, you feel mildly disturbed upon awakening. On the high side of the scale, you are jolted awake from your personal horror movie, with your heart racing, brow sweating, and mouth as dry as cotton, feeling as if you've seen a ghost.

Suggestion: Ask yourself the question *"What fear, resentment, or limiting belief is my subconscious mind attempting to release?"*

Mantra: *"I can't heal what I can't feel."*

Integration Dreams (aka "Artist")

You are an infinite being, housed within a finite space known as your body. If you've ever dabbled in metaphysics, you know that you are connected to everything and everyone. You are a microcosm of humanity. Not just the heroic, brave, saintly aspects, but the villainous and the thieving as well, and everything in between . . . all the aspects that you are proud to be associated with, and others you'd prefer not to touch with a ten-foot pole. Any association you deny, the dark and seedy, or even the extremely wise and noble, will rattle your cage during the night until you face and embrace that it is you.

Your integration dreams are like your inner Artist that sees every color on your human palette as beautiful. Your Artist does not see the pastel colors as more interesting than the dark tones, or the muted colors as more fascinating than the bright tones. In fact your Artist is a master of blending the colors of your inner rainbow, shadows with light and light with shadows, to paint the masterpiece of your life.

In the dreamtime, your Artist rescues colors that you have rejected, lost, or disowned and returns them to the palette of your heart so they can be integrated. Reconnecting can at first be disorienting, uncomfortable, and even disturbing. However, once you've adjusted, you'll discover new dimensions of yourself, and a greater mastery within.

A few years ago, Melanie was in the middle of an extremely painful argument with her best friend, Sharon. Harsh words were spoken over what seemed to be irreconcilable differences, and it felt as though the bridge of their friendship was burned to a crisp. Melanie couldn't understand why Sharon was *"Being such a drama queen!"* Melanie had utter disdain for Sharon's reaction; disowning it in herself, and without knowing it, she was projecting it onto Sharon. Well, Melanie's integration dream gave her a wake-up call she'll never forget.

Melanie's Integration Dream

> I walked into a room where a couple of women were talking; they stopped when they saw me come in and told me that they no longer wanted to work with me because they didn't like being around me. I was devastated and heartbroken. I yelled, "This is betrayal!" and thought to myself, "This must have been how Sharon felt."

Melanie woke up with tears stinging her face, and a newfound compassion for Sharon. Sharon had been playing out an aspect of humanity that was too painful for Melanie to admit was within herself. Melanie called to tell Sharon of this dream. Melanie said, "I understand why you were so upset, and I am so sorry that my actions hurt you. Please forgive me." Sharon did and was grateful that Melanie finally understood her. The interesting thing is that not only did Melanie gain back her best friend, but she reclaimed an important aspect of herself.

When: Integration dreams take place anytime, but usually within the last two hours of sleep.

Telltale Signs of an Integration Dream: You dream that you or someone else is acting out in an extreme way, or you have a judgmental reaction to the behavior of someone in your dream.

Suggestion: Open your mind to the possibility that every character in your dream is you. I know this may be difficult if you dream of a scary, needy, vicious, jealous, vindictive, or even an extremely virtuous, successful, or heroic person. Know that this character isn't *all* of you, but a part of the infinite spectrum of humanity that is within you. Embrace the missing color and feel compassion flood your being. As you do this you will be making great strides in the reclamation of your wholeness and oneness.

Mantra: *"Face and embrace the fact that there is no such thing as an ugly color!"*

Breakdown/Breakthrough Dreams (aka "Construction Worker")

As a spiritual being having a human experience, you are constantly moving from glory to greater glory. In other words, once you get comfortable and cozy in one identity or life construct, you can bet your bottom dollar that your ol' friend Change is going to pay you a visit. You can either welcome Change with open arms, or he will huff and puff and . . . well, you know the rest.

Most human beings cling ferociously to a mere semblance of life, and try (unsuccessfully) to avoid change/death/transition/transformation at all costs. We tend to think that our lives should always be characterized by having it all together—thus the human comedy.

During a particularly challenging transition in my life (challenging only because I was resisting it), I had the following breakdown/breakthrough dream that gave me quite a chuckle.

Kelly's Breakdown/Breakthrough Dream

I was walking through the airport while there was construction going on. Scaffolding, chain saws, hammering, sawdust everywhere; it was a horrible mess. I noticed a sign that read "Pardon the Mess. Renovations in Progress."

Being at the airport meant that soon I would be taking off, traveling toward adventures untold, and I was walking through a great transition that I judged a shameful mess. When in actuality, something wonderful was in the process of being created . . . so what was all the drama about? The dream gave me an empowering and reassuring context to hold on to while I went through that particular transition, and through the many transitions I've ventured through since.

When: Breakdown/breakthrough dreams can take place anytime, but you are most likely to remember the ones you have just before awakening.

Telltale Signs of a Breakdown/Breakthrough Dream: You dream of disaster, death, fires, tornadoes, floods, earthquakes, structures falling down and/or being rebuilt.

Suggestions: Inquire within as to what structure in your life is breaking down or being reconstructed (relationships, work, home, creativity, health, finance, etc.). Once you've identified this, ask yourself the following questions: *"How can I most powerfully participate in the releasing of my old attachments?"* and *"How can I most powerfully participate in the creation of what is next for me?"*

Mantra: *"Pardon the mess. Renovations in progress."*

Recurring Dreams (aka "Secret Agent")

Your recurring dreams are like a Secret Agent, on a mission for the SIA (Subconscious Intelligence Agency). The mission: to deliver a message to your conscious mind that will either clear up an issue from the past or move you toward a more desirable future, should you choose to accept it. Until the mission is accomplished, the Secret Agent will try again and again until the message is received and decoded successfully.

Jacqueline's Recurring Dream

> My husband is leaving me for another woman . . . he is walking out the door, with a look of repulsion. He says, "You're too needy, clingy, and insecure . . . I can't take it anymore . . . get a life!"

Jacqueline told me she was desperately in love with her husband and had built her entire life around him. At least once a week for three years this nightmare would awaken her. And she was progressively becoming more insecure. She felt certain and terrified that it was just a matter of time before her husband would actually leave. I asked her, "What message do you think your recurring dream is trying to send you?"

She replied, "My dream seems to keep telling me to get a life . . . a life outside of my husband. Maybe that would make me less needy and clingy."

"Bravo," I cheered. "What might 'getting a life' look like?"

Jacqueline replied after some thought, "Well, I used to love to dance before we got married. But my husband has two left feet, so I've given it up because I feel uncomfortable dancing with other men . . . I feel like I'm being unfaithful."

"What about belly dancing?" I suggested. "You don't have to dance with a partner to enjoy that form of dancing; in fact, it's usually an all women-sisterhood-solo kind of thing."

Jacqueline soon began belly dancing and within a short time she became quite masterful. She started performing and developed a large circle of friends and a very active social life. A year later, she was glowing. I asked her if her recurring dream was still haunting her. At first she looked at me blankly as if she had no idea what I was talking about. Then she laughed as she remembered. "Oh that! I haven't had that dream in ages! And, by the way, my relationship is better than ever. My husband loves coming to see my performances and is so proud of me. He's never been more affectionate and expressive with his emotions. Since I 'got a life' apart from him, I feel that he finally appreciates me!"

To reveal the message your recurring dream has been working so hard to send, inquire into its intent. While you contemplate and meditate on the familiar scenes and re-create its feeling tone, ask yourself, *"What message is my recurring dream trying to send?"* In Jacqueline's case, the message was directing her to develop an independent sense of self. However, the message of your recurring dream might be to forgive someone, to recognize your gifts, to pursue a particular type of employment, to alter your life direction, or to heal a lingering wound.

When: Recurring dreams take place anytime during the sleep cycle; however, they will tend to create a visitation pattern that is consistent.

Telltale Signs of a Recurring Dream: You have the same dream over and over again. Even if it is not exactly the same dream, it can be a repetition of a similar dream theme (e.g., *"I am always competing with someone; it's always different, but I'm always trying to win and prove that I'm the best." "I am being criticized by different people, but it always feels the same." "I keep attending a graduation; it's always a different type of ceremony."*).

Suggestion: Contemplate the following questions: *What is the goal of this dream? What is the message it is trying to send me?* Dreams recur because your attitudes, responses, and habitual anxieties haven't changed. Recurring themes change and transform when *you* change and transform.

Mantra: *"What I resist persists."*

When You Can't Rid Yourself of That Recurring Dream

If you've determined that a dream is a recurring dream, it might require additional attention to resolve the challenge, trauma, or difficulty underlying the dream. This section will help you decode the message that has been delivered by the SIA.

1. Ask yourself: What need is my most primitive self/ego striving to fulfill (attention, love, adoration, security, support, food, sex, respect, glory, fame, freedom, etc. . . .)?
2. Once you identify the missing need, visualize your need being met, and embody the feeling of fulfillment.
3. Once you feel that your need is met, ask yourself, "Now what?" Allow the question to take you deeper into the core of the need/want/desire. Most people fight for their limitations, clinging to their pain because it is familiar. Continue with the "Now What?" questioning until your most stuck, stubborn, rigid, cynical, and resigned aspect of self has been illuminated.
4. Revel in the clarity, peace, and satisfaction of knowing that the goal of your SIA has been accomplished.

Precognitive Dreams (aka "Fortune-teller")

A world-renowned psychic once said that he wasn't so much of a psychic as an observer of patterns. He said that he could pick up a person's energy in this moment, combine it with his understanding of the predictable patterns and archetypes that most human beings gravitate toward, and, in an instant, predict the person's future. This is how your own inner Fortune-teller works. While you are asleep and your conscious mind is dormant, your Fortune-teller tiptoes outside and observes your life from afar, gaining an objective perspective of your patterns and primary archetypes. From your current patterns, your Fortune-teller attempts to predict the future and prepare you for what is likely to come.

Joe's Precognitive Dream

I was lying in a field of grass. A bluebird flew down and pecked a hole between my eyes and nose, and pulled out a long worm. A Navajo medicine man appeared and told me, "Don't be afraid, the bluebird is taking disease out of you."

A few days after Joe had the dream, a mole started to grow between his eyes and nose, exactly where the bird had pecked at him in his dream. When he went to see a doctor (a thin, *bird*like man), the doctor immediately detected cancer and said, "We need to operate right away because this type of cancer spreads quickly." During the surgery, *a long, wormlike cancer* was extracted.

Joe was not the type of man to easily go to the doctor. Had it not been for his precognitive dream giving him the message, it might have been too late for him.

When: Precognitive dreams usually take place during the middle of your sleep cycle; for example, if you go to sleep at 10:00 p.m., your Fortune-teller will usually pay you a visit between 1:00 and 4:00 a.m.

Telltale Signs of a Precognitive Dream: You dream of people, places, and situations that are future extensions of what is currently taking place in your life (e.g., you've been working hard on a project at work and you dream that you get a raise).

Suggestion: If your dream is desirable, then you can feel validated and reassured that you are in the right place at the right time, on track with fulfilling your heart's and soul's desires. If your dream is undesirable, ask yourself *"What pattern needs to be changed?"* and begin taking action to break your current pattern and develop new ways of being that are empowering.

Mantra: *"Change my pattern, change my future."*

Prophetic Dreams (aka "Angel")

Prophetic dreams are our own personal burning bushes that can, if we heed their messages, teach us more than any book, class, or teacher ever can.

John's Prophetic Dream

> I was in a classroom. There was a big blackboard, and the Dalai Lama was teaching the class. He drew a horizontal line dividing the blackboard into two halves. He told the students to write everything that was good in life above the line (e.g., friends, sunshine, weekends, etc.), and to write everything that was bad in life below the line (headache, war, crime, etc.). Then the Dalai Lama walked up to the blackboard and erased the line that separated the two polarities. With his famous smile he said, "Good and bad is an illusion. Everything in life is all a part of the inseparable oneness that connects us all. Your compulsion to label things good or bad is the cause of your suffering. Erase your labels and erase your suffering."

John awoke from this dream feeling clear, inspired, and enlightened from his own private tutorial with the Dalai Lama himself.

When: Prophetic dreams can take place anytime, but you will tend to remember the ones that take place during the last two hours of sleep.

Telltale Signs of a Prophetic Dream: You dream of a wise, loving being (e.g., Jesus, Mother Mary, Krishna, Sai Babba, Buddha, Mother Teresa, Ammachi, Gandhi, or a departed loved one) and you feel that you've been given a gift or taught an invaluable life lesson.

Suggestion: A prophetic dream is often very literal, requiring a minimum of interpretation and a maximum of meditation. Make the dream a real part of your conscious reality by writing down its message, sharing it with your friends and other dream adventurers, and, most of all, recalling the feeling tone of the dream often. And don't forget to take the action that it inspires!

Mantra: *"I let this angel groove inspire my every move."*

Wish Fulfillment Dreams (aka "Genie")

A wish fulfillment dream, like a genie in a bottle, aligns you with the resonance of your heart's and soul's desires. Just as people who are wealthy attract more wealth to themselves and happy people attract more circumstances to themselves that make them happy, when you move in the direction of your dreams by acting as if they've already come true, you add velocity to the process of manifestation. Wish fulfillment dreams are a powerful key to your ability to manifest that which you desire.

Wish fulfillment dreams might include dreams about an upcoming vacation, an ideal scene at work, or the resolution of a conflict that you've had with a sibling. Because your subconscious mind cannot discern between actual events and that which is vividly imagined, your wish fulfillment dreams actually create an energetic map that can lead you from where you are to where you would like to be. Whereas your venting, processing, integration, and breakdown/breakthrough dreams help you to release that which is in your way of having your greatest and fullest life experience, your wish fulfillment dreams help to take you the rest of the way toward manifesting your desires.

Sadie had been dating her boyfriend, Joe, for three years and was ready to settle down and get married. Joe, though in love with Sadie, was a bit, shall we say, commitment phobic. Because money was a struggle for both of them, Joe's excuse for prolonging the wedding was that he wanted to be financially secure before saying "I do." Sadie began to clip out images from magazines that reflected the life of her dreams and to read literature that helped connect her to her source and self-esteem before she went to sleep. She was attempting to saturate her subconscious mind with the wonderful feelings and images that she desired to create in her life.

Sadie's Wish Fulfillment Dream

On bended knee, my boyfriend, Joe, proposed to me on the doorstep of a beautiful mansion. I excitedly nodded my head and cried, "YES!" Then I asked him, "Whose house is this?" He handed me a key and replied, "It's yours!" I walked into the mansion and began to weep. It was the most beautiful house I'd ever seen, with vaulted ceilings, marble floors, skylights, and sunlight pouring in through bay windows. When I went to put the key in my purse I noticed my purse was overflowing with hundreds of hundred-dollar bills. I cried tears of joy. I felt like I'd won the lottery emotionally, spiritually, and financially.

When she awoke, her pillow was drenched with tears, and although she was a bit disappointed it was only a dream, the feeling of fulfillment was so profound that it uplifted and altered her perception and has stayed with her years after.

Because of her dream, Sadie got to experience the feeling of fulfillment even though her actual life circumstances hadn't changed at all, and her desperation about getting married was replaced with an inner knowing that her destiny was indeed unfolding fortuitously. Sadie's contentment made her magnetic, and within a few years she became happily married, bought a beautiful home, and is making more money than she ever has. But the most important aspect of this story is the fact that because she maximized the gift of her wish fulfillment dream she was able to feel fulfilled independent of her undesirable circumstances. And from this place she was magnetic (not resistant) to the circumstances she desired.

When: Wish fulfillment dreams can take place anytime, but you will tend to remember the ones that take place during the last two hours of sleep.

Telltale Signs of a Wish Fulfillment Dream: You feel happy, joyous, optimistic, hopeful, and more aligned with the energy needed to actualize your desires in your waking reality.

Suggestions: Before you go to sleep saturate your consciousness with the wonderful feelings and images you desire to create in your life. Clip out images from magazines that reflect the life of your dreams and read uplifting, inspirational literature. Recognize your wish fulfillment dream as an affirmation of who you are and of what you are capable of being. Don't disregard this as "just a dream." Recognize the power and gift of your mind's ability to create the experience of this desirable circumstance. Identify the qualities you embodied during this dream and carry them with you as you move throughout your day. Allow this heightened state to energetically lead you, step by step, toward the "real life" fulfillment of your desires.

Mantra: *"I move in the direction of my dreams and act as if they've already come true."*

The Emotions of Shadow and Light

> *Either everything is a miracle, or nothing is a miracle.*
> —ALBERT EINSTEIN

The five-thousand-year-old Chinese oracle, the I Ching holds balance as one of its major tenets. It says that within all things exist the masculine and feminine, the good and bad, the light and dark . . . all under the umbrella of balance, unity, oneness, wholeness, and inclusivity. You could say the same about dream symbols. As I mention in the "Integration Dreams (aka 'Artist')" section, shadows lurk within all "positive" symbols, and virtues shine within all "negative" symbols. For example, the symbol of a "gun" might initially strike you as a "bad" symbol because it implies killing and murder. However, it might also represent a tool for liberation, killing a negative habit or tendency so that you can be free. Or a dream of "flying" might initially appear to be a "good" symbol that represents liberation and joy. However, the shadow side of a flying dream might be an indication that you are being too flighty in your life, and ungrounded and unwilling to face reality. Ultimately, from the highest perspective, we throw the labels of "good" and "bad" away (as in the prophetic dreams example with the Dalai Lama) and simply call it all energy, growth, and expansion.

Your emotions leave clues about the deeper meaning of a dream as a whole as well as the significance of the specific symbols. If you are on an enchanted island, but you are fraught with fear, this dream will have an entirely different meaning than it would if it felt like paradise. You could be hitchhiking alongside a dark, lonesome highway, but if you feel hopeful about something wonderful coming around the bend, this changes the entire context of your dream. When you can identify the emotional tenor of a dream (joy, sadness, fear, regret, guilt, hope, excitement, gratitude, dread, or ecstasy) you have an important clue toward solving its mystery.

Dream Interpretation System: From Confusion to Fusion

Now that you know how to classify your dreams and understand the important role that emotions play, and how to see their light side and shadow, you are more than halfway to your goal of understanding the valuable gifts of your dreams. The following dream interpretation system will take you the rest of the way.

As soon as you wake up, write down everything you remember from your dreamtime in as much detail as you can: who, what, where, when . . . and be sure to include your emotions (happy, sad, heartbroken, ecstatic, overjoyed, disappointed, ignored, hopeful) as well as the type of dream you think it was.

1. On a sheet of paper or in your dream journal, make three columns with the following labels:

   Symbol   My Interpretation   Dictionary Definition

2. In the first column, make a list of the most significant words from your dream. For example, you dreamed: *My house is under construction, and I am climbing up and sliding down the scaffolding like it's a jungle gym. I put pillows on the ground so I won't get hurt when I slide down.*

Symbol	My Interpretation	Dictionary Definition
House		
Construction		
Scaffolding		
Jungle gym		
Pillows		
Ground		
Slide		
Down		

3. In the second column, using the first thought method, write your hunch about what each symbol means (write down the first thing that comes to mind . . . no overthinking or overanalyzing).

Symbol	My Interpretation	Dictionary Definition
House	My life	
Construction	Change/renovation	
Scaffolding	Support with change	
Jungle gym	Play—childlike	
Pillows	Cushion, buffer	
Ground	Get grounded—reality check	
Slide	Fun—having a good time	
Down	Down to the nitty-gritty	

4. In the third column, write an abbreviated version of *The Dreamer's Dictionary* definition next to its symbol.

Symbol	My Interpretation	Dictionary Definition
House	My life	Belief structures/ context for life
Construction	Change/renovation	Transformation/ breakdown/ breakthrough
Scaffolding	Support with change	Creation of new thought structures and beliefs

Jungle gym	Play—childlike	Freedom/adventure in the mind's jungle
Pillows	Cushion, buffer	Rest assured, all is well; comfort and support
Ground	Get grounded— reality check	Foundation
Slide	Fun—having a good time	Loss of control
Down	Down to the nitty-gritty	Depth—the heart of the matter

5. Read the words in the second and third columns as if you were reading a sentence. Keep in mind your emotions (fun) and the type of dream (breakdown/breakthrough). With your intuition as your guide, tell the story of your dream, for example: "*My life, belief structure,* and *context for life* are under *construction.* I'm in the midst of *change,* which I am normally very uncomfortable with, but I am having fun with the *renovation* and *transformation* I am undergoing . . . even the *breakdowns and breakthroughs* are exciting. I can *support* myself as my life changes and reflects more *supportive thought structures and belief systems* by remembering to have fun. If I *lose control* as I *get down to the nitty-gritty of my new foundation,* I will remember this *reality check* to *comfort* me and to remind me to *rest assured* that *all is well.*

6. Share your dreams with other dream enthusiasts. In the telling of a dream, a deeper layer of clarity will begin to emerge, new clues that you hadn't noticed before will suddenly "pop" into view. Exchanging thoughts and ideas about dream symbols with a sacred circle of "Dream Weavers" can be nothing short of illuminating. The more you do this (just like building a muscle) the sooner you will begin to get a broader, richer, and deeper understanding of the language of your *strange dreams*!

DREAMER'S DICTIONARY

ways, and influenced in a way that could be harmful to you. Perhaps you are overstressing through feelings of overwhelm or of being overpowered by someone in your life. If you dream that you are the ab-

AA Dreams of AA signify support and that you are taking steps in the right direction. They are either a wake-up call to join this 12-step program, or to step up your participation in your spiritual path. See *Alcohol* and *12-step Program*.

Abandonment If you dream of being left behind, then this is a venting dream helping you to release your abandonment issues. A dream of abandonment is giving you the message that when you stop leaving yourself, as in energetically abandoning yourself, then your fears of others leaving you will leave you. The dream could also denote that you are abandoning an aspect of the past that no longer serves you, or that you desire freedom from responsibilities, worry, control, and inhibitions.

Abdomen The abdomen represents the third chakra, the solar plexus, self-empowerment, and creativity. If you dream of pain in your stomach, you are processing through your blocks to creativity and self-empowerment. See *Stomach*.

Abduction Dreams of abduction symbolize a fear of being carried away and influenced in a way that could be harmful to you. Perhaps you are processing through feelings of overwhelm or of being over-powered by someone in your life. If you dream that you are the abductor, then the dream reflects your desire to control a person or situation in your life. See *Kidnap*.

Abortion Dreams of an abortion are about the elimination or interruption of a new relationship, idea, project, or a literal pregnancy. Your subconscious mind may be telling you that just because you are going through a challenge, don't throw the baby out with the bathwater. If there is sorrow or fear connected to the dream, then take heart in knowing that which is real can never die because the soul lives on forever.

Absence Dreams of the absence of someone you love denote that you are grieving and/or processing a loss and/or transition in your relationship. They are also a reflection of your feelings and attitudes about commitment and a message to become more present in your life.

Abundance Dreams of abundance signify that conditions of wealth abound, and that love, success, fortune, and good things are coming into your life. You are awakening to your infinite nature. See *Wish Fulfillment Dreams,* page 18.

Abuse Dreams of abuse are venting dreams about control, or the lack thereof. If you dream of being the victim of abuse, then you are venting your connection to the victim archetype and are coming to terms with your own power. You are realizing that it is time either to stand up for yourself or to remove yourself from a nonsupportive situation. If you dream of being the abuser, then you are venting your frustration and rage at feeling out of control. Your subconscious mind may be cautioning you to take responsibility for your feelings and actions and treat others the way you'd like to be treated. Dreams of abuse also reflect the way you treat yourself. See *Venting Dreams,* page 8.

Abyss A dream of an abyss means that you are connecting with your deeper nature, going beyond the superficial to where your inner rivers run deep and you feel your connection with the soul of the world. If you are afraid of this abyss, then the dream is assisting you to process fears of death, overwhelm, inadequacy, or your own powers.

Accelerator Dreams of an accelerator symbolize the need for speed and your desire to move forward in your life with velocity toward your goals.

Accent An accent in a dream denotes qualities of the country in which the accent is heard. Perhaps you have a desire to stand out in a crowd. Also, a dream about an accent can represent your desire to connect to your heritage or family bloodline.

Accessories Dreams of accessories signify that you are aware of magic that lies in the details of your life, love, affection, and a desire to stand out and have a touch of style. Alternatively, dreams of accessories could represent a feeling of insecurity that would cause you to overcompensate for what you feel is missing. See *Bling Bling.*

Accident A dream of an accident signifies that you need to pay more attention to what you are doing. This venting dream also indicates a desire for perfection and a fear of making a mistake.

Accordion Dreams of an accordion represent festivities, happiness, and joy. The movement of the accordion suggests that you are connecting with the cycles of life. See *Musical Instrument.*

Accosting If you are accosted in your dream, then you are releasing your fear of being harmed, hurt, or overpowered. If you dream of accosting someone, then you are exposing and/or releasing aggression and your need to control in a way that has negative consequences.

Account Dreams of an account are about self-worth, checks, and balances. Consider if your emotional/spiritual account is abundant, overdrawn, or balanced. Dreams of an account may be a message to give yourself credit where credit is due, and to be more generous with praise and acknowledgment.

Accountant Dreams of an accountant represent the need to connect with the aspect of you that is logical, reasonable, detached, organized, and detail oriented. This dream may signify that it is time to get into balance with your giving and receiving.

Accusing To dream of accusing reflects guilt, blame, shame, and an unwillingness to take personal responsibility for your life. Dreaming of this offers you the opportunity to own an aspect of your power that you have yet to embrace as you come to realize that blaming or accusing someone for your pain only adds insult to injury.

Ace An ace signifies success and that you are tapping into your natural genius that will help you win in the game of life. You are feeling like a winner. See *Gambling* and *Trump Card.*

Achievement Dreams of achievement denote that you have been pushing yourself to discover your personal best and are striving for excellence. A dream of achievement may be a message to celebrate your accomplishments and to prepare for success that is forthcoming. See *Wish Fulfillment Dreams,* page 18.

Acid Dreams of acid mean that your anger and unexpressed emotions are eating at you. Your subconscious mind is telling you to find a healthy form of expression.

Acne Dreams of acne represent shame, self-criticism, unexpressed rage, and that something is boiling under the surface and it is ready to be popped.

Acorn Dreams of an acorn symbolize great potential. Because the blueprint for the oak tree resides within this tiny seed, an acorn represents the fact that your highest destiny is already alive within you.

Acrobat To dream of an acrobat symbolizes flexibility and your ability to accommodate the desires of the people in your life. It can be symbolic of being head over heals in love with someone.

Across Dreaming of someone being across from you can represent qualities that person is mirroring back to you. He or she may be reflecting your beauty, or an aspect of your shadow you have yet to embrace.

Acrylic Nails Dreams of acrylic nails reflect manufactured ambition and a message to soften your approach to reaching for what you want in life. See *Finger* and *Nail*.

Act To dream of putting on an act represents inauthenticity and fear that if you let your true feelings show you will be rejected. A dream of an act is bringing to light the roles you play to get what you need and want in life. See *Mask* and *Play*.

Actor/Actress Dreams of an actor or actress represent the archetypes you embody, or the roles you play in life. If you dream of an actor or actress you admire, the dream is revealing qualities that you like most about yourself or aspire to embody. If the actor or actress represents qualities that you dislike, then the dream is assisting you to embrace your shadow. See *Famous, Celebrity*. See also *Integration Dreams*, page 10.

Adam and Eve Dreams of Adam and Eve symbolize sexual innocence, temptation, and having all your needs met but your still wanting more. You are on a quest for knowledge and you are expanding and exploring your boundaries. These dreams may be telling you to appreciate what you have instead of coveting that which you don't. See *Yin and Yang*.

ADD/ADHD A dream of ADD or ADHD denotes that you've been allowing yourself to become distracted from your goals. Perhaps you've lost your focus, and the dream is giving you the message to seek support in getting yourself back on track.

Addiction Dreams of addiction are about insatiability or the need for comfort, a quick fix to take the pain away. Keep in mind that within all addictions is a craving for a higher source. See *AA, Drugs* and *12-step Program.*

Address Dreams of an address represent your place in life, your influence on others, your career, status, your self-concept, and identity. If you dream of a former address, then you are releasing past identities or you may be processing moments from the past when you lived at this address. Consider what the numbers add up to. See *Number.*

Administrator Dreams of an administrator signify that you are taking responsibility for your life and assuming your authority. These dreams might also reflect your issues with authority figures.

Admiral Dreams of an admiral signify that you are standing at the helm of your life, claiming your authority, power, confidence, seaworthiness, and leadership.

Adolescence Dreams of adolescence denote that you are in touch with your passion, eagerness, impetuousness, sexuality, and perhaps rebellion against social rules. Also, you may be going through a transition and a growth spurt, and you are feeling geeky and awkward in your own skin. See *Breakdown/Breakthrough Dreams,* page 12.

Adoption If you dream of being adopted, then you are grappling with feelings of belonging, abandonment, betrayal, and worthiness. If you dream of adopting a child, this may reflect that you are adopting a new habit or point of view.

Adult Dreaming of an adult signifies that you are embracing the process of growing, the courage it takes to be responsible, mature, and sensible. For some, being an adult represents freedom; for others it represents a burden.

Adultery Dreams of adultery represent your internal struggle with loyalty, guilt, shame, commitment, and promiscuity. Perhaps there is a quality that is missing from an intimate relationship of yours or in your business, and dreaming of adultery is showing you what qualities to cultivate within yourself. If you are grappling with "the grass is greener" syndrome, a dream of adultery may help you to process your feelings and give you a clearer perspective before you do something that you might regret.

Adventure If you enjoy an adventure in a dream, then this indicates a positive and healthy approach to change. If you do not enjoy an adventure you dream of, then this indicates your resistance and re-action to changes that are taking place in your life.

Adversary See *Enemy* and *Integration Dreams,* page 10.

Adversity Dreams of adversity reflect your resistance to change and an unwillingness to accept what is. Because solutions are inherent in every problem, dreams of adversity denote your desire to find the solutions you seek. See *Breakdown/Breakthrough Dreams,* page 12.

Advertisement Dreams of an advertisement signify that you are promoting and selling yourself, and that you desire recognition and status. Dreaming of an advertisement may be cautioning you to read between the lines and to not be easily seduced by the market-ing campaigns of the people and products in your life. Alterna-tively, the dream may be a headline written for you from your higher self. See *Sign.*

Advice The advice that you give to someone in a dream is always in-tended for yourself. Consider the advice and take your own medi-cine.

Aerobics Dreams of aerobics are a sign to get your life into shape and to get a jump on your mental, emotional, spiritual, and physi-cal fitness. See *Exercise* and *Step Aerobics.*

Affection Dreams of kisses, hugs, and compliments symbolize affin-ity, love, and connection. Consider the person for whom you are feeling affection and remember that that person reflects an aspect of you that you adore. See *Kiss.*

Affiliate Link Dreams of an affiliate link signify that you are ac-tively supporting people and are being rewarded for it. You are real-izing the reciprocation process—that which you give comes back to you tenfold. See *Karma.*

Afraid If you dream of being afraid, then you are venting your feelings of overwhelm and inadequacy to handle the circumstances you face. See *Venting Dreams,* page 8.

Africa Dreams of Africa symbolize a desire to get in touch with your heart's desires and your wild, authentic, untamed nature. See *Chakra* (4th) and *Heart.*

Afterlife Dreams of the afterlife represent your awareness of a light at the end of the tunnel. You are recognizing a larger perspective of life beyond the confines of the ego, and that heaven is at hand now. See *Death, Heaven,* and *Reincarnation.*

Afternoon Dreams of the afternoon represent illumination, inspiration, and activity. If you dream of a weekday afternoon, then this symbolizes business and productivity. If you dream of a weekend afternoon, then this reflects your need to take a relaxing break.

Age If you dream of being a particular age, then you may be processing your concern about the aging process or dealing with the issues and concerns related to that age. See *Adolescence, Birthday, Middle Age, Number,* and *Old Age.*

Agenda Dreams of an agenda represent order and organization of your time, energy, thoughts, and plans. Dreaming of someone having an agenda can also be cautioning you to read between the lines and practice discernment. See *Diary.*

Agent Dreaming of an agent or advocate represents your own inner support for your product, service, or who you are. A dream of an agent can also be a wish fulfillment dream about your desire for support in your life and in making your dreams come true. The agent in a dream can represent the aspect of yourself that has healthy self-esteem.

Agreeing Because all the characters in your dreams are you, if you are in agreement with someone in a dream, then this represents inner synergy. Consider the feeling tone of the dream, and whether you are agreeing submissively or willingly.

Agriculture Dreams of agriculture symbolize success, abundance, health, and bounty. These dreams might be suggesting that you get back to basics and become grounded in order to receive the fruition of your hard work. See *Farm/Farmer, Food,* and *Harvest.*

"Aha" Moment Dreams of an "aha" moment symbolize illumination, clarity, and awakening. Pay particular attention to the context of the "aha" moment. See *Lucid Dreams*.

AIDS Dreams of AIDS are about sexual shame, blame, or guilt. Perhaps you are venting out feelings of helplessness, defenselessness, and an inability to stand up for yourself. See *Disease*.

Air Dreams of air signify springtime and youthful innocence, and that you are discovering a fresh outlook on life. Perhaps you are embarking upon a new project that has you walking on air. Also, air is associated with the breath, which is synonymous with spirit. If the air in a dream is pure, this means your spirit feels light and clean. If the air is unclean, then this indicates that you have been weighed down by negativity and it's time for a breath of fresh air. See *Spring* and *Wind*.

Air Conditioner Dreams of an air conditioner mean that you are adjusting your inner temperature. For example, if you were running too hot and heavy, allowing passion and impetuousness to overheat you, then you instinctively know to cool off in order to achieve balance.

Air Force Dreams of the air force signify that you may be forcing your spiritual beliefs onto other people. Or perhaps you are asking for higher guidance as you fight for what you think is right. See *Air, Airplane,* and *Military.*

Airplane Dreams of an airplane represent your desire to see life from a higher view, to move out of the mundane ego experience of life, and to begin to take action to live on a higher plane. Dreaming of an airplane can also signify that a dramatic life change is on the horizon. If the plane is in turbulence, this represents your control issues—that you are trying to stabilize your spiritual life, and that a deeper commitment to your spiritual practice is in order. If the plane is still on the ground, then you are being guided to have patience. If you are soaring through the air, then your goals are in midflight, and you are well on your way to manifesting your soul's desires.

Airport Dreams of an airport symbolize your spiritual center, the place from which you depart and land. This is where you refuel to prepare for your next adventure or flight of fancy. A dream of an airport can also be predicting a major change in your life.

Aisle If you dream of an aisle, then this represents order and a desire for symmetry and precision in your life as you move through into a new life experience. An aisle can also symbolize division, a divide between opposing aspects of yourself. Walking down an aisle represents focus, clarity, and commitment. See *Ceremony* and *Wedding*.

Alarm Dreams of an alarm are a message to pay attention and be alert because something important is happening.

Album Dreams of an album symbolize memories and nostalgia. Perhaps you are remembering a past event in order to embrace its lesson and/or blessing. See *Gallery* and *Treasure*.

Alchemist/Alchemy Dreams of an alchemist symbolize your ability to transform a negative situation into one that's advantageous to you. Acknowledging that your awareness turns dross to gold.

Alcohol Dreams of alcoholic beverages represent a desire for escape, freedom, diversion, and a peak experience. Perhaps dreaming of alcohol is revealing that you've been numbing your pain and that it is time to soberly deal with the facts of your life. See *AA*.

Alibi Dreams of an alibi signify that you are hiding something. Maybe you are making excuses to yourself for why you aren't showing up in life the way that you know you can. Consider the reason for the need of an alibi.

Alimony Dreams of alimony signify that you are honoring past commitments or your karmic debt. Or perhaps you are dealing with unhealed energy that is still lingering from a past relationship.

Alive If there is someone who is dead in real life who is alive in a dream, then you are realizing that your connection with that person is still very much alive. See *Awake*.

Allergy If you dream of an allergy, then you may be feeling claustrophobic because of stifled expression or repressed emotions. See *Sick*.

Alley Dreams of an alley are integration dreams reflecting your unrecycled thoughts and feelings, and the clutter that is behind the scenes in your life.

Alligator Dreams of an alligator symbolize the predatory energy in your life, or your fear of being eaten alive, overpowered, or pulled into the swamp of your fears. They could be venting dreams helping you to release your fear about the abuse of power. See *Animal*.

Allowance Dreams of an allowance symbolize issues of worth, abundance, deservedness, and energy exchange. They are showing you how much prosperity you feel you are worth and how much good you will allow yourself to receive.

Ally Dreams of an ally may be a message for you to become your own best friend and stick up for yourself and recognize your beauty and innocence. See *Friend*.

Almond Because of its husk, dreams of an almond represent the substance hidden behind a rough exterior, like an ego that guards an open and loving heart. You are realizing that you cannot judge a book by its cover, but that you must look beyond the surface to discover the treasure within. See *Nuts*.

Alphabet Dreams of the alphabet signify that you are spelling out your feelings and thoughts in a desire to be understood. These dreams may be telling you that if you keep communication simple, it is more apt to be understood.

Altar Dreams of an altar signify that you are devoted to altering your spiritual life and that you have a desire to connect with your higher self. See *Sacrifice*.

Aluminum Dreams of aluminum signify that you are preserving and protecting your emotional well-being from a chilly disposition or from a heated argument.

Amateur Dreams of an amateur reflect your frustration with your learning curve or the amateur skill level of someone you are working with. They also may be suggesting that your actions are lacking patience and compassion. See *Mistake*.

Amazon.com Dreams of Amazon.com represent curiosity and a desire for knowledge, information, and entertainment. They are telling you that all information resides within your own mind.

Ambassador Dreams of an ambassador signify that you are stepping into leadership and becoming a role model. They may be giving you the message to be responsible and aware that you are acting on behalf of all whom you represent.

Ambulance Dreams of an ambulance are a sign that help is on the way and you would be wise to get your ego out of the way and allow care to be given to the part of you that has been harmed.

Ambush If you dream of an ambush, then you may be contemplating a surprise attack on someone in order to gain leverage in your life. Or you may be venting out feelings of being ganged up on, or that you fear being overpowered or outnumbered.

America Dreams of America signify freedom and expression, and that the land of opportunity resides within you. You are realizing the opportunity to pursue your passion and fulfill your potential that is in your hands.

American Express Card Dreams of an American Express card denote that you shouldn't leave home without connecting to your spirit and making sure that you carry your sense of self, spirit, and purpose with you at all times. See *Credit Card.*

American Idol If you dream of *American Idol,* then you are dreaming of having your talent fully expressed and recognized. It could also be suggesting that it is time to get off the couch and onto the stage. See *Fame* and *Idol.* See also *Wish Fulfillment Dreams,* page 18.

Ammunition Dreams of ammunition signify that you are on the defensive in your life. Perhaps you've been firing verbal attacks or feeling the need to protect yourself from caustic energy that is being fired at you.

Amputation To dream of an amputation symbolizes a need for integration because you've been feeling scattered or cut off from your source. A dream of amputation can also be showing you where you give your power away. See *Body.* See also *Integration Dreams,* page 10.

Amusement Park Dreams of an amusement park symbolize your connection with your childlike, playful essence and to the joy of being alive. Perhaps they are a message for you to enjoy your life, even the ups and downs and highs and lows. See *Park* and *Roller Coaster.*

Anchor Dreams of an anchor symbolize your desire for a relationship, a job, or a situation that is solid and stable, and that can ground you in place. Alternatively, dreams of an anchor can represent that you are being weighed down by an obligation or person.

Consider the feeling tone of the dream to discern its message. See *Commitment*.

Ancient Dreams of something ancient signify that you are realizing the elder aspect of yourself, your connection to the part of you that is ancient and wise. Things that are ancient or antique represent importance and value because they have stood the test of time. See *Antiques* and *Elder*.

Anesthesia Dreams of anesthesia denote that you may be numbing out your physical or emotional pain. Keep in mind that you cannot heal what you cannot feel. These dreams may also be a sign to call on your support system to see you through a challenging time in your life. See *Addiction* and *Drugs*.

Angel Dreams of an angel mean that assistance is yours for the asking. You are tapping into your own healing abilities, your higher guidance, and the realization that you are loved, adored, and always being guided. See *Miracle*. See also *Prophetic Dreams,* page 17.

Anger Dreaming of expressing anger is a healthy way to vent your frustrations and hurt feelings in a way that may be socially unacceptable in real life. Keep in mind that your anger, if channeled properly, can be the creative fuel you need to manifest your heart's desires. See *Venting Dreams,* page 8.

Anger Management If you dream of anger management, then this symbolizes a need to take responsibility for your power and energy and funnel your frustration into productive outlets.

Animal Dreams of an animal signify that you are connecting with your wild side, basic instincts, and survival needs. Consider the type of animal. See *Zoo*.

Ankle Dreams of an ankle symbolize flexibility. They are a message for you to relax and go with the flow of life. If you dream that your ankle is broken, then this reflects that you are resisting where life is moving you and that your rigidity is making it difficult for you to proceed. See *Body*.

Anniversary If you dream of an anniversary, then you are connecting with the rewards of your staying power and the strength of your commitment and fortitude. See *Birthday* or *Wedding*. See also *Wish Fulfillment Dreams,* page 18.

Announcer Dreams of an announcer symbolize the aspect of you that is objective and impartial, and it is delivering a message to you loud and clear.

Anorexia Dreams of anorexia symbolize self-control, austerity, self-sacrifice, and a desire for perfection. They are giving you the message to get back into balance and feed your soul.

Antelope Dreams of an antelope symbolize knowledgeable and decisive action.

Antenna To dream of an antenna symbolizes connection to your intuition and telepathy. It is a message to pay attention to all communication that you are transmitting and receiving.

Antibiotics Dreams of antibiotics symbolize a desire for healing solutions, health, and well-being. They could be suggesting that you take preventive care to avoid the need for antibiotics in the future. See *Medicine*.

Antidote A dream of an antidote denotes that you are in the process of discovering answers because subconsciously you know that within every challenge resides a solution. See *Band-Aid* and *Cure*.

Antiques Dreams of antiques signify nostalgia, style, elegance, and a reverence for tradition. Perhaps you are reconnecting with your old-fashioned values, or your dreams are telling you that you are living in the past.

Antiseptic Dreams of an antiseptic are a message to take preventive measures that will protect you from getting hurt in a relationship or your career.

Antlers Dreams of antlers symbolize protection, bravado, and the desire to seem more powerful than you actually are. Antlers, like antennas, can also symbolize intuition.

Ants Dreams of ants signify that you've been taking the little things in life for granted, sweating the small stuff, and being easily bugged by life's minor annoyances. They can be a message to respect the details in life because it is the little things that make a difference. Also, dreams of ants are telling you that your patience will pay off in time, and that when you engage in teamwork, you will move mountains.

Anxiety Dreams that carry an anxious feeling represent resistance to your life circumstances or that you are grappling with your fears. See *Venting Dreams,* page 8.

Anxiety Attacks If you dream of an anxiety attack, then you are confronting your fear of death and being out of control. The dream is showing you that you've been out of sync with the grace and ease of your true being. Consider that if your mind is powerful enough to create anxiety, imagine what else it can create for you if you focus on what you would prefer to manifest.

Ape Dreams of an ape show that you are connecting to your primal feelings, sexuality, power, and perhaps feeling a desire to dominate and express the largess of your being. See *Animal.*

Apocalypse Dreams of an apocalypse are helping you process through an ego-annihilating experience. They also reflect that you are on the verge of a major transformation. See *Breakdown/Breakthrough Dreams,* page 12, and *Venting Dreams,* page 8.

Apostle Dreams of an apostle signify that good news is coming your way. A dream of an apostle can be alerting you to pay attention to a guru/teacher that will be appearing in your life, or that the guru/teacher that you've been praying for is you. See *Ambassador* and *Angel.*

Appendix Dreams of pain in the appendix are venting dreams that are assisting you to move past feelings of self-denial, anger, and resentment that are rooted in your family history. The more acute the pain, the more acute your self-disdain.

Appetite Dreams of an appetite mean that you have a zest for life. Consider what it is—validation, love, support, stimulation, recognition, etc.—you are hungry for.

Applause Dreams of applause symbolize your desire for approval and positive feedback or to give praise, recognition, and acknowledgment.

Apple A dream of an apple symbolizes fertility, health, the divine feminine, or the vagina. Whether you are male or female, dreams of a ripe, juicy red apple may suggest that it is time for you to celebrate your femininity. If an apple is unripe or bitter, then the dream is cautioning you to be patient in your endeavors. If an apple is rotten, then you've been neglecting your inner goddess.

Apprentice To dream of the television show *The Apprentice* or of actually being an apprentice signifies that you are learning, growing, and applying your talent in the real world. A dream of an apprentice may be giving you the message to follow in the footsteps of a master. See *Donald Trump*.

April Dreams of April represent the beginning of a new chapter in your life and the joy of new love. They are giving you the message to be patient with the new seeds of future visions that have recently been planted. See *Rain* and *Spring*.

Apron Dreams of an apron signify that you are connecting with your maternal energy and are perhaps cooking up something delicious in your life. Because an apron is worn around the waist and covers your first three chakras—the root, sacrum, and solar plexus—this dream of an apron suggests a desire for protection against spills, thrills, and sexual projections.

Aquarium Dreams of an aquarium represent your desire to contain the ocean of your emotions and control the passion of your sexual expression. See *Fish* and *Water*.

Aquarius To dream of the Aquarius astrological sign signifies that you are connecting with your spiritual, mysterious, and imaginative nature. It may be giving you the message to find a healthy and productive outlet for your creativity.

Arch To dream of an arch suggests that you are connecting with or desiring connection with the feminine aspect of your being, that you are craving safety, nurturing, and support.

Archery Dreams of archery signify that you have single-minded focus and are on track with your visions and goals. See *Goddess* (Artemis).

Architect Dreams of an architect denote that you are taking responsibility for your life and are creating the blueprint for your dreams and goals. When you have these dreams, perhaps you are in the midst of manifesting or building a career or relationship.

Arena Dreams of an empty arena signify that you are going to be entering a challenging period of your life. If an arena is filled, then they are about your being in a situation that is calling for your competitive nature to kick in. See *Sports* and *Stadium*.

Arguing To argue in your dream reflects your internal struggle with your own conflicting needs and belief systems. You are grappling with your inner polarities and paradoxes, attempting integration and synergy. See *Integration Dreams,* page 10.

Aries Dreaming of the astrological sign Aries denotes rank, spontaneity, dynamism, naïveté, and idealism. See *Fire, Spring,* and *Ram.*

Ark Dreams of an ark symbolize your awareness of your inner sanctuary that will always carry you through the turbulent waters of life. Perhaps you desire to be in a partner*ship,* realizing the strength and benefits that a relationship can bring you, or you are developing balance and synergy between your masculine and feminine energies.

Arm Dreams of an arm signify that you are reaching for something, and/or that you have the ability to embrace and extend yourself to another. If the arm is broken, then there is a break in your ability to embrace, hold, or envelope something or someone. The right arm represents giving strong support. The left arm represents receptivity and the ability to lift, push away, or hold something or someone. If the arms are crossed, then this represents protection and boundaries. If the arms are open, then they represent that you are open-hearted and trusting of the people in your life.

Army Dreams of an army signify that you are preparing for an attack or that you are feeling a threat to your survival or well-being. See *War.*

Arrest Dreams of being arrested symbolize a fear of being caught, found out, discovered, and punished. They can also mean that you are blaming and judging others.

Arrow Dreams of an arrow represent direction, focus, and the ability to be clear about where you are going. Arrows are symbolically connected with the goddess Artemis, who is the archetype of independence and focus, and one who goes after her dreams. An arrow is also associated with Eros, the Greek god of love, which can mean that you are in the honeymoon stage of romantic love. See *Archery* and *Goddess* (Artemis).

Art/Artist Dreams of art are a message for you to express your unique, creative style of expression. Perhaps art you dream about is the inspiration for a piece of art you are being guided to create in your waking life.

Arteries Dreams of arteries signify affluence and that you are in the flow of life. If you dream that an artery is blocked, then you are resisting your creative flow of joy, vitality, and abundance, and the dream is a sign to take action to clear out all nonsupportive energy from your life that would impede your flow.

Arthritis Dreams of arthritis signify that you are having difficulty asking for what you really want and you are resisting reaching for your dreams.

Ashes Dreams of ashes symbolize completion, transformation, death, and rebirth.

Asia Dreams of Asia symbolize discipline, manners, and technology. See *Karate.*

Assassin/Assassination Dreams of an assassin symbolize extreme, calculated self-defense, and perhaps an attempt at killing off an undesirable aspect of yourself. See *Killing.* See also *Integration Dreams,* page 10.

Asthma If you dream of having asthma, this signifies that you are grappling with feelings of unworthiness, being smothered, and that there is not enough room for you to be completely yourself. Breath is associated with spirit or life force, so dreaming of having asthma may be giving you the message to reclaim your power and life force. See *Air.*

Astrologer/Astrology Dreams of an astrologer represent your desire to understand the outcome of a situation and may be an exploration of your own psychic and intuitive gifts. Also, dreams of the zodiac or your astrological sign represent success in your career, relationships, and fortune, and that you are synergizing with the healing energy of the planets, elements, cycles, and seasons. See *Aquarius, Aries, Cancer, Capricorn, Gemini, Leo, Libra, Pisces, Sagittarius, Scorpio, Taurus,* or *Virgo.* See also *Prophetic Dreams,* page 17.

Astronaut Dreams of an astronaut signify that you are breaking through barriers, shooting for the stars, and realizing that even the sky is not the limit.

Athlete Dreams of an athlete signify competition, a desire to become your personal best, and that you are striving for success. Perhaps you are working toward your goals and are stretching beyond what you thought you were capable of.

Atlas Dreams of an atlas can refer to Atlas, the Greek God depicted carrying the world on his back, which represents your concern for the people of this world, and is possibly a suggestion to explore new territory. See *Codependence* and *World*.

ATM Dreams of an ATM symbolize quick access to power, energy, knowledge, and resources. Pay attention to the PIN number; the number might be valuable to you. See *Money*, *Number*, and *PIN*.

Attack Dreams of an attack are about suppressed emotions. You are realizing that what is suppressed must eventually express itself. The message of dreams of an attack may also be to prepare you to protect yourself from negative projections coming your way, or to find a healthy outlet for your stress. See *Anger* and *Victim*.

Attic Dreams of an attic symbolize higher consciousness, wisdom, and resources. If a house represents your body, then the attic represents your mind and your belief systems. See *House*.

Attraction Feeling attracted to someone in a dream symbolizes connection, resonance, affinity, and unification with aspects of yourself you have projected onto this person. See *Love*.

Auction Dreams of an auction represent opportunistic thinking, and mean that you may be selling your talent to the highest bidder, and grappling with integrity issues and worthiness.

Audience Dreams of an audience symbolize a feeling that you are performing in your life and being judged and evaluated. Perhaps you are feeling the need for reassurance and validation.

Audition Dreams of an audition represent control, security issues, and a desire for acceptance.

Aunt Dreams of an aunt represent feminine endearment and nurturing, maternal support.

Aura If you dream of seeing someone's aura, this represents seeing that person's energetic essence, his or her soul, the truth about the person regardless of his or her words, demeanor, or reputation. If the aura has a color, see *Color*, *Light*, and *Spirit*.

Author Dreams of an author signify personal power, and when you write something in a dream, you are attempting to *right* something that went wrong. Consider the words you have written.

Autograph The act of writing your name in a dream is symbolic of sharing your energy with someone. If you receive an autograph you are connecting with the person and are allowing the person to make an impression on you.

Autopsy Dreams of an autopsy represent acceptance and/or denial regarding a present situation or end of a relationship. You are wanting to understand what went wrong.

Autumn If a dream takes place in autumn, then this represents introspection, intuition, preparation, depth of feeling, maturity, middle age, and means that you are gathering things together and moving inward. A dream taking place in autumn is giving you the permission to reap the rewards of your labor and focus on *being* instead of *doing*. See *Middle Age* and *West*.

Avalanche Dreams of an avalanche signify that you are feeling overwhelmed with too many tasks, releasing frozen emotions, hitting a breaking point, and you are no longer able to suppress your emotions. See *Breakdown/Breakthrough Dreams,* page 12.

Awake Dreams of being awake represent mastery, advanced awareness, and enlightenment. To become aware of what was previously a blind spot means that you are coming into clarity and having a spiritual awakening. See *Lucid Dreams*.

Award Dreams of an award symbolize success, fortuitous events, and acknowledgment. You are coming into a feeling of worthiness. See *Wish Fulfillment Dreams,* page 18.

Ax Dreams of an ax represent an ending, a severed bond, and a drastic halt to a pattern or person in your life that is unhealthy. See *Knife*. See also *Integration Dreams,* page 10.

B

Baboon Dreams of a baboon signify that you are in touch with a playful aspect of yourself. They may be telling you to stop taking yourself so seriously.

Baby Dreams of a baby symbolize innocence, vulnerability, untapped potential, and dependence. They might be telling you that a baby is on the way or that perhaps a new project or relationship is forthcoming. See *Child, Infant, Pregnant,* and *Spring.*

Babysitting Dreams of babysitting symbolize vigilance and perhaps a message for you to take care of the aspect of you that is the most vulnerable. If you dream that someone is babysitting for you, this represents an inability to fully express your wishes.

Bachelor Dreams of a bachelor symbolize opportunism and a desire to be socially free without commitments. They could be a call to stop playing the field and prepare for deeper responsibilities in your career and relationships. See *Peter Pan* and *Prince.*

Back Dreams of a back represent your ability to stand up for yourself. If your back is tall and straight, then this is a sign of confidence and self-assuredness. A hunched back is a sign of a defeatist attitude, shame, or embarrassment. If your back is against a wall, then you feel bullied. Or you may be feeling that someone is backing you up, supporting you in your life. If you turn your back, then you are leaving an old way of being behind. See *Lower Back* and *Upper Back.*

Backdoor Dreams of a backdoor symbolize an escape and looking for a way out.

Backward If you dream that someone or something is going backward, then this symbolizes rebellion, feeling out of style, or being attached to outmoded ways of the past. Perhaps a dream of going backward is telling you that you are going in the wrong direction, that you are off track, and that you are going against the flow, or perhaps that you are being contrary and rebellious. See *Rewinding.*

Bacon A dream of bacon represents wealth and abundance, your feelings and attitudes about bringing home the bacon and providing a living. See *Food.*

Badge Dreams of a badge represent your identification with a particular role in life, and/or the need for proof of your authority. Consider the type of badge and its affiliation. See *Certificate.*

Bag Dreams of a bag symbolize beliefs, ego attachments, and memories that you carry with you. If a bag is closed, then its contents are sacred or secret. If a bag is open, then this is a sign that you have been careless and reckless with that which is most valuable to you.

If a bag is empty, then this means that you are feeling disillusioned with the accomplishment of egoic goals. See *Box*.

Baggage Claim Dreams of baggage claim symbolize karma and the anticipation of what is coming to you. See *Karma*.

Bait Dreams of bait reflect your issues of power, whether you are trying to get energy from someone, or struggling to keep your energy intact. A dream of bait may be showing you that you are falling hook, line, and sinker for someone's strategy—perhaps an advertising campaign has lured you into buying something you don't need, or a person has seduced you into a situation that is not good for you. If you dream of dropping the bait, then you are trying to hook someone into doing your will.

Baker/Baking Dreams of a baker or of baking symbolize nurturing and self-love, and that you are cooking up loving, nurturing, delicious creations in your life. They could also be about money (dough) coming into your life. See *Art/Artist* and *Food*.

Balcony Dreams of a balcony symbolize the need for a higher perspective, and a message to step out of your internal myopic perspective and look at things objectively. You are getting a fresh perspective, a second wind, and an expanded view on your life circumstance. If a house represents you, then the deck is the aspect of you that is objective because it resides outside the confines of your normal point of view.

Bald Dreams of baldness denote that you are feeling exposed and vulnerable. For some the loss of hair equates a loss of power and/or sexual virility. Alternatively, a bald head symbolizes an exposed crown chakra, which signifies that you have an openness to higher consciousness and enlightened thoughts. See *Chakra* (7th).

Ball Dreams of a ball are associated with play, games, and friendly competition. If you have a ball, then it is your turn to make a move. If the ball is in someone else's court, then wait until that person makes a move. A ball also represents the circular, infinite cyclical nature of life, the world, the globe, wholeness, and completion.

A dream of a ball, a gala, symbolizes a rite of passage, the celebration of a turning point in your career, a relationship, or your vitality. See *Ballroom*.

Ballerina Dreams of a ballerina signify that you have grace, ease, and balance as you move through life. They may be a sign that your discipline is paying off. See *Dancing*.

Balloon Dreams of a balloon symbolize freedom and feeling as if you were floating on air. You may be feeling so high that you have lost touch with reality and these dreams are a message to stabilize your bliss and get grounded. See *Bubbles* and *Flying*.

Ballot Dreams of a ballot signify that you are in touch with your judgments and that you want to make your opinion count. Perhaps you are being cautioned to make sure to judge fairly before you cast your vote for someone or something in your life.

Ballroom Dreams of a ballroom symbolize wealth, elegance, and a forthcoming festive occasion.

Bamboo Dreams of bamboo signify that you are realizing the spiritual strength, focus, and simplicity that can lead to enlightenment.

Banana Dreams of a banana represent a sweet, delicious taste for life. The banana is also synonymous with the male phallus, representing fertility, sexual pleasure, and fulfillment. If you slip on a banana, then you are feeling reckless and ungrounded. See *Fruit*.

Band-Aid Dreams of a Band-Aid represent your desire for a quick fix to a problem, perhaps a temporary mend for a deep pain. A dream of a Band-Aid may be asking you to consider the deeper wound that wants to be healed. It also may signify that the healing process has already begun.

Bank Dreams of a bank signify that you are processing through your issues of financial security. Perhaps you are reevaluating where you've been investing your time, energy, and resources. A dream of a bank can also be pointing you toward a prosperous future. Consider the feeling tone.

Bankrupt Dreams of being bankrupt denote that you are at the end of an unworkable, fear-based pattern. Perhaps they are showing you that it is time to cultivate healthier patterns of manifestation and abundance.

Baptism Dreams of a baptism signify rebirth and forgiveness, and that you are recognizing your sacredness. See *Infant* and *Water*.

Bar Dreaming of a bar or nightclub represents a desire to cut loose from the rigors of daily life. If you dream of falling off the wagon, then you are venting and releasing your fear of falling back into old patterns of unhealthy living.

Barber Dreams of a barber signify that you need an ego boost and that you are concerned with your appearance. They can also represent a change in your identity, that you are cutting away your attachment to your former self. See *Hair* and *Hairdresser.*

Barbershop Dreams of a barbershop symbolize a desire for camaraderie, fraternity, and support. See *Barber* and *Metro-sexual.*

Bare Feet Dreams of bare feet symbolize being grounded and connected with your natural essence.

Bargain Dreams about looking for a deal or finding a bargain can reflect that you are frugal and opportunistic. Perhaps a dream of finding a bargain is also calling attention to your feeling of unworthiness. Consider the feeling tone. See *Money* and *Shopping.*

Barn Dreams of a barn symbolize a storehouse for your animal instincts, power, and resources. Perhaps you are feeling the need to restrain your wild side. See *Chakra* (1st and 2nd) and *Farm/Farmer.*

Barricade Dreams of a barricade signify a desire for protection and firm boundaries, or that your ego's defensiveness is keeping love, intimacy, and opportunity at bay.

Barrier Dreams of a barrier denote resistance to your circumstances or that there is a challenge to overcome. You are grappling with a growth opportunity that once overcome will make you stronger, clearer, wiser, and better.

Bartender Dreams of a bartender symbolize a friendly, superficial aspect of you that is serving up a facade or smoke screen that may be keeping you from having a profound relationship with reality. See *Alcohol* and *Bar.*

Baseball Dreams of baseball reflect competition and that you are taking the challenges thrown your way and attempting to hit them out of the park. A dream of a baseball can also have sexual connotations. The bat is a phallic symbol and the glove represents the female genitalia. See *Sports.*

Basement Dreams of a basement symbolize your unconscious desire to embrace your shadow. Secrets, sexual obsessions, and desires are hidden in the basement of your subconscious mind and it can be worthwhile and empowering to investigate and excavate the treasures buried there. See *Goddess* (Persephone). See also *Integration Dreams,* page 10.

Basket Dreams of an empty basket symbolize either receptivity or feelings of emptiness. If a basket is filled, then whatever the basket is filled with represents the type of abundance you are experiencing in your life. Also, if you dream of weaving a basket, then this symbolizes your ability to weave together seemingly random and misplaced aspects of yourself into a unified, wholesome container. Consider the feeling tone. See *Goddess* (Athena). See also *Integration Dreams,* page 10.

Basketball Dreams of a basketball signify that you are goal oriented, focused, and/or willing to jump through hoops to please someone or to achieve a goal. See *Sports.*

Bat If you dream of a baseball bat, it is either a symbol of a weapon to defend yourself with, or a message to knock your challenges out of the ballpark. A bat is also a phallic symbol. See *Sports.*

If you dream of the flying mammal, see *Vampire.*

Bath Dreams of a bath signify that you need to cleanse away the clutter, debris, and stress from your life. You are in the process of washing your troubles down the drain and returning with a clean slate. A dream of a bath suggests every moment contains a new beginning. A bath can also represent nurturing, pampering, and self-love.

Bathroom Dreams of a bathroom symbolize releasing and letting go of toxic feelings and thoughts that no longer serve you. See *Venting Dreams,* page 8.

Bathtub In dreams, a bathtub can symbolize a womb, and dreaming of a bathtub signifies that you are feeling contained as you are cleansed in a healing environment. See *Water.*

Battery Dreams of a battery represent your ability to finish a task or to achieve your goals. If you dream that batteries are running low, then this symbolizes your need for downtime to recharge and plug into that which stimulates and revitalizes you.

Bay Dreams of a bay symbolize emotional calm, serenity, and gentle femininity. They may be suggesting that you have been keeping your true feelings at bay in order to avoid deeper and more challenging emotions.

Beach Dreams of the beach signify your desire for growth, change, and expansion, and that you are on the threshold of understanding your inner mystery. You are exploring the realm of your sexuality, recognizing your synergy with the tides and cycles. Dreaming of the beach can also mean that you are coming into great wealth represented by the innumerable grains of sand. See *Ocean* and *Sand*.

Beads Dreams of beads worn as decoration around the neck represent embellishment of the throat chakra. They are calling attention to your need to strengthen and add confidence to your self-expression and communication. See *Jewelry* and *Throat*.

Bear Dreams of a bear symbolize power, strength, fierce protection, and custodianship of your family. Perhaps you are feeling the need for solitude and to be uninterrupted in your emotional cave. See *Animal*.

Beard Dreams of a beard signify that you are hiding and covering up, and creating a mystique. A beard also symbolizes mystery, wisdom, and masculinity. See *Mask*.

Beast Dreams of a beast symbolize suppressed anger, and your wild, untamed dark side that you have yet to integrate and embrace. See *Animal* and *Shadow*. See also *Integration Dreams*, page 10.

Beauty Dreams of beauty represent creativity, passion, appreciation, and affinity.

Beauty Shop Dreams of a beauty shop symbolize the need for a self-esteem lift and a luxurious pampering. They are nudging you to make the most of your natural resources and gifts.

Beaver Dreams of a beaver signify that you are building walls for protection and setting boundaries for space. In Native American traditions, dreams of the beaver were considered auspicious and a blessing for the dreamer. Consider the feeling tone.

Bed Dreams of a bed represent comfort, relaxation, rejuvenation, sexuality, intimacy, and privacy. A bed is considered the safest place in the world, the place where you allow yourself to be the most vulnerable. This is the place where the veil is thinnest between the conscious and unconscious. Dreams of a bed can also signify that you are taking responsibility for your choices, as in you made your bed, now lie in it.

Bed and Breakfast Dreams of a bed and breakfast, or a B&B, symbolize the need for R&R, to get away and be nurtured and taken care of. See *Hotel.*

Bedroom Dreams of a bedroom symbolize a need for recharging your batteries, or perhaps a desire for sex, privacy, and/or intimacy. See *Room.*

Bedspread Dreams of a bedspread symbolize protection for your vulnerability and sensitivity. A bedspread can also represent warmth and security.

Beef Dreams of beef denote that you are upset at someone and you are dealing with unfinished business. See *Food.*

Beehive Dreams of a beehive signify activity and productivity, and that you will soon be working synergistically with a group. Such dreams may be telling you that you will thrive in a buzzing community, or alternatively, that you have to get out of the hive in order to be more productive in your business. If the beehive is turned upside down, then this represents anger, frustration, and the fear of being ganged up on by an angry mob.

Beer Dreams of beer symbolize intoxication, and mean that you are intentionally not wanting to deal with reality and face life soberly and lucidly. See *Alcohol.*

Bees Dreams of bees represent industriousness, self-sacrifice, fertility, and pregnancy. If you dream of a queen bee, then this represents power and matriarchy, and means that perhaps you are afraid someone's temper will sting you.

Beetle Dreams of a beetle symbolize disorder and a lack of cleanliness in your life, or that you are becoming aware of your resilient survival instincts. Alternatively, native people in the Amazon consider beetles to be sacred travelers from other dimensions that venture between our world and the afterlife to remind us that life is eternal. Dreams of a scarab signify that you are protected from harm, and that you are aligned with the sacred and the mystical. Consider the feeling tone. See *Goddess* (Persephone).

Beggar Dreams of a beggar symbolize poverty and victim consciousness. They may be showing you that it is time for you to own your power and give yourself the change you have been begging other people to make for you. See *Homelessness.*

Beginning Dreams of beginning something symbolize hope, faith, inspiration, and passion. They may be showing you that a new chapter lies ahead. See *Baby.*

Bell Dreams of a bell symbolize a warning, an awakening, or a reminder that it's time to take action. For some, the ringing of a bell represents an angel getting her wings, signifying that you will be acknowledged for your good work and heroic deeds.

Belly Button Dreams of a belly button represent connection with your mother or the Mother Goddess, maternal nurturing, and support. The belly button is also associated with the second chakra, or sacrum, which symbolizes life force and sexuality. See *Chakra* (2nd).

Belly Dancing/Belly Dancer Dreams of belly dancing or of a belly dancer represent sensuality, sexuality, and a desire for the expression of your goddess femininity in your life. See *Goddess.*

Belt Dreams of a belt signify that you are pulling yourself together, or holding back your personal power and individuality. If a belt is tight, it represents restriction or lean times. If a belt is loose, it represents vulnerability. Consider the feeling tone. See *Chakra* (3rd).

Bench Dreams of sitting on the sidelines or on the bench symbolize frustration, and mean that it is time for you to take the time to watch, learn, and reevaluate your life strategy. See *Dugout.*

Bending Dreams of bending can mean that you are testing the flexibility of your boundaries. They can also be showing you where you are being coerced or seduced, or are using your will in an attempt to influence others. The bend of a bow represents the inhale before the exhale, the necessary withdrawal of energy in order to reemerge more powerful than before. See *People Pleaser.*

Best Man Dreams of a best man symbolize honor, support, nobility, self-sacrificing, and the personification of friendship. See *Wedding.*

Beverage Dreams of a beverage denote a thirst for knowledge and nurturing, that you are drinking in all that life has to offer. If the beverage is warm, then you are drinking in that which warms your heart. If the drink is cold, then you are feeling relieved.

Bible Dreams of these sacred holy scriptures represent the power of the written word and the importance of chronicling your life. The Bible is also an invitation for you to reconnect with the Christ consciousness within yourself and to take your spiritual practice to the next level. See *Christ*.

Bicycle Dreams of a bicycle symbolize moving ahead and mean that you are in sync with the cycles of life. A racing bike represents competition that is animating and inspiring you to be your best, or that you are in a hurry for change. If you are riding for pleasure, then you are enjoying the phases of life without stress or worry. If this is a tyke bike, then you are reconnecting with your youth, and finding your sense of balance.

Big Dreams of something big symbolize power and influence. If you are small in comparison to something big, this represents feelings of intimidation and inadequacy. However, if you are big in comparison to the size of your challenge and/or the people you are dealing with, this represents that you feel capable, superior, powerful, and possibly overly qualified. See *Supersizing*.

Bill If you dream of paying a bill, then you are balancing your karma, reciprocating energy, wanting to even the score. If you are reacting to a bill that needs to be paid, then you are processing through and venting out feelings of insufficiency and lack. See *Money*.

Billboard A dream of a billboard is a sign for you to pay attention to the messages the universe is sending you. Consider the message that is written on the billboard.

Billiards Dreams of billiards signify that you are feeling competitive. See *Gambling* and *Las Vegas*.

Bindis Dreams of these ornaments for your forehead and third eye signify that you are accentuating your intuition, compassion, and wisdom.

Binoculars Dreams of binoculars symbolize a desire and/or the ability to see clearly into your own future or perhaps other people's business. See *Magnifying Glass* and *Voyeur.*

Bird Dreams of birds represent imagination, intuition, angels, creativity, and a desire for freedom. Perhaps you are in the midst of leaving the nest toward a more expansive reality. If the bird in a dream is injured or caged, this signifies that your freedom feels thwarted. The dream may be suggesting that you open up your cage, spread your wings, and venture out beyond your self-imposed restraints.

Birth Dreams of a birth represent renewal, transformation, a fresh start, and the manifestation of a creative project or a new opportunity for more life to be experienced and expressed. See *Baby, Infant,* and *Lamaze.*

Birth Control Dreams of birth control symbolize your ability to take control of your life. A dream of birth control may be gifting you with the realization of the responsibility required in the domain of parenthood. It could also reflect that you are blocking or manipulating the flow of your creativity, sexuality, or love. You are taking responsibility for your creative power and having a say where your creative juices will flow.

Birthday Whether it is your birthday or the birthday of someone else, a dream of a birthday represents a leap in consciousness or growth. Consider the feeling tone. See *Graduation* or *Party.*

Biting To dream of biting someone or being bitten is about your desire to leave your mark, to ingest life and to experience life fully. If you dream of a poisonous creature biting you, then this represents your awareness that you are being influenced in a nonsupportive way. However, if you enjoy the sensation of being bit, you may be in the process of being influenced in a beneficial way. See *Teeth.*

Black Dreams of the color black signify that which is mysterious, secretive, seductive, unknowable, a shadow aspect of your power that has not yet been realized. See *Integration Dreams,* page 10.

BlackBerry Dreams of a BlackBerry, a small phone/organizer/address book, signify that you are realizing the enormous power you have in the palm of your hand. See *World Wide Web.*

Blackboard A dream of a blackboard signifies a profound message for you. Consider the message written on a blackboard. If it is a clean slate, then this represents that you have an open mind. If you are writing on a blackboard, then you have a message that you want to share. If someone else is writing on a blackboard, then you are allowing another to influence you. See *PowerPoint Presentation.*

Blanket If you dream of a blanket, you are feeling comforted, loved, and protected. If you are looking for a blanket, you are seeking shelter, femininity, nurturing, and a warm hug of reassurance.

Blend/Blender Dreams of a blender signify that you are mixing in with the crowd, integrating and connecting with your community, or that you are mixing opposite aspects of your self together and integrating your polarities. A dream of a blender may be showing you the importance of maintaining your autonomy while blending in with a group. Consider the feeling tone. See *Integration Dreams,* page 10.

Blessing To dream of a blessing is an auspicious sign that you are recognizing and acknowledging the divine. See *Bodhisattva.* See also *Prophetic Dreams,* page 17.

Blind Dreams of being blind symbolize an unwillingness or inability to see what is happening right in front of your eyes. Perhaps you are processing your shock at being blindsided or overwhelmed by circumstances in your life. These dreams could be helping you to see that your insight, intuition, and gut feelings may be more accurate than what your physical eyes may see.

Blindfold Dreams of a blindfold signify that you may be purposefully ignoring your intuition. If you dream that you are being blindfolded, then the dream is showing you that you may be following someone blindly, or giving up your control issues and learning to trust. Consider the feeling tone.

Bling Bling Dreams of bling bling symbolize your fascination with materialism, wealth, and making a good appearance. Perhaps you have the desire for attention or to look more successful than you actually are. See *Accessories.*

Blipverts A dream of these short and seemingly random video images is your subconscious deprogramming, cleansing, and releasing the data it received during the day. Consider the content and feeling tone to discern the message. See *Processing Dreams,* page 7.

Blister A dream of a blister signifies that something or someone is rubbing you the wrong way. The dream is showing you that an emotional explosion will erupt if the situation isn't corrected. Consider where the blister is on your body to discern the dream's message for you.

Blizzard A dream of a blizzard signifies that you are moving through an emotional storm, and to keep moving and seek help during this challenging time so as to not freeze in your tracks. See *Breakdown/Breakthrough Dreams,* page 12.

Block Dreams of building blocks symbolize strategic movement toward the fulfillment of your goals and dreams. However, dreams of a roadblock signify that you are resisting abundance, success, and/or love. See *Constipation* and *Traffic.*

Blockbuster Video Dreams of Blockbuster Video represent your desire for either escapism or knowledge. You are being presented with a myriad of choices. Consider the movie you pick and the feeling tone of the dream. See *DVD, Movie,* and *Videotape.*

Blog A dream of a blog or literary diary represents a desire to stand on a soapbox and share your private thoughts with the public. The dream symbolizes nakedness and a drive to connect with people based on what you truly feel and think.

Blond Hair Dreams of blond or fair-colored hair symbolize naïveté, innocence, youth, being an "air head" or angelic. They may be suggesting that it is time for a change. Don't take things so seriously and have some fun. See *Hair.*

Blood Dreams of blood symbolize life force, power, and connection to your family or spiritual source. Consider what part of the body is bleeding and the feeling tone. See *Holy Grail* and *Wine.*

Bloom A dream of a flower in bloom symbolizes manifestation and the fulfillment of your dreams and goals. The dream also reflects a desire to be validated, supported, and recognized. Perhaps it is suggesting that you are blossoming into maturity and coming into your own. See *Garden.*

Blossom Dreams of a blossom signify that opportunities are coming into fruition and expansion in your career and/or relationships. See *Adolescence* and *Bloom.*

Blouse Dreams of a blouse represent your self-image. If a blouse is buttoned, then it represents modesty. If a blouse is loosely opened, then it symbolizes sexual freedom and liberation. See *Clothes* and *Shirt.*

Blue Dreams of the color blue symbolize clarity, peacefulness, and truth. A dream of blue may also be drawing attention to an underlying sadness. Consider the feeling tone. See *Chakra* (5th), *Sapphire,* and *Throat.*

Boat Dreams of a boat signify that you are floating just above the depths of your unconsciousness and the mysterious ocean of your sacred feminine nature. A dream of a boat can also symbolize your ability to flow with the currents of life or can reflect how you handle commitments.

Bodhisattva Dreams of a bodhisattva signify that you are connecting with your loving, angelic, and compassionate nature. Consider the feeling tone and the message brought to you by these dreams. See *Angel.* See also *Prophetic Dreams,* page 17.

Body Dreams about your body signify what is personal, essential, natural, sexual, and sensual about you. Dreams of your body also symbolize your self-image. See *Abdomen, Arm, Back, Buttocks, Ear, Eyes, Finger, Head, Leg, Lips, Neck, Nose, Penis, Throat, Toes, Vagina,* and *Naked.*

Bodyguard Dreams of a bodyguard symbolize a need for safety, protection, and defense against an actual or perceived threat. They may be suggesting that you need to take some preventive health measures. See *Boundary.*

Body Piercing Because metal is a conductor of energy, heat, and power, dreams of piercing one's body symbolize the desire to amplify power or rank within a social circle. The significance of the piercing is based upon which part of the body is pierced.

Boiling Dreams of boiling water signify that you are going through a transformation. You are purifying, altering, and/or heating things up in your life. Dreaming of boiling can also symbolize anger that is within you. Consider the feeling tone. See *Blister.*

Bolt If you dream of a bolt, then the dream signifies that you are trying to hold things together, maybe a relationship, or perhaps you are repairing a project, job, or belief system. The dream may be giving you the message that it is time to simplify your life by getting down to the nuts and bolts of the matter, or to bolt, as in get out of there.

If you dream of a lightning bolt, see *Lightning*.

Bomb Dreams of a bomb symbolize transformation—old structures, ideas, or relationships being blown to bits, and the radical destruction of old patterns. You are dealing with explosive emotions; however, if you catch your emotions before they erupt, then you can channel your anger in a direction that empowers your dreams to come true. See *Anger Management* and *Death*.

Bone Dreams of a bone symbolize your core, your soul essence, and/or the foundational principles of your life. Bones are also symbolic of strength, courage, and determination. If you dream of a broken bone, then this is about the structure of your belief system being fractured or broken. See *Skeleton*. See also *Breakdown/Breakthrough Dreams,* page 12.

Bonus A dream of a bonus signifies that a surprise is forthcoming and that you will be rewarded for your efforts. The dream may be preparing you to uplevel your self-worth and deservedness.

Boob Job As in any dream of cosmetic surgery, a dream of a boob job represents a lack of self-worth, a desire for perfection, and an external solution for an internal wound. The dream could represent a desire to enhance your ability to nourish and to be nourished. See *Breasts* and *Cosmetic Surgery.*

Book Dreams of a book symbolize the letter of the law, your worldview, inherited wisdom, and/or memories. A book represents a belief system, a point of view that you believe in, rebel against, and/or throw at someone. Consider the type of book and its message. See *Writing.*

Boomerang Dreams of a boomerang symbolize instant karma, what goes around comes around. You are realizing the full circle of life and recognizing the fairness and balance in the universe.

Boot Dreams of wearing boots represent strength, defense, power,

and machismo. Perhaps you are giving someone the boot and setting clear and nonnegotiable boundaries. You will show up grounded
and in a position of strength in an upcoming negotiation. See *Shoe*.

Booty Call Dreams of a booty call symbolize the need or desire for
instant gratification. Perhaps you are grappling with a conflict between your sexual longings and your desire to be respected.

Borrowing Dreams of borrowing something denote a need for energy that isn't yours, a desire to expand and grow, a need for support
or to support someone else who is in need.

Boss Dreams of a boss or an authority figure reflect your issues,
thoughts, and feelings about being in power or being at the mercy
of a powerful person. See *Employee/Employer*.

Botox Dreams of Botox represent a desire for a quick fix, an emotional bypass, and eternal youth. These dreams may be showing
you that you are operating under the false idea that if you keep the
wrinkles away you keep the aging process at bay. Consider the feeling tone. See *Cosmetic Surgery*.

Bottle A dream of a bottle represents nurturing and sustenance, depending on its contents. If you dream of a baby bottle, then it is a
symbol of nurturing empowerment. If you dream of a beer or wine
bottle, then it means that you are attempting to nurture yourself
while keeping at arm's length from reality. If you dream of a message in a bottle, consider the message to be a profound insight regarding your current circumstances.

Bottom Dreams of being at the bottom represent the end of a cycle.
If you dream of hitting the bottom, you have completed a particular pattern and are ready to reach for something higher.

Boundary A dream of a boundary symbolizes your attitudes and
feelings about saying no. You are learning to set healthy limits, allowing yourself to have some alone time, learning to speak up for
yourself, and protecting yourself against a real or perceived threat.
Also, a fortress could represent your desire to hold tight to your
ideals and patterns as you fight against change. Alternatively, a
dream of a boundary may be showing you that you may have set
too many boundaries and are keeping intimacy, love, and opportunities at bay.

Bouquet Dreams of a bouquet of flowers represent love, appreciation, respect, celebration, congratulations, and admiration. You are realizing a successful accomplishment. See *Flowers*.

Bowing A dream of bowing to someone suggests either a deep appreciation or an unwilling submission.

Bowl Dreams of a bowl symbolize receptivity and the ability to hold a space for someone, or for yourself. If a bowl is empty, then the dream is revealing that you are hungry for attention, energy, recognition, and/or acknowledgment. If a bowl is full, then the dream represents abundance. Consider the contents.

Bowling Dreams of bowling symbolize focus and concentration on a goal. They may be suggesting that you will strike it rich if you engage in life and get out of your rut. See *Sports*.

Box Dreams of a box represent a belief system or a surprise gift. A box might also represent repressed emotions, feelings, and/or cherished memories. An open box represents a paradigm shift or out-of-the-box thinking. Consider the feeling tone. See *Drawer*.

Boy Dreams of a boy symbolize connection with your youthful male essence, playfulness, sense of adventure, and creativity. They may be suggesting that it is time to let loose and play with abandon. See *Child, Knight, Peter Pan,* and *Son*.

Boyfriend A dream of a boyfriend represents your connection to the boyfriend archetype and desire for young love, romance, innocence, passion, and sexual exploration. If it is of a boyfriend of yours or of someone you know, you may be processing your feelings about that person. See *Prince*.

Bra Dreams of a bra symbolize support or embellishment of your femininity. If you are wearing your bra in public, then the dream is about public disclosure of your personal feelings, wearing your heart on your sleeve, or perhaps shame or embarrassment about your true feelings being revealed in public. If the bra is strapless, then you have a lack of support in your life. If the bra is padded, then you are embellishing or covering up your feelings of inadequacy. See *Clothes* and *Underwear*.

Bracelet If you dream of wearing a bracelet on your right hand, then this signifies that you are reaching for what you want in life. If the bracelet is worn on your left hand, then you are waiting for what you want to come to you. If it is a charm bracelet, then consider the symbolic nature of the charm(s).

Braces Dreams of braces symbolize correction and support. Perhaps you are realigning a pattern or habit that has taken you off track. If you dream of braces on your teeth, then you are working to improve your communication skills. If you dream of braces on your legs, then you are learning to stand up for yourself. If you dream of a back brace, you are learning to stand up straight, to be proud and confident. See *Mouth* and *Teeth*.

Braid A dream of a braid symbolizes integration, unification, synergy, and the weaving together of different aspects of yourself. If a braid is tight, then there may be fear holding you together. If a braid is loose, then you are peaceful and comfortable as you blend together your many qualities and talents. Pay attention to what materials are woven into the braid. If a braid is made of your hair, then you are strengthening your personal power. See *Goddess* (Athena) and *Weaving*.

Brain Dreams of a brain symbolize your thoughts and beliefs, logic, reasoning, order; your mental processing. They may be showing you that it is time to use your head, or alternatively, that you are overusing your head and it might do you good to allow your heart to do the thinking. Consider the feeling tone. See *Computer* and *Head*.

Branches Dreams of branches signify family connection and history, and that you are reaching out for support. If there are no leaves on the branches, then you have completed a cycle, and your relationship or job may be coming to an end. See *Arm* and *Tree*.

Brass Dreams of brass symbolize the coming together of diametrically opposed personalities or energies to perform a function in unity. See *Metal*. See also *Integration Dreams,* page 10.

Bread Dreams of bread symbolize money, abundance, life, support, and wealth. If bread is moldy, then it represents stinginess and a fear of spending. If bread is crusty, then it is about releasing your old belief systems about money. If you are breaking bread with someone, then you are sharing your wealth, and realizing that more will be added unto you. See *Baker/Baking.*

Breakdown Dreams of a breakdown signify that you are in the midst of a major transformation, processing your way through the changes in your life, and breaking out of a pattern or identity that no longer fits you. You may be discovering that what you thought was the worst thing that could ever happen is actually a blessing in disguise. See *Breakdown/Breakthrough Dreams,* page 12.

Breakfast Dreams of breakfast symbolize the first thoughts that you feed yourself, your intuitive beliefs. If you dream of eating a healthy breakfast, then you are feeding yourself positive affirmations about your life and vice versa. Consider the types of food you are eating. See *Food.*

Breaking Dreams of something breaking symbolize the ending of a pattern, relationship, or career. They reflect your relationship with change. Consider the feeling tone. Also, they could be giving you the message to put on the brakes, to slow down, or take a time-out.

Breakup If you dream of a breakup, it signifies that you are recognizing the completion of a cycle. This is not necessarily an indication that an entire relationship needs to end, just the unhealthy patterns. See *Breaking.*

Breast Feeding Dreams of breast feeding symbolize being cared for and nurtured. They reflect your desire to connect with the Goddess and to be mothered or to mother someone else. As well, they can be calling attention to an aspect of you that is in need of support.

Breasts Dreams of breasts represent nurturing, sexuality, femininity, and mothering. Full, ripe breasts represent abundance, prosperity, and seduction. Small breasts symbolize ripening femininity or perhaps a lack of nurturing in your life. See *Boob Job.*

Breath Dreams of breath symbolize your life force, your spirit, and your connection to your source and power. If you are holding your breath, then the dream may be suggesting that your stubbornness is keeping you from accomplishing what you truly desire. If you are breathing too hard or fast, then you are moving too fast and you might consider becoming more balanced so you can catch up with yourself. Pay attention to the feeling tone and quality of the breathing. See *Air*.

Brick Dreams of a brick or bricks signify that you are focused on the building blocks of a relationship or business venture. These dreams forecast a successful outcome. Alternatively, a brick can represent stubbornness. Consider the feeling tone. See *Foundation*.

Bride Dreams of a bride are very auspicious and represent your connection to the divine feminine and to your commitment to a life larger than your individuality. They can also symbolize partnership and your feelings and attitudes about marriage. See *Fairy Tale, Goddess,* and *Wedding*.

Bridesmaid Dreams of a bridesmaid symbolize support. If you are a bridesmaid, then you are processing your feelings and attitudes toward being in a secondary position. If you are the bride, then your bridesmaid symbolizes that you are supported and are connected to your female intuition. See *Sister* and *Wedding*.

Bridge Dreams of a bridge represent connecting one place in consciousness to another, one relationship to another, or one aspect of yourself to another. If you successfully cross a bridge, then you have left the past behind. If a bridge is broken or in need of repair, then it is suggesting that you need to slow down in a new relationship or business venture. If a bridge is burned, then it means a relationship has been severed. Consider the feeling tone to discern its message for you.

Briefcase Dreams about a briefcase, the container for important documents, represent your feelings and attitudes about your career and identity. A lost briefcase represents a transition in your career. See *Purse* and *Luggage*.

Broken Dreams of something being broken signify that you are feeling fragile and vulnerable, and that you are at the end of a cycle. Keep in mind that the places within you that have been broken, when repaired, become the places of your greatest strength and wisdom. Consider what has been broken. See *Accident, Breakdown,* and *Breaking*.

Bronze Dreams of bronze represent protection, strength, and preservation. See *Metal*.

Broom Dreams of a broom signify either that you are getting swept away in the moment or that it is time to clean up your act and resolve issues of the past. A dream of a broom can also be calling attention to your connection with the mystical and magical crone aspect of yourself. See *Crone* or *Witch*.

Brother If you dream of your brother, it can be a literal dream about him, the qualities he represents to you, or that which you project upon him. If you don't have a brother, then the dream can be symbolic of brotherly love, being a "soul brother," having a trusted bloodline with a man, or your connection to the brotherhood of man. See *Boy, Family,* and *Son*.

Brown Dreams of the color brown symbolize that which is plain, functional, and earthy. They could be a call for you to become more grounded. See *Chakra* (1st) and *Color*.

Bruise Dreams of a bruise signify that you have survived a painful experience, and that you have unhealed issues. Pay particular attention to the body part that is bruised. See *Body*.

Brunet Hair Dreams of brunet or dark-colored hair represent seriousness, intelligence, and groundedness. Brunet hair also symbolizes the sexually mysterious and possibly the dark side of a person. See *Black* and *Hair*.

Brush Dreams of a brush symbolize a desire to clean up your act and make a good appearance or impression.

Bubbles Dreams of bubbles signify that you are feeling light and joyous. They are foretelling a short but intensely joyful relationship and are a call for a spontaneous celebration of the present moment. See *Balloon* and *Champagne*.

Bucket A dream of a bucket signifies compassion and that you are a caring person. Consider the contents of the bucket.

Buckle Dreams of a buckle signify that you are holding or fastening things together, whether a relationship, a business situation, or a family dynamic. Because a belt buckle goes around your waist (1st chakra), dreaming about one represents survival issues. If you are unbuckled, you are throwing caution to the wind and living dangerously. Consider the feeling tone. See *Belt*.

Bud Dreams of a bud symbolize potential, the beginning stages of a

romance or a creative endeavor. A bud can also symbolize blossoming sexuality. A dream of a bud is telling you to have patience with
the process you are in because everything will blossom in its time.
See *Blossom, Seeds,* and *Spring.*

Buddha Dreams of the Buddha symbolize enlightenment, being in
this world but not of it, self-mastery, and knowing the truth of
beauty, love, and oneness beyond appearances. You are awakening
your ability to remain connected to your God/Goddess self while you
walk here on the earth, experiencing freedom from the trappings of
the world. See *Dalai Lama.* See also *Prophetic Dreams,* page 17.

Buddy List Dreams of a buddy list, as in your online IM, represent
your connection with friends and family. If your buddy list is
empty, this dream may be suggesting that it is time to communicate
with your tribe. If your buddy list is overflowing, then you may be
dealing with issues of quantity versus quality. See *Friend, Instant
Messenger,* and *Text Messages.*

Buffalo Dreams of a buffalo symbolize abundance. If there is a
white buffalo in a dream, it is telling you that your prayers will be
answered.

Bug Dreams of a bug denote that something or someone is distracting or irritating you. They are a call to focus your attention on your
major goals and not to sweat the small stuff. Recognize that distractions offer you an opportunity to master your attention and to live
your life as a living meditation. A bug can also represent a computer
virus, or a sign that if you don't take precautions you will get sick, as
in "catching a bug." See *Ants* and *Virus.*

Bugle Dreams of the sound of a bugle symbolize a wake-up call. Pay
particular attention to what happened after the appearance of the
bugle; therein lies the main message of the dream. See *Alarm.*

Building Dreams of building signify creation, and manifestation,
and that you are making things happen in your life. See *Architect.*
See also *Breakdown/Breakthrough Dreams,* page 12.

Dreams of a building symbolize your body and/or your life. If you
are in the lower levels of a building, then this represents your exploration of the foundational, primal, sexual, and instinctual aspects of
yourself. If you are on the top of a building, then you are connected

to your higher awareness, solutions, and spiritual realizations. If you are halfway up, then you are either feeling stuck in the middle or you are finding a balance between higher consciousness and mundane reality. Because a building represents your body or your life, the condition of the building is very telling. If it is in ruins, then this shows you have a lot of work to do to get your life up to code. If it is under construction, then your life is in the midst of an inner renovation and your belief systems are being transformed. If the building is in pristine shape, then so are your body and your life.

Bulb Dreams of a lightbulb represent a great insight, idea, or solution. See *Light*.

If you dream of a plant bulb, it represents the budding potential of your mind, body, and spirit, or the growth of a project, a baby, and/or a relationship. See *Bud*.

Bull Dreams of a bull symbolize energy that is masculine and unbending. You are venting pent-up feelings of anger and hostility. Perhaps your subconscious is calling you to stand up for yourself. A dream of a bull also may be suggesting that you slow down in a new relationship or business venture. Don't be a bull in a china shop. See *Taurus*.

Bulldozer Dreaming of a bulldozer is about destruction that leads to new life. Perhaps you are leveling an old structure so that something new can be built or created. See *Steamroller* and *Wrecking Ball*. See also *Breakdown/Breakthrough Dreams,* page 12.

Bullet Dreams of a bullet signify that you are trying to hit your mark. Perhaps you are feeling on the defensive or venting out anger or frustration. If you are shooting bullets, then you are expressing your rage or desire to kill off an undesirable aspect of yourself or of your life. If you are on the receiving end of the bullet, you are feeling guilty about an indiscretion. See *Gun* and *Killing*.

Bungee Jumping Dreams of bungee jumping signify that you are living on the edge, taking risks, and experiencing emotional highs and lows. They can also be about your reticence to make a commitment, or to *take the plunge.*

Buoy Dreams of a buoy symbolize optimism and an attitude of gratitude that will always help you to rise above your pain. A buoy can also be a marker, an indication of your progress, or emotional boundaries, and it can be a sign to alert you when you've gone off the deep end.

Burial Dreams of a burial signify that you are putting to rest habits and behaviors that no longer support you. You are coming to completion, and letting something or someone go. A dream of being buried alive is a venting dream about the fact that you have not been fully living. It is a wake-up call to live today as if it were your last. See *Death* and *Funeral*.

Burning Dreams of a burn or of something burning symbolize transformation, initiation, destruction, healing, purification, alchemy, passion, and releasing that which no longer serves you. Burning also represents intense passion, sexual feelings, and intense romantic love. See *Fire*.

Burning Man Dreams of the Burning Man experience symbolize a desire to burn away your ego defenses and to connect with your innate sense of freedom, creativity, unity, and self-expression.

Bus See *Shuttle*.

Business Dreams of your business are processing dreams helping you to sort out and solve unresolved issues of the day. A dream of business could also be giving you the message to *get down to business* and take your work more seriously. See *Work*. See also *Processing Dreams,* page 7.

Business Card A dream of a business card is about your public persona and your attachment to your title and credentials. It could also reflect credentials that you wish you had. Consider what is written on the card.

Butcher Dreams of a butcher symbolize your ability to separate your heart from what you have to do. This is about your ability to cut someone out of your life if that person isn't healthy for you. You are setting boundaries without compassion or sensitivity. If you normally have a hard time setting limits or boundaries, then this extreme archetype might be helpful for you to call upon. However, if you are normally cold and able to chop people out of your life without caring, then the dream is suggesting that sensitiv-

ity and empathy is necessary for you to achieve intimacy in relationships.

Butter Dreams about butter represent good fortune. They can also
be showing you that you have been buttering someone up or that
someone's compliments may be disingenuous.

Butterfly Dreams of a butterfly symbolize transformation, freedom,
expansion, and full self-expression. You are spreading your wings
and flying to the heights of your creative expression. A dream of a
butterfly is telling you to embrace all the cycles of your life and appreciate the present moment.

Buttocks Dreams of the buttocks can represent issues of support,
sexuality, or body image. The details of a dream and the feeling
tone will help you find a more decisive message.

Button Dreams of buttons denote closure, or perhaps that you are
covering something up. If you dream of unbuttoning your clothes,
then you are opening yourself to intimacy and are removing your
armor. If you dream of buttoning up your clothes, then you are
hiding or defending yourself.

Buying Dreams of buying signify that you are taking responsibility
for your life. Also, a dream of buying something can be suggesting
that you have bought into an idea and are allowing yourself to be
influenced. Consider what you are buying. See *Retail Therapy* and
Shopping.

Buzzard Dreams of a buzzard signify that you or someone in your
life is preying on those who are energetically weaker and smaller—a
buzzard is an ominous symbol for death, decay, destruction, and
the end of a cycle. See *Shadow*.

C

Cab Dreams of being a passenger in a cab signify that you are allowing other people to influence your direction in life. If you are
driving a cab, then this means that you are influencing the direction
of other people's lives. See *Car*.

Cabin Dreams of a cabin symbolize self-reliance, independence, social reclusivness, connection to the simple things in life. Dreaming

about this cozy place nestled in the woods represents a sanctuary in the midst of the wild world you live in. You are finding your center, a haven you can come home to wherever and whenever you want.

Cabinet Dreams of a cabinet symbolize your body and your life. If a cabinet is locked, then it represents family secrets and mythology. If a cabinet is open for display, then it represents your desire to express the truth. If it is a governmental cabinet, then you are processing feelings and opinions about the government or of other people running your life. However, if you dream that you are part of the cabinet, then you are stepping into leadership and taking responsibility for your life.

Cable Dreams of a cable signify that you are getting hooked up, fixed up, or plugged into a love/partnership arrangement. You are either finding your creative outlet or finding a creative partnership for your business. If a cable is strong, then it represents strength, stamina, and durability in the partnership. If a cable is frayed, then it represents vulnerability, weakness, and fragility in the relationship. See *Communication, Plug, Television,* and *Wire.*

Cactus Dreams of a cactus symbolize your egoic defense mechanisms that keep people and opportunities at bay. Cactus can also represent good karma and reassurance in your ability to survive extreme circumstances. See *Boundary* and *Desert.*

Café Dreams of a café symbolize your attitudes and feelings about social/communal situations. An outdoor café represents intimacy, romance, and stimulation. See *Restaurant* and *Starbucks.*

Caffe Latte Dreams of a caffe latte symbolize the desire for a buzz and socialization, and to energetically keep up with the high expectations you have for yourself. See *Espresso* and *Milk.*

Cage A dream of a cage signifies that you are feeling trapped, smothered, stuck, powerless, and/or victimized. Perhaps you have a desire to break out of, leave, fight, or flee a situation you are in. For a more precise understanding of a dream of a cage, identify who is jailed and who is the jailer. If you put a wild animal into a cage, this means either that you are gaining mastery over your animal instincts or that you are suppressing them. Consider the feeling tone of the dream.

Cake Dreams of a cake symbolize celebration, acknowledgment, and reward for your hard work. Things will now come easily to you as you are realizing that you can have your cake and eat it too.

Calculator Dreams of a calculator are about your concern for the way things are adding up in your life. You are carefully thinking through your problems and choices, accessing your logic, and taking stock to make sure your energy is being properly allocated. Consider the numbers on the calculator as well as the feeling tone. See *Number*.

Calendar A dream of a calendar signifies that you are counting the days for an event or situation to unfold. The dream may be a message for you to make every day count. See *Cycle* and *Seasons*.

Calf Dreams of a calf symbolize youthful vitality, innocence, immaturity, flexibility, inexperience, and connection with your own childhood and vulnerability. If you dream of a white calf, then your prayers are being answered. See *Buffalo*.

Camcorder Dreams of a camcorder are symbolic of being able to view yourself objectively, and your desire to keep memories alive, to own and recapture time. See *Movie* and *Photograph*.

Camel Dreams of a camel signify that you are able to survive extreme circumstances. You have the inner resources within you to make it through any challenging time, as well as the patience and perseverance to make it through a drought. Your oasis is within you. See *Desert* and *Oasis*.

Camera Dreams of a camera signify your desire to capture time, and that you are holding tightly to your past memories. If you are the one handling a camera, then you are processing feelings of being on the outside looking in. If you are the one being photographed, then this is about self-love. If you are avoiding having your picture taken, you are trying to maintain your privacy. See *Photograph*.

Camouflage Dreams of camouflage mean that you are hiding, wanting to blend in or be unnoticed because perhaps you feel your survival is an issue. You may feel it is unsafe to let the full spectrum of your colorful expression shine through. See *Chameleon*.

Camp Dreams of a camp signify your desire for connection to the outdoors and adventure, and that you are living on the edge.

Camping also represents simplicity and your connection to your survival skills.

If a dream is of a military camp, see *Army* or *Navy.*

Campaign A dream of a campaign represents a platform upon which you base your life. The dream may be telling you that it is time to identify your higher purpose. If you already know what your higher purpose is, the dream may be an affirmation that you are on the right track.

Campfire Dreams of a campfire symbolize transformation, intimacy, warmth, and closeness with yourself, your tribe, family, or community. See *Goddess* (Hestia).

Can Dreams of a can symbolize preservation. If you dream of a tin or aluminum can, it means that you *can* do whatever it is you set your mind to.

Canal Dreams of a canal are about the female genitalia, the feminine principle of openness, receptivity, flow, and intuition. They can signify that you are in the flow of romance, passion, sexuality, or manifesting your dreams.

Canary Dreams of a canary signify assistance, and that you are calling out for help. They can also be about the healing power of sound. See *Bird* and *Singing.*

Cancer Dreams of cancer represent unexpressed emotions, guilt, anger, resentment, and a deep fear of the repercussions of fully expressing your feelings. You may be allowing guilt to eat away at you. See *Aids, Disease,* and *Sick.*

Astrologically, Cancer represents sensitivity, empathy, and someone who puts his or her imagination to use. Dreams of cancer may be guiding you to spend time with people who understand, love, and nurture you. Set boundaries, but be cautious of too much armor.

Candle Candles in dreams symbolize power, energy, heat, and the amplification of energy. They signify good luck and clarity of intent. If a candle is extinguished in a dream, then you are surrendering your attachment to a goal or romance. If a candle is burning from both ends, you are overextending yourself and need to find balance—otherwise you will burn yourself out. See *Light.*

Candy Dreams of candy signify that something sweet is happening in your life. Or candy can represent a bribe to get the child within you to do something he or she may or may not want to do.

Cane Dreams of a cane symbolize support during a vulnerable time and/or the need for someone or something to lean on. See *Railing*.

Cannibal Dreams of a cannibal symbolize your fight for survival at all costs. A cannibal also represents power, control, and a battle for energy. See *Animal, Fight* and *Flying*. See also *Venting Dreams*, page 8.

Cannon Dreams of a cannon symbolize power, destruction, defense, a loud presence, and perhaps a tendency to fight fire with fire. See *Breakdown/Breakthrough Dreams*, page 12.

Canoe Dreams of a canoe symbolize that you are going with the flow of life and keeping up with current trends. Alternatively, they might be guiding you to get back into harmony with your nature instead of going against it. See *Boat*.

Canopy Dreams of a canopy symbolize royalty, protection, and a veil of secrecy. See *Bed*.

Canteen Dreams of a canteen symbolize a need to keep emotionally hydrated and creatively juiced. If a canteen is full, you are capable of quenching your own thirst and tending to your own needs. If a canteen is empty, you are going through a creative dry spell, processing feelings of lack, and you are thirsting for acceptance, support, and/or creative inspiration. See *Thirst*.

Canvas If you dream that a canvas is blank, then you have a new opportunity ahead of you. If a canvas is filled, then you are filled with creative ideas. If what you see on a canvas pleases you, then you feel good about the current status of your creativity and/or life. If you don't like what is on a canvas, or if it won't wash off, then there is something uncomfortable for you to face and embrace before you can erase it and move on. See *Art/Artist*.

Canyon Dreams of a canyon are a message for you to be still and collect your thoughts and composure while taking time away from the hustle and bustle of the world. You are indulging in an exploration of your feminine side, your receptivity, and introspection. See *Grand Canyon*.

Cap Dreams of a cap symbolize preservation or suppression of your potential, capabilities, and possibilities. A cap signifies that you may be keeping things a secret until you are ready for them to be revealed. See *Hat, Lid,* and *Roof.*

Capricorn If you dream of the astrological sign Capricorn, then you are connecting with the aspect of you that is capable, hardworking, determined, dominant, and tyrannical. The dream may be telling you to recognize your natural leadership and/or to empower others to lead. See *Astrologer/Astrology.*

Captain Dreams of a captain signify that you are taking control of the vessel of your life, and are coming to the awareness that you are responsible for how you navigate through it.

Captive Dreams of a captive express your control issues or your fear of being controlled by a person, job, or situation. They are helping you to vent out and process through the victim/perpetrator polarities within you.

Car A dream of a car symbolizes your body and your identity. If a car is in good shape, then this dream is a reflection of your self-care. If a car is in need of repair, then so are you. If a car is being worked on, then this suggests that you are undergoing a transformational overhaul. Dreams of being in a car mean that you are being carried from one place of consciousness to another. If you are driving, then this signifies that you feel in control. If you are a passenger, then the dream may be telling you that you have abdicated responsibility and are in a state of passivity or surrender. Consider whether or not you like *where* you are being driven to, *how* you feel about *what* you are being driven in, and *how* you are being driven.

Carbs/Low Carbs Dreams of carbohydrates (carbs), energy that burns fast, symbolize easy money or an overnight relationship. If you dream of being on a low-carb diet, it represents your desire to lose emotional baggage. Dreams of any diet are about discipline, which if taken to an extreme can lead to deprivation and imbalance. A dream of being on a high-protein, low-carb diet can also symbolize a subconscious desire for more substance and solidity and less fluff in your life. See *Diet.*

Carburetor A dream of a carburetor is about an aggressive and explosive aspect of your personality that is kicking in because you need to accomplish something quickly. The dream could be suggesting that balance is needed.

Cards Keep in mind that life is 10 percent the cards you're dealt, and 90 percent how you play them. A dream about cards is about how you play the game of life and your desire to see the future. If there is a card up your sleeve, then you are hiding something or keeping secrets. If all your cards are on the table, then you are being honest about your intentions. Pay attention to what cards are being revealed. See *Ace, Club, Diamond, Gambling, Heart, Number, Spade, Tarot,* and *Trump Card.*

Carnation Dreams of a carnation vary in symbolism based upon its color: *red*—compassion; *pink*—I'll never forget you; *purple*—capriciousness, caution; *striped*—sorry I can't be with you, "Dear John"; *white*—innocence; *yellow*—playfulness.

Carnival Dreams of a carnival are calling you to live life to its fullest and honor life's rites of passage. They may also indicate that something exciting is forthcoming. There is a shadow side to a carnival as well, which may be telling you to look beneath the surface of the "eye candy" in your life. Consider the feeling tone of the dream. See *Mardi Gras.*

Carousel Dreams of a carousel symbolize the cycles of life. If you are riding a carousel, then you are participating in life's passages. If you are watching a carousel, then you are not participating, but rather watching life pass you by. In that case, the dream is telling you to take a more active role in your life. If the dream is of a carousel at an airport's baggage claim, then it is about patience and being reassured that that which is yours cannot pass you by. See *Baggage Claim* and *Seasons.*

Carpenter Dreams of a carpenter symbolize your ability to take life into your own hands and create your life the way you want it to be. Generally they are calling you to enjoy fully the abundance that surrounds you.

Carpet Dreams of a carpet signify that you are cushioned from life's hardships, that you are enjoying luxury and comfort. Consider the condition of a carpet, its color, the room that it is in, and whether or not you are hiding something under the carpet. If it is a magic carpet, then you are rising above troubles, overcoming obstacles, and getting a higher view. See *Rug*.

Carrot Dreams about carrots signify that you are on a path toward a desired outcome or goal, focused on a reward for your hard work. Perhaps you feel that the goal is out of reach, and that you are chasing after something that is outside of yourself. If you dream that a carrot is in your possession, then congratulations, you have what you've been looking for. A carrot can also be a phallic symbol, showing you that you are being seduced.

Cartoon Character Dreams of seeing someone as a cartoon character signify that you don't take that person seriously or that you think he or she is laughable. To see a specific cartoon character in a dream means that you are embracing the larger-than-life qualities that you ascribe to that character. Consider the qualities that the cartoon character represents to you.

Carving Dreams of carving are about shaping life to your liking. You may be carving out a niche so that you can leave your mark on the world. If you are carving meat, then you are dividing up your power and energy and preparing to share it with others. Carving something can also reflect criticism, as in cutting something or someone down to size. See *Knife*.

Cash Dreams of cash symbolize power, freedom, energy, and security. Also cash, as opposed to checks and credit cards, represents having energy and power that you can use spontaneously with anonymity. You are feeling in control of your life. See *Money*.

Cashier Dreams of a cashier signify that you are connecting with your internal money manager and processing your issues with money. They can also be a message for you to pay an emotional debt and/or that you are paying the price for your choices in life. See *Karma* and *Money*.

Casket Dreams of a casket symbolize your feelings and attitudes about death, change, and transition in relationships or business. Dreams of a casket are also about being contained and supported while you move from one phase of your life to the next. See *Death*.

Castle Dreams of a castle forecast wealth and prominence. Also, dreams of a castle are a sign that your wishes will come true. See *Fairy Tale*.

Castration Dreams of castration symbolize disempowerment, invalidation, rejection, and criticism. You are either rejecting yourself or invalidating someone else. See *Testes*.

Cat Dreams of a cat represent your feminine essence and sensuality. Perhaps you have been cautious, skittish, aloof, mysterious, mischievous, and/or curious lately. Cats also represent other dimensions and are considered to have the ability to travel between the third, fourth, and fifth dimensions. A black cat may be reminding you to pay attention to your intuition. See *Animal*.

Catechism Dreams of this Catholic training ground for children represent spiritual inquiry, foundations of spirituality, and ritualistic repetition. Consider the feeling tone of the dream and your associations with Catholicism. See *Catholicism* and *School*.

Caterpillar Dreams of a caterpillar signify that you are in the midst of a great transformation, and that you are realizing the value of every stage of growth. The caterpillar stage of growth is about budding potential and beauty and the importance of honoring the ordinary and mundane aspects of your life. These dreams can also be a suggestion to take your time and not rush a new relationship. Consider the feeling tone. See *Breakdown/Breakthrough Dreams*, page 12.

Cathedral Dreams of a cathedral symbolize elaborate spirituality and outward devotion to your religious or spiritual path. They could also represent your attachment to the outer accoutrements of your spirituality. A dream of a cathedral is asking you to make sure that your spiritual walk matches your talk. See *Church*.

Catholicism Dreams of Catholicism signify that you are connecting to your spiritual roots, devotion, suppression of your natural urges, conformity, rules, and piety. Perhaps you are realizing strength in tradition and the value in ceremony. Alternatively, a dream of Catholicism might also represent rigid ideas and issues of integrity. Consider the feeling tone. See *Pope*.

Cattle Dreams of cattle signify that you are going along with the crowd, following the leader, and feeling a lack of individuality. They may be telling you to maintain your individuality as you proceed with your projects and relationships. Alternatively, you might be discovering strength and power in your affiliation with a group or tribe. Consider the feeling tone. See *Cow.*

Caught   If you dream of being caught, this is calling attention to your lack of integrity in an existing personal relationship or business venture. The dream is suggesting that you should clean up your thoughts and deeds. Perhaps someone or something has hooked your attention and you've been caught in or seduced into a web. To be caught in a dream can also mean that you have been running from responsibility and neglecting a decision that you are now being forced to deal with. If you catch something, this represents your willingness and capability to get what you need in life. See *Thief.* See also *Venting Dreams,* page 8, and *Integration Dreams,* page 10.

Cave   Dreaming of this prehistoric hiding place can represent a respite, a place of a rich inner life, hidden treasures, and your need for safety. Perhaps a dream of a cave is suggesting that you take time away from your busy life to process your feelings and plan your strategy for your next venture. Or it may be telling you to give other people in your life the dignity of their own space when they need it. A dream of a cave also represents a desire to go back to the womb. See *Dugout* or *Hermit.*

CD   Dreams of a CD symbolize your ability or desire to control your emotions, people, events, and the sound track of your life. If you are burning a CD, then this represents your ability to create what you want in life and to capture what is pleasing. See *Circle* and *Music.*

Ceiling   Dreams of a ceiling signify that you are becoming aware of real or imagined restrictions, as well as a desire to be protected. A low ceiling denotes that you are feeling cramped or stifled in your expression and in your ability to progress. A high ceiling represents lofty thoughts, open-mindedness, and feeling that there is room to grow and advance. See *Cap, Lid,* and *Roof.*

Celebration Dreams of a celebration signify that you have successfully achieved a level of growth, learning, and/or accomplishment. This is your subconscious saying congratulations for your progress and for the lessons you have learned and earned. Pay particular attention to what the celebration is honoring. See *Party.*

Celebrity Dreams of a celebrity symbolize power, influence, glamour, and strolling down the red carpet as your greatest, most celebrated self. Because every character in a dream is you, consider that the qualities of the celebrity and the role he or she plays in a dream are revealing an aspect of you.

Celery Dreams of celery signify that you are of good stock, strong, and healthy. See *Vegetables.*

Celibacy Dreams of celibacy symbolize your fear of having power or the fear of losing power. They could be a call for more discipline or for more release. Consider the feeling tone. See *Tantric Sex.*

Cellophane Dreams of cellophane symbolize your attempt at preserving your talents, gifts, or resources. You also might be processing through and venting out feelings of being invisible, unimportant, and dispensable. See *Transparent.*

Cell Phone Dreams of a cell phone represent telepathic communication. Significant aspects of these dreams are the person you are calling and/or who is calling you, whether or not you are able to reach the person, and the status of your connection (four bars, three, two, or one, or none). Consider what is being communicated. See *Text Message.*

Cemetery Dreams of a cemetery represent change or the ending of a relationship or business affair. You may be grieving and moving through the bittersweet sorrow of missing your connection to a loved one or releasing a deeply held attachment. See *Death.*

Center Dreams of a center symbolize the essence of control and essential survival issues. If you are in the center of a situation, then your choices will either create a sense of unity and interconnectivity or chaos.

Ceremony Dreams of a ceremony represent an initiation or completion of a chapter of your life. Perhaps you are celebrating or honoring a rite of passage from one incarnation to the next. To ceremonialize something in waking life or in a dream is to make it sacred and to evoke your higher nature. Dreams of a ceremony also mean that you are bringing your focus to a particular commitment. See *Graduation, Ritual,* and *Wedding.*

Certificate Dreams of a certificate are about approval, respect, authority, and authenticity. Perhaps they reflect your desire to show the world that you are worthy. If you've been waiting for a certificate to feel worthy or to begin doing your life's work, then here it is.

Cesarean Dreams of a cesarean birth, or C-section, signify that you are slicing through barriers to attain your next level of awareness. Perhaps you are attempting to force or prematurely extract a creative process or you are saving a project or relationship by the skillful use of your will. See *Birth.*

Chain Dreams of a chain symbolize your connection to people and events and your interconnectivity with all life. Pay particular attention to what you are chained to. It may be time for change and a rearrangement of agreements and commitments. Consider the chain reaction, the cause and effect that your actions have on the people around you. See *Caught* and *Karma.*

Chair Dreams of a chair symbolize authority, the opinions that prop you up, and the ideas that uphold your position. They may be guiding you to relax, sit down, and rest. Alternatively, they could be showing you that if you are resting on your laurels you could become sedentary. It may be time to stand up and be counted. An overstuffed chair represents an overstuffed sense of importance and ego. A hard and straight chair denotes uptight, inflexible, and rigid beliefs.

Chakra Dreams of these energy centers in your body represent distinct qualities and themes that are associated with the area of the body and/or color that appears in a dream. A dream may be suggesting an overemphasis or imbalance in one of your chakras, or perhaps a suppression of energy. Keep in mind that the ideal state is equanimity, balance, flow, and honoring of all centers as sacred. For more in-depth understanding, see the corresponding area of the body as well as the color.

Chakra	Placement in the Body	Qualities/ Attributes	Color
1st/Root	Base of spine	Connection to the earth, survival instincts	Brown
2nd/Sacrum	Lower abdomen	Sexuality, passion, life force	Red
3rd/Solar Plexus	Upper abdomen	Self-confidence, personal power	Orange
4th/Heart	Heart/chest	Love, commitment, integrity	Green
5th/Throat	Throat	Communication, self-expression, manifestation	Blue
6th/Ajna	Head	Intuition, wisdom	Violet/ indigo
7th/Crown	Above the head	Spirit awareness, enlightenment	White

Chalice Dreams of a chalice symbolize immortality and a thirst for spiritual nourishment. If you are drinking from this sacred goblet, you are in the midst of a rite of passage, transforming, and connecting with the divine Feminine. Dreams of a chalice are suggesting that you make room for more abundance and opulence to come into your life. Also, a silver chalice represents justice and that the truth will always prevail. See *Cup* and *Holy Grail*.

Chalk Dreams of chalk symbolize a temporary marker, and that which can be easily erased. Chalk is usually something associated with school that involves learning from a teacher. You are growing and making progress.

Challenge Dreams of a challenge signify that you are in the midst of a growth opportunity to deepen, strengthen, and perfect levels of mastery. Perhaps you are realizing a form of angelic support that will reveal your blessing in disguise.

Chameleon Dreams of a chameleon symbolize your desire to fit in and be accepted or approved of. They are showing you that you have the ability to intuitively know how to behave appropriately in any situation. Alternatively, dreams of a chameleon show you that you have an authentic and unique expression that also needs to be expressed. See *People Pleaser* and *Rainbow.* See also *Integration Dreams,* page 10.

Champagne Dreams of champagne symbolize celebration, bubbly and happy times. You are having a toast to yourself, which foretells of success. The popping of the cork can also symbolize the sexual act or need for emotional or physical release. See *Ceremony.*

Champion Dreams of a champion signify that you are accessing your hero archetype and realizing your willingness to become the best you can be. Perhaps you are realizing and receiving the support that you need. See *Cheerleader* and *Hero.* See also *Wish Fulfillment Dreams,* page 18.

Chandelier Dreams of a chandelier represent extravagance, grandeur, and illumination. If a lightbulb represents an "aha" moment, then a chandelier reflects grand-scale inspiration. See *Light.*

Chapstick Dreams of Chapstick represent honest expression and freedom from speaking dryly and dispassionately. They are telling you to say what you mean, and mean what you say.

Charcoal Dreams of charcoal represent a quickening, an amplification, and enhancement of the fire of your desire, passion, and transformation.

Chariot Dreams of a chariot represent a mode of transportation between the earth and otherworldly places. They can represent the journey of transformation from hope to pain and back again. A dream of a chariot can also indicate whether or not you are driving or being carried by another, relinquishing control and responsibility, or returning to your childhood.

Charity Dreams of charity symbolize your connection with your divine nature and indicate that blessings are coming your way. In dreams or in real life, acts of charity connect you to great abundance. Dreams of being the recipient of charity could reflect your ability to receive, or might be revealing issues of victimhood. Consider the feeling tone.

Chart Dreams of a chart signify that you are monitoring your progress in an organized and controlled way. Also, you may be feeling the need to know where you stand in a relationship or your job. See *Map*.

Chase Dreams of chasing or of being chased signify that you believe that what you need is out of reach, that you are being seduced by the thrill of the hunt, or that you are running from an undesirable aspect of yourself or from an adverse influence. Keep in mind that what you resist persists.

Chat Room If you dream of being in a chat room, then it represents connecting with aspects of yourself that you have not yet met. Pay particular attention to the content of a chat; the words are the prime message in the dream. A chat room also reflects a desire for anonymity, intimacy at a safe distance, and a desire for connection with people that share a mutual interest. A dream of a chat room may be advising you to venture out and take your chats to the next level. See *Internet*.

Cheating Dreams of cheating symbolize a poverty-consciousness, fears of being victimized, and an unwillingness or inability to trust yourself. If you are afraid someone will cheat you, listen to your instincts and recognize that the people in your life are mirrors of your self. See *Insider Trading*.

Check Dreams of writing a check for services rendered reflect your feelings about money and self-worth issues. If you are receiving a check, then the feeling tone of these dreams will reflect your level of receptivity. The amount of a check will reflect your feelings of deservability.

Checkers Dreams of checkers signify competition and strategy, and that you are playing a game and attempting to anticipate your opponent's next move. You are feeling challenged and are attempting to make a winning move in your life. See *Game*.

Checkmate Dreams of checkmate are about moving on to the next phase of your life: success, victory, or defeat depending upon the feeling tone. See *King* and *Queen*.

Checkout If you dream of being at the checkout stand of a grocery store, then it means that your karmic debt is being paid into and that you are taking responsibility for your actions. On the other hand, it could represent that you have been checking out, as in not being present. If this is the case, then this may be a call to be aware of that which you are disassociating from.

Cheerleader Dreams of a cheerleader symbolize your inner champion and your ability to pull yourself up by your bootstraps. Your enthusiastic belief in yourself and the people you are rooting for will ensure success and victory.

Cheese Dreams of cheese symbolize nurturing wisdom. Swiss cheese represents vulnerability; Brie represents elegance and decadence; Cheddar represents wholesome, basic sustenance for your soul.

Chef Dreams of a chef symbolize mastery in your ability to nurture and feed souls. Perhaps you are blending together the ingredients of your personality with the chemistry of other people into a delicious creation. See *Shaman.* See also *Integration Dreams,* page 10.

Cherry Dreams of a cherry symbolize virginity, innocent sexiness, the vagina, the hymen, and immeasurable value and sweetness. Consider the feeling tone. See *Food* and *Fruit.*

Cherub Dreams of a cherub symbolize your closeness to God. A dream of a cherub could be a prophetic dream where an important message is being delivered to you. See *Angel.* See also *Prophetic Dreams,* page 17.

Chess Dreams of chess symbolize strategy, patience, and slow, deliberate moves in your decision-making process. They could also reflect discipline, intelligence, and the manipulation of power and energy. See *Checkmate.*

Chest Dreams of a chest, as in a physical body, represent the cover over your heart. Perhaps you are feeling protective or defensive about allowing your heart to be open. If you dream of a pirate's treasure chest, then this symbolizes wealth and treasure. If it is a buried chest, then you are keeping your talent buried. See *Breasts* and *Heart.*

Chestnuts Dreams of chestnuts are associated with Christmas, heat, emotional warmth, and nurturing. Chestnuts are also a symbol of foresight and can be calling you to plan ahead.

Chewing Dreams of chewing represent a need to understand something and to figure out what you need to do in a relationship or business venture. You are working out the details and ingesting the energy of a new situation before you make a move. Chewing gum represents anxiety. See *Digesting*.

Chicken Dreams of a chicken mean that you are feeling fearful. They are telling you that it is time to come to your senses, meditate, and find your center. The message of these dreams is to move through your fear.

Child Dreams of a child symbolize new life, innocence, and connectivity to everyone and everything. Your subconscious is giving you a message to integrate feelings of unbridled joy, fun, and unlimited creativity into your serious adult endeavors. If you dream that you are a child, then this is about your need or desire to be taken care of, pampered, and babied. See *Baby* and *Spring*.

Chili Dreams of chili symbolize fuel and energy. Dreams of chili peppers symbolize something spicy and exciting happening in your love life. See *Food*.

Chimney Dreams of a chimney represent the release of pressure, anger, and frustration. They are telling you that you need to find a healthy way to release pent-up energy. See *Anger*.

China Dreams of China symbolize ancient tradition, discipline, and a value of the mental process over the emotional. See *Orient*.

If you dream of dining on fine china, it is foretelling a successful business arrangement.

Chocolate Dreams of chocolate symbolize a reward for good work and possibly a substitute or metaphor for love. Something sweet is coming your way. See *Candy*.

Choir Dreams of a choir symbolize strength and power in numbers and that you are never alone. A choir also is symbolic of spiritual fortitude and religious fervor. See *Angel, Music,* and *Singing*.

Choking Dreams of choking signify that there is something in your life that is hard to swallow. The throat is your avenue of communication and manifestation, so choking means that there is something you are holding back or afraid to express and/or manifest. A dream of choking may be suggesting that you find a safe means of expression, for example, a venting letter that is never sent, or that you share what is stuck in your throat with a trusted friend, therapist, or life coach.

Chord Dreams of hearing musical chords, or notes, signify that something or someone is resonating or not with you. Consider the way the sound makes you feel. See *Music.*

Christ Dreams of Jesus Christ are about divine guidance, unconditional love, wisdom, and inspiration. See *God.* See also *Prophetic Dreams,* page 17.

Christmas Dreams of Christmas represent the birth of the sacred within the human. For some, however, Christmas is synonymous with materialism, shopping, and the pressure of gift buying. To the inner child, Christmas is symbolic of joy, magic, enchantment, and the belief that anything is possible. Consider the context and feeling tone of the dream.

Church Dreams of a church symbolize your relationship with spirituality, religious attitudes, and beliefs. Consider the feeling tone. See *Cathedral, Ceremony,* and *Temple.*

Cigarette See *Smoking.*

Cinderella Dreams of Cinderella signify victimhood, and innocence, and that you have a spiritual strength, even when your circumstances look bleak. See *Fairy Tale* and *Midnight.*

Circle Dreams of a circle represent wholeness, infinity, cycles, unity, and your connection with the feminine essence. If something is in the center of a circle, it represents wisdom, spirit, and that which is most important to you. A circle can also represent repetition. See *Wheel.*

Circumcision Dreams of circumcision symbolize emasculation, extreme self-denial, and/or a desire to cut off masculine aggressiveness and power. See *Castration.*

Circus Dreams of a circus represent your unconscious desire to connect with or express aspects of your genius that you deem freakish. Perhaps you are afraid people will judge you for being over the top if you truly express your uniqueness. See *Animal* and *Circus.*

Cirque du Soleil Dreams of the Cirque du Soleil signify that you are thinking out of the box, discovering skills and talents that are unique to you, and that you are realizing your bizarre, one-of-a-kind mastery and expression. See *Circus*.

City Dreams of a city signify productivity and high energy, and perhaps that you are feeling out of touch with nature and caught up in a high-tech, low-touch world. They will also reflect your attitudes about community.

Clam Dreams of a clam symbolize that you are feeling secretive and closed off. They can also symbolize money and may be forecasting that you will soon be coming into wealth.

Clamp Dreams of a clamp represent being closed up emotionally, your lips sealed, and your secrets safe. Perhaps you are feeling shut down, protected, and afraid of exposure.

Class If a dream of a class takes place in a school, it signifies learning and growing, and that you are grading and evaluating your performance. If you dream of being unprepared or late to class, you are venting out feelings of inadequacy, shame, and low self-esteem. If a dream is about class as a social rank or status, see *High-class, Low-class,* or *Middle Class*.

Claw Dreams of a claw signify that you are feeling protective and defensive, and are attempting to set boundaries. You are in touch with your animal/survival instincts. A dream of a claw is also giving you the message to release your fears and let go of a person or situation you are holding on to.

Clay Dreams of clay represent creativity, suggestibility, and a vulnerability to outside influence. Consider if you are being molded or are the one doing the shaping.

Cleaning Dreams of cleaning symbolize integrity, purification, healing, and transformation. The act of cleaning represents restoring yourself to your natural luster. If you are cleaning something, you may be attempting to correct a wrong, make amends, or tie up loose ends.

Cleopatra Dreams of Cleopatra represent your connection to matriarchal, feminine power, the occult, and a desire to be respected as a powerful force.

Clergy Dreams of clergy reflect your personal morality, righteousness, tradition, judgment, and rules put into action.

Cliff Dreams of a cliff signify that you are living on the edge and taking risks that may put you into a dangerous position. Perhaps it is time to make an important decision, to leap and build your wings on the way down. Consider the feeling tone. See *Gambling*.

Climb Dreams of climbing mean that you are gaining success despite opposition.

Clip Art Clip art in a dream represents the desire to express yourself quickly and visually and to be understood in a way that transcends words. Consider the art or picture in the dream. See *Art/Artist*.

Clitoris Dreams of a clitoris symbolize your ability to give and receive pleasure, a desire for creative stimulation, and sexual expression. See *Sex* and *Vagina*.

Clock Dreams of a clock represent concern about time, worry that you'll be late, and stress about the passage of time, time running out, or being behind schedule. To want to know what time it is represents a desire for lucidity and that it is time for a reality check. See *Calendar, Time,* and *Watch*.

Closet Dreams of a closet symbolize a place where your secret life, shadow, and clothes/costumes hang behind closed doors. They may be revealing your unintegrated aspects of self that yearn to be exposed proudly in the light of day. If a closet is cluttered, then it's time to take an inventory of what to keep, what to release, and what to wear. See *Clothes*. See also *Integration Dreams,* page 10.

Clothes In a dream of clothes, each type has its own significance. The clothes you wear in your dream are always a statement about your feelings, attitudes, and position in life. Consider how the clothes and their colors made you feel. See *Blouse, Bra, Color, Dress, Pants, Suit,* and *Underwear*.

Cloud Dreams of a cloud symbolize a block in a relationship or business venture. This setback is temporary; keep breathing, and find your sense of well-being. Consider the feeling tone. It will reveal the way you handle disappointments and temporary setbacks. See *Rain*.

Clover (Four-leafed) Dreams of a four-leafed clover signify good luck and fortune, and that your wishes are coming true. If you dream of fields of clover it represents abundance, freedom, and expansion. See *Wish Fulfillment Dreams,* page 18.

Clown Dreams of a clown are a message to see the comedy in the drama of life. They can also be a warning to look behind the mask of laughter that is worn by a close friend, or to lighten up and stop taking things so seriously. However, dreams of a clown may be showing you that too much joking indicates insecurity, or that you have been wearing a mask to cover up your sadness. Consider the feeling tone of the dream to discern its significance. See *Fool.*

Club Dreams of a club signify strength in numbers and support, and that your affiliation with like-minded individuals will be promising. Perhaps you are realizing a need to network to improve your net worth. See *Family* and *Stick.*

Clue Dreams of a clue reflect that you are connecting to your inner detective, taking nothing at face value, reading between the lines, and discerning fact from fiction in your life. You are moving toward an "aha" moment where everything will ultimately make sense. See *Coyote.*

Coal Dreams of coal symbolize fuel, energy, and your connection to an outdated power source. Your subconscious mind is giving you the message to seek a more efficient use of your energy and that there is a more graceful, joyful way for you to get what you need in life.

Coat Dreams of a coat represent warmth, comfort from the cold, and a desire for emotional support through a chilling time. You are allowing yourself to be comforted and reassured that all is well.

Coat of Arms Dreams of a coat of arms symbolize connection with your family tree, pride in your heritage, and awareness and appreciation of the strength of your lineage.

Cobra Dreams of a cobra symbolize your sacred sexuality and kundalini energy. Be cautious of being seduced into situations that aren't healthy for you. You are dealing with temptation, being charmed and mesmerized, and perhaps giving your power away. You are learning to keep your circle of power even when you are extremely attracted to someone. See *Kundalini* and *Snake.*

Cobwebs Dreams of cobwebs signify that you are discovering a part of your power and wisdom that has been long forgotten, neglected, or discarded. They can also represent seduction and your ability to lure people. See *Shadow, Spider,* and *Web.*

Cocoa Dreams of cocoa or hot cocoa represent love, reward for hard work, and nurturing. See *Chocolate.*

Coconut Dreams of a coconut represent that you are being hard-headed and stubborn. Perhaps your ego has been bruised and you've been protecting your vulnerability with a tough shell.

Code Dreams of a code symbolize an important clue in the case of your own self-revelation. Something important is being delivered to you. Pay attention to the details, the numbers, and letters. See *Letter* and *Number.*

Codependence Dreams of codependence signify insecurity and low self-esteem, and that you are allowing your disempowering beliefs to injure you and/or the other people with whom you are entangled. They are alerting you to cultivate your own sense of self, boundaries, authenticity, self-respect, and faith in your higher power.

Coffee Dreams of coffee symbolize a desire for creative stimulation, to wake up and get in the game. See *Starbucks.*

Coffin See *Casket.*

Coil Dreams of a coil symbolize sexual energy springing into action, repetition, and flexibility. See *Circle, Kundalini,* and *Spiral.*

Coin Dreams of coins represent your opinions, as in giving your two cents. Something either makes sense (cents) or it doesn't. Perhaps you are nickel and diming your way through life, and the dreams are a message for you to avail yourself to a more abundant perspective. If you dream of a gold coin, then this symbolizes a golden opportunity coming your way. See *Money.*

Cold Dreams of a cold represent overwhelm and the need for a break, relaxation, and time to assimilate all that is going on around you. You also might be feeling neglected, unappreciated, and left out in the cold. If you dream of the temperature being cold, then this is your emotional barometer alerting you that you've been getting the cold shoulder or that you've been experiencing emotional chilliness and a loss of connection.

Collage Dreams of a collage, like those of a quilt, symbolize a collection of memories, visions, dreams, and aspirations. Your creative dreams are coming together piece by piece. See *Quilt.*

Collagen Dreams of collagen injections symbolize restoration, a desire for eternal youth, and a willingness to endure pain for beauty. Perhaps you are struggling with the aging process or you are in the process of discovering that your true value and beauty increase with age and wisdom.

Collar Dreams of a collar symbolize power, control, passive/aggressive behavior, and a desire to take the lead. If you are wearing a collar, then you are submitting to someone's will. If you are leading someone else by the collar, then you are taking the lead and asserting dominance over someone.

Collection Dreams of a collection signify that you are gathering your resources, holding on to a past identity, and/or cherishing a precious aspect of yourself.

Collection Agency Dreams of a collection agency symbolize debt and that you may be lacking integrity with the people in your life. Perhaps you have taken without reciprocation, or you have given and you are resentful, or you are in the process of gaining back the power you've given away. See *Karma.*

College Dreams of college represent that you are learning and developing a degree of recognition and authority. You are realizing that in the school of life you are turning your challenges and lessons into blessings. See *Class, School, Student,* and *Teacher.*

Collision Dreams of a collision symbolize an intersection of energy that is either serendipitous or injurious. If someone is hurt in a collision, as in an auto accident, this can represent a wake-up call, telling you to pay attention and become more responsible. See *Accident.*

Colonel Dreams of a colonel symbolize authority, power, and a desire to give orders and/or rank high in your chosen field.

Color If a person has a colorful personality or is particularly colorful in a dream, it represents significance, passion, aliveness, and brilliance. Dreams that feature a specific color signify strong feelings and creativity, and symbolize that you are in or are moving toward a creative peak. In the Hindu chakra system, each color has a very specific meaning, placement in your body, and emotional/physical/spiritual functionality. For a specific color, look up its entry. See *Chakra*.

Comb Dreams of a comb mean that you are in the process of cleaning up your act, preparing to present yourself publicly. Also, dreams of a comb represent investigation, reading between the lines, not taking things at face value. You are untangling a mystery with a fine-tooth comb.

Comedy Dreams of a comedy symbolize your ability to see the comedy in the tragedy of life, and to find the tragedy in the comedy, which is a mark of genius.

Comet Dreams of a comet signify that you are flying high, having a peak experience, and soaring to successful new heights in your career and/or a relationship. You are really taking off, expressing your power as the star that you came here to be.

Commitment Dreams of a commitment symbolize your willingness to take things to a deeper level in a relationship, your career, or spiritual practice. See *Marriage* and *Vows*.

Committee Dreams of a committee symbolize an integration of all your sub-personalities. You are bringing together all aspects of yourself into agreement, realizing that you can move mountains when you are aligned.

Commotion Dreams of a commotion represent restlessness, transformation, and a disturbance. Perhaps an aspect of you that has been neglected is vying for your attention. See *Transformation*.

Commune Dreams of a commune symbolize integration, partnership, mutuality, and synergy within your various aspects of self. Perhaps you are recognizing where your strengths are valued and where you could benefit from the strengths of others. See *Integration Dreams*, page 10.

Communication Dreams of communication symbolize a desire for connection, understanding, and relationship. For many, saying "I understand you" is synonymous with saying "I love you."

Companion See *Marriage* and *Relationship*.

Compass Dreams of a compass represents a desire to know where you are and whether or not you have chosen the correct path. According to Native American traditions, all roads lead to the same place. If a compass is clearly pointing in a specific direction, there are interpretations for you to consider. See *East, Medicine Wheel, North, South, True North,* and *West.*

Completion If you dream of completion, then this reflects your feelings and attitudes about death. Keep in mind that the end is always the beginning of something new. See *Death* and *Graduation.*

Complexion Dreams of a complexion vary depending upon the skin type you dream of. If you dream of an oily complexion, then you are stressed out from working too hard and not giving yourself enough self-love. If you dream of a dry complexion, then you are allowing fear to hold you back and dry out your passion. See *Face* and *Pimples.*

Composing Dreams of composing symbolize harmony among the different aspects of yourself. You are creating and expressing the music of your soul. Perhaps dreams of composing are forecasting romance and that you will soon be making beautiful music with a partner. See *Music.*

Computer Dreams of a computer represent your unique access to the universal mind. Throughout all eastern religions, including Hinduism, Buddhism, the Goddess religions, even Masonry, there is the belief in the one supreme mind and being that interconnects us all. The computer is often used as a symbol of the one mind and your desire to connect and express yourself to others. See *Internet.*

Concealer Dreams of concealer makeup are about your desire to blend in, cover up your flaws, maintain a false image of perfection, and/or connect with your youth. See *Cosmetics* and *Mask.*

Concert Dreams about a concert signify synergy in your life and within yourself, and that everything is coming together for you. You are in a period of lucrative creativity. See *Music.*

Concrete Dreams of concrete symbolize a solid, substantial foundation. Concrete can also symbolize an agreement, a commitment, a promise, or a partnership that is based in integrity.

Condiment Dreams of a condiment symbolize your need for embellishment or enhancement to bring out the full flavor of a situation you are in. See *Ketchup, Mayonnaise,* or *Relish.*

Condom Dreams of a condom signify that you are taking sexual responsibility and that you are owning and managing your power. A condom also symbolizes protection. Perhaps you are dealing with a fear of intimacy, or of impregnating someone else with your energy. Maybe you are resistant to starting something you don't feel prepared to finish. A dream of a condom also represents your ability to be lucid in a situation where it is tempting not to be. See *Birth Control.*

Conductor Dreams of a conductor are about your ability to take charge of your life, and to stay on track with your dreams, goals, and aspirations. Perhaps you are being cautioned to read the signs and pay attention to the guideposts along the way. See *Railroad Tracks.*

If you dream about an electrical conductor, see *Copper, Train,* and *Wire.*

Conference Call Dreams of a conference call or teleconference represent simultaneous telepathy and connectivity with many people, or with many aspects of yourself. Dreams of a conference call can also represent successful activity in your business. See *Teleseminar.*

Confession Dreams of a confession symbolize the exposure of secrets and the release of shame, guilt, or blame. Perhaps a dream of a confession is suggesting that you make amends for your misdeeds, forgive yourself, and practice discernment about whomever you share your secrets with. See *Mistake.*

Confetti Dreams of confetti symbolize a surprise, a celebration, joyous frivolity, and optimism about the future. See *Party.*

Connection Dreams of a connection signify that you are in resonance with your purpose for being alive, your soul mate, or your higher power.

Conspiracy Dreams of a conspiracy symbolize a guilty conscience. Perhaps you are indulging in negative thoughts that make you feel that the world is against you. Keep in mind that the entire universe is conspiring on behalf of your greatest good.

Constipation Dreams of constipation signify that you've been suppressing your power, holding back your creative impulses, and keeping a backlog of negative energy. Perhaps you've been stuck in unworkable patterns, and your subconscious mind is giving you the message to vent daily, to become regular with your emotional purges.

Construction Dreams of construction signify that your life is in the midst of repair and re-creation. At this time you probably don't feel like presenting yourself to the public. A dream of construction is giving you the message to pull back from social engagements until your inner life is finished being remodeled. See *Breakdown/Breakthrough Dreams,* page 12.

Consultant Dreams of a consultant signify that you are connecting to your wisdom, knowledge, and genius in the area of your expertise. To dream of seeking a consultant is a message from your subconscious mind to seek help, support, and guidance. Keep in mind that asking for help is not a sign of weakness, but a sign of strength because it allows you to learn and grow.

Consumption Dreams of consumption symbolize a hunger or thirst for what you need or desire. You may be processing feelings of hoarding, clinging, or taking more than your share for fear that there is not enough to go around.

Container Dreams of a container signify that you are being nurtured, held, and protected. If a container is empty, then you are dealing with issues of lack or loss. If a container is full, then you are feeling abundant and complete. Consider the contents for more insight into the significance of the dream. Also, a container can be a nurturing space that holds you while you develop to a certain level.

Contest Dreams of a contest represent inspiration to be your best combined with a competitive spirit. Perhaps you are comparing yourself with someone in your life, striving to win and be number one. A dream of a contest may indicate that you are under the false impression that you are either better than or not as good as the people in your life. See *Goddess* (Athena) and *Sports*.

Contract If you dream of signing a contract, then the dream represents your feelings about commitment, and means that you are coming to realize the value of your word. See *Promise*.

Convent According to the feeling tone, dreams of a convent can symbolize a profound commitment to your spiritual life. They could also be showing you where you deprive yourself, cut yourself off sexually, and keep passion at arm's length under the guise of being morally superior. See *Catholicism*.

Convention Dreams of a convention signify synergy, unity, and inner harmony, and that many aspects of your self are coming together. See *Party*.

Conveyer Belt Dreams of a conveyer belt symbolize a desire for efficiency, effortlessness, machinelike functionality, and a high degree of organization in your life structures. Or perhaps they are showing you that you lack passion in your current endeavors and that you are mindlessly going through the motions. See *Robot*.

Cook/Cooking Dreams of a cook symbolize the aspect of you that is maternal, nurturing, and knows what is best for you to ingest. These dreams may be a message from your subconscious mind to be more mindful about the energy that you take in, and to be more responsible for what you feed yourself mentally, spiritually, physically, and emotionally.

Cookie Dreams of a cookie symbolize your just desserts, a sweet reward for your hard work. If you dream of baking cookies, then this represents that you are manifesting and creating something in your life that is sweet and wonderful. See *Fortune Cookie*.

Copper Dreams of copper symbolize that you are conducting yourself in a positive, healing, and balanced way. See *Metal*.

Copying Dreaming of copying what someone else is doing represents a lack of originality and trust in your natural genius and skill. If you dream that someone is copying you, then you are on your way to great success, because to be copied is the greatest form of flattery. See *Xerox*.

Coral Dreams of coral signify that you are connecting with lessons and blessings that have come from your deepest pain.

Cord Dreams of a cord symbolize your connection and/or attachment to a person, habit, thought pattern, or belief system. Consider whether this connection is energizing or draining you. See *Codependence* and *Umbilical Cord*.

Cork Dreams of a cork signify that you have been holding back your emotions and expression. They are giving you the message to find a healthy way to release your energy, whether via a trusted friend or a journal, before you pop. Alternatively, a dream of a cork might be showing you to use discernment with your expression and to keep a lid on your emotions until the timing is right.

Corkscrew Dreams of a corkscrew signify that you are unraveling feelings that have been bottled up for a long time.

Corn Dreams of corn symbolize gold, wealth, health, and riches. They are a sign that abundant blessings are yours and that you'll be rewarded for your hard work. See *Harvest*.

Corner To dream of turning a corner signifies that you are making progress and that you are growing and advancing in untold ways. You may be surprised by what meets you at the intersection of destiny, fate, and serendipity; after all, luck happens when preparation meets opportunity. You are coming into your area of expertise, the area of life in which you have a corner on the market. Alternatively, a dream of a corner can represent feeling trapped, stuck, or boxed in. Consider the feeling tone.

Coroner Dreams of a coroner symbolize helpful and supportive energy to assist you in releasing habits, conditioning, and even relationships that no longer serve you. See *Goddess* (Persephone).

Corpse Dreams of the corpse of someone you know represent the completion of a relationship you once had with that person, and perhaps the end of a particular pattern of relating. Dreams of a corpse can also represent a loss of passion for being alive. See *Death* and *Goddess* (Persephone).

Corral Dreams of a corral symbolize your power circle, personal responsibility, and integrity. They are giving you the message to rein in your energy and focus on what needs to be done. See *Horse* and *Ranch*.

Cosmetics Dreams of cosmetics signify that you feel the need to embellish your natural way of being, that you desire to attract attention, or that you want to cover up perceived flaws so that you will appear better than you actually are. These dreams may be revealing your public persona versus your true self or your feelings about self. If makeup is excessive it can be a mask that hides the vulnerability of the true self that lies within. See *Concealer, Eyeshadow, Foundation, Lipstick, Mascara,* and *Mask.*

Cosmetic Surgery Dreams of cosmetic surgery represent a desire for a shortcut to rapid transformation. Because the body holds your memories and energetic patterns, when you dream of "cutting" something out of your body or off of your skin, consider this to be a venting dream whereby your subconscious mind is attempting to release shame or pain that is either held in or represented by this area of your body. If you have undergone any cosmetic procedures, dreaming of the surgery could be assisting you to assimilate your experience. See *Integration Dreams,* page 10.

Costco Dreams of Costco reveal your attitudes and feelings about abundance, and that you are feeling the need to stockpile and store up for lean times. See *Shopping.*

Costume Dreams of a costume symbolize your desire to be seen in a particular type of role or as a particular archetype. Depending upon the feeling tone of the dream, your subconscious mind may be revealing the type of person you are aspiring to become. See *Clothes* and *Dress.*

Cot Dreams of sleeping on a cot represent a bare-bones approach to nurturing and self-care.

Cotton Dreams of cotton represent a desire to soften the rough edges of life. Cotton can symbolize that you have a gentle approach that is accessible, warm and fuzzy, huggable, and cozy. See *Pillow.*

Cotton Candy Dreams of cotton candy symbolize a treat, reward, joyous occasion, and connection to your inner child.

Couch Dreams of a couch signify that you are experiencing comfort, luxury, ease, confidence, support, and extravagance in your life. See *Furniture.*

Cough Dreams of a cough signify that words are being caught in your throat, and that you are resisting saying what you mean or meaning what you say. See *Throat.*

Counselor Dreams of a counselor symbolize your higher self and your connection to your own higher wisdom. See *Life Coach.*

Country Dreams of country dancing, clothing, or lifestyle denote that you are getting back to basics, becoming grounded, and appreciating an uncomplicated way of life.

If you dream of a foreign country, see *Foreign*.

Couple Dreams of a couple symbolize your feelings, attitudes, and opinions about relationships, partnerships, romance, love, and marriage. Perhaps you are working through obstacles to intimacy and love. See *Marriage*.

Court Case To dream of a court case is about judgment and forgiveness. You are deciding a verdict upon yourself or someone who you feel has wronged you. You are processing your feelings of guilt versus innocence. See *Judge* and *Jury*.

Cousin Dreams of a cousin symbolize closeness, familial affinity, and telepathy. See *Family*.

Cover Dreams of a cover represent protection or hiding. Because a cover can make something more beautiful than it would otherwise be, a dream of a cover may be about your attempt to fit in by hiding your uniqueness. Consider what is being covered.

Cow Dreams of a cow symbolize sacredness and maternal qualities. Since cows produce milk, which is converted to many of the dairy products that sustain us, a cow is associated with providence, nourishing, food, and life itself. See *Cattle* and *Milk*.

Cowboy/Cowgirl Dreams of a cowboy or cowgirl signify that you are connecting with the rough, rugged, grounded, natural aspects of yourself. Perhaps you are learning to rope in your wild desires and corral them into manifestation. See *Country*.

Coyote Dreams of a coyote symbolize connection to your inner trickster. Perhaps you are being sneaky and beating around the bush. Also, a dream of a coyote signifies that you are being initiated into your next level of spiritual growth. See *Animal*.

Crab Astrologically speaking, dreams of a Crab represent extreme empathy and depth of feeling. Perhaps they are showing you that you have been crabby and are taking things too personally.

Crack Dreams of a crack represent an end of a cycle, and that there is something new emerging. If something falls or slips through a crack, then a dream of a crack is about your fear of losing something that you value. See *Breaking*.

If you dream of the drug crack, see *Drugs*.

Cradle Dreams of a cradle symbolize maternal yearnings, your desire to nurture or be nurtured and to protect or be protected.

Craigslist Dreams of Craigslist represent ease of accessibility for anything that you need or want. You are realizing your fraternity with the global community and that you have the world at your fingertips as you see the value in sharing resources with others. See *Commune*.

Crane Dreams of this bird symbolize that major changes, transformation, and breakthroughs abound. See *Bird*.

Crash If you dream of a crash, it symbolizes that you've been falling asleep at the wheel of life and have been cruisin' for a bruisin'. If you dream of a car crash, see *Accident* and *Collision*. See also *Breakdown/Breakthrough Dreams,* page 12.

Crater Dreams of a crater symbolize an old wound or emotional scar. See *Canyon*.

Crawl Dreams of crawling signify that you are beginning a new venture. You may be realizing the need to have patience with yourself while you learn a new skill.

Crayon Dreams of a crayon signify childlike expression and that you are allowing space for your innocent brilliance to create magic in your life.

Crazy If you dream you are feeling crazy, the dream may be telling you that you are overwhelmed and need a break to get back into balance. Keep in mind that what may appear crazy to the judgmental mind may actually be brilliantly artistic to the soul. See *Insane Asylum*.

Cream Dreams of cream denote that you are wanting the best things in life. You have a desire to balance the sweet with the bitter, and you are coming into a rich time in your life. See *Gravy*.

Creativity To dream that you are using your creativity or problem-solving abilities means that you are in touch with your feminine essence, and your ability to think outside the box. This can be a valuable asset to you in your everyday life, as long as you find a practical way to honor it so that it may become manifest.

Credit Dreams of credit symbolize appreciation, gratitude, and the value and worth you give to yourself. You are realizing that what you appreciate appreciates in value.

Credit Card Dreams of a credit card reflect your feelings, attitudes, and opinions about borrowed wealth, abundance that isn't really yours, money and the ease and power and/or struggles it brings. They may be warning you to be mindful of your spending, and to consider whether or not a relationship or project you are investing in is worth it. See *Accountant.*

Cremation Dreams of a cremation represent completion and the end of a cycle. Perhaps you are coming to accept ashes to ashes, dust to dust, and the temporal nature of life. You are realizing that the ego diminishes to dust in the light of the fire of transformation and only that which is real remains. See *Breakdown/Breakthough Dreams,* page 12.

Crest Dreams of a crest are about having a peak experience, riding the wave of your spirituality, and reveling in a moment of illumination. You are awakening to the grandeur of your being, so allow this experience to be a ray of light to guide you through dark times. If you dream of a family crest, then the dream is about family pride, honor, and respect for your tribe. See *Coat of Arms.*

Crew Dreams of a crew symbolize power in numbers. If a crew is working together in harmony, then the dream represents productivity, and that the whole is greater than the sum of its parts. If a crew is disharmonious, then the dream signifies inner chaos and that it is time to regroup.

Cricket Dreams of a cricket signify wisdom, and that you are attuned to the wisdom and music of nature, your instincts, and the still-small voice within you that guides you to the right people, places, and things at the right time.

Criminal Dreams of a criminal mean that you are grappling with guilt and shame about something you have done. Forgive yourself and make amends for your misdeeds as you forgive those who have trespassed against you.

Crippled Dreams of being crippled or seeing someone who is crippled signify injured emotions, and that you are relating to yourself as your wounds, as opposed to relating to yourself as a whole and complete being. Perhaps you are suppressing your self-expression and feeling a sense of diminished self-worth. Consider the area of the body that you dreamed was crippled. See *Body*.

Critic Dreams of a critic symbolize a fear of exposure, of making a mistake, and/or looking foolish. Dreams about your inner critic usually show up when you are in the midst of expansion and/or taking a risk. Your inner critic is synonymous with your primitive survival mechanism that wants you to stay intact. Keep in mind that you have to be willing to be bad at something before you can be good.

Crocodile Dreams of a crocodile signify anger that can eat a person alive, and that an unintegrated shadow aspect of you is sneaking up on you from the murky swamp of your unconscious. These dreams are giving you the message to begin releasing your anger in a healthy way. A dream of a crocodile could symbolize that you have been harboring suppressed anger at an authority figure.

Crone Although scary, a crone in a dream is a symbol of great wisdom and empowerment. Often a crone is synonymous with a witch, which traditionally represents darkness, jealousy, vindictiveness, or evil. A metaphysical interpretation of a crone, however, is that she is a primary instigator of spiritual growth that ushers a person who is stuck in his or her unconscious innocence to find his or her conscious power. See *Witch*.

Crop Dreams of a crop symbolize your awareness of the truth that you reap what you sow. Dreaming of a crop could be telling you to be careful of what you ask for because you just may get it.

Crop Circle Dreams of a crop circle are a direct message from your higher self and reflect your awareness of higher life forms. They are telling you to pay attention to the mystical and magical aspects of life that show up in the most mundane places and situations. See *Geometry*.

Cross Dreams of a cross signify that you are dealing with your cross to bear, or you are grappling with your religious and spiritual affiliation and devotion. They may be suggesting that it is time for you to sacrifice short-term pain for long-term gain, or that you will ascend from this difficult time you are moving through. See *Christ*.

Crossroads If you dream of being at a crossroads, then you are at a choice, and it is time for you to connect with your inner guidance to make a decision that will impact the rest of your life. A dream of being at a crossroads may be getting you to realize the consequences of your actions and choices.

Crosswalk Dreams of a crosswalk signify that you are following the rules, staying within the lines, and perhaps being overly careful. Or, they may be a message to be more careful.

Crow Dreams of this bird that is known for flying between the worlds of life and death reflect your feelings and attitudes about death, your shadow, change, and transformation. See *Bird*.

Crowd Dreams of a crowd symbolize your relationship with groups of people. If you are going along with a crowd, then the dream may be showing you that it is time to express your individuality. If you are fitting in and enjoying yourself, then the dream reflects your ability to harmonize and be supported. If you feel out of place in a crowd, then you may be dealing with pressure to conform and/or to exert yourself. A crowd represents powerful energy, either supportive or unsupportive, depending upon the consciousness and intent.

Crown Dreams of a crown symbolize higher wisdom, nobility, rank, beauty, self-esteem, authority, and prominence. They may be a message for you to respect yourself because the best is yet to come—your crowning glory. See *Chakra* (7th) and *Tiara*.

Crucifix See *Christ, Cross,* and *Crossroads*.

Crucifixion Dreams of the Crucifixion signify that you are dwelling inside your deepest existential pain. You are processing and venting out your fear that others will turn on you, crucify you, and vilify you. Keep in mind that immediately following the Crucifixion is the Ascension, which reflects that your true self cannot be harmed. See *Cross*.

Cruelty Dreams of cruelty are venting dreams that are helping you to release your criticism and lack of respect toward yourself and others. See *Hate*. See also *Integration Dreams,* page 10.

Cruise Dreams of a cruise signify that leisure time is in store for you, an opportunity to coast for a while. They are giving you the message to relax, eat, drink, and be merry. You've left the shores of your normal, grounded life and it is time to set sail into uncharted waters. However, if you continue to procrastinate and always take the easy way out, you may be cruisin' for a bruisin'.

Crust Dreaming of crust can represent the upper crust, or that you are yearning to be a part of high society. Or it can reflect your feeling about getting the leftovers in life, crumbs and crust and scraps. A dream of crust is a venting dream helping you to release your feelings of unworthiness.

Crutch Dreams of a crutch signify that you've been relying too heavily upon that which may eventually weaken you. Keep in mind that the use of a crutch is appropriate during a transition; however, becoming dependent upon it is not. Dreaming of a crutch is a message for you to find your strength from the inside. See *Addiction* and *Codependence*.

Crying Dreams of crying signify that you are healing, grieving, cleansing, and releasing that which no longer supports you as you make room for that which does support you. Consider that this might be a *cry* for help and that you would be wise to seek support to help you through a challenge you are going through. Keep in mind that you can't heal what you can't feel. See *Venting Dreams,* page 8.

Crystal Dreams of crystals symbolize your eternal self. These conductors of energy represent the amplification of your intent and your ability to bring forth your goals, visions, and desires into realization. A dream of crystals is showing you that you are harmonizing and attuning yourself to your highest and greatest possibilities.

Cucumber Dreams of a cucumber symbolize health and vitality. Because a cucumber can also be a phallic symbol, perhaps you are desiring or exploring healthy sexual expression. See *Vegetables.*

Cuddling Dreams of cuddling signify a desire for tender loving care, and that you are either desiring or allowing yourself to feel nurtured, safe, and cared for. You are feeling in sync with the universe and you have an inherent sense that all is well.

Cul-de-sac Dreams of a cul-de-sac signify stagnation and that perhaps you are feeling stuck in a pattern, or have come to a dead end in a job, relationship, or situation in your family life.

Cult Dreams of a cult denote that you are faced with issues of whether or not to surrender your individuality or to hold on and risk feeling separate, alone, and fragile. A cult dream is reminding you to be true to yourself, and that you are coming to terms with your feelings about power, worship, mob mentality, leadership, and self-responsibility. See *Crowd* and *Guru*.

Cunnilingus If you are a woman, dreams of cunnilingus symbolize empowerment, celebration of your sexuality, and finding pleasure in life. If you are a man, dreams of cunnilingus symbolize your desire to please or win over the women in your life. You may also be finding pleasure as you explore the sensuality, receptivity, and sensitivity of your inner female. See *Tongue* and *Vagina*.

Cup Dreams of a cup symbolize your capacity to understand and hold a space of compassion and empathy for another's feelings, views, and attitudes about abundance. If a cup runneth over, then dreaming of this signifies that you are thriving in prosperity. If a cup is empty, then it means that you are either feeling empty or available to receive. See *Chalice*.

Curb Dreams of a curb mean that you are bumping up against your edge. Perhaps it is time to either curb your enthusiasm or, alternatively, not allow naysayers to block your joyous and adventurous spirit from its full expression.

Cure Dreams of a cure reflect your awareness that inherent within every challenge resides a solution. Your challenges are pushing you to discover answers and wisdom you never knew you possessed.

Curfew Dreams of a curfew symbolize restriction and a fear of being shut out of your social circle if you don't conform. They can also be about acceptance or rebellion toward your own self-imposed standards, limitations, or boundaries.

Curling Dreams of curling something are about adding energy to it. Whether you dream of curling hair or a ribbon, you are adding bounce, vibrancy, and vitality to all that you do.

Curls Dreams of curls, because of their circular nature, represent connection to your feminine nature and to the cyclical nature of life. See *Spiral*.

Cursing/Cursed If you dream of cursing at someone, then you are venting out your anger, frustration, and displeasure. If someone is cursing at you, then you are venting out feelings of being attacked and criticized. A dream of being cursed is a venting dream that is helping you to release any projected negativity and guilt you may have taken on. See *Karma*. See also *Venting Dreams,* page 8.

Curtains Dreams of curtains are about revealing or concealing. Open curtains represent an invitation for opportunities to come your way. Closed curtains mean that you are hiding something. If you are drawing curtains, then you are declaring a project or relationship complete. Lace curtains signify that you are concerned with appearances.

Curves Dreams of curves signify that you are accessing your femininity, operating in a soft, nonlinear way that is intuitive and holographic.

If you dream of Curves, as in the workout gym for women, the dream may be suggesting that you begin to work through your goals to achieve the success you desire. See *Goddess* (Aphrodite).

Cut Dreams of a cut symbolize an ending, a break, or a time-out from a relationship, your job, or a daily routine. See *Breaking* and *Knife.*

Cutting and Pasting Dreams of cutting and pasting symbolize that you are editing, organizing, and rearranging your thoughts and maybe even your life.

Cycle If you dream of a cycle, then you are coming to terms with the beginning, middle, or end of a process you are in. Keep in mind that the only thing you can count on is change. A dream of a cycle may be a call to find your rhythm within the cycles and seasons of your life so that you will be filled with grace as you progress and grow. See *Bicycle, Menstruation,* and *Seasons.*

Cymbal Dreams of a cymbal are your subconscious mind's way of telling you to pay attention, to wake up, and to heed the signs that are presented to you. See *Music.*

D

Daisy Dreams of a daisy symbolize playfulness, innocence, royalty, and romance. See *Flowers.*

Dalai Lama Dreams of the Dalai Lama symbolize forgiveness, compassion, and enlightenment. They may be revealing your ability to smile even when you've lost everything, because you know that your sustenance does not come from this world. The message in these dreams should be highly regarded. See *Buddha, Christ,* and *Smile.* See also *Prophetic Dreams,* page 17.

Dam Dreams of a dam signify that you are holding back your feelings, bottling up your emotions. Perhaps you've been overwhelmed by your life circumstances and you need some support to release your feelings in a healthy way. See *Depressed/Depression.*

Dance Floor Dreams of a dance floor symbolize your creative expression. If a dance floor is filled, then it represents the collective energy of all aspects of you dancing at the same time. If a floor is empty, then consider that you need some alone time to rejuvenate, or that you need to energize your creative spirit and begin making joy a priority in your life. See *Ballroom.*

Dancing Dreams of dancing represent your self-expression, and a desire to be unabashed, uninhibited, sexual, passionate, and primal. They are fortuitous dreams, telling you that if you give yourself permission to be more of yourself, you will magnetize partnerships that will support you in your creative expression. If you are dancing with someone, you are harmonizing with the energy that person represents. See *Ecstasy.*

Danger Dreams of danger are venting dreams to assist you in releasing negative and destructive thought patterns. They may be forewarning you to take preventative measures to avoid an undesirable situation. See *Venting Dreams,* page 8, and *Precognitive Dreams,* page 15.

Dark Dreams of anything dark symbolize shadow aspects of you that want to be integrated into the light of your being. Anything dark can also represent a personal challenge, the mystery of an unsolved puzzle, or an unconscious aspect of you. See *Shadow.* See also *Integration Dreams,* page 10.

Dart Dreams of a dart signify that you are attempting to make your mark on this world, to hit the bull's-eye, and to get it right. If you are throwing darts at someone, then this represents resentment, blame, or jealousy. If someone is throwing darts at you, then this reflects unresolved shame or guilt. Remember, that which you put out comes back to you tenfold. See *Arrow* and *Karma*.

Date Dreams of going on a date represent that romance is in the air. You are feeling adventurous and willing to expand your horizon. If you dream of a date on a calendar from the past, then this symbolizes a time in your past with which your subconscious mind is wanting you to connect and/or resolve. If the date on a calendar is in the future, then this is a precognitive dream and you would be wise to pay attention to it. For further exploration, add up the numbers of the date and look at the entry for the total. See *Number*. See also *Precognitive Dreams,* page 15.

Dating Service Dreams of being enrolled in a dating service represent your need or desire for guidance with romantic issues and/or help with finding a mate. See *Match.com*.

Daughter To dream of a daughter represents the archetype of a young girl within you who is vulnerable, insecure, and in need of support, care, and direction. The qualities ascribed to the daughter in a dream represent your maternal yearnings for a daughter and/or guidance and insight regarding your actual daughter.

Dawn Dreams of dawn symbolize hope, inspiration, and the joyous anticipation of a new beginning. If you are just coming through a challenging time, a dream of dawn is giving you the message that the light at the end of the tunnel is upon you. See *Sun* or *Sunshine*.

Day Dreams of activity taking place during daylight signify that which is exposed and revealed, as opposed to dreams of activity that take place at night. If you dream of a cloudy or rainy day, then it represents loss and struggle. If you dream of a sunny day, then it signifies clarity and hope, and that you have a new lease on life. See *Dawn* and *Light*.

Deaf Dreams of being deaf signify that you may be turning a deaf ear to criticism or unwarranted opinions about your life choices. Perhaps you are blocking out feedback that you fear might steer you away from your authentic path. Your subconscious mind may be telling you that you are being stubborn and rigid, and that you need to develop some listening skills.

Death Dreams of death are very common in that it is the job of your subconscious mind to keep you alive, so your dreams are assisting you to process your fears of death and dying. If you dream of your own death, then you are contemplating the value and impact of your life. Dreaming of someone else dying is about transformation and change in your relationship with that person, not necessarily a forecast of a literal death (though sometimes it is). You might also be venting out your fears of losing someone you love. Often a dream of death represents the ending of a chapter in a person's life, and that a new cycle is about to begin. A dream of death is suggesting that you consider what aspect of your life is ending, how you can harmoniously participate in completing this cycle, and what new beginning is wanting to come into your life. See *Fire* and *Transformation*.

Debt Dreams of a debt suggest that there is energy that you've taken but have not yet repaid. A debt dream could be bringing to your attention an unresolved issue that requires forgiveness or an amends. Your freedom is awaiting you. See *Karma* and *Money*.

Decaffeinated Dreams of decaffeinated beverages signify that you are making healthy choices in your life, choosing to be calm and balanced as opposed to stressed and frantic. See *Coffee*.

Decay Dreams of decay signify that you have allowed an aspect of your upkeep to slip. Perhaps you have allowed negative thoughts and/or behavior to fester. Your subconscious mind is alerting you to take care of yourself and take the action necessary to bring yourself back into balance.

December Dreams of December symbolize holidays, family reunions, and traditions. If it is June and you dream of December, then it denotes a desire for downtime and family time. For further clarification, consider what winter and the holidays mean to you. See *Christmas*.

Deck See *Balcony*.

Decorations Dreams of decorations or enhancements made to a space or body signify that you are ceremonializing, beautifying, embellishing, and bringing out its natural glory.

Deep Dreams of something deep, like a pool or ocean, represent importance, impact, an intimate bond, your participation in life, and/or your level of sensitivity. The deeper you go, the more profound the pain and the gain.

Deer Dreams of a deer symbolize a gentle spirit, a precious, wise, loving, and fragile heart. You need to be mindful of your naïveté making you vulnerable to sudden, unexpected predators.

Defeat Dreams of defeat are venting dreams that are helping you to release a defeatist attitude. Keep in mind that the game isn't over until you declare it to be over. Dreams of defeat may be prompting you to rethink your strategy and realize that the darkest hour is just before the dawn. See *Game.*

Defense Dreams of being on the defensive signify that you are venting out your fears, insecurities, and feelings of inadequacy. Dreams of self-protection signify not feeling safe, and that you are doing battle with your unintegrated shadow. See *Integration Dreams,* page 10.

Deformity Dreams of deformity signify that there is an aspect of you that you have not yet embraced. Perhaps this is an aspect that you are ashamed of because it does not fit the status quo. An abnormal growth or development could mean an aspect of your genius that has not yet been integrated and/or accepted by you. Acceptance has to begin with you. See *Crippled.*

Delay Dreams of a delay denote that there is something blocking you from moving forward. Perhaps you are venting out self-sabotage mechanisms, and feelings of being unprepared, insecure, or afraid of success.

Demand Dreams of making a demand signify clarity about what you want and what you don't want, and that you are no longer willing to remain passive. You are coming into your power and authority.

Dentist Dreams of a dentist mean that there is an incomplete communication between you and an associate, friend, or lover. Your subconscious mind is prompting you to forgive, make amends, and/or cultivate a healthier and more effective way of communicating. See *Teeth.*

Depressed/Depression Dreams of being depressed signify that you are venting out unhealed emotional wounds and self-punishment that have been dampening your spirit. They are giving you the message that you've been suppressing your passion, and it is time for a change.

Descending Dreams of descending are about your coming down to earth, becoming grounded, embracing your humanity and your three-dimensional needs, wants, and desires. If it feels that you've descended into the underworld, see *Depressed* or *Goddess* (Persephone).

Desert Dreams of the desert symbolize "no-man's land," the drought before the rain, and the darkest hour that is before the dawn. You may be experiencing hardship, loneliness, trial and tribulations, and a loss of passion because you are not who you used to be and you are not yet who you are becoming. A dream of a desert is giving you the message not to give up five minutes before the miracle, because once you make it through the dry spell, you will be greatly rewarded with the character, strength, and the wisdom you learn and earn.

Design Dreams of a design mean that you are becoming aware of the divine design for your life. Just as there is a pattern of the oak tree within the acorn, a dream of a design is about your ability to connect with the pattern and design of your life. It is also a message for you to realize the power of your mind to create your life the way you desire it to be. See *Director*.

Desk A dream in which there is a desk signifies discipline, authority, and your dedication to your career, and/or that you are processing data that took place at work. If a desk is overcrowded with papers and files, then the dream is telling you it is important for you to become more organized. If there is nothing on a desk, then the dream is suggesting that perhaps you are too rigid and organized and it's time for you to take some creative risks. See *Business* and *Work*. See also *Processing Dreams,* page 7.

Despair Dreams of despair are venting dreams helping you to release your negative thought patterns and low self-esteem so that you may realign with your passion and aspirations. See *Depressed/Depression*.

Desperate Housewife Dreams of a desperate housewife, or of the show *Desperate Housewives,* denote your connection to the dark side of femininity: vindictiveness, competition, beauty used as a weapon, and victimization. See *Drama Queen/Drama King* and *Karma.*

Dessert Dreams of dessert represent celebration, festivities, and a reward for hard work or accomplishment. Consider whether you were able to savor the flavor of a just dessert, or if you were too pre-occupied with guilt to truly enjoy it.

Detective If you dream of a detective, it signifies your vigilance and objectivity and that you are looking for clues to resolve a mysterious happening in your life.

Detour Dreams of a detour signify that an unexpected change is forthcoming. Perhaps you are releasing feelings of frustration at thinking you were on a direct path from A to B. Keep in mind that this detour or change is part of your path, and that the more you embrace life's journey with a flexible and adventurous spirit, the more you will reap the rewards of success and joy along your path.

Devil Dreams of the devil denote that you are grappling with temptation to do something you deem morally wrong versus what your conscience knows to be right for you. A dream of the devil can also be a venting dream that is assisting you in releasing feelings of separation and a lack of trust in the higher good of this universe. See *Shadow.* See also *Integration Dreams,* page 10.

Devotee Dreams of a devotee signify power issues, and that you may have abdicated your power and personal responsibility to a person or organization and are experiencing harmful consequences. However, if you are feeling devoted to a relationship or a higher calling, then dreaming of a devotee is reflecting and affirming your purpose for being alive. See *Love.*

Devouring Dreams of being devoured are about feeling over-whelmed or being overpowered by another's will. If you dream of devouring something or someone, you are taking its energy, seeking superiority and dominion over it. The dream is giving you the message that without mutuality or equality, you will ultimately find yourself unbalanced and disempowered. See *Eating.*

Diamond Dreams of a diamond represent your multifaceted nature, and the fact that there are many sides of you with many different perspectives. A diamond also symbolizes a promise that is lasting and timeless. Your subconscious mind is giving you the message to remember that you are precious, invaluable, brilliant, and sparkling in your unique way. See *Alchemist/Alchemy* or *Jewelry.*

Diapers Dreams of diapers symbolize protection, release of negativity, and perhaps an inability to control your feelings and urges. They could be reflecting a place within you that is immature and in need of personal responsibility. Alternatively, they may show that you are purifying and releasing ways of the past. See *Faces.*

Diary Dreams of a diary represent your secret thoughts and your true perception of life. If a diary is locked, then you have secrets that you don't want anyone to know about. If it is unlocked, then you feel like an open book. If you are reading someone else's diary, then you are prying where you don't belong. Dreaming of a diary also may be a message for you to be mindful with whom you share your secrets. See *Agenda.*

Dice Dreams of dice signify that you are going out on a limb and taking your chances. Consider whether you are being adventurous or foolhardy. See *Gambling* and *Luck.*

Dictionary Dreams of a dictionary represent your search for understanding. You desire to make sense of your life, and you are coming to realize the importance and power of your words. If you dream that you are reading a dictionary, then the words you read are a message to explore and possibly to take literally. See *Spell.*

Diet Dreams of being on a diet signify discipline, control, and sacrifice, and that you are becoming mindful about your consumption of energy, food, and entertainment. You are learning to say no to that which is not healthy for you so that you can say yes to that which supports you.

Diet Coke Dreams of drinking Diet Coke signify that you are ingesting information that is refreshing, reinvigorating, and stimulating but not necessarily healthy for you.

Digesting Dreams about digesting food signify that you are processing and taking in information, choosing what to keep or what to eliminate.

Digging If you are digging in a dream, then you are looking for secret or hidden information. The dream could signify your search for depth and meaning in your relationships, or that you are trying to get to the bottom of an important issue.

Digital Dreams of anything digital or digitized symbolize a desire to step outside of the linear, stair-step approach to life and explore that which is holographic and instantaneous.

Dim Light Dreams of a dim light denote that you are feeling uninspired or burned out because you've been overusing your wattage. You need some downtime to unplug from the frenzy of your life.

Dining Dreams of dining symbolize your need for soul food that takes place during social gatherings. Consider what you are eating and whether your current social circle is nourishing your soul. If it is not, a dream of dining is giving you the message to choose another experience from your social menu.

Dining Room Dreams that take place in a dining room represent common bonds. You are ingesting a similar ideology and belief system with the people with whom you are dining. If a dining room is empty or chaotic, then you are dealing with unresolved family issues.

Dinner Dreams of dinner represent family time, a social time to bond and pass around stories of the day. You are feeding yourself the belief systems of your family or tribe. See *Family.*

Dinosaur Dreams of a dinosaur symbolize outdated systems and prehistoric ways of thinking. They are a symbol that it is time to change your obsolete and clumsy ways of doing things and take the risk of trying something new.

Diploma Dreams of a diploma signify that you've officially completed a level of learning. You've earned your stripes with regard to a certain obstacle, goal, or pursuit. See *Graduation.*

Directions Dreams of directions can represent clues about where to go, what to do, and how to do something in your waking life. See *Compass, North, South, East,* and *West.*

Director Dreams of a director signify that you are experiencing uncertainty about where you are going in life and are connecting to the aspect of yourself that sees the big picture and has a sense of order, of what you should do, of where things should go, and of the way your life movie should be played.

Dirt Dreams of dirt indicate that there is an aspect of your life that needs to be cleaned up. Perhaps there is an amends that needs to be made, or a person to forgive. If you dream of dirt that won't rub off, then you are dealing with an issue of shame or blame that requires that you go deep, all the way to the roots to heal. Also, dirt is related to the element of earth, which is a message from your subconscious mind to get real, be grounded, and connect with your roots. See *Earth*.

Disagreeing Dreams about disagreeing signify your own internal struggle regarding your conflicting needs. See *Fight*.

Disappearing To dream of something suddenly disappearing signifies that you feel that something is missing in your life. Also, it means you are coming to terms with impermanence, change, and the illusive, mysterious nature of life.

Discovery Dreams of making a discovery signify that you are opening up to new regions of yourself.

Disease Dreams of a disease signify that you've been going against your grain, ignoring your instincts, and indulging in fearful thoughts. You are venting out a negative influence that someone or something has had on you as you realize that your thoughts have a viral effect on everyone around you. A dream of a disease may be a message for you to take care of your health in order to avoid challenges that could arise from an imbalance. If you are dealing with an actual disease, the dream could be helping you to heal or gain an insight into its remedy. See *Disease* and *Sick*. See also *Venting Dreams,* page 8.

Dish Dreams of a dish symbolize your ability to take in the nurturing that is around you. Broken or chipped dishes represent a break in your ability to receive. See *Bowl* or *Plate*.

Dishwasher Dreams of a dishwasher symbolize cleansing your relationship to that which feeds you. You are removing all that is in the way of your ability to receive, or you are clearing your plate to give yourself a break from your busy schedule.

Disneyland Dreams of Disneyland symbolize your connection to your inner magic kingdom, to your imagination, and to your inner child.

Dissecting Dreams of dissecting, or splitting something apart, signify either your quest for knowledge or that your inner critic is tearing you apart.

Distance If you dream of being physically distant from someone or something, you may be feeling disconnected from that person or thing, that you are holding back your feelings, or awaiting objectivity, clarity, and certainty before making a choice.

Ditch Dreams of a ditch reflect that you are in the midst of a difficult challenge. Being stuck in a ditch represents a lack of foresight, and that you are learning from your mistakes. See *Quicksand*.

Divine Dreams of something or someone that is divine symbolize being of the spirit, and perhaps being able to see the future. You are tapping into your infinite source, supply, and consciousness, seeing beyond your fear and limited views. See *Prophetic Dreams,* page 17, or *Precognitive Dreams,* page 15.

Diving Dreams of diving into a pool signify that you are committing yourself, immersing your self wholeheartedly into a belief system, relationship, or project.

Dizziness Dreams of being dizzy symbolize a loss of center and self. It is high time for you to get grounded and back to nature. A dream of dizziness is a message for you to meditate, come back to your senses, and proceed from a centered place.

DMV Dreams of the Department of Motor Vehicles represent your feelings and attitudes toward bureaucracy. You may be experiencing stress and frustration as you await mobility or a license to take control of your life. See *Car*.

Dock Dreams of a dock symbolize a transition space between your conscious and unconscious, and the mundane and the mystical where the veil between worlds is thin. Perhaps you are coming back to shore to rest and incorporate what you've learned from your voyage into the deep end of your emotional ocean. See *Bridge*.

Doctor Dreams of a doctor represent your intuition, wisdom, and the aspect of yourself that diagnoses your ailments, makes you better, puts on an emotional Band-Aid, and gives you the medicine you need.

Dog Dreams of a dog typically symbolize unconditional love, loyalty, fidelity, a best friend, philanthropy, and the wild, protective nature that keeps threats away or at bay. If a dog in a dream is angry or vicious, then this represents hostility and your need for protection and boundaries. Dreams of a nice dog mean that you are connecting to your sweet, innocent vulnerability.

Doll Dreaming of this pretend baby represents budding maternal instincts and desires. It could also be about idealizing someone or yourself. You are attempting to live up to an impossible standard of perfection. See *Stepford Wife.*

Dolphin Dreams of a dolphin symbolize multidimensional wisdom, intelligence, love, sensuality, playfulness, and healing. You are connecting with your most joyous, enlightened aspect of self. A dream of a dolphin means that healing, either physically or psychically, is taking place within you. See *Angel.* See also *Prophetic Dreams,* page 17.

Dominoes If you dream of playing dominoes, it symbolizes that you are taking responsibility for your actions, realizing that everything you do creates a chain reaction that sets a whole world into motion.

Donald Trump Dreams of Donald Trump represent wealth, status, power, and perhaps a fear of being fired or a dread of having to fire someone. You are realizing the Midas touch. See *Wealth.*

Donkey Dreams of a donkey symbolize your willingness to help out and do your share, or maybe more than your share. They may be showing you that perhaps you've been taking on other people's burdens as if they were your own. Or perhaps you are venting out the embarrassment of feeling like a fool or an ass. See *Codependence.*

Door As is true in real life, a door allows one to enter from one place to another. An open door is an invitation; a closed door is a sign that the time is not right to proceed, or that an opportunity is not the right one for you. A closed door also represents privacy, aloneness, aloofness, and possibly rejection. Keep in mind that the door that is right for you will open for you. See *Knock.*

Doorbell Dreams of a doorbell signify that opportunity is ringing, and you are being alerted that someone or something is at the door of your heart.

Doormat Dreams of a doormat mean that you've been allowing people to walk all over you. You are afraid of saying no for fear that you will not be loved. Low self-worth has you putting up with intolerable circumstances. It is time for you to dust yourself off and stand up for what you need and want. A welcome mat signifies that you are receptive to the blessings of this universe and to new opportunities, and that you have an open-door policy to life. Consider the feeling tone. See *Rug*.

Dormitory Dreams of a dormitory signify that you are dealing with a lack of privacy, continuous disruptions, and a party atmosphere. You are growing into the responsibility of being able to fully own your space and take control of your life.

Double If you dream of two of something, then it signifies partnership or double the intensity of the symbol. For example, if you dream of two birthday cakes, then the dream symbolizes twice the celebration or double the pleasure. See *Twins* and *Two*.

Dove Dreams of a dove symbolize peace and freedom. A dove is also the Christian symbol for Jesus and/or Christ consciousness as well as the Masonic symbol of power.

Down Dreams of feeling down, falling down, or going down a staircase or in an elevator signify that you are getting down to the heart of the matter and discovering the truth of a situation. Alternatively, you could be giving in to depression or negativity. Or your dream could be saying that you need some downtime to rest and connect with your deeper feelings and intuition.

Downloading Dreams of downloading software or information signify that you are tapping into quantum consciousness. They are showing you how quickly and easily information can be transmitted into the database of your mind. Consider the content of what you are downloading. A dream of downloading can also reflect that which you are venting and releasing.

Dragon Dreams of a dragon symbolize the power of your subconscious mind, your mysterious, primal energy, sexuality, and rage.

They are giving you the message to harness this power to assist you in attaining self-mastery; otherwise, you might spend your life hiding, suppressing, and feeling victimized by the gift of your power. A dragon can also represent your biggest challenge, and the wisdom you earn as you deal with it will make you a hero/shero.

Drain Dreams of a drain represent a leak in your energy. They are giving you the message to more powerfully manage your power and not give it away so easily. See *Circle*.

Drama Queen/Drama King If you dream of a drama queen or drama king then this is your wake-up call to remind you that you are more than your passion, excitement, or sorrow. See *Actor/Actress*.

Drapes Dreams of drapes in a bedroom symbolize secrecy, privacy, and modesty with regards to intimacy and sexuality. Drapes in a living room or family room symbolize a desire to preserve family secrets.

Drawbridge Dreams of a drawbridge signify that you are creating rigid boundaries regarding whom and what you allow into your life, rejecting energy that is nonsupportive of you. They also might mean that unresolved trust issues may be keeping you from allowing love and intimacy in your life.

Drawer Dreaming of a drawer represents a space within you that is not normally in view, your secret, sacred world, and perhaps a virginal aspect of you. Consider the contents of a drawer; if the drawer is locked, then they are taboo. Dreaming of a drawer may be informing you to integrate the contents of the drawer into your outward personality. See *Pandora's Box*. See also *Integration Dreams*, page 10.

Drawing Dreams of drawing signify that you are coming to realize your ability to have a vision, make a plan, and create your life. See *Art/Artist* and *Design*.

Dreaming To dream of dreaming is quite common and it represents your subconscious becoming aware of itself. Becoming lucid during your unconscious sleep state is the beginning stage of self-mastery as you learn to bridge your conscious mind to your subconscious mind.

DreamWorks To dream of Steven Spielberg or of his motion picture production company is about opening your creativity to the skies and beyond. You are beginning an out-of-the-box creative exploration, realizing that your fantasy life could translate into a profitable career.

Dress The type of dress you wear in a dream reflects your self-image and/or the image you want others to have of you. If you dream of wearing a dress, then you are outwardly wanting to express your femininity, vulnerability, softness, and sensuality. See *Clothes, Costume,* and *Uniform.*

Dressing Dreams of dressing signify that you are suiting up and showing up in life, preparing to present yourself in a way that represents the image you show to the world. You are covering up your nakedness and authenticity with a socially acceptable exterior. The clothes you choose to wear are significant and say a lot about how you want the world and your peers to see you. If you dream of getting "dressed up," then you are preparing yourself energetically to make an impression. The dream may be a symbol that good news is forthcoming and will be worth celebrating. See *Clothes.*

If you dream of dressing for a salad, see *Salad Dressing.*

Drill Dreams of a drill signify that you are intent on getting your point across and making an impression. Perhaps you are questioning and drilling someone for answers, being overly forceful.

Drinking Drinking in a dream indicates that you are thirsting for connection, mental stimulation, or a spiritual connection. If a drink is satisfying, then you are content with the answers, energy, and substance you are receiving. If a drink does not satisfy your thirst, then you are still on a quest to find the answers or energy you need to quench your thirst.

Drive-through Dreams of a drive-through restaurant signify convenience and expeditiousness, and that you are having a quantity versus quality experience, a desire for instant gratification without nutrition.

Driveway Dreams of a driveway symbolize the need for a rest and pause between spurts of energy. A driveway is a home base for your vehicle (body) that moves you through life.

Driving Dreams of driving can symbolize your ambition and drive to succeed. Whoever is driving or in the driver's seat is influencing your direction and/or is in control of your life. See *Car.*

Drowning Dreams of drowning signify that you are feeling overwhelmed and that you have been indulging in negative, fear-based emotions. Dreaming of drowning is helping you to release your fear of being unable to keep your head above water. See *Venting Dreams,* page 8.

Drugs Dreams of drugs represent a desire for a self-destructive vacation from reality to escape your mental, emotional, or physical pain. See *AA.*

Drum Dreams of a drum signify that you are in touch with your soul's unique rhythm, creativity, and artistic expression. You are dancing to the beat of your own drum, daring to be the authentic individual that you are. See *Heartbeat* and *Musical Instrument.*

Drunk Dreams of being drunk symbolize that you are looking for love and/or God in all the wrong places, thirsty for something that will fulfill your soul. These venting dreams may be helping you to release toxic ways of being, to wake up, and soberly face your life. See *AA, Alcohol,* and *Drugs.*

Dry If you dream that something is dry, as in dry weather, a piece of meat, or dry land, then it reflects that you've been going through a dry spell and are dealing with the facts of life, going through the motions without joy, passion, or spice.

Dry Cleaning To dream of dry cleaning signifies that you are suiting up and showing up in your life, being pressured to look your best, and putting on a good appearance.

Duck Dreams of a duck mean that you are feeling vulnerable, like a sitting duck to potential threats and/or predators. They may be giving you the message to duck criticism or attacks by not taking them personally.

Duet Dreams of a duet symbolize your desire for a partnership that makes beautiful music together. They are telling you that when you are in the right relationship, intimate or business, both people feel more powerful and capable than they would feel separately. See *Music.*

Dugout Dreams of a dugout signify that you are preparing yourself to get out on the playing field of life. You are becoming mentally ready to take a swing at the curveballs life throws your way.

Dungeon Dreams of a dungeon symbolize your unexplored subconscious, shadow side, and unintegrated aspects of your consciousness. There is a great deal of unintegrated power, wisdom, and talent that you have yet to uncover. See *Basement, Dragon, Goddess* (Persephone), and *Shadow.*

Dusk Dreams of dusk, the transition time between day and night, mean that you are in the twilight of your life, of a relationship, or of a project that you've been working on. This time of day reflects wisdom, reflection, and hindsight.

Dust Dreams about dust represent an existential awareness of the temporality of our human experience. You are realizing that souls live forever, but bodies end in dust. If something is dusty, then it means it has been neglected, abandoned, unused, and it is old or outdated.

DVD If you dream you are watching a DVD it reflects a high regard for the content of a clear message, and your ability to observe your life with clarity (high resolution), as in the shamanistic practice of "soul retrieval," whereby you witness your life and reclaim any personal power that was lost, stolen, or given away. See *CD.*

Dwarf Dreams of a dwarf signify that you have become small energetically. You have lost or abdicated your power to someone which has left you feeling insecure, diminished, and insubstantial. Perhaps these dreams are showing you that you've been downplaying your talents and gifts. Dreams of dwarfs also signify that you are connecting with a magical, childlike aspect of yourself.

Dynamite Dreams of dynamite are venting dreams about exploding with anger or passion, and/or out-of-control feelings that have been bottled up but can no longer be contained.

E

Eagle Dreams of an eagle symbolize a higher view. In Native American spirituality eagle medicine represents a powerful force that is extremely wise with keen vision and strong soaring flight.

Ear Dreaming of an ear symbolizes your desire to amplify your innate ability to hear what is going on around you. Dreaming about an ear can also forecast a memorable occurrence. See *Hearing*.

Earrings Dreams of earrings signify that you are accentuating your ability to hear the voice of your higher self and/or to allow the truth and wisdom of your inner voice to ring.

Earth Dreams of the earth represent your foundation, and the belief systems that uphold your life. Your subconscious mind is reminding you to keep your feet on the ground. The earth is also symbolic of your mother or the maternal, nurturing energy you have received in life. Sometimes the things that are the most important for your survival are the things you most take for granted. Your subconscious mind may be giving you the message to be grateful for the people in your life who are there for you unconditionally and to treat them with the respect they deserve. See *Dirt*.

Earthquake Dreams of an earthquake represent enormous change and transformation taking place in the foundation of your life. Your belief systems are being rattled, perhaps so that you can find what is truly solid within you. See *Breakdown/Breakthrough Dreams,* page 12.

Earwax Dreams of earwax symbolize blockages to hearing and that you are resisting advice.

East Dreams of the east signify that you are coming into a new chapter in your life. Your subconscious mind is giving you permission to have beginner's mind, and to be open to inspiration.

Easter Dreams of Easter symbolize resurrection, eternal life, renewal, and rebirth. If you've just gone through a dark night of the soul, take heart in knowing that you are undergoing transformation, and you will come through better and brighter than ever before. See *Spring*.

Eating Dreams of eating signify that you are hungry for energy, power, and connection to your source. Perhaps you are yearning for stimulation. Keep in mind that you are what you eat, so be aware of the beliefs and energy you allow yourself to ingest. See *Food*.

eBay Dreams of shopping or selling on eBay represent your connection with the world and with unlimited opportunity. Pay attention to the feeling tone of the dream to see whether it is telling you to monitor your shopping, or to prepare for a great opportunity. Consider what you are shopping for and/or what you are selling. See *Retail Therapy*.

E-book Dreams of an e-book symbolize your need or desire for instant gratification, knowledge, and ease of transmission of information. You are aware of your connection to the one mind and one database of information to which we are all connected. You are also realizing your ability to download information simply by directing your attention to the place it resides in consciousness.

Echinacea Dreams of echinacea represent holistic healing and your desire for improved health and stimulation.

Echo Dreams of an echo symbolize instant karma: what you send out immediately returns to you. You are the one you've been calling for, the one with all the answers you seek.

Ecstasy Dreams of ecstasy represent an experience of your potential, your creative brilliance, your sexuality, and your eternal and authentic nature. Allow these dreams to be a touchstone of your true nature, the feeling tone of your spiritual expression, and/or a window to insight and enlightenment.

Editing/Editor Dreams of editing or an editor signify your desire for perfection, and/or that you may be second-guessing yourself. Alternatively, dreams of an editor signify that you are taking responsibility for the power of your words, and you are coming into a position of power regarding the role you play in influencing people. See *Critic* and *Gatekeeper*.

Egg Dreams of an egg or eggs represent fertility in business, conception, ideas, partnership, and the potential for success. They may be cautioning you not to put all your eggs into one basket. If you dream that there is egg on your face, there may be something you are afraid people will find out about you. An egg is also a symbol of your ego, the fragile, breakable, vulnerable shell that protects the golden life within you. Consider the feeling tone.

Eggshell Dreams of walking on eggshells represent insecurity and vulnerability. You are tiptoeing through a very precarious situation, attempting to do and say all the right things and not break your egoic illusion of your fragile ego or the egos of those around you.

Ego Dreams of the ego represent your unconscious desire for fusion and integration with your shadow and light, humanity and spirituality. The exposure of the ego in all of its grandiosity, defensiveness, and outrageous demands is very healthy as long as your intent is wholeness and integration.

Egypt Dreams of Egypt are symbolic of wealth, power, and the afterlife. See *Afterlife, Cleopatra,* and *Pyramid.*

Eight A dream featuring the number 8 represents infinity, eternity, regeneration, success, the dollar sign, material wealth, competition, ambition, and intense efficiency with regard to manifestation. Material rewards are of utmost importance to you, and this may be a sign that dedication to such gains and success may be becoming an obsession.

Eighteen Dreams of the number 18 represent the turning point from childhood to adulthood. You are stepping into responsibility.

Elasticity Dreams of elasticity signify flexibility, and that you are able to bend and contract easily. Be cautious of being spread too thin or being pulled too tight. Setting healthy boundaries will help you to snap back into place. See *Codependence.*

Elbow Dreams of an elbow represent your ability to protect yourself, to set boundaries, and to bend to accommodate other people's desires. The universe may be nudging you to change directions, and be open and flexible to input from others.

Elder Dreams of an elder signify that you are tapping into your wisdom, the "wizard" that has the benefit of age and perspective to yield an empowering and wise point of view. See *Crone.*

Election Dreams of an election represent choice, options, and responsibility. A dream of an election represents your ability to vote and recognize the opinions of all aspects of you. You are coming to the awareness of the impact that your choices have on the people in your life. See *Voting.*

Electricity Dreams of electricity symbolize power, aliveness, energy, and the chemistry that takes place when opposites attract and come into harmony. You are in a relationship, project, or time in your life that is synergistically stimulating and that is sparking your creativity.

Elephant Dreams of an elephant are a fortuitous sign that there is something important for you to remember. The Hindu god Ganesh, depicted as an elephant, is the deity of wealth, prosperity, and great abundance. Dreams of elephants also represent the ability to break down barriers and challenges to success, as well as the ability to truly own one's power, strength, and greatness.

Elevator Dreams of moving up in an elevator signify that you are elevating rapidly and moving up in the world. You now know where the buttons are, so you are advancing with a sense of confidence and control over a situation. If you are moving down, then you know what to do to switch directions to elevate your position. Also, if you are moving down, it can signify either your interest in understanding the foundation of a situation you are in, or that you are allowing fear and negativity to bring you down.

Elevator Speech Dreams of a thirty-second elevator speech represent clarity, cohesiveness of thought, and purpose. You are experiencing confidence, boldness, and power as you elevate in status and/or in consciousness.

Eleven Dreams of the number 11 represent illumination and spiritual awareness. They are a sign to trust your intuition, visions, and your humanitarian nature. See *Ace*.

Eleven/Eleven If you dream of "Eleven/eleven," then it represents a divine opportunity that is opening up for you that will bring you great blessings. See *Angel*.

Elf Dreams of an elf signify that you are connecting with a very magical and playful aspect of yourself. The large ears on an elf represent attunement to the still-small voice within.

Elixir Dreams of an elixir represent alchemy; you are changing and transforming from the inside out. The elixir that you dream of ingesting is reacquainting you with your divine nature, eternal youth, and healing abilities.

Eloping To dream of eloping reflects your need or desire for privacy and secrecy to protect the vulnerability and sacredness of your vows or deepest feelings from scrutiny, judgment, or fanfare. Perhaps you are also rebelling against and/or rejecting tribal or familial values and customs.

Eloquent Dreams of being eloquent, saying what you mean and meaning what you say, represent clarity, certainty, and passion about who you are, why you are here, and what you want to do.

E-mail Dreams of e-mail represent communication, and a desire to reach out and touch people. They also represent efficiency and expeditious interactions from a distance. E-mail can also symbolize a kind of aloof intimacy and/or unwanted communication. See *Letter.*

Embarrassment Dreams of embarrassment signify that you are releasing shame for doing or saying something foolish.

Embryo Dreams of an embryo signify that you are embarking on a new project or relationship, and perhaps you are feeling that you are being born again. See *Baby.*

Emerald Dreams of an emerald symbolize successful love, domestic bliss, and loyalty. You are combining your intelligence with discernment, and making the right choice with regard to love and relationships. See *Green, Ireland,* and *Jewelry.*

Emergency Dreams of an emergency signify that you are releasing stress, anxiety, hurry, and worry. They may be flagging you down to pay attention to aspects of yourself that have been ignored for too long, and that now have an urgent need to be paid attention to. A dream of an emergency is a wake-up call. If you are dialing 911, then you are calling out for help. You are in a situation that leaves you feeling helpless and you need support to return to balance. See *Hospital.*

Emergency Exit Dreams of an emergency exit are your subconscious mind's way of telling you to leave a job, relationship, or unhealthy situation you are in immediately.

Emotions The expression or release of emotions is very typical and healthy in dreams. Often, because of the lack of inhibitions in the dream state, you might experience extremes that your ego does not allow you to explore in your waking state. Emotions release psychological pressure and allow you to awaken in the morning feeling refreshed, invigorated, with a clean clear slate. See *Afraid, Angry, Ecstasy, Happy, Jealousy,* and *The Emotions of Shadow and Light,* page 20.

Employee/Employer If you dream of working for someone else, it can mean that you are venting out feelings of powerlessness, suppression, resentment, and restlessness because you have not yet fully come into your power. Keep in mind that frustration can be the catalyst for you to make positive and necessary changes in your life. Alternatively, dreams of being an employee might represent your feelings of service and support. If you dream of being an employer, then it reflects that you are coming into your power, and you are grappling with your feelings about having authority and responsibility.

Empress Dreams of an empress symbolize feminine power, status, rank, service, and sovereignty. An empress represents the ego and a desire to impress. An empress also represents your feelings toward your mother, nurturing, and your creative impulses. See *Queen*.

Empty Dreams of feeling empty signify that you've not been tending to your needs, you're running on empty, your tank is low, and you are processing and releasing feelings of emptiness, loneliness, and lack of connection to your purpose. They are telling you that it is time to fill your well with soul food that will nurture your body, mind, and soul. See *Low Tide*.

Encyclopedia Dreams of an encyclopedia represent the awareness of your connectivity to all knowledge and resources. You are realizing the value of your own inner wisdom and that knowledge is power.

End To dream of an ending represents completion, the culmination or achievement of a goal. You are realizing that there is no such thing as an end, because in the life/death/life cycle, an end always precedes a beginning. You may be grieving for the parting of ways between you and a loved one, but you can take heart in knowing that the love you shared lives forever. See *Breakup*.

End Table An end table represents support, strength, and convenience. Consider what is on an end table or if it is empty. See *Drawer, Furniture,* and *Table*.

Enema Dreams of an enema signify that you are receiving assistance in releasing, purifying, cleansing, and flushing out your toxic thoughts and emotions that are keeping you energetically clogged.

Enemy Dreams of a person who is an enemy represent your shadow and an opportunity for self-integration, empowerment, and realization. If you inquire into the qualities that the person represents (e.g., stubbornness, deceitfulness, selfishness, insensitivity, etc.), become willing to see where in your own life you show the same qualities, and forgive yourself, then you will begin to powerfully integrate the shadow energy and truly receive the gift of the dream. If you do this you may discover that your enemy is offering you a great gift. See *Shadow.* See also *Integration Dreams,* page 10.

Energy See *Blood, Emotions,* and *Power.*

Engagement Dreams of an engagement represent courting, responsibility, devotion, and connection, that you are preparing to make a big commitment. See *Commitment* and *Wedding.*

Engine/Engineer Dreams of an engine signify that you have the power and energy to move, manifest, go where you want to go, and do what you want to do. You are driven, inspired, goal oriented, and ready to take control of the course of your life, making sure that you are on track with your goals. A dream of an engine may be showing you that you are being controlling and overbearing. See *Blood, Emotions, Power,* and *Train.*

Enron Dreams of Enron signify a misuse of power, and that karma eventually catches up with you. An Enron dream could be a call to remain spiritually balanced and keep integrity as you expand into more and more of your power.

Entertainment Dreams of entertainment represent a desire for amusement, distraction, or education. If you dream of doing the entertaining, see *Actor/Actress* or *Host.*

Entrance Dreams of an entrance represent the beginning of a new chapter in your life, starting anew. If you are making an entrance, it is about getting attention and wanting others to notice you, a desire to feel important.

Envelope Dreams of an envelope signify that an important and surprising message is forthcoming.

Epidemic Dreams of an epidemic represent news that spreads like wildfire, whether it is good news or gossip. You are realizing the oneness of life, and that what affects one of us affects us all, because ultimately there is only one of us here. See *Viral Marketing* and *Virus.*

Epilepsy Dreams of epilepsy signify that you are feeling a loss of control, resisting the flow of life, and adding insult to injury by indulging in self-criticism. They are prompting you to discover ways to harmoniously engage in life, to live life on life's terms, and to embrace yourself.

Epstein-Barr Virus Dreams of Epstein-Barr virus or chronic fatigue syndrome, represent depression, a need for deep rest, and the inability or unwillingness to process data that has been piling up in your mind. They also are about procrastination, exhaustion, and frustration, which reflects a need to set better boundaries and to begin to take care of yourself. See *Depressed/Depression* and *Disease*.

Equinox Dreams of an equinox symbolize balance of power within you, equality between the masculine and feminine energies, and an embrace of your light and dark aspects. See *Yin and Yang*.

Errands Dreams about running errands, either those you've completed or those you actually need to do, signify that you are processing the data of the day. They reflect your desire to get it all done, to catch up, and keep your head above water. See *Processing Dreams,* page 7.

Escalator Dreams of moving up on an escalator signify that you are rising gracefully to new heights, that you are climbing the ladder of success with relative ease. You know where you are going and you're moving to the top. If you are moving down, you are either going in the wrong direction or you are exploring the depths of your nature.

Escape Dreams of an escape signify that your survival is at stake, or that you've perhaps just had a close brush with danger. They are a warning that if the situation you are in is not supporting your well-being it is time to leave. Alternatively, what you resist persists, so face and embrace your fears in order to erase them, and then replace them with that which empowers you.

Espresso Dreams of this extreme coffee drink symbolize your need for the energy to express yourself, a desire to externalize your feelings and desires, and put your dreams into motion. See *Coffee*.

Europe Dreams of Europe represent your affinity or connection to old civilizations, history, and a variety of languages, people, and culture.

Evergreen Dreams of an evergreen signify that which is constant, forever, eternal, and everlasting, as in unconditional love. Perhaps your subconscious mind is giving you the message to appreciate and not take for granted the wonderful aspects of your life that are always there. See *Tree*.

Evil Dreams of evil represent that which is fear based and ignorant. Note that *evil* is *live* spelled backward, which means that *evil* is the inversion of your life force, your natural inclination toward light being misdirected. Perhaps you've been devastated and are grappling with your faith in a beneficent universe. Your dreams are assisting you with your soul-searching for the answers to your questions about who you truly are and why you are here. See *Devil*. See also *Venting Dreams,* page 8.

Evite If you dream that you receive an evite, then the dream is inviting you to get out, be adventurous, explore new terrain, and say yes to the opportunities presented to you. If you dream that you are sending an evite, then you are telling the universe that you want more social interaction, an expanded social circle, and/or a desire to meet a special someone. See *Invitation* and *Match.com*.

Exchange Dreams of an exchange reflect your opportunistic desires as well as a desire for order and balance. You may be grappling with a need for fairness that has not been met, or you are having a "grass is greener" experience.

Execution/Executioner Dreams of an execution symbolize rejection and punishment. Perhaps you are venting out your disdain for a person or an aspect of yourself of which you are ashamed. Dreaming of an execution might reflect your rejection of your intellect and logic (cutting off your head) in favor of your emotions and feelings. Keep in mind that a house divided against itself cannot stand. Integration of all aspects of yourself is the goal to self-realization. Dreams of an executioner represent the aspect of you that is the most critically judgmental. There is an aspect of your life or a person in your life that you find you want to reject and push away. See *Critic* and *Cut*. See also *Integration Dreams,* page 10.

Exercise Dreams of exercise represent a desire to get moving, to exercise your beliefs and thoughts, and to get blood flowing in the areas that have been sedentary. They may be a message for you to exercise your rights, your vote, or your say in the matter at hand.

Exhaling Dreams of exhaling represent relief because you are realizing you can finally relax, and know that everything is working out.

Exile Dreams of exile represent disdain for an aspect of yourself. Keep in mind that what you suppress must express. See *Castration*. See also *Integration Dreams,* page 10.

Exit Sign Dreams of an exit sign signify completion, finality, closure, and that it is time to leave. See *Backdoor* and *Emergency Exit.*

Exorcism If you dream of an exorcism, you are releasing attachment to nonsupportive energy and connection to negativity so that you can return to your divine nature. See *Phoenix.*

Experiment See *Gambling* and *Laboratory.*

Expert Dreams of an expert signify that you are connecting with your mastery and genius, recognizing that what you are best at is what you can teach others. See *Higher Self.*

Explosion See *Venting Dreams,* page 8.

Express Dreams of an express lane or express service signify that you are in a rush and are living life in the fast lane. They are giving you the message to take time to smell the roses and find balance in your busy life. Perhaps you are in the midst of a great growth spurt.

Extraction Dreams of an extraction signify that you are removing an undesirable habit, relationship, or aspect of your life. They reflect that you are in the midst of major change and transformation. You are learning to say no to what is undesirable and nonsupportive in order to bring into your life that which is desirable and supportive. See *Operation.*

Ex- (Wife, Husband, Boyfriend, or Girlfriend) Dreams of an ex are about venting, sorting out, and processing your ties to your former lovers. You are realizing that those relationships do not end when the divorce papers are signed. Often an ex represents a part of your shadow that you must face and embrace, erase and eventually replace. See *Integration Dreams,* page 10.

Eyes Dreams of eyes signify that you are in touch with your intuition, and your ability to see what is really going on. In a dream, if an eye is cloudy, then you are not seeing your life situation clearly, perhaps because it is cluttered with unresolved emotional issues. If you are able to see another person's point of view, then you are compassionate. If you are nearsighted, then you are able to see only your own myopic perspective, and you would be wise to consider the opinions and points of view of the people in your life. If your vision is clear, then you trust your vision and intuition. See *Vision*.

Eye Shadow Dreams of eye shadow, or any eye makeup, symbolize your desire to see and be seen, to be recognized and noticed. See *Cosmetics* and *Eyes*.

F

Fabric Dreams of fabric signify that you are decorating, enhancing, and making your life as beautiful as you can with the raw materials you have. Dreaming of fabric can also mean that you may be covering something up that you want to hide, as in "fabricating the truth."

Facade Dreams of a facade represent protection, defensiveness, a veneer, social mask, or ego. You are becoming aware that what is going on behind the scenes is distinct from the appearance on the surface.

Face Dreams of your face symbolize your presentation to the world, your self-image, your concerns with your reputation and the way others perceive you. Perhaps these dreams are giving you the message that it's time to face facts, not take things at face value. If you can't see a person's face, then he or she represents your feelings about anonymity.

Face-lift Dreams of a face-lift signify that you are contemplating taking drastic measures to recapture your youth. Perhaps you are unable or unwilling to face your own mortality and your own aging process. This dream may be revealing your preoccupation with your facade and a lack of attention to your inner worth and value. Alternatively, you might be attempting to uplift your spirits and see things from a different perspective. See *Cosmetic Surgery*.

Factory Dreams of a factory symbolize your inner space of creation, manifestation, and plans for the successful output of your dreams and aspirations. Alternatively, if you dream of working in a factory and being a cog in a wheel, then you are feeling suppressed with regard to your creativity.

Fainting If you dream that you are fainting, then you are probably having a blood sugar drop. This can also represent that you are feeling overwhelmed. See *Breakdown*.

Fair If you or someone else is being treated fairly or unfairly in a dream, then it is about justice, equality, balance, and karma.

If the dream is of a country fair or carnival, see *Amusement Park*.

Fairy Dreams of fairies represent your connection to the realm of magic, enchantment, and miracles. They are either beckoning you to delve more deeply into your magical inner life, or letting you know that fairies are assisting you in a current life circumstance. See *Angel*.

Fairy Tale Dreams of an idealistic story of romance and happily ever after represent great or unrealistic expectations of love and life, and a childlike view which is innocent. You may be in the honeymoon stage of a romance. True love does exist, and there is a reward for your virtue, but you have to earn it, even after you walk into the sunset.

Faith Dreams of faith in a higher power or in yourself represent the strength and growth of your spirit. When you allow yourself to have faith in the goodness of this universe, you naturally embody a confidence that supports you in rising to the occasion of any situation you may encounter.

Fake Dreams of a fake represent discernment and your ability to see and know the difference between that which is authentic and that which isn't. These are a wake-up call to acknowledge that your true self is good enough as is and doesn't need a mask. See *Facade* and *Mask*.

Falcon Dreams of a falcon signify that you are in touch with the hunter within you, the predator that is able to swoop down from above and seize your prey. See *Bird*.

Falling Dreams of falling signify a feeling of loss of control, a lack of confidence, and that you are losing your step as a result of not having your feet firmly planted on the earth. They mean that you are overwhelmed with the events in your life. Falling can also be symbolic of surrendering your control to something or someone more powerful than you.

If your dream is set in or about the season of fall, see *Autumn*.

False To dream of something false represents your quest for something true and real. In order to do this you must be willing to read between the lines and discern fact from fiction. See *Facade*.

False Teeth Dreams of false teeth signify that you need assistance processing and chewing on the events of your life. See *Teeth*.

Fame Dreams of fame signify validation of your worthiness, and that you are moving toward higher levels of success and societal status. Keep in mind that fame is a fickle, elusive ego trick to teach you that all recognition is worthless without your own self-approval. Dreaming of fame is giving you the message to develop a sense of worthiness by taking esteem-able action. See *Award*. See also *Wish Fulfillment Dreams,* page 18.

Family Dreams of family symbolize loyalty, strength, unconditional love, and deeply rooted belief systems from your tribe. They could be an indication that healing among your family members is taking place or is forthcoming. If you dream of a particular family member, it can literally be that you are processing the details of your recent interactions with that person, or you are beginning to disidentify with your family mythology as you begin to autonomize and discover your own beliefs and attitudes. Also, because as every character in a dream is a reflection of you, consider the qualities and attributes you ascribe to that family member and realize that you are grappling with this aspect of yourself. See *Aunt, Brother, Father, Grandfather, Grandmother, Mother, Sister,* and *Uncle.*

Famous Dreams of a famous person in a dream may be guiding you to reach your dreams and recognize yourself. See *Actor/Actress, Celebrity,* and *Fame.*

Fan If you dream of being someone's number one fan, then you are putting someone above you, living vicariously through that person. If this helps you to grow, then this is positive and supportive.

However, if you are placing someone on a pedestal and put yourself beneath that person, then a dream is giving you the message to get on with the business of maximizing *your* potential.

If a dream is of a fan that circulates air, it is about a change in the air, a change in perspective that happens when you take a breather. See *Air.*

Fan Club Dreams of a fan club signify that you are connecting with your own cheering section, being championed to victory or being the wind beneath someone else's wings. You are developing self-esteem so as to be bold as you make progress every day toward your passion. See *Fan.*

Fare Dreams of paying a fare represent that you have to pay the price to have what you want in life, and that it is up to you to discern whether or not the price is too high or if it's fair. See *Money.*

Farm/Farmer Dreams of a farm represent how well you care for your basic needs, your animal instincts, and your level of attunement to the seasons and cycles of life. They are telling you to get grounded, because you reap what you sow. Dreams of a farmer symbolize the simple, no-nonsense aspect of you that lives close to nature and has its feet on the ground.

Fast Food In a dream, eating fast food can mean that you are feeding yourself energy that if consumed over a long period of time could have diminishing returns for your body and your body of affairs.

Fasting Dreams of fasting indicate self-discipline. If you are abstaining from food or thoughts that are unhealthy for you, then dreaming of fasting indicates that you are releasing and detoxifying impurities from your system, that you are releasing what you don't want so that you can feast on what you do want.

If you dream about rapid movement, see *Express* or *Fast Lane.*

Fast Lane Dreams of driving in the fast lane, or the number one lane, signify your competitive edge and that you are driven to be number one. These are processing dreams, allowing you to decompress all the high-speed activities from your life on the edge and in the fast lane. See *Express.*

Fat Dreams of being fat represent extreme sensitivity and a need for protection from adverse elements. Perhaps you've been engaging in overindulgence, stuffing your feelings, and creating a cushion to hide behind. Dreams of fat can also forecast wealth and abundance.

Father Dreams of a father, or your father, can be about your feelings and projections about the father archetype or God. A father generally represents support, protection, and heroism. If a dream is a pleasant one where a father is amiable, then it signifies that you are in balance and harmony with the father/masculine/God aspect of yourself. If a father character is malevolent, it means a distrust of God/the universe, your own father, or the father aspect of yourself, as in the ability to provide or protect yourself from harm. See *God* and *King*.

Faucet If a faucet in a dream is flowing, then it means that abundance and creativity are flourishing in your life. If a faucet is leaky, then your power source is going down the drain. If a faucet is broken, then you are in need of repair in the abundance area of your life. Dreams of a faucet can also represent mastery over your emotions, as in your ability to turn them on and off. See *Water*.

Favor Dreams of asking for a favor reflect your comfort level in asking for help or support. They are auspicious dreams where you are aware of the positive energy that is available for the asking.

Fax Dreams of a fax represent sending and receiving messages, communication, and telepathy. A very specific interchange is taking place between you and an old friend. See *E-mail* and *Phone*.

Fear Dreams of fear are venting dreams. Your dreams are a safe place to explore and release your deepest fears that reside in the darkest shadows of your subconscious. When your fears are faced and embraced, they can then be erased and replaced with positive energy that supports your well-being. See *Venting Dreams,* page 8.

Feast Dreams of a feast usually signify your awareness of something wonderful being prepared for you, or that you are preparing to bestow something wonderful upon another. If you are seated at a feast, partaking in a joyous manner, then this symbolizes your ability to enjoy the fruits of your labor. If you are uncomfortable at a feast, then you are grappling with issues of deservedness and abundance. The message of a dream of a feast is to revel in your

well-earned success and share to it with others. See *Food*. See also
Wish Fulfillment Dreams, page 18.

Feather Dreams of a feather represent your connection with your
lightness of being. They are about the wisdom that comes from
gaining a higher view, seeing the big picture, and connecting more
closely to your higher source for inspiration. If you have a feather in
your cap, then you are feeling proud as you are being recognized for
an accomplishment. Because birds of a feather flock together, dreaming of a feather could also symbolize your desire for a harmonious
relationship. See *Bird*.

February Dreams of February are associated with Valentine's Day,
love, romance, and passion. You are acknowledging those you love
or you are pining for love. See *Eros* and *Fairy Tale*.

Feces Dreams of feces signify that you are releasing and letting go of
what is in the way of your being fully in your power. You are purifying, healing, and cleansing your mind, body, and spirit and are entering into a powerful time in your life.

FedEx Dreams of FedEx represent your desire to have a message or
communication delivered quickly, with a guarantee. Consider the
message that is being sent and why it is so urgent. See *Express* and
Instant Messenger.

Feeding Tube See *Life Support*.

Feet If you dream of clean feet, then you have pure intentions. If
feet are dirty, then a dream is telling you to release your nonsupportive thoughts, beliefs, and feelings. The washing of someone
else's feet shows service, devotion, and a passion for caring for
the well-being of others. Tantric teachings say that the feet are the
point where the human and the divine intersect. You are becoming
grounded. See *Bare Feet*.

Fellatio Dreams of fellatio signify that you are empowering your
inner masculine energy. They can also represent submission or empowerment, depending upon the feeling tone in the dream. See *Sex*.

Fence See *Boundary* and *Wall*.

Feng Shui Dreaming of feng shui symbolizes your desire to be rid of
clutter in your life, emotionally and physically, and to connect with
your natural sense of order, clarity, abundance, and success.

Fern Dreams of a fern represent your fascination and curiosity with life. See *Flowers* and *Plant*.

Ferris Wheel Dreams of a Ferris wheel represent joy, fun, celebration, repetition, and the cycles of life. You are going around in circles; perhaps you are stuck in the past, or trying to re-create and relive an enjoyable time from your history. See *Carnival, Wheel,* and *Wheel of Fortune*.

Ferry Dreams of a ferry symbolize assistance in crossing into the unknown and the mysterious waters of your subconscious. If your car is on a ferry, you are bringing your sense of self with you as you transition from one shore of your being to another. See *Boat*.

Fertilizer Dreams of fertilizer represent that you are setting the foundation for your heart's desires to grow to fruition.

Fever Dreams of a fever signify anger, and that you are burning up with resentment, anger, or passion.

Fiber Optics Dreams of fiber optics symbolize unity, oneness, and instant gratification. They also represent instantaneous transmission of information, the realization that everything is happening now, and there is only one of us here. See *Light*.

Fiddle Dreams of a fiddle symbolize your feelings of importance, esteem, and status. Notice whether or not you are playing first or second fiddle. Perhaps a dream is telling you that you have been fiddling around and not taking your life seriously. See *Foreplay* and *Musical Instrument*.

Field Dreams of a field represent an open space for you to create, manifest, and grow the life you desire. See *Farm/Farmer*.

Fig Dreams of a fig represent sweetness and the female genitalia, fertility and sexuality.

Fight Dreams of a fight represent that you are venting out aggression, resentment, rage, and hostility toward yourself and/or others. Keep in mind that your anger and willingness to fight for what you believe in are the energy you need to make positive changes in your life. See *War*. See also *Venting Dreams,* page 8.

Files Dreams of files, or of filing, represent your mental process: logic, order, and reasoning. Your subconscious mind is attempting to support you in getting a handle on all the data in your life so that you can properly categorize people, places, things, and events of your life in a way that they make sense to you, and you can feel in control of your life.

Finding A dream of finding a new object, person, or thing signifies that you are discovering new aspects of yourself and are reconnecting with something you thought was lost, stolen, or missing. The dream is giving you the message that everything is coming together for you.

Finger To dream of pointing a finger is to blame, scorn, look for fault, or put your finger on the answer. A finger may be symbolically pointing you toward a particular direction to move toward in life. If you dream of an injured finger, then you are processing your hurt feelings for having been blaming, shaming, or fault finding. See *Hand*.

Fingernails Dreams of fingernails symbolize protection and your ability to fend for yourself and take what you need. If you dream of short fingernails, then this is about feeling vulnerable and/or functional. If you dream of long fingernails, then this is about elegance and/or your ability to protect yourself. If fingernails are dirty, this represents a lack of hygiene or care for personal appearance. If the fingernails are polished and clean, this means you care about being presentable, professional, making a good appearance, and having your act together.

Fingerprint Dreams of your fingerprint represent your unique, one-of-a kind, creative essence and nature. You are connecting to your soul and your authentic way of doing things. You are putting your finger on the way that works best for you.

Finish Line Dreams of a finish line signify a mark of completion, achievement, and success. Consider whether or not you have won. See *Death* and *End*.

Fire Dreams of fire represent change, transformation, passion, love, sexuality, energy, and destruction. They also represent energy that feels out of control in your life. A change is coming, a rite of passage in which you are stepping into the fire of initiation, burning away all that is impure so all that remains is solid, real, golden, and immortalized. If a fire is contained in a hearth, then it represents keeping the home fires burning, warmth, security, and domestic tranquillity. See *Goddess* (Hestia).

Fireman Dreams of a fireman show you how you handle the heat of passion, love, sex, and success. They may also be about looking for someone to rescue you from going down in flames. The fireman archetype is also your inner hero, the warrior part of you that is willing to go through fire to do what he has to do for love, life, and passion.

Fireplace Dreams of a fireplace signify contained heat, and that you are feeling safe enough to allow your home fires to burn. You are connecting to your nurturing side and domestic tranquillity. See *Goddess* (Hestia).

Fire Wall Dreams of an Internet fire wall represent boundaries to protect people and information that is valuable to you. You are feeling on the defensive, afraid of being harmed or corrupted by a negative influence or virus. A ring of fire in a sacred ceremony creates a safe space that deflects and dissolves any unwelcome energy.

Fireworks Dreams of fireworks symbolize passion, love, romance, ecstasy, celebration, and bliss. You are realizing your independence and interdependence, and are feeling free to love as fully as you choose. See *Fairy Tale.*

Fish Dreams of fish, because they are aquatic, represent the feminine essence and are the symbol of the Christ. A fish is also a sign of the creative element in life and going with the flow. In addition, fish can represent sperm and perhaps the subconscious desire for a baby, as well as for unconscious wisdom that you have yet to understand. See *Salmon* and *Swimming.*

Fishbowl Dreams of a fishbowl signify that you are revealing your true feelings, emotions, and intentions. Perhaps you are feeling exposed and emotionally naked.

Fisherman Dreams of a fisherman are about your ability to care for yourself, and knowing how to access the resources you need to survive and thrive. Perhaps it's time to pass on what you know to others and teach them to fish for themselves.

Fishing Pole Dreams of a fishing pole signify desire, and that you are extending yourself, putting your desires "out there," hoping for a bite. A fishing pole is also a symbol of the penis, a desire for sex, intimacy, and/or fertility. Or perhaps in a dream you are fishing for clues or answers to the issues and challenges you are dealing with.

Fishnet Dreams of a fishnet symbolize your ability to lure in energy. Because fishnet stockings are alluring and used to catch or hook men, dreams of a fishnet can symbolize attraction, seduction, and the awareness of the energetic nets that you set. See *Web*.

Fist Dreams of a fist represent anger, aggressiveness, intimidation, arrogance, stress, preparation for a fight, restraining anger, and feeling powerful. You are in a power struggle, and you are dealing with issues of machismo, strength, combat, competition, and intimidation. See *Fight*.

Five Dreams of the number 5, according to the I Ching, symbolize rebellion and leadership. They are about a great learning opportunity and change taking place in your life.

Flag Dreams of a flag represent an affiliation of which you are proud. Perhaps these dreams represent familial or national pride, or maybe you desire to outwardly share your innermost feelings and beliefs. If a flag is being waved, then you are proud of what the flag represents. If a flag is being burned, then you are ashamed or against what the flag represents. If a flag is white, then you are declaring surrender.

Flame Dreams of a flame symbolize a ceremony or ritual. The lighting of a flame represents heating up an intention or adding fire to a desire. A flame can represent passion, enthusiasm, and commitment. A violet flame represents St. Germain, the saint of safety, divine security, protection, and transformation. See *Fire*.

Flashlight Dreams of a flashlight symbolize your spiritual awareness, giving you the ability to navigate through the dark times and find your way to the light at the end of the tunnel. Your subconscious mind is giving you hope, connection to the light of your being, and the message that you will make it through this transition and come into a greater degree of power, clarity, and focus.

Flat Dreams of feeling flat or of something becoming flat are about a loss of confidence, power, energy, or momentum. If you dream of a flat tire, you are feeling discouraged about your direction in life.

Fleet Dreams of a fleet signify unity, synergy, power in numbers,

FLOWERS   143

abundance, supply, and that the fulfillment of your desires is within reach. Consider the type of fleet it is.

Fleet Week Dreams of fleet week represent celebration, honor, and recognition of the aspect of you that courageously and heroically engages in life.

Flight Attendant Dreams of a flight attendant represent angelic assistance helping to make your journey to higher consciousness as smooth as possible. You are realizing that you are never alone, because divine assistance is always at hand. See *Angel.*

Flip Dreams of a flip represent the heights of enthusiasm, joy, success, and celebration. A flip hairstyle represents perkiness, bounce in the step, joviality. If you "flip off" someone, you are angry and sending a message of hostility.

Float Dreams of floating symbolize grace and ease in the midst of your journey. You are in need of a time-out so that you can feel supported and carried by the universe and your higher power. If you dream of a parade float, then you are being celebrated, honored for your accomplishments, and uplifted in a state of grace. See *Flying.* See also *Wish Fulfillment Dreams,* page 18.

Flock Dreams of a flock represent synergy, harmony, and alignment of all aspects of you moving in the same direction at the same time. See *Bird* and *Flying.*

Flood Dreams of a flood signify that you are feeling overwhelmed emotionally, overpowered, and out of control of your life circumstances. Also, the floodgates of your heart may be opening and you may be feeling flooded with more abundance of joy than you can handle. Or your subconscious mind may be preparing you to be overtaken with love. See *Breakdown/Breakthrough Dreams,* page 12.

Floor Dreams of a floor symbolize the foundation principles of your life and your support system, which holds you up and gives you a sense of safety and security. See *Earth* or *Feet.*

Flour Dreams of flour mean that you are rising to the occasion and you are in the process of making some dough (money) and being elevated in status as you do something you love.

Flowers Dreams of flowers signify beauty, and that you are accentuating the positive and ceremonializing or ritualizing life's passages.

If you are gathering flowers, then this is an indication of prosperity. A seed being planted, taking root beneath the soil, shooting up through the ground, and blossoming into a flower is quite a symbolic journey and metaphor for all of life. Each flower has a specific significance.

Flunking Dreams of flunking symbolize failure, losing, self-rejection, and not making the grade. Dreaming of flunking is about feelings of inferiority, overwhelm, or feeling that you are in the wrong class and not engaged in your area of expertise.

Flute Hearing a flute in a dream symbolizes harmony in your life, spirited joy, and aliveness. See *Musical Instrument* and *Penis*.

Fly Dreams of a fly signify a desire for eyes in the back of your head. You are accessing your acute awareness and survival skills. Or something or someone is being a nuisance, distraction, and irritant. You are realizing that your persistence is annoying the people in your life. This is a call to take a hint and buzz off.

Flying Dreams of flying represent freedom, joy, expression, feeling light, confidence, creativity, independence, and awareness of a higher perspective. You desire freedom from physical constraints or limitations as you connect with your true spiritual essence and access your true potential.

Flypaper Dreams of flypaper signify that you are feeling stuck, trapped, tricked, obligated, victimized, or caught.

Fog Dreams of fog represent difficulty seeing or thinking clearly. This dream is sending you a message to hold off on making major decisions. Navigate your way slowly through this period of your life. Your dreams may be telling you to connect with your meditative or spiritual practice in order to gain clarity.

Following Dreams of following are a sign that you are being influenced, perhaps giving up your personal power. If you dream of being followed, then it may signify that you are coming into your power. See *Cult* and *Victim*.

Food Dreams of food represent nourishment and influence. If you are cooking food, you're the one giving nourishment. If you are eating food, you are receiving nourishment, energy, stimulation, praise, acknowledgment, and influence. Every type of food represents a specific type of support for your body, mind, and soul. See *Bread, Breakfast, Chef, Cook/Cooking, Dessert, Dinner, Lunch, Meat, Potato, Starch,* and *Vegetables.*

Fool Dreams of a fool, or of being foolish, are a message not to take yourself too seriously. Often a trickster makes an appearance in a dream as a symbol of great growth and transformation. In the tarot, the fool symbolizes the beginning of your journey, your child essence, innocence, and eagerness to embark upon the adventure of your life. Also, a fool can represent enthusiasm, fool's luck, and even manipulative, trickster tendencies. See *Clown.*

Foot Dreams of a foot represent the blueprint for the entire human body and your grounded sense of self. They are a call to keep in step with the rhythm of life. See *Feet.*

Football Dreams of football are about tackling life's problems head-on. The game of football is an expression of masculine energy primarily reflecting that you are moving past obstacles and knocking down whatever is in the way to get past the goal line of your desires. If you dream of an actual ball, then this could be a sign that you are being abused, kicked around, piled upon, thrown, and treated harshly. Consider the feeling tone. See *Sports.*

Footprints A dream of footprints represents that you are being supported by a higher power, being carried by your ancestors, angels, and by divine guidance. In your darkest hour, know that you are not alone. Recognize how far you've come; you are leaving your legacy. See *Angel* and *Feet.*

Forehead Dreams of a forehead represent the sixth chakra in the Hindu chakra system, which represents divine insights, wisdom, intuition, and the third eye that sees beyond appearances of doubt, fear, and separation.

Foreign Dreams of anyone or anything foreign denote that you are expanding your horizons. When you remove yourself from your day-to-day life, and explore new and foreign terrain, you are able to bring back a wealth of information and perspective that enriches and benefits your life. A dream of something foreign also denotes that you may be feeling out of your element, away from your tribe; you are in the midst of a transition, learning and discovering aspects of yourself you never knew existed. As you evolve, you may be feeling unfamiliar in your own skin, going through an identity crisis because you are not who you used to be and you are not yet who you are becoming. Keep in mind that wherever you go, home resides within you. See *Stranger* and *Travel.*

Foreplay Dreams of foreplay are about flirtation, desire, seduction, romance, courtship, preparing for union, sex, connection, and feeling your beauty and sexuality.

Forest Dreams of a forest signify that you are discovering unexplored regions of your psyche, your hidden power, animal instincts, magic, and enchantment. Dreaming of being in a forest can also mean that you are in the thick of the details of your life and unable to see the forest for the trees. As well, a forest represents that you are moving through a rite of passage, testing your wits and resourcefulness in order for a great transformation to occur.

Forgetting If you dream of forgetting something or someone, then this usually indicates a venting dream where you are releasing your fear of actually forgetting. Perhaps you are overwhelmed and/or the reason you are forgetting is because this is not something or someone that is very important to you, perhaps this is something you are forcing yourself to do out of obligation.

Fork Dreams of a fork represent a tool for allowing and receiving energy. If you are at a fork in a road, you are contemplating an important decision. Keep in mind that you cannot make a mistake. If someone is speaking with a forked tongue, this is about communication that is coming from fear, duplicity, and an internal split.

Form Dreaming of a form means things are beginning to take shape and your ideas and plans are coming together. It is a sign that it is all working out. If you are filling out a form, you are taking official steps to have what you want and desire.

Formula Dreams of a formula signify that you are cracking a code and finding the answers you desire. See *Code.*

Fortune When dreaming of a fortune, you are accessing your abundance, inheritance, and wealth consciousness, and coming into an experience of your soul. You are dealing with issues related to prosperity, power, energy, and love. See *Wish Fulfillment Dreams,* page 18.

Fortune Cookie Dreams of a fortune cookie represent your belief in fate, destiny, and good luck. Pay attention to the words on the slip of paper inside; they may be an important message for you. See *Prophetic Dreams,* page 17.

Fortune-teller Dreams of a fortune-teller represent your connection to your most mystical, intuitive, psychic aspect of self. They are your link to your own psychic gifts and abilities, as well as your attempt to predict your future. If you don't like the psychic's prediction, the action you take today will affect the way your destiny plays out tomorrow. See *Precognitive Dreams,* page 15.

Forty For some, forty is considered the midlife point where life truly begins. If you dream of being forty, you are now prepared to do what you came here to do, and this is your time to shine. Forty is the mystical number that represents total transformation, incubation from one form to another.

Forum Dreams of a forum represent sharing, learning, expanding, growing in community, and strength in numbers. Exponential collective wisdom is here for you, accessible to you and within you now.

Foundation Dreams of a foundation symbolize your life philosophy, your survival tools, your home base. They represent the basis, the ground floor upon which all else depends, what is crucial to you. If a foundation is solid, then there is security and support for the structures that will be built upon it. If a foundation is weak or flimsy, then the rest is in jeopardy of falling apart. See *Floor.*

Fountain Dreams of a fountain are about overflowing abundance, joy, and effervescence. You are connected to your source and supply that never run out.

Fountain of Youth Dreams of a fountain of youth symbolize your desire for eternal youth, vitality, innocence, and play. You are aware of the fact that if you are engaged in living your bliss, then you can virtually age backward. You have found a way to tap into your inner spiritual wellspring. See *Fountain.*

Four Dreams of the number 4 represent physicality and the mundane world. Perhaps you are striving for perfect balance, stability, symmetry, and strength. Four also represents your home and your connection with the four directions and the four elements. See *North, South, East,* and *West,* and *Air, Earth, Fire,* and *Water.*

Fox Dreams of a fox signify that you are connecting to the part of you that is sly, cunning, shrewd, clever, opportunistic, predatorial, tricky, and nonconforming. See *Animal.*

Fragile Dreams of something fragile signify that you are feeling vulnerable, as though you could easily break. Interestingly, your sensitivity can also be the source of your greatest strength. Dreaming of something fragile is a message for you to handle your dreams and desires with care.

Frame If you dream of a picture frame, then it underscores or adds importance to the picture within the frame. Dreams of a frame can also be calling your attention to observe your frame of reference, point of view, or paradigm. Perhaps you are feeling framed or set up, or a frame could be bringing objectivity to your typical point of view, or showing you a new and more enlightened perspective in order for you to have compassion for another's view. See *Glasses.*

Franchise Dreams of a franchise represent wealth, expansion, and success. You are empowering others to partake of your success and/or perhaps you should consider jumping on the bandwagon of someone else's success.

Frappuccino Dreams of a frappuccino represent a quick jolt in your spirits. Perhaps you are mixing up frozen emotions so they can be expressed and released. See *Espresso* and *Frozen.*

Fraud Dreams of a fraud are venting dreams about being victimized and/or releasing your guilt for doing something out of alignment with your own moral code. They may be assisting you to grapple with your issues of short-term gratification.

Freckles Dreams of freckles symbolize the kiss of an angel, a blessing, and good luck. If you dream of someone with freckles and you find that person attractive, then he or she represents a child or an angel. However, if you find the freckles unattractive or unappealing, then they represent a mark or judgment against the person. Freckles are a tiny mark of imperfection, an acknowledgment that you are a perfectly imperfect, fallible human being.

Freedom Dreams of freedom symbolize a desire for a reprieve, to fly, move away from all responsibilities or ties that bind; you are seeking an escape. Dreams of freedom are a reminder and an affirmation that your soul is always free.

Freeway A dream of a freeway signifies the need for speed, and that you are on the fast track to success. You may be feeling impatient for the quickest route from A to B.

Free Will A dream of free will may be showing you that every crossroads you are at is a choice; you have the ability to choose to be in bondage or to set yourself free. Thus there is no one else to blame for any circumstance because you are responsible for your life, for every situation and its outcome. Besides being the lead actor, you are the director and writer of your life movie. This is a sign that if you don't like the way your life is going, you have the power to change it.

Freezer Dreams of a freezer signify preservation, and that you are putting your feelings on ice until the moment is right to let them express.

Freight Dreams of freight can signify abundance, and that your ship has come in. Freight can also represent all of the baggage you've acquired in your life, and that perhaps it is time to take stock of that which weighs you down and that which supports your journey. Perhaps you are evaluating the emotional baggage you've inherited and realizing that it is time to lighten your load.

French Fries Dreams of French fries symbolize little habits and unhealthy indulgences that start off small but can accumulate over time and become harmful and even addictive. As in every treat or splurge, moderation is the key. See *Food* and *Frying*.

French Kiss Dreams of a French kiss denote a passionate connection and romance. The use of the tongue in a kiss represents a deep, unspoken communication of affinity and desire. See *Kiss*.

Frequent Flier Miles If dreams of flying represent freedom and connection with your spirit, then frequent flier miles represent a reward for your spiritual work, a bonus for your good karma and your ability to frequently fly above the mundane and connect with a bigger, more spiritual vantage point.

Friend To dream of a particular friend is about processing your relationship with that person. A friend or even someone you dream of being friendly with symbolizes supportive and harmonious aspects of yourself.

Frog Dreams of a frog represent the need to look beyond the surface of what you see; the frog may be a prince, and your current challenge might be a blessing in disguise. A frog also represents renewal and reproduction. See *Shadow*. See also *Integration Dreams,* page 10.

Frozen Dreams of feeling frozen reflect emotions that have been buried deep down, that you have been in shock and have a backlog of unprocessed feelings.

Fruit Dreams of fruit symbolize abundance, sweetness, and wealth, as in the horn of plenty. Fruit, such as a cherry, peach, apple, plum, or banana can also represent reproductive organs or be phallic symbols. Perhaps you are desiring fertility and/or to see the fruit of your labor. Fruit as well signifies a sacred offering or appreciation for a spiritual teacher or deity. Each fruit has its own significance. See *Apple, Banana, Fig, Grapefruit, Grapes, Lemon, Melon, Peach, Pineapple,* and *Strawberry.*

Frying To dream of frying food denotes that things are heating up in your life and/or that you are nurturing yourself, perhaps not in the healthiest of ways. Because fried food is deliciously unhealthy, a dream of it can signify that there may be relationships and/or habits that you have been indulging in that give you short-term gratification but could be destructive to you in the long run.

Fuel Dreams of fuel denote energy and power. If you have enough fuel, you can make your dreams come true. If you feel that your tank is running on empty, a dream of fuel is giving you the message to take some downtime to turn within to realign your connection to your inner power source. See *Gasoline* and *Power.*

Fugitive Dreams of a fugitive signify rebellion, a fear of being caught, and the fact that you may be harboring guilt or shame about something you did or didn't do.

Full Dreams of feeling full signify that you have completed something and arrived at your limit. You have come full circle and have fulfilled your mission and cycle. If you are feeling full, then you may be at a saturation point. If there is a glass or container that is full in a dream, then this symbolizes prosperity, abundance, and an optimistic outlook on life.

Full-time If you dream of working full-time, then you may be processing through feelings that relate to your job, perhaps feelings that you are giving it too much of yourself. You may be reevaluating your appropriation of time and energy. See *Processing Dreams,* page 7.

Fun Dreams of having fun and frivolity are about a desire to connect with your spirit and to take yourself lightly. Perhaps these dreams illustrate a desire to return to youth. Keep in mind that fun is rarely about circumstances and always about your state of mind, and it is ever available.

Funeral Dreams of a funeral represent transformation and your issues with death, completion, endings, and sickness. Perhaps you are appreciating the preciousness of a person who has died, or whose death you are preparing to mourn. If you dream of your own funeral, then this is a profound opportunity to recognize your value and worth, to make critical changes, and to align your life with your higher purpose. You are laying the past to rest, releasing grievances, resentments, disagreements, and coming to terms with something that has been unsettling. You are achieving completion, resolution, and finality, as well as processing your feelings about death and attachments to life. A dream of a funeral is a wake-up call to appreciate the gift of life. See *Death.*

Fungus Dreams of fungus signify that you have been neglecting certain aspects of your well-being. Perhaps you have been indulging in negative, self-deprecating thought forms or relationships. Dreams of fungus are also showing you that life continues to emerge even from decay. They are about the life/death/life cycle, the fact that nothing ever dies, and that there is always a growth opportunity hidden within all things that appear to be decayed.

Fur Dreams of fur represent comfort, shelter from the cold, security, and being taken care of and pampered. They also symbolize a desire for extravagance, wealth, and status.

Furnace Dreams of a furnace signify that things are heating up, and that romance and passion are around the corner. They are telling you that it is time to radiate your light. Or, they might reflect that you have too many blankets on you as you sleep.

Furniture Dreams of furniture generally represent that which is solid in your life, that which upholds you, doesn't let you down, displays your relics and achievements. Furniture varies in meaning based upon the function it serves. See *Bed, Cabinet, Chair, Couch, Dresser, End Table,* and *Table*.

Fuse Dreams of a fuse represent synergy, cooperation, and working together. Separate aspects of you that may have been *con*fused are now coming together and fusing. A dream of a fuse also denotes that you are connecting with ideas, insights, and inspirations that feel electrifying. You may be in a position to have to reject or refuse something or someone. See *Energy*.

Future Dreams that take place in the future are your projections based on your intuition, desires, hopes, dreams, or past experiences. See *Fortune-teller*. See also *Precognitive Dreams,* page 15.

G

Gallery Dreams of a gallery represent that your life is a work of art/heart. You are desiring recognition and an opportunity to display your achievements, your most prized experiences, and your moments of illumination.

Gambling Dreams of gambling signify that you are taking your chances and living on the edge. Perhaps you are risking the safety of your life alone to venture forth into a relationship, or you are taking a risk in your career. You are realizing that nothing ventured means that nothing can be gained. You believe in yourself and are stacking the odds in your favor. See *Las Vegas*.

Game Dreams of a game symbolize play and competition. To be engaged in a game means that you have a playful attitude. Dreaming of a game may be giving you the message to engage and play wholeheartedly with the awareness that life is really a game, or to realize that you can win at this game called life only when you can be in the world but not of it. Alternatively, dreaming of a game may be showing you that you haven't been taking your life seriously, and your frivolity has become a defense mechanism that stands in the way of your ability to live an authentic and powerful life.

Game Boy Dreams of a Game Boy signify that you are honing your mental skills and the desire to battle at a safe distance. Perhaps they are telling you that you are playing mind games. See *Game*.

Gang Dreams of a gang are about power through affiliation, safety in numbers, and the loss of individuality for the greater good and strength of a gang. Perhaps they are revealing that you've been engaged in a mob mentality and you should begin to discern your individuality from the powerful collective consciousness. See *Crowd* or *Family*.

Gangrene Dreams of gangrene mean that you've been pessimistically projecting into your future. You are purifying and cleansing poison from your body, mind, and spirit so that you can consciously choose thoughts that are in harmony with your well-being. See *Venting Dreams,* page 8.

Gangster Dreams of a gangster signify that you identify with machismo and violence as a tactic for persuasion. They are giving you the message that there is a price you pay for power via fear and intimidation. See *Criminal* and *Victim*.

Gap Dreams of a gap denote that you are feeling distant or separate from other people. If a gap is narrowing, you are getting closer, more intimate, or maybe you are fearing that time is running out. If a gap is widening, accept the fact that you may be on different paths from your partner, but ultimately all paths lead to the same place.

Dreams of the Gap store represent casual comfort, ease, and a desire to bridge the gap between races, sexes, and religions.

Garage If you dream that your car is parked in a garage, then this is a message to take a break, giving your car (body) a rest to recuperate and rejuvenate. Because a garage can also be used as a storage area, a place for things that are not useful to you in your life right now, dreaming of one may be showing you your untapped resources.

Garbage Dreams of garbage reflect useless energy that can be recycled, like compost, into fertilizer for something new. They are suggesting that it is time for a change, that you consider releasing habits, plans, and ties that are no longer supportive to you in order to make room for that which is supportive. See *Recycling*. See also *Processing Dreams,* page 7.

Garbage Can If you dream a garbage can is empty, you have either done your emotional cleansing or you have yet to begin. If a garbage can is filled, then your negative feelings, memories, attachments, and emotions need to be released. Identify what it is that you are throwing away.

Garden Dreaming of a garden is about the state of your life, your level of fruition, abundance, and manifestation. If a garden is flourishing, it is because you are on track and being true to your nature. If a garden is unkempt, it is symbolic that you need to pluck the weeds that don't serve you and plant the seeds of your creative dreams and aspirations. See *Flowers, Fruit,* and *Harvest.*

Gardener Dreams of a gardener symbolize the pragmatic aspect of you that is down to earth and grounded. You are aware of what is working in your life and what is not. You realize what new seeds need to be planted and what weeds need to be eliminated. A dream of a gardener represents your connection to the natural world, and how to nurture life into existence and reap the harvest of your work.

Gargoyle Dreams of a gargoyle symbolize protection and defensiveness that are based in fear. You are feeling threatened and have a desire to keep away adverse energy in order to protect something sacred, secret, and private.

Garlic A dream of garlic signifies that you are cleansing, energizing, and providing a shield of safety and protection around you.

Gasoline Dreams of gasoline symbolize the fuel and energy you need to participate in life. You are activating your drive for success, seeking sustenance and power. Alternatively, these dreams may be showing you that to get your juice for life you are attached to an old paradigm that has diminishing returns. You may be living in the dark ages and stuck in the past in a relationship that is running on fumes. See *Fuel.*

Gas Station Dreams of a gas station represent a source that fills you up emotionally, mentally, spiritually, or financially.

Gate Dreams of a gate represent an opportunity for an opening in your life. Or a gate could represent a barrier that stands between one realm and another and/or what separates or protects you from a great challenge or a great blessing. See *Boundary* and *Door.*

Gatekeeper Dreams of a gatekeeper represent your ability to discern what is healthy for you and what isn't, what energy to allow in and what to keep out.

Gathering See *Party.* See also *Integration Dreams,* page 10.

Gauge Dreams of a gauge symbolize your inner measuring stick that tells you how well you are doing. If a gauge indicates your tank is full, then you are in a state of abundance. If a gauge reflects that your tank is empty, then it is time to refuel and reconnect with your power source.

Gavel Dreams of a gavel denote order, attention, power, and respect. Your words are law. See *Judge.*

Gear Dreams of a gear signify forward motion, and that you are moving ahead quickly or slowly, depending upon the gear you are in. If you are in high gear, then you are making rapid progress. If you are in a low gear, then you are moving more slowly and steadily, paying attention to details but not necessarily making rapid progress.

Geese Dreams of geese signify that there is power in your ability to become synergized. If you dream of geese flying in formation, then this represents that you are understanding the order and harmony of the universe and you are maximizing all aspects of yourself for the greater good. See *Bird* and *Flock.*

Geisha Dreams of a geisha symbolize connection to your femininity, sensuality, and service. You may be deliberately using your femininity and/or playing a subservient role in hopes of winning someone's affection, getting your needs met, or seducing someone.

Gemini Dreams of the astrological sign Gemini symbolize twins, which could be suggesting that you are dealing with two-faced gossip or dealing with your inner polarities: from happy/sad, to extroverted/introverted, to masculine/feminine, to child/elder, etc. See *Goddess* (Persephone).

General Dreaming of a general means you are coming into your authority, paying attention to your position in life, taking orders from your higher self, saluting your divinity, standing in your power, and taking responsibility for your life. See *Military*.

Generator Dreams of a generator signify that you are connecting with your power, your inner source of heat, energy, life force, passion, and the persistence it takes to build dreams into reality. See *Furnace* .

Generous Dreams of generosity reflect that you are feeling full, overflowing, abundant, and capable of giving and sharing resources. You are becoming aware of the fact that when you give, it comes back to you tenfold.

Genitals Dreams about genitals represent sexuality, reproduction, life force, sexual feelings, desire, vulnerability, mating, and pleasure. If you dream of the genitals of someone to whom you are attracted, then this represents your connection to that person and desire for a more intimate exchange. However, if you dream of seeing the genitals of someone you don't like or aren't attracted to, then this may be helping you to process or vent out a traumatic sexual experience. See *Ovaries, Penis, Sex, Testes,* and *Vagina*.

Geodesic Dome Dreams of this vaulted structure made of lightweight straight elements that form interlocking polygons represent a desire for safety and security. You are dealing with a structure, a person, or situation that may appear to be flimsy but is extremely strong and resilient. Don't be fooled by appearances. See *Pyramid*.

Geometry Dreams of geometry symbolize your desire to make logical sense out of the random and complicated relationships and circumstances of your life. They reflect your awareness of the sacred order of the universe, and that you are realizing that ultimately everything measures up.

Germ Dreams of a germ symbolize adversarial energy. You may be feeling defensive and protective about getting sick or being adversely affected by someone's negative or pessimistic influence.

Ghost Dreams of a ghost represent your shadow side attempting to integrate with your light, or an aspect of you that is in search of completion. If a ghost is someone you recognize, such as a deceased family member, then that person may be trying to send you a message or teach you something. See *Prophetic Dreams,* page 17, and *Integration Dreams,* page 10.

Giant Dreams of a giant symbolize power, strength, and dominance. They are about how you handle and manage your power. Consider whether you abuse it or if you use it to empower those around you. If you feel small in comparison to a giant, then you are venting your feelings of inferiority, inadequacy, victimhood, and powerlessness.

Gift Dreams of a gift symbolize an insight, idea, or pregnancy. If you dream that you are giving a gift, then this signifies that you are acknowledging, showing love and appreciation toward someone. And because everyone in your dream is you, you are acknowledging yourself. If you dream that you are the one receiving a gift, then this is about a desire to be recognized, acknowledged, loved, and appreciated by others. A dream of a gift could also be a message for you to realize that your presence is the greatest gift you can give those you love. See *Wish Fulfillment Dreams,* page 18.

Giraffe Dreams of a giraffe represent compassion and wisdom. They reflect your desire to open your heart in compassion and to reach, stretch, and expand your point of view. A giraffe's long neck represents wisdom, flexibility, and an ability to see many points of view.

Girl Dreams of a girl represent your connection to the youthful, feminine, innocent, impetuous, playful, and vulnerable aspect of you. See *Goddess* (Persephone).

Girlfriend If a girlfriend is a love interest in a dream, then it is about passion, mutual interest, and chemistry. You are processing and expressing your feelings about a relationship. If a dream is about an ex-girlfriend, see *Ex-.* If this is a friend, see *Friend.*

Glamour Dreams of glamour represent beauty as power, a desire to amplify your energy and status by enhancing your attractiveness. They could perhaps be showing you that you've allowed a romanticized physical ideal to become more important to you than the authenticity that resides within you. Dreams of glamour also signify that your eyes may be playing tricks on you, that you are allowing the smoke and mirrors of a person's facade to distract you from the truth.

Glass Dreams of glass signify that you are feeling fragile, vulnerable, breakable, and transparent. They can also represent clarity or distortion of perception. Consider the feeling tone of the dream. If a glass is half empty, then you are dealing with feelings of lack and deprivation. If a glass is half full or full, then you feel abundant, powerful, wealthy, and that your needs are being met. If a glass is broken, then you feel shattered. See *Broken*.

Glasses A dream that features glasses represents either that you are seeing a situation clearly or that you *need* glasses because your vision is skewed. In the latter case, the dream is a message to get a better perspective, a message to see the forest for the trees and the truth of the situation.

Glitter Dreams of glitter symbolize magic, sparkle, luster, a desire for attention, fame, fortune, recognition, and abundance. They are telling you to not be fooled by appearances because all that glitters may not be gold. See *Glamour* and *Las Vegas*.

Glove Dreams of a glove symbolize physical, mental, or emotional protection. Your hands symbolize your ability to reach for what you want in life, to have and to hold, and gloves are a way of keeping a distance or softening your approach. Margaret Thatcher was known for having a steel fist in a velvet glove. You may be keeping yourself at arm's length from what you really want or need, either because of formality or a fear of intimacy. See *Condom*.

Glue Dreams of glue signify that you are feeling bonded, attached, and/or stuck in a relationship or commitment. Perhaps it is time to leave but fear has you unable or unwilling to release yourself from a sticky situation. In order to become unstuck, release your attachment to the outcome, and allow your heart to be your guide. See *Codependence*.

Goal Dreams of a goal, as in a sport, represent focus, concentration, sacrifice, intention, and your ability to keep your eyes on the prize. If you dream of completing a milestone, this signifies that you are moving in the direction of your dreams.

Goat Dreams of a goat reflect that something is eating at you or that someone's got your goat. You are letting things make you feel bad. Dreaming of a goat is giving you the message to take responsibility for the situation you are in and to stop blaming or making anyone your scapegoat. Alternatively, it might signify that you are climbing upward toward status and recognition. You are butting your way with machismo through the obstacles to your success. In the Hebrew tradition it is believed that he who dreams about goats shall be blessed throughout all his years. See *Capricorn.*

God Dreams of God represent your connection to your ultimate power source and the infinite, unconditional love and intelligence that govern the universe. You are feeling sourced, empowered, filled with grace and miracles as you awaken to your highest nature and creative expression. Dreams of God may be an opportunity for you to process your issues with God, religion, dogma, and your spirituality. See *Energy* and *Light.*

Goddess A dream of a goddess is prophetic and powerful, and filled with wonderful insights relating to the divine feminine, the maiden, maid, crone, and sacred sisterhood. Dreams of a goddess represent your desire to connect with a higher aspect of yourself, your greatest potential. You are evoking divine assistance or a higher view into your life. Each goddess archetype will evoke within you a distinct power and energy. Following are the seven primary Greek and Roman goddesses, the gifts they offer you if you are fortunate enough to be visited by them in the dreamtime, and the primary dream symbols accorded to them.

> *Aphrodite/Venus*—goddess of love, sensuality, beauty, passion, sexuality, and freedom. She is the muse of creativity and inspiration. Symbols: *scalloped shell, sweet fruit, nectar, dolphin, gold coins, swan, myrrh*
>
> *Artemis/Diana*—goddess of the hunt, wildlife, and independence. She is a humanitarian and caretaker of those less fortunate. Symbols: *bow and arrow, bear, hound, moon, stag*
>
> *Athena/Minerva*—goddess of wisdom, discernment, success, and leadership. She is business minded and competitive. Symbols: *olive tree, owl, shield, lightning bolt, loom, Parthenon*

Demeter/Ceres—goddess of harvest and fertility. She is the mother and nurturer of children. Symbols: *cornucopia, poppy, sickle, wheat*

Hera/Juno—goddess of marriage, primarily identified with the role of wife and partnership. She is known for being the woman behind the man. Symbols: *peacock, throne of gold and ivory, cuckoo, temple, two gold rings, wind*

Hestia/Vesta—goddess of the hearth and home. She makes a house a home and her qualities include domesticity, introversion, meditation, mindfulness, and nest maker. Symbols: *flaming hearth, globe, altar, vest, locked box, shelter*

Persephone/Proserpina—goddess of death, the underworld, renewal, and transformation. She is the maiden who assists you in the embracing of your shadow side. Symbols: *pomegranate seeds, narcissus flower, gates, chariot, two faces, spring*

Goggles Dreams of goggles for seeing underwater represent the ability to see what is beneath the surface of your true feelings, into your subconscious and your most intimate feelings. You realize the ability to read between the lines and understand esoteric knowledge.

Gold Dreams of gold denote wealth, abundance, opulence, your soul, talents, and gifts. You are realizing that you are in the midst of a golden opportunity.

Goldfish Dreams of a goldfish signify the wealth and richness of your emotions and your inner life, that you are recognizing the value of introspection and connection to the divine feminine within the deep end of your ocean.

Golf Dreams of golf signify that you are focused and concentrated on your goals and desires. You have a desire to be in the zone. See *Sports* and *Zone*.

Golf Club Dreams of a golf club represent your will and ability to get into the swing of things. Within a golf bag are several different types of clubs that are appropriate for the various situations presented within the game of golf. This is symbolic of the variety of inner resources that you have at your fingertips to apply to the variety of challenges presented within the game of life. See *Golf*.

Gondola Dreams of a gondola symbolize a desire for romance, sexual foreplay, and the honeymoon stage of love. See *Boat* and *Fairy Tale.*

Gong Dreaming of the sound of a gong is about the calling of spirits, a spiritual ceremony, and a call to connect to your center. Sometimes, however, the sound of a gong, as in Chuck Barris's *Gong Show,* represents rejection. Consider the feeling tone of the dream to discern its meaning for you.

Good Dreams of feeling good or of doing a good job are about balance, harmony, and being in sync with your destiny.

Good-bye Dreams of good-bye signify completion, leaving, fulfillment, nostalgia, and dealing with issues of attachment. You've come to the end of an interaction. Perhaps you are in a transition between one chapter of your life and another, and you are dealing with issues of completion and closure.

Google If you dream of Google, then it represents your quest for knowledge, answers, and research, and your desire to investigate what is behind the scenes in your pursuit of self-understanding. Consider what it is you are looking up.

Gossip In a dream, if you are the one gossiping about someone, then you are being warned to beware of the consequences. Gossip is a red-flag indication of insecurity and a flaw in one's own self-esteem. If you are the one being gossiped about, then know that it is a backhanded compliment.

Government Dreams about the government represent your rules for life and your own moral code of conduct or belief system; a higher order of laws, rules, and structure from which to love and abide, spiritually, emotionally, or physically. You may be processing your feelings about your current government and its policies, and your feelings of activism, apathy, or rebellion.

Gown Dreams of a gown symbolize a special occasion or a rite of passage. A gown is an outer reflection of an inner preparation for the next level of your evolution in consciousness. See *Bride, Dress,* and *Goddess.*

GPS Dreams of a GPS, a global positioning system, represent direction in life, being on track, knowing where you are going, being on target and aligned with your higher vision.

Grade Dreams of a grade represent your judgments, criticisms, and assessments of yourself and/or the people in your life. You are processing feelings of anxiety, inferiority, or superiority. Consider what and/or who is being evaluated and what grade is given.

Graduation Dreams of a graduation signify completion and the fulfillment of a cycle. Your subconscious mind is telling you that you can now move on and prepare for the next series of opportunities and challenges life has in store for you.

Grain Dreams of grain are associated with harvest, reaping what you sow, abundance, and your visions coming into fruition. Dreams of grain represent the macrocosm within the microcosm; that within a tiny grain of sand exists the entire shore of life. Your subconscious mind is telling you that it's the little things that count the most, and to pay attention to the details. If you are going with the grain, then you are in sync/harmony with the universe. If you are going against the grain, then you are feeling disharmonious, you are struggling and learning the hard way. See *Bread* and *Goddess* (Demeter).

Grammy Dreams of any award represent recognition of excellence and/or a desire to become masterful in a given field. Because the Grammy is an award for music, in a dream it represents your own recognition of the magnificence of the music of your soul.

Grand Anything grand, in a dream, whether it is a grand piano or grand-scale event, implies great, large, oversized, over-the-top, important, and majestic.

Grand Canyon Dreams of this national wonder symbolize a great womb, a container that is feminine, receptive, magical, and a powerful space of nurturing. The Grand Canyon is a message for you to stand in awe of your own natural beauty, to appreciate the years and lifetimes of spiritual growth that have brought you to this place of evolution.

Grandfather Dreams of your grandfather can signify the mature masculine aspects of yourself or elder consciousness, or that you are processing your relationship with your grandfather. The grandfather archetype represents the sky, the all-seeing, and all-knowing, the wise part of yourself. A grandfather can sometimes represent God. Dreaming of a grandfather may be an opportunity to grapple with your feelings toward God, male elders, or about aging. See *King*.

Grandmother Dreams of a grandmother represent the mature, wise, feminine elder within you, the one who tells the truth and loves you unconditionally. If you dream of your grandmother, it signifies the qualities she represents to you and the feelings you have for her. In general, dreams of a grandmother are about wisdom, the earth, and nurturing, and are a message to take care of your natural, earthly resources. See *Crone*.

Grant If you are the grantee in a dream, you are allowing yourself to receive the abundance, love, support, creativity, and resources the universe has in store for you. If you are the grantor, you are expressing the joy and blessing of service and generosity.

Grapefruit Dreams of grapefruit signify that which is bitter but healthy for you, such as constructive criticism and hard work. You are swallowing a bitter pill and dealing with tough love, which is a blessing once it is ingested.

Grapes Dreams of grapes signify decadence, lavishness, abundance, juiciness, and sweetness of life, and that you are enjoying earthly pleasures. If you are feeding grapes to someone other than yourself, this could be a form of seduction. Grapes also are associated with wine, intoxication, and drunkenness. See *Wine*.

Grass The green color of grass in a dream signifies that you are grounding yourself in wealth and abundance. Dreams of managed and cared-for grass represent growth, new developments, and carefree feelings. If grass is overgrown or unkempt, then it means that you've been taking something important for granted. If it appears that grass is greener somewhere else, then it is a message for you to appreciate what you have. Consider the feeling tone. See *Green* and *Marijuana*.

Grasshopper Dreams of a grasshopper signify that you are tapping into your inner voice of wisdom, guidance, and higher consciousness.

Gratitude Dreams of gratitude signify that you have a great attitude. When a person is grateful, he or she is full of greatness and elevated to a state of grace.

Grave See *Death* and *Funeral*.

Gravy Dreams of gravy denote excess, abundance, wealth, plenty, and that you have or will be receiving more than you need. You are reaping and enjoying the rewards of your hard work.

Gray Dreams of gray, neither black nor white but somewhere in between, signify that you are unsure about how you feel, that you are on the fence feeling confused, murky, or even depressed. Gray matter represents your brain, mental processes, logic, and thinking. Dreaming of gray matter is giving you the message that you need to organize your thoughts systematically so that you can make a decision.

Grease Dreams of grease signify that you are receiving assistance in moving forward in your life. Perhaps you are receiving financial support or encouragement to grease your wheels as you progress on your path.

Greece Dreams about Greece represent philosophy, theater, education, spirituality, and morality. You are connecting with the consciousness of great scholars, gods, and goddesses that have gone before you. See *God* and *Goddess*. See also *Prophetic Dreams,* page 17.

Green A dream that features a significant amount of the color green symbolizes good health, nature, healing, positive change, new beginnings, and springtime. Green can also represent money, envy, and naïveté.

Greenhouse Dreams of a greenhouse signify that you are in the midst of an intense growth spurt. You are taking particular care of your self-growth, nurturing, and healing.

Green Light Dreams of a green light mean that all lines of traffic have opened up for you and the universe is motioning you to go forward with your dreams. See *Green*.

Grid Dreams of a grid signify your ability to make sense out of the circumstances and events of your life. You are able to maintain objectivity about the patterns, cycles, and systems in your life.

Griddle Dreams of a griddle signify that you are creating something delicious and cooking up something nurturing. See *Breakfast* and *Kitchen*.

Grip Dreams of a grip symbolize a desire for control. You are wanting to get a handle on the circumstances and relationships in your life that feel out of hand. See *Hand*.

Grocery Cart Dreams of a grocery cart signify that you are receiving assistance in accumulating what you need to survive. You are acquiring sustenance, nurturing, and support. If a cart is empty, then you are feeling either deprived or available to become full. If a cart is full, then your cup runneth over, and you are coming into your power.

Grocery Store Dreams of a grocery store symbolize plenty, abundance, wealth, and prosperity, the ability to provide for yourself. You are realizing that the fulfillment of your needs is at your fingertips. Consider what you buy at a grocery store because that is significant. See *Shopping*.

Grotto Dreams of this secret chamber signify mysteries, and that you are realizing your connection with your shadow side and becoming aware of the deepest, innermost, sacred aspects of your nature.

Ground Zero In relation to the events of September 11, 2001, dreams of ground zero represent an uprooting and/or crumbling of that which appeared to be solid and indestructible. A dream of ground zero is a breakdown/breakthrough dream, as in the Buddhist deity of death and destruction that is an essential catalyst to transformation and change. It can symbolize the necessity to come down to earth and connect with what is truly important in life and for you to reassess your values. It could also signify that you are processing and venting out your feelings about the events of September 11 or the war on terrorism. See *September 11* and *World Trade Center*. See also *Venting Dreams,* page 8.

Group Dreams of a group denote a power and energy that is much stronger than that of an individual. If you are a part of a group, you will feel strengthened, empowered, and supported. If you don't feel that you belong to a group, then you are dealing with feelings of intimidation, domination, fear of losing your individuality, and freedom. See *Crowd, People,* and *Team*.

G-spot Dreams of a G-spot signify erotic, sexual pleasure, and that you are right where you are supposed to be in your life, right on target, hitting the bull's-eye in a relationship and in your career. See *Wish Fulfillment Dreams,* page 18.

Guest If you dream of being a guest, then the dream is about the comfort you are receiving. If you are a host to a guest, you are the provider of the space. There's always a bit of mystery and guesswork in dealing with a guest, which signifies that you are feeling stiff, awkward, and formal in your own home (self).

Guide Dreams of a guide symbolize your higher self which embodies wisdom, confidence, clarity, certainty, and the answers to your questions, and is familiar with the terrain you are traveling. They are giving you the message that it would be wise to incorporate a higher perspective into your daily travels along your life's path. See *Angel* and *Higher Self.*

Guillotine Dreams of a guillotine represent severe criticism and rejection of yourself or someone in your life. Perhaps you are disowning your mental processes and are in an unhealthy imbalance between your thoughts and feelings.

Guinea Pig Dreams of a guinea pig signify an adventurous spirit and that you are willing to experiment, take a chance, try something new, and make a breakthrough. See *Gambling* and *Laboratory.*

Guitar Dreams of a guitar signify that you are in harmony with life, and are attuning to your natural rhythm. If a guitar is acoustic, then it signifies your natural beauty and authenticity. If a guitar is electric, then it is showing you that you are connecting with energy that is penetrating and shocking. A guitar is also a phallic symbol. See *Music* and *Musical Instrument.*

Gum If you dream of your gums or of having gum problems, then you are feeling indecisive, having difficulty chewing on your problems, and feeling vulnerable like a baby. In a dream, if you are chewing gum, then you are nervous or worried. Chewing gum, for some, is also a sign of immaturity and disrespect. You could also be in a sticky situation. Consider the feeling tone.

Gun Dreams of a gun signify a desire for power over life and death, and that you are feeling desperate about asserting your boundaries to get what you need or want.

Guru Dreams of a guru signify that you are connecting with your wisdom, guidance, and higher knowing, and you are realizing that you always have the answers to your questions and challenges. See *Prophetic Dreams,* page 17.

Gutter Dreams of a gutter symbolize a low point in your life. You are hitting bottom and are off track. You are realizing that sometimes you have to hit rock bottom before you know which way is up. Now you can begin to build yourself back up. See *Poverty.*

Gym Dreams of a gym mean that you are growing, strengthening, and improving your body, mind, and spirit. You are getting stronger as you work out the details of your life. Or dreaming of a gym may be a literal message for you to get to a gym.

Gypsy Dreams of a gypsy signify that you are predicting the future, living on the edge, and traveling with the wind. If you've been feeling stuck, you are connecting with your desire for freedom. If you've been a wanderer for too long, you may desire predictability and stability. See *Precognitive Dreams,* page 15.

H

Hacker See *Parasite* and *Virus.*

Hair Dreams of hair symbolize memory and power. If you dream that your hair is longer than it currently is, then your power is increasing. If it is shorter than it currently is, then you are either afraid of losing your power or attractiveness or you are boldly willing to start again. If you are washing your hair, then you are cleansing your attachments and any unclean associations you have with power, sexiness, or attractiveness. If you are losing hair, then this represents feeling naked, defenseless, and vulnerable. If your hair is disheveled, then you are feeling wild, unorganized, and cluttered. If your hair is coiffed, then you are making a good appearance. If hair in a dream has a distinct color or style, see *Blond Hair, Brunet Hair, Curls, Gray, Red,* or *Straight.*

Haircut Dreams of a haircut symbolize transformation. A new look symbolizes a new outlook on life. See *Hair* and *Hairdresser.*

Hairdresser Dreams of a hairdresser signify that you are being nurtured and taken care of. If your hair is being cut, this signifies that you are being supported in your transformation. Because a hair-dresser is altering and cleaning up your hair, which is associated with the seventh chakra, a hairdresser can also symbolize one who influences your higher thoughts and opens you up to spiritual insights and ideas. See *Hair* and *Haircut*.

Half Dreams of cutting something in half symbolize a context where you are sharing with someone with whom you are in a relationship. Eating half of something can also denote discipline. If you dream of getting only half of something but you wanted the whole thing, this represents feeling unfulfilled.

Halloween Dreams of Halloween signify that you are embracing and bringing awareness to the different masks you wear and to the social roles you play. A dream of Halloween is about embracing your shadow, the aspects of yourself that are the most difficult to love, in order to fuse, unify, and integrate all aspects of yourself. Consider the feeling tone. See *Ghost, Mask,* and *Shadow.* See also *Integration Dreams,* page 10.

Hallucinogenics/Hallucinations Dreams are hallucinations and projections of our unconscious mind. However, if you dream of hallucinogenics/hallucinations, this signifies the expansion of your mind, openness, compassion, understanding, wisdom, and that you are delving into foreign regions of your mind and spirit. See *Drugs.*

Hallway Dreams of a hallway signify that you are on the verge of stepping into a whole new space, because the hallway is the transition place between where you've been and where you are going. You are preparing for change, gearing up for a life-altering occurrence. See *Threshold.*

Halo Dreams of a halo symbolize your ability to see the angelic, divine aspect of a person. See *Angel* and *Aura.*

Ham Dreams of a ham denote insatiability, a desire to be the center of attention, and/or to take more than your share. You are hogging all the room, dominating the space, and/or are living high off the hog.

Hammer Dreams of a hammer signify persistence and relentlessness, and that you are using force and aggression to express yourself to get what you want. Your desire to be understood may be causing you to hammer your point home or to hammer someone else with your questions.

Hamster Dreams of a hamster signify that you are engaged in activity without a higher vision or a plan, that you're feeling as though you've been putting out a lot of energy but not getting anywhere.

Hand A hand symbolizes the ability to get a handle on life and take control. Also a hand symbolizes applause, assistance, as in giving someone a hand, or being handy, as in capable, knowledgeable, and useful. Your left hand is receiving and connected to your mother. Your right hand is demonstrative, influenced by and connected to your father or the right hand of God, helpful, active. Consider the feeling tone of the dream to discern its significance.

Handcuffs Dreams of handcuffs are about restraint, punishment, control, restriction, and holding back. You are grappling with feelings of guilt and shame. See *Prison*.

Handle Dreams of a handle signify self-control and that you are giving yourself a lift and elevating yourself to a higher level. They are giving you the message to grab hold of life, and get a grip on the issues that have gotten out of hand.

Handsome Dreams of someone who is handsome signify attraction and appeal, and that you are receiving an intuitive yes to move forward toward the person or situation. They are also about connecting with your own inner beauty. (If you see it, you be it.)

Hanging If you dream you are hanging, then this signifies that you have lost touch with the ground beneath you and are suffering the consequences. Perhaps you are feeling punished and judged cruelly. A dream of hanging may be suggesting that you've been thinking too much and you are hanging yourself with your own self-destructive thoughts of guilt and fear. A drastic change is at hand. If you dream of hanging your laundry, then you are exposing your secrets. See *Killing*.

Hangover Dreams of a hangover represent exhaustion as you burn the candle at both ends; you are dealing with the consequences for ingesting information or the overindulgence of nonsupportive people or habits in your life. It is time for some changes in your lifestyle. See *Alcohol* and *Drunk*.

Hanukkah Dreams of the Festival of Lights represent celebration, victory, miracles, light, family bonding, and appreciation, and the ability to take the resources you have and turn them miraculously into all that you need.

Happy Dreams of feeling happy signify that you are at the right place at the right time. You've achieved contentment and are on track with your life. Happiness is a demonstration of balance and inner harmony. See *Wish Fulfillment Dreams*, page 18.

Harassment Dreams of sexual harassment, or any kind of harassment/ violation, are about the disrespect of personal boundaries and wanting to take another's power. If you feel harassed, create firm energetic boundaries so that your energy cannot be harmed. This challenge is showing you where you give your power away or where you try to take it from others. See *Rape*.

Harbor Dreams of a harbor signify a respite from the stormy seas of life. They could be a message for you to connect with a trusted friend to help you get through a challenging time, or to be a safe harbor for someone in your life who is going through a rocky time.

Hard Dreaming of something hard represents your power, reliability, strength, or stubbornness. Alternatively, it could be an expression of a difficult time that you are moving through.

Hardware Dreams of hardware symbolize tools of change, power, and resources. You are realizing your ability to construct, remodel, and repair your life the way you desire it to be.

Harem If you are a man dreaming of a harem, this is about the desire for adoration, sexual pleasure, attentiveness, and reassurance of your masculinity and virility. If you are a woman dreaming of being a member of a harem, then you are grappling with your identification with the prostitute archetype. See *Dancing* and *Prostitute*.

Harness Dreams of a harness signify that you are trying to rein in your wild inner horses, and get a grip on and focus your energy toward the direction you want it to go. Perhaps they are giving you the message to bite your lip and practice discretion. Alternatively, if you feel as though you've been too harnessed, perhaps it is time to let go of your inhibitions, reconnect with your wild nature, take the reins of your life, and run free for a while. Consider the feeling tone.

Harp Dreams of a harp signify that you are connecting with the wisdom and music of your angels. You are resonating with your heavenly nature and vibration that are peaceful and serene. Perhaps you are experiencing a spiritual awakening, and attuning to your higher self. See *Angel, Music,* and *Musical Instrument.*

Harvest Dreams of a harvest signify that your hard work is paying off, that it is time to reap what you sow, and enjoy the fruits of your labor. See *Garden.*

Hat Dreams of a hat symbolize the way you want others to see you. Also a hat represents your egoic thoughts, opinions, judgments, and ideas. If a hat has a logo or a picture on it, as in a fireman's hat, a fez, or baseball cap, this could be about your affiliation or job. A hat can also be a disguise, a distraction, or an extension of your beliefs. As well, a hat can signify that you feel the need to protect yourself from the influence of those around you. See *Chakra* (7th), *Crown,* and *Yarmulke.*

Hatchet Dreams of a hatchet signify that you are chopping down debris that stands in the way of your ability to access your true path. Perhaps you are cutting through the jungle of your mind to find certainty and clarity. See *Killing* and *Knife.*

Hate Dreams of hate denote judgment, hurt, and unprocessed pain. Often hate stems from unrequited love, betrayal, or a deep soul mate connection that did not meet your needs. This also may be an aspect of yourself that you have rejected. See *Integration Dreams,* page 10.

Haunted Dreams of something haunted symbolize your shadow and fear-based negative thoughts that are eating at you and feeding off your fear. If you've done something in the past that you regret or feel ashamed of, it may be haunting you until you are able to make amends. See *Ghost* and *Shadow.* See also *Venting Dreams,* page 8.

Hawaii Dreams of this tropical paradise symbolize being nurtured by nature and paradise; you are connecting with your inner beauty and bounty. See *Island.*

Hawk Dreams of a hawk signify that someone or something is trying to send you a message. They are telling you to connect with your higher view, to become aware of the magic of life that is coming to you, and to develop the strength and resources necessary to carry you through your current challenge. Your hawkeyed view is your key to accessing your intuition. See *Bird.* See also *Prophetic Dreams,* page 17.

Hay Dreams of hay symbolize a desire for gold, warmth, and riches. You are preparing the way for wealth to enter your life. See *Bed* and *Gold.*

Head Dreams of a head symbolize your thoughts, opinions, critical functions, higher wisdom, awareness, self-perception, and ability to think, reason, be logical, and make sense out of situations. If a head is down, then this represents shame, embarrassment, and inferiority. If a head is held high, then you are feeling confident and proud. If a head is disconnected from a body, then this reflects a lack of integration between your thoughts and feelings. If something is over your head, then it may feel too lofty or difficult to understand. If a head is bigger than normal, then you are feeling cocky and overconfident, and have an overblown ego. See *Chakra* (7th).

Headphones Dreams of headphones denote being in your own little world, socially reclusive, and dancing to the beat of your own drum. You are connecting to your own creativity and rhythm. See *Head* and *Music.*

Headrest Dreams of a headrest signify that you are thinking nurturing thoughts, and taking your higher awareness seriously. They also can be about giving your head a rest from having to figure everything out and from having to know the answers. The best solutions come when you are on a mental vacation and you allow your intuition to inform you.

Healer Dreams of a healer symbolize your inner shaman/goddess that knows just the right soul medicine to prescribe for any challenge or imbalance you face. Healing is at hand. See *Doctor.* See also *Prophetic Dreams,* page 17.

Hearing Dreams of hearing sounds or words demonstrate great sensitivity in the dreamer; they are about clairaudience, the gift of hearing your inner guidance, or being psychically led via your sense of hearing words and sounds. Consider the words that you hear as a literal message from your subconscious mind.

Hearing Aid Dreaming of assistance in hearing symbolizes a desire to hear beyond the spoken words, and read between the lines. You may be grappling with your difficulty in hearing or listening to people's criticism, gossip, or negativity. See *Deaf.*

Hearse Dreams of a hearse signify that you are moving toward death, completion, and/or putting an aspect of your life to rest. You are processing your issues about death and mortality. If you are driving a hearse, you are in control of your transition process and you are lucid, awake, and aware.

Heart Dreams of a heart symbolize love, willpower, commitment, and the strength of love. You are realizing that when you put your heart into a relationship or a project, the power of the divine channels through you and miracles take place. If you dream of a broken heart, then you are grieving over attachments from a previous relationship, and dealing with issues of betrayal, thwarted intentions, and unfulfilled desires. See *Love.*

Heartbeat Dreams of a heartbeat signify that you are in touch with your passion, love, and the rhythm of your creativity. If you dream that your heart is racing, then you may be processing nervousness, stress, or infatuation. If you dream that there is no pulse, then you are feeling a lack of passion, or you are dying to your former identity in order to be made anew.

Heat Dreams of heat represent passion, sexuality, energy, and power; being engaged in activity that warms your soul. Sometimes heat, like chemistry, happens when opposites attract or have friction. You might also have too many blankets on you as you are sleeping. See *Fire* and *Generator.*

Heater Dreams of a heater symbolize a desire to melt the emotional chill in the air. They reflect your need for support to feel comfortable and reassured. They also signify a desire for friendship, intimacy, sensuality, and sexuality.

Heaven Dreams of heaven, or of feeling heavenly, symbolize an ideal experience of who you really are, your higher self. Dreaming of heaven is a transformational dream in which you are liberated from your fear and distortions and elevated to a higher consciousness of oneness, love, and bliss. See *Ecstasy* and *Love.*

Heavy Dreams of feeling heavy signify that you are experiencing pressure, feeling weighed down, burdened, overly responsible, somber, and depressed. Perhaps you have fallen under the illusion that you have to carry the weight of the world or more than your share to be loved. A dream of feeling heavy is a sign to delegate and share the load.

Heel Dreams of a heel symbolize vulnerability, as in an Achilles' heel. Or they could be cautioning you to speak mindfully so as to not be a heel.

Height Size in dreams represents importance. The bigger something is, the more important and valuable it is to you. Dreams of something tall suggest that you are at the height of your self-esteem and success. If you are taller in a dream than you normally are, you are confident in your power, authority, and mastery. If you are shorter in a dream than you normally are, then you are feeling a lack of confidence or importance. See *Giant* or *Short*.

Heir Dreams of an heir signify that you are coming into your inheritance of riches, power, wealth, and talent. You are processing all that you have inherited from your family bloodline. A dream of an heir could also be a spiritual dream where you are awakening to the fact that you are a descendant of the divine, and worthy of all good things in and of this earth.

Helicopter Dreams of a helicopter symbolize freedom that is in your control as you rise above the mundane and seek a higher view. You are feeling adventurous. See *Airplane.*

Hell Dreams of hell are venting dreams of your greatest fears and most disassociated shadow figures. A terrifying dream such as a dream of hell is a golden opportunity for you to embrace your shadow and become, as in the story of the goddess Persephone, a fully integrated being who is a force to be reckoned with. When you take your fears and face and embrace them, then you can erase them, and replace them with energy that supports you. See *Death, Devil, Ghost,* and *Goddess* (Persephone). See also *Venting Dreams,* page 8, and *Integration Dreams,* page 10.

Helm Dreams of a helm signify that you are taking control of your life, or a relationship, and owning your power and responsibility. You are rising to meet your challenges. See *Captain* and *Ship*.

Helmet Dreams of a helmet signify that you are protecting your mind from adverse thoughts, criticism, and judgments, and being responsible for the vulnerability and suggestibility of your open mind. See *Hat*.

Help If you are reaching out for help, assistance, intervention, support, with an SOS, or a 911, then you are connecting with the benevolence of the universe, and accessing a source that is greater than you. Alternatively, a dream of help is showing you the perils of remaining associated with a feeling of powerlessness and victimhood. Perhaps it is time for you to pull yourself up by your bootstraps and access your inner hero. See *Emergency* and *Victim*.

Hemorrhoids Dreams of hemorrhoids signify that you are holding back your true feelings, sitting on the action you know you must take, and that you are avoiding coming to terms with an unhealthy relationship in your life. You are feeling stressed and burdened because you have been procrastinating dealing with an important yet uncomfortable confrontation.

Hen Dreams of a hen signify that you are being overly vigilant, worried, nitpicking, protective, nosy, fear based, and maternal.

Henna Dreams of henna, used for Mehndi, or sacred body art, symbolize adornment of the flesh, self-love, decoration, beauty, romantic love, and ceremony. You are preparing for a ritual, ceremony, or rite of passage. See *Art/Artist, Red,* and *Tattoo*.

Herb Dreams of an herb reflect your connection to the elements, that you realize a natural cure for a challenge and that the solution you seek resides within you. See *Flowers*.

Hermit Dreams of a hermit symbolize your need to take time for yourself. Or if you've been in isolation, playing it safe, and avoiding intimacy for too long, they could be showing you that it is time to come out and be part of the living and take a risk. A hermit also can signify that you are in a period of self-reflection where you are reevaluating all that you've learned and are trying to find a sense of inner peace. See *Cave* and *Island*.

Hero/Heroine Dreams of a hero/heroine symbolize your higher self, your innate healing ability, and your mastery over any challenge you face. Perhaps you are exalting your natural genius to its fullest potential, going beyond the physical limitations of being human, and realizing that love can move mountains. These dreams may be indicating your attachment to the role of rescuer or of needing to be rescued. Consider the feeling tone of the dream to discern the significance. See *Codependence* and *Higher Self.*

Herpes Dreams of herpes symbolize sexual shame, blame, punishment, and victimization. It is time to embrace your sexuality as a sacred and divine gift. See *Venereal Disease.*

HGH Dreams of HGH, the human growth hormone, are about a desire for eternal youth. They also represent your very own fountain of youth that you access whenever you follow your bliss. See *Fountain of Youth* and *Peter Pan.*

Hiccups Dreams of hiccups signify that you are dealing with overcoming a slight obstacle to your goal. Your subconscious mind may be telling you to breathe deeply and remain persistent, and you will get through the challenge.

Hidden Dreaming of something hidden is exposing a mystery whose time has come to be faced, embraced, erased, and replaced. Once you have done this, what was formerly hidden becomes integrated into your life, you become more powerful and peaceful, and the world around you will mirror your integration and self-acceptance. See *Hermit.* See also *Integration Dreams,* page 10.

Hieroglyphs Dreams of hieroglyphs represent a secret language or code that your subconscious is speaking to you in, or perhaps they are connecting you to a past life. They may also be expressing to you the importance of telling your story so that future generations will understand your legacy. Alternatively, they may be telling you that it is time to update your communication style.

High Dreams of a high signify that you are having a peak experience and are at the top of your emotional wave. They are a sign that great things are happening to you in your relationships, achievements, and spiritual mastery. The more centered you are, the more you can remain grounded and stabilized in your joy.

High-class Dreams of being high-class signify that you are living up to your potential, realizing that you deserve the best. See *Integration Dreams,* page 10.

Higher Self Dreaming of your higher self is very auspicious in that you are connecting with your inner wisdom, guidance, and clarity. See *Prophetic Dreams,* page 17.

High School Dreams of high school signify that you are learning, growing, and grappling with issues relating to independence and dependence. You may be sorting through and integrating your own high school memories, traumas, and learning opportunities. Consider the importance placed upon your role in life or in high school, e.g., jock, nerd, popular kid, valedictorian, etc. See *School.*

High Tide Dreams of high tide symbolize fulfillment of a project or desire. You are coming into abundance and your cup runneth over. See *Celebration.*

Hike Dreams of a hike symbolize your willingness to climb and your ability to take the action necessary to rise to the occasion presented to you.

Hill Dreams of a hill signify that you are dealing with the ups and downs of life, and struggling with a minor obstacle to overcome. You are realizing that the challenge will make you stronger, smarter, and more resourceful. See *Mountain.*

Hip Dreams of your hip symbolize your ability to sway with the current trends of life and your ability to be hip to changes. Your hip is in your second chakra, your life force, which represents the need to check in with your gut instinct about a decision you have to make.

Hip-hop Music Dreams of hip-hop music denote the need for a healthy, creative outlet for your angst, pain, suppression, and victimhood.

Hippie Dreams of a hippie symbolize peace, free love, and nonviolent rebellion and perhaps passive aggression. You are connecting with the aspect of you that would rather make love than war.

Hippopotamus Dreams of a hippopotamus show you that you have a wonderful balance between your masculine energy, which can be dominating and intimidating, and your feminine energy, which can flow with the stream of life.

History Dreams of history are about your feelings and attitudes that relate to the particular period of which you are dreaming. These dreams may be assisting you in learning from your past. If you are continuing to relive your own history, then you need to heal the reoccurring issues in order to move on, create a future, and move in the direction of your dreams. See *Mythology*. See also *Recurring Dreams,* page 13.

Hit Dreams of violence reflect protection, aggression, anger, and out-of-control feelings. If you get a hit of intuition, then you would be wise to pay attention to the message. Also, dreaming of a hit may be forecasting that you will be creating a hit song, movie, or project that hits a home run, or hits the mark and becomes a great success and victory. Consider the feeling tone.

Hobby Dreams of your hobby are clues to your bliss, passion, talent, and purpose for being alive. Don't be surprised if a hobby you dream of or one you dabble in during your real life is really a lucrative career in disguise.

Hoe Dreams of a hoe represent assistance in tilling the soil of your field of dreams. You are plucking weeds of doubt, planting seeds of inspiration, and using your inner resources to make your dreams come into fruition. This also might be wordplay for a *whore.* If so, see *Prostitute.*

Hold Dreams of having or wanting to take hold of someone or something are about your desire for connection, attachment, control, and/or ownership. They may be showing where you are needy and insecure, or passionate and committed. Consider the feeling tone of the dream to discern the significance. See *Hand* and *Hug.*

Hole Dreams of a hole signify receptivity and femininity, and that you are holding a space for new life to come in. However, if you dream of feeling empty, hungry, or needy, then you are venting out feelings of lack or loss. Keep in mind that as you grow in your realization of your spiritual wholeness, you will realize that you are never empty.

Holiday Dreams of a holiday signify that you are giving yourself permission to relax, have fun, and unwind. This is a special time in your life to be fully enjoyed. See *Celebration, Christmas, Hanukkah,* and *Kwanzaa.*

Hollow See *Death, Empty,* and *Hole.*

Hollywood Dreams of Hollywood symbolize a desire to be discovered and recognized. They are a message for you to recognize yourself and take the initiative to bring your talents into fruition. Perhaps you are coming to the spiritual awareness that underneath it all you are a one-of-a-kind star. See *Actor/Actress* and *Celebrity.*

Hollywood Walk of Fame Dreaming of walking among the stars is about desiring closeness to greatness. Perhaps you are recognizing that you are not so different from the gods and goddesses of Hollywood. This dream may be giving you the message to express your unique creative genius. Or it may indicate an overemphasis on worldly recognition. See *Celebrity.*

Holy Communion Dreams of Holy Communion are about the awareness of your oneness with God, spirit, and humanity.

Holy Grail Dreams of the Holy Grail signify that you are connecting to your sacredness, the meaning of life, and/or your life's quest. Dreaming of the chalice that contained the blood of Christ is about recognizing your own divine bloodline, and the fact that you are made in the image and likeness of the Divine. See *God, Goddess,* and *Jesus.*

Home Dreams of a home symbolize domestic stability. The shape, size, and decor of a home is often how you see yourself. If you are uncomfortable with a home, then this indicates that self-improvement is needed. The activities taking place in the place of domesticity are very telling. If you dream of your childhood home, then it represents either nostalgia or unresolved childhood issues. If it is your future dream home, then it represents a positive outlook on the future. See *House.*

Homelessness Dreams of being a homeless person signify disconnection to your center, your true self, and your purpose on this earth. You feel ungrounded, cast out, victimized, and helpless. You may be in a transition period and are feeling homesick for heaven. See *Gypsy.*

Home Run Dreams of a home run signify success and victory, and that you are knocking your problems out of the park, taking what is thrown at you and handling it powerfully and covering all your bases. You are feeling victorious because you are doing your very best. A home run can also be symbolic of a desire for a sexual experience.

Homeschooling Dreams of homeschooling may be assisting you to process your feelings and associations with the concept or the reality of homeschooling. They also reflect your awareness that the greatest learning takes place within the home. Perhaps you are reviewing what you learned as a child from your parents. Dreaming of homeschooling means you are taking a proactive approach to the information you are receiving, as well as taking responsibility for what you teach and how you influence those around you. See *Home* and *School*.

Home Shopping Network Dreams of the Home Shopping Network symbolize a fascination with all that glitters, sales, marketing, convenience, luxury, and instant gratification. See *Bling Bling, Retail Therapy,* and *Shopping*.

Homosexual Dreaming of a homosexual is about processing your relationship with your sexuality and/or your same-sex parent, or exploring the realm of homosexuality. Depending upon the emotional context, a homosexual dream could denote self-love and adoration, or fear/defensiveness/disdain of the opposite sex. Because we all contain masculine and feminine energy regardless of our sex, a homosexual dream could represent an imbalance of an aspect of your nature, unresolved issues with your parents, or the freedom and self-love to explore beyond the boundaries of society's parameters. Consider the feeling tone of the dream.

Honey Dreams of honey symbolize sweetness, pleasure, flattery, healing, and the nectar of life. You are connecting with the essence and substance of your soul. See *Bees* and *Gold*.

Hood Dreams of a hood symbolize a desire to be incognito, anonymous, and secretive. Perhaps you are feeling ashamed or guilty for something you've done. If so, then these dreams are giving you the message to make amends and/or forgive yourself.

Hook Dreams of a hook symbolize seduction, manipulation, and your ego tricks to lure someone in. Or perhaps they are exposing that which seduces and/or captures your attention.

Hoop Dreams of a hoop symbolize your connection to the circular, cyclical nature of life. Perhaps you are feeling that you are going around in circles, or that you are jumping through hoops to get someone's attention or to prove your worthiness. If you dream of a basketball hoop, then you are shooting for a goal on which you are focused.

Horizon Dreams of a horizon signify that you are awakening to a larger perspective as you glimpse the big picture of your life. The sun coming up in the east signifies hope, faith, and renewal.

Horn Dreams of a horn are symbolic of an important announcement calling you to pay attention. See *Music* and *Musical Instrument.*

Horse Dreams of a horse symbolize sensitive, compassionate strength, and untamed sexual energy. If you dream of stealing someone's horse, then this represents jealousy and an attempt to take that person's power. If you dream of a black horse, then this represents your connection to the place within you where the answers live. If you dream of a yellow horse, then this represents illumination and inspiration. If you dream of a red horse, then this represents playfulness, humor, and balancing hard work with joy. If you dream of a white horse, then this represents balance, wisdom, and power. See *Animal* and *Stallion.*

Horseshoe Dreams of a horseshoe symbolize good luck and fortune.

Hose If you dream of a leak in a hose, then this symbolizes a leak in your creativity or life force. If you dream that a hose is channeling water in heavy thrusts, then this represents your life force is in full expression. It may also be showing you the importance of channeling your energy, creativity, and sexuality in a direction that uplifts and energizes you.

Hospice Dreams of a hospice symbolize your wisdom and tender loving care as you transition from one stage of life to the next, or as you cope with the mortality of a loved one.

Hospital Dreams that take place in a hospital signify that you are healing, repairing, or nursing back to health a sick or wounded aspect of yourself, hospicing the old and midwifing the new.

Hospitality Dreams of hospitality are symbolic of feeling gracious and generous, wanting to share and be of service and make others feel at home.

Host Dreams of a host symbolize leadership, power, and maturity. You are claiming responsibility for all the various aspects of yourself, integrating and shepherding yourself into synergy. If you dream of a Web site host, then this is about being on a similar wavelength with someone, sharing energy, power, and resources.

Hotel Dreams of a hotel signify that you are in a transition, feeling a sense of impermanence and detachment. You may be coming to realize and accept the transitoriness of this life and learning to be at home wherever you are. If you dream of a five-star hotel, then it signifies that you are moving through life in luxury and style. If you dream of a cheap hotel, then you are moving frugally through this period of your life.

Hot Sauce Dreams of hot sauce symbolize passion, romance, and a desire to add spice to your life, and push yourself to the limit to see how much heat you can stand. Because hot sauce goes on your food into your mouth, this is about ingesting passion and/or speaking passionately about your feelings.

Hound Dreams of a hound signify that you are focused, determined, and hunting. You are on the scent for what you want. See *Dog*.

Hourglass Dreams of an hourglass symbolize your relationship with time—perhaps fear that time is passing too quickly or too slowly. An hourglass can also symbolize a situation that has turned upside down, the reversal of time, and a return to your beginning, from fullness to emptiness and back again. An hourglass figure is a shape that many women aspire to and men desire.

House Dreams of a house symbolize your self, your life, your body, and how you see yourself. If your house is clean and in order, then you are on track and healthy. If your house is in disrepair and cluttered, then you've got some sorting out to do, people to forgive, and amends to make. See *Home*.

Housekeeper Dreams of a housekeeper are symbolic of self-transformation and keeping your mental and emotional house in order, and cleaning, polishing, dusting, and removing the negative thoughts that clutter your body, mind, and spirit.

HOV Lane Dreams of an HOV lane signify that you are gaining speed through life because when you are unified within yourself, the gridlock of life is eliminated.

Howard Stern Dreams of this radio personality and shock jock may symbolize your shadow, the aspect of you that is a sexist, chauvinistic voyeur. See *Celebrity.*

Hug Dreams of a hug symbolize a desire for reassurance, support, acceptance, love, harmony, and integration. They may signify that you are giving all these qualities to yourself. The qualities of a person you are hugging are the qualities you are embracing and resonating.

Humvee Any type of car that you dream about reflects the way you get by in life, your identity and persona. If you are driving a Hummer or a Humvee, this represents the desire for a powerful, intimidating presence. You may be wasting a lot of your natural resources being so defensive. A Humvee also means that you are extremely driven to succeed.

Hunger Dreams of being hungry can literally reflect a drop in your blood sugar level, or they can signify desire and passion, and that you are yearning for emotional, physical, mental, or spiritual fulfillment. See *Eating* and *Food.*

Hunting Dreams of hunting signify that you are on the prowl for energy and power. The way you hunt says a lot about your survival mechanisms. You are becoming aware of the effectiveness of your survival skills. See *Stalking.*

Hurdle Dreams of a hurdle reflect your feelings and attitudes about challenges. You are facing a setback or difficulty that is a blessing in disguise because it will help you to build stronger and more powerful spiritual, mental, and emotional muscles.

Hurricane Major transformation is in the air. Your entire foundation is being blown to bits. Keep in mind that only love is real, and all that is unreal is being blown away. A dream of a hurricane may be giving you the message to develop a spiritual/meditative practice that assists you in identifying with the center, not the circumference, of life. See *Breakdown/Breakthrough Dreams,* page 12.

Hurt Dreams of being hurt signify that you are venting and processing a painful experience from the past. When you realize that only your ego can be hurt and that your truest self cannot be threatened or harmed, velocity is added to your healing process. See *Venting Dreams,* page 8.

Husband A dream of a husband symbolizes the provider/protector aspect of yourself. If you are an unmarried man dreaming of being a husband, then you are processing your aspirations/hopes/fears of one day being married. If you are a married man, then the dream can represent that you are dealing with the pressure of being the breadwinner. If you are a married woman, then this can represent your idealized husband versus the day-to-day reality, with its expectations and demands, of your actual husband. If you are an unmarried woman, this may be your hope, fantasy, or "dream" of what your future husband will be.

Hut Dreams of a hut are symbolic of simplicity, closeness to nature, and vulnerability to the challenges of life.

Hybrid Car Dreams of a fuel-efficient car represent a desire to conserve energy, and are an indication that you are globally aware, mature, responsible, conscientious, and mindful of natural resources, namely, *your* natural resources (time and money). See *Car* and *Solar Power.*

Hyena Dreams of a hyena symbolize an ability to find humor in the midst of a painful situation or that your humor is masking your pain. Consider the feeling tone. See *Animal.*

Hypnosis Dreams of hypnosis signify that you are feeling suggestible to someone else's influence and perhaps you are afraid of losing control. If you dream of being in hypnosis and you are receiving empowering suggestions, then you are deepening your ability to access your greatest potential. If you are not feeling empowered by the suggestions you receive, then dreaming of hypnosis is giving you the message to set energetic boundaries. See *Boundary.*

Hypocrite Dreams of a hypocrite denote that you are processing through and bringing to your awareness your conflicting needs so that you can walk your talk and talk your walk, being in sync with your mind, body, and spirit. If you are judging someone else's hypocrisy, be aware that you wouldn't be so emotionally charged by this unless the behavior mirrored your own shadow.

Hysterectomy Dreams of a hysterectomy signify that you are disconnecting yourself from your feminine, maternal urges. If you've actually undergone a hysterectomy, then you are processing your experience with the procedure and you are connecting with the crone archetype. See *Crone*.

I

iBook See *Book, Computer,* and *Laptop*.

Ice Dreams of ice symbolize frozen emotions, sexual inhibitions, insecurity, and unhealed wounds.

Iceberg Dreams of an iceberg are symbolic of your deepest existential pain. If you dream of the tip of an iceberg, then you are just beginning to understand your pain. The fact that you are dreaming about this reflects that the thawing process has begun, and with some self-love and understanding your natural genius will soon find its way into expression.

Ice Cream Dreams of ice cream are symbolic of a treat, reward, and celebration.

Idle If you dream of being idle, then this signifies that you are stuck in gear and out of step with your natural rhythm and momentum. Alternatively, what might appear to be idleness, laziness, or procrastination might simply be that you are awaiting clarity.

Idol Dreams of an idol signify that you are putting someone on a pedestal. They denote that you've been projecting greatness onto someone else other than yourself, putting that person above you. See *American Idol, Fame,* and *Pedestal*.

Ignition Dreams of an ignition are symbolic of the spark, inspiration, and catalyst that you desire to get your creative juices and/or sexuality revved up. An ignition also signifies that you are preparing to start over, to begin a new project or get involved in a new romance.

Image Dreaming about your image signifies that you are grappling with your ego, and your perception of what you should look like,

be like, and have. Perhaps you are processing out a fear that someone will find out your walk doesn't match your talk and you have
an inner desire to have your insides match your outsides. See *Ego.*

Immigration Dreams of immigration represent the process of
transformation from one state of consciousness to another. You are
processing grief and loss for the past as well as joy and hope for a
brighter future.

Implant Dreams of an implant mean that you are additionalizing,
maximizing, and embellishing yourself for a desired effect. For
example, if you dream of breast implants, you have a desire to uplevel your femininity, sexiness, or attractiveness. If you dream of receiving an alien implant, then you are venting your feelings of
being violated and influenced in nonsupportive ways. See *Cosmetic
Surgery.* See also *Venting Dreams,* page 8.

Impotence Dreams of impotence signify that you are feeling cas-
trated, powerless, insecure, and afraid of making a mistake. You are
venting out and releasing feelings of being unsupported, of being
unable to express yourself, of negative judgments, and of extreme
self-criticism.

Incense Dreams of incense signify the element of air, which represents clarity of thought and that you are opening your mind to
possibilities beyond your normal scope. Incense is also associated
with a spiritual or religious rite of passage, and a change in the air.
See *Air.*

Incest As disturbing as it may be, it is fairly common, from time to
time, to dream of your family members in a sexual context. Don't
take your dream literally because, as in any sex dream, it is about
connecting and energetically merging with the parts of you that
they represent.

Incinerator Dreams of an incinerator symbolize transformation.
You are releasing and burning away all that no longer serves you.
See *Fire.*

Incubation Dreams of incubation signify that you are preparing,
gestating, and getting warmed up for the next stage/incarnation of
your life. See *Time-out.*

Independence Dreams of independence signify that you are finding your own voice, exploring your unique expression apart from your family and/or tribe, and discovering autonomy from your intimate relationships. You are realizing that you are free to create the life you desire.

Indian Dreams of an American Indian symbolize spirituality, connection to the Great Spirit, and a reverence for animals, the earth, and the earth's elements. Dreams of an Indian from India symbolize spirituality and connection to the Buddha, Krishna, and the Dalai Lama.

Indigestion Dreams of indigestion suggest an unwillingness or inability to stomach the events of your life. Your ability to digest is blocked either by your fixed ideas about the way you believe things should be, or because your life circumstances are shocking to you and you need some time to process and make sense of everything.

Indigo Dreams of the color indigo symbolize spirituality, metaphysics, and tranquillity. See *Color.*

Indigo Child Dreams of an Indigo child are about your connection with your interdimensional power, talent, and wisdom while maintaining your innocence. Your subconscious mind is giving you the message that you are wise beyond your years and that you are here with a higher purpose.

Infant Dreams of an infant are symbolic of purity, innocence, and the need for assistance and support from others in order to make it through to the next level of evolution. They may be giving you the message to joyously trust the unfolding of the events of your life.

Infection Dreams of an infection signify that the negative thoughts you have been indulging in are beginning to fester. They are showing you the power of your mind and thoughts. Because you were able to manifest an expression of your fears, consider what you could manifest or create when you are focused on that which brings you joy. Keep in mind that where attention goes, energy flows and results show. See *Disease.*

Inheritance Dreams of an inheritance forecast wealth, prosperity, and abundance coming into your life. Keep in mind, of the one to whom much is given, much is expected. Dreaming of an inheritance represents your awareness of your connectivity to the bounty of this universe. See *Wish Fulfillment Dreams,* page 18.

Initiation Dreams of an initiation signify that you are at the beginning of a new chapter in your life. They are giving you the message to see the challenges that you've been facing as part of your initiation process, preparing you for the next level of your evolution. See *Fire* and *Graduation.*

Injury Dreams of an injury signify an overuse of energy and that you are out of balance. They are a red flag alerting you to pay attention and sync up with your natural rhythm. See *Accident.*

Ink Dreams of ink symbolize communication, permanence, a contract, or a promise. See *Pen* and *Tattoo.*

Insane Asylum Dreams of an insane asylum are venting dreams that signify that you are overwhelmed and are feeling out of control with the events of your life. You may be processing your shame about expressing your true feelings, and being seen as weird, strange, or an outsider. See *Crazy.*

Insider Trading Dreams of insider trading are a message from your subconscious mind to maintain your integrity. See *Karma* and *Prostitute.*

Instant Messenger (IM) A dream of Instant Messenger symbolizes your desire and/or telepathic ability to send and receive communication quickly. It could be a processing dream whereby your subconscious is attempting to organize the daily events of your life, or it could represent an irritation at having your creative flow be interrupted. See *FedEx.* See also *Processing Dreams,* page 7.

Insulation Dreams of insulation signify that you are padding yourself, wanting protection, warmth, and nurturing. Perhaps you are having the foresight to prepare for potential lean times. If you are too protected, then you may be attempting to escape or hide from intimacy. See *Fat.*

Interior Design Dreams of interior design are symbolic of your sensitivity to the space that surrounds you, whether it is the physical space or the people with whom you associate. If the space around you feels good, then this represents that you have created a life that works for you. If the space around you is displeasing, then a dream of interior design is alerting you to make changes in your life. Consider the feeling tone of the dream as well as the room(s) being designed. See *Feng Shui, Home,* and *House.*

Internet   Dreams of the Internet symbolize having the world at your fingertips, and your connectivity to everything, everyone, all the time; it is a net in which all solutions you seek are caught. See *Computer.*

Internet Café   Dreams of an Internet café symbolize public privacy and a desire for stimulation while connecting with the world of possibilities.

Interruption   Dreams of an interruption reflect the way you handle distractions. Perhaps you are venting your frustration at the circumstances in your life that vie for your attention. See *ADD/ADHD.*

Interview   Dreaming of an interview symbolizes integration, wisdom, and healing in that two aspects of yourself, the interviewee and the interviewer, are seeking to find common ground and unity. If you are being interviewed, then you are accessing your wisdom, sitting in the seat of authority. If you are the interviewer, then this represents your curious nature, and that you are learning something new about yourself and life. See *Job Interview.* See also *Integration Dreams,* page 10.

Intimacy   Dreams of intimacy denote a desire for closeness, and to know and be known. Intimacy could be wordplay for *into-me-I-see,* the desire to have an authentic connection with yourself. See *Sex.*

Intruder/Intruding   Dreams of an intruder signify that you are processing and venting your fears of being hurt or having your boundaries violated. An intruder can also represent your unintegrated shadow that will continue to threaten you until you face and embrace it. If you are the intruder in a dream, then it is giving you the message to go only where you are invited, and not to waste your time and energy where they are not desired or appreciated. See *Integration Dreams,* page 10.

Intuition   Dreams of intuition signify clarity, higher guidance, lucidity, and enlightenment. Allow them to give you permission to follow your intuition. Consider the message you receive to be significant. See *Precognitive Dreams,* page 15.

Invalid Dreams of an invalid symbolize an unused or apparently broken aspect of your being that is in need of repair. They are giving you the message to be aware that just because something may be broken does not invalidate its purpose or relevance in life. See *Crippled* and *Sick.*

Invasion Dreams of an invasion signify that you are feeling overwhelmed and inundated with the opinions and energies of other people. They are giving you the message to set energetic boundaries to keep yourself centered and balanced in the midst of a challenging time.

Invention A dream that features an invention forecasts a great breakthrough and that you are on the cutting edge of genius, tapping into new and inventive ways to grow, learn, and create solutions. Consider the invention in the dream and its practical applications in real life. It might be your million-dollar idea. See *Processing Dreams,* page 7, and *Wish Fulfillment Dreams,* page 18.

Inventor Dreams of an inventor represent your connection to your natural genius and creativity. You are realizing the value of your "mistakes." Your subconscious mind is giving you the message that it is through your experiments, both the successful ones and the unsuccessful ones, that you earn your genius and make your greatest contributions to life.

Investment To dream of making an investment is about creating a bond and being attached and plugged into the energy of something or someone. If it is about a relationship that you are investing your energy into. See *Commitment* and *Relationship.*

If it is about a financial investment, see *Money.*

Invitation If you dream of receiving an invitation, it signifies that your presence, energy, gifts, and talents are being recognized and are in demand. If you dream of sending out an invitation to a particular person, then you are desiring connection with the part of you that that person represents. Consider the qualities of the person or people you are inviting. See *Evite.*

In Vitro Fertilization Dreams of in vitro fertilization signify that you are asserting your will in the creation of a baby, project, or relationship. You are not taking no for an answer with regard to the obstacles and challenges you face in creating and fulfilling your desires. See *Pregnant*.

iPod Because music represents a medium that greatly influences feelings, moods, attitudes, and thoughts, dreams of an iPod signify that your ability to have mastery and control of your emotions, moods, and thoughts is in the palm of your hand. See *Music*.

Ireland Dreams of Ireland, or any Irish association, symbolize a lighthearted approach to life, frivolity, storytelling, and perhaps your realization that the pot of gold is right where you are. See *Clover* and *Leprechaun*.

Iron/Ironing Dreams of the element iron symbolize strength and power, unbendable, inflexible, stubborn energy. They may be showing you that you have too many irons in the fire. Dreams of ironing clothes are about your ability to press through the wrinkles, challenges, and struggles of your life.

Irrigation Dreams of irrigation signify that you are watering the seeds of your desires. Your subconscious mind is giving you the message to go ahead and have a good cry, let your tears water the seeds of your field of dreams. See *Water*.

Island Dreams of an island are symbolic of being in your own little world, reclusive, distant, lonely, protected, aloof, and independent. Because islands are formed from centuries of volcanic eruptions, these dreams symbolize beauty created by apparent disaster, and are symbolic of how growth can seem to be slow and arduous, but that if you stick with it, it will eventually pay off. See *Hermit*.

Itch Dreams of an itch are symbolic of feeling unsatisfied with your current circumstances; you are wanting more and realizing your unfulfilled desires. Keep in mind that just as within an oyster sand acts as an irritant that creates a pearl, an itch signifies that positive transformation is in process in your life.

Itinerary A dream that contains an itinerary symbolizes your desire for control, order, a schedule, and an understanding of the time and space in which you are traveling.

I.V. Dreams of being fed intravenously symbolize your attachment or addiction to the support of a person or situation in your life. See *Crutch* and *Life Support.*

Ivory Dreams of ivory symbolize virginity, purity, and vitality.

Ivy Dreams of ivy symbolize wedded love and fidelity.

If it is poison ivy, see *Poison Ivy.*

Ivy League College Dreams of an Ivy League college symbolize a desire for the best in life, prestige, academic hierarchy, intelligence, and status with regard to education.

J

Jack Dreams of a jack symbolize support to elevate to a higher level, the desire for assistance to repair what has been broken, or the desire to get out of a ditch. Perhaps they are showing you that you are a jack-of-all-trades. If this is the case, then it may be time to focus upon that for which you have the greatest passion and natural genius, or accept the fact that you are a Renaissance man or woman, and diversification is your specialty.

Jade Dreaming of jade, or of what the Mayan culture called the "dream stone," is a sign of lucidity and supernatural support to assist you in bridging the gap between your awakened reality and your dreamtime. Jade also represents confidence, self-sufficiency, and the ability to transform cherished desires into physical reality.

Jail/Jailer Dreams of a jail or a jailer signify that you are coming to grips with the part of you that holds you captive behind bars of guilt and shame. You are realizing the key that will set you free is in your own hands, and it lies within your ability to make amends, and forgive yourself and those who have harmed you. See *Prison.*

Jam Dreams of jam signify that you are in a sweet but sticky situation; because you've spread yourself too thin, now you're stuck. Jam also represents precious memories preserved in the photo album of your mind that get sweeter with time.

If the dream is about a traffic jam, see *Traffic.*

Janitor Dreams of a janitor denote that you are wanting to clean up your act, make amends, and find forgiveness. They also represent your desire or compulsion to clean up after someone else's messes, or cover for his or her mistakes. See *Codependence.*

January Dreams of January symbolize resolutions, starting anew, having a clean slate, and connecting with your intentions. Depending upon where you live in the world, January will also symbolize a particular season. See *Spring, Summer, Fall,* or *Winter.*

Jar Dreams of a jar signify that you are feeling contained, bottled up, and unable to express yourself. Perhaps you are preserving your feelings until the moment is right.

Jaw Dreams of a jaw symbolize communication. If you dream of lockjaw, then this denotes anger, frustration, stress, and resentment, and that you've put a lock on joy. It could be suggesting that it is time to be more mindful about your communication patterns. See *Lockjaw.*

Jealousy Dreams that expose your jealous feelings can be a catalyst for you to move forward, onward, and upward toward the creation of the life you desire so that you can actualize the qualities that you admire in another. Keep in mind that if you see it, you can be it.

Jellyfish Dreams of jellyfish symbolize feelings of helplessness and powerlessness. Perhaps you are feeling spineless about your effectiveness in a current challenge. These dreams may be giving you the message to watch your step and walk mindfully through this difficult time.

Jesus Dreams of Jesus represent unconditional love. Whether or not you are Christian, dreaming of Jesus signifies that you are connecting with your higher consciousness and your ability to see through appearances to the heart of the love beneath pain and suffering. See *God* and *Sacrifice.*

Jewel Case Dreams of a jewel case for a CD symbolize your ego, protection, and defense mechanisms that ensure your well-being.

Jewelry Dreams of jewelry symbolize extravagance, prosperity and abundance, lavishness, and qualities you cherish. If you dream of your family heirlooms, then you are realizing inherited wisdom. If you dream of being in possession of a valuable piece of jewelry, then you feel connected to your natural inheritance and to the priceless wonder that you are. Jewelry can represent an aspect of you, a proud achievement, a precious memory, a friendship that is priceless to you, your talents, resources, wisdom, or the qualities that you treasure, such as kindness, compassion, honesty, etc. Dreaming of jewelry is telling you to acknowledge where you sparkle, what is rare and invaluable about you. See *Amethyst, Bracelet, Diamond, Earrings, Emerald, Gold, Jade, Necklace, Opal, Pearl, Ruby, Sapphire, Silver,* or *Turquoise.*

Job Dreams featuring your job are assisting you to process thoughts, feelings, challenges, and unfinished business regarding your work and business relationships. If you don't have a job, then these dreams may be helping you become clear about what type of job you should pursue. See *Processing Dreams,* page 7.

Job Interview If you dream of interviewing for a job, the dream is helping you to put your best foot forward, and see that you will soon be recognized for your talents. If you dream of interviewing an applicant, then you are realizing that you have a choice to discern who and what you want in your life. See *Audition* and *Interview.*

Jockey Dreams of a jockey symbolize harnessing and focusing the energy, power, and passion of your animal instincts toward a particular goal. Also, because jockeys are usually diminutive in their physical stature, they can represent your inner child and your childhood dreams. See *Goddess* (Artemis) and *Short.*

Jogging Dreams about jogging may be a message to integrate more exercise into your life, to increase your creative stamina, or to run in the direction of your dreams. See *Exercise.*

Joints Dreams of joints signify issues of bending your will, flexibility, and your issues of control with regards to the changes of life.
    If you are dreaming of marijuana, see *Marijuana.*

Joke A dream of a joke that makes you laugh is a sign of genius, intelligence, joy, and that you have a great sense of humor.

Journalist Dreaming of a journalist signifies that you are interested in people and value the lessons and blessings of everyday life. Alternatively, it may signify that you've been nosy, gossiping, and perhaps overly fascinated with human drama, and in some cases you've been looking for trouble. Consider the feeling tone of the dream to discern the significance. If you dream of being interviewed by a journalist, then this represents that you will soon be valued, honored, and heralded as important. If you are the one doing an interview, then you are seeking the truth, and trying to get to the bottom of a story. See *Drama Queen/Drama King, Interview,* and *News.*

Journey Dreams of a journey, whether you are planning a trip or are in the midst of one, represent excitement, adventure, an open mind, and a departure from your everyday life. They reflect your willingness to do what it takes to move from one place in consciousness to another. A dream of a journey symbolizes a change in your life direction, that you are open to unlimited possibilities, and that you are going places, learning, growing, and preparing to meet new people. Perhaps it is also reflecting that you are exploring your inner self and traveling to new and different regions within your body, mind, and spirit.

Judas Dreams of Judas signify your fear of being betrayed, or that you are dealing with a betrayal that has already taken place. They are giving you the message: to thine own self be true. See *Venting Dreams,* page 8.

Judge Dreams of a judge symbolize justice, fairness, or criticism. Consider the feeling tone. See *Critic.*

Judgment Day Dreams of Judgment Day represent an opportunity to find yourself innocent, to discover either that you've been doing the best you can or that there are areas of your life that need to be improved or amends that you need to make. You are coming to terms with death, your beliefs about the afterlife, spirituality, God, and your own self-judgments. A dream of Judgment Day is giving you the message that it is time to connect more solidly with your higher purpose. See *Apocalypse.*

Jug Dreams of a jug are symbolic of your ability to nurture yourself. Consider the contents of the jug. If a jug is empty, then you are dealing with an unfulfilled need and you are coming to terms with how to fill it. If a jug is full, then you have the ability to wet your whistle and quench your own thirst for creative stimulation, fun, excitement, and nurturing. See *Drink* and *Thirst.*

Juggling Dreams of juggling signify that you are multitasking, and that you are feeling on the verge of being out of control with too many balls in the air. It is time to deal with your messiah complex: attempting to be all things to all people. A dream of juggling may be giving you the message that it is time to drop a few things, and learn to say no every once in a while. See *Codependence*.

July If you live in America and you dream of the Fourth of July, then this represents independence, freedom, *inter*dependence, and the passion to live your dreams. If you see skyrockets in your dreams, then you are in love or lust and/or are having a burst of creativity. See *Fireworks*.

Jumping Dreams of jumping signify that you are excited about your life. If you are jumping from one thing to the next, then you are being compulsive. However, if you are making a leap, then this represents that you are taking a leap of faith, or making a quantum leap. Dreaming of jumping is giving you the message to live fully, to leap and know that the net will appear.

June Dreams of June symbolize weddings, joy, passion, union, summertime, and frivolous fun in the sun. See *Goddess* (Hera).

Jungle Dreams of a jungle signify that your most primal feelings and urges are rising up from your unconscious to be integrated with your conscious mind as you are connecting with your deepest desires and passions. You may be charting your way through a challenging time in your life and you are feeling out of your element. See *Integration Dreams,* page 10.

Jungle Gym Dreams of a jungle gym signify freedom and play, and that you would be wise to allow your inner child to go wild. Because when you do, your inner child will lead you through the jungle of your mind to your greatest solutions and insights.

Jury Dreams of a jury denote that you are putting your power outside yourself, allowing your self-perception to be influenced by the opinions of others. A jury can also represent the many voices of your own sub-personalities. See *Judge*. See also *Integration Dreams,* page 10.

Justice If you dream about wanting justice, then you are concerned with fairness, balance, and equality. Perhaps you are venting out and processing through a situation in your life that feels unfair. You are realizing that there is a cosmic balancing act and an ultimate justice system in the higher order of the universe. See *Karma*.

K

Kaleidoscope Dreams of a kaleidoscope symbolize creative imagination and inner delight. The dominant colors in a kaleidoscope play an important role in the meaning of a dream. Your patterns and life structures are altering before your eyes. See *Color.*

Kama Sutra Dreams of this ancient Hindu manual of sexual positions symbolize a desire for sexual variety, to celebrate your body, and to integrate the sacred and the sexual within you. See *Sex.*

Kangaroo Dreams of a kangaroo represent feminine power. The large feet on a kangaroo symbolize being powerful and grounded. A kangaroo's bouncing signifies buoyancy and that you are jumping for joy and leaping into the unknown with both feet. The pouch of a kangaroo represents protection and nurturing, and that you desire a maternal, safe place to hide. See *Jumping.*

Karaoke If you dream you are singing at a karaoke bar or with a karaoke machine, you are expressing your desire to be heard and to passionately express your full voice. Consider the song being sung.

Karate Dreams of karate signify fighting, that you are coming into your power, and that you have a desire to break through obstacles in your ability to defend yourself. They are also about mental discipline, commitment, diligence, strategy, and focus. A black belt is a sign of mastery in the art of defending yourself, and a white belt is a sign of a novice. Consider the feeling tone of the dream.

Karma Dreams of karma represent your desire for fairness, justice, and/or retribution. You are aware of a higher order and spirituality, and that you reap what you sow.

Keeping To dream of keeping something denotes your desire for a person or thing you want in your life, or gratitude and/or attachment for what you already have. You might be grappling with issues of responsibility, deservedness, and worthiness regarding that which you already have.

Keepsake Dreams of a special memento are about good luck, empowerment, and a reminder that you have a charmed life. If you are searching for a lost keepsake, you are trying to reconnect with a special and important part of your soul.

Kelp Dreams of kelp symbolize a tangled relationship that you are feeling stuck in and unable to leave. Sea kelp contains a protein that can be nutritious for the hair and skin, representing the fact that sometimes relationships that appear to be undesirable on the surface are helping you to sort out important soul lessons beneath the surface. See *Weed*.

Kennel Dreams of a kennel signify that you are in a holding pattern, feeling helpless as you await rescue. Perhaps you are feeling trapped against your will because you've allowed your animal instincts to be bound and suppressed.

Kernel Dreams of a kernel represent the seedling of an idea before it pops, just before an "aha" moment. A kernel also is symbolic of golden ideas. See *Corn* and *Seeds*.

Kerosene Dreams of kerosene are symbolic of the fuel for passion, the catalyst for the fire of your creativity, passion, sexuality, and transformation. They denote your desire to raise the level of intensity in a current relationship or business endeavor.

Ketchup Dreams of ketchup are about feeling the need to add flavor and spice to your life. They can also mean that you are feeling behind and that you need to *catch up*. See *Blood, Condiment*, and *Tomato*.

Kettle Dreams of a kettle signify that your creativity is percolating and that you are waiting for the appropriate time to express your anger or passion. If you suppress these feelings for too long, you will blow. Perhaps it is time to blow the whistle on an unacceptable situation in your life.

Key A key is a symbol of power, freedom, and solutions. In the I Ching (the ancient Chinese oracle), the keeper of keys is the one who contains wisdom and wealth in great measure. You have the key that can open up any locked-up area of your mind, body, or spirit and set you free. A key also represents the penis and sexual intercourse. Consider the purpose of the key.

Keyhole Dreams of a keyhole signify that you are awaiting entrance and/or connection to someone or something. A keyhole represents the feminine principle of holding space, the vagina, awaiting masculine energy to enter, and feeling the anticipation of a great opportunity.

Key Word Dreams of a key word are about the power of words and your ability to attract what you are focused upon. A key word also represents your inner radar and your ability to identify what you need and want. Consider what a key word is. See *Search Bar*.

Khaki Dreams of khaki signify that you are attempting to blend in, remain incognito, and camouflage your self-expression. They may be showing you the value in being an observer or listener, or they may be telling you to blend in because your security depends on it.

Kick Dreams of a kick signify aggression and defense, or that you are initiating a project or relationship, as in "kick starting" or "kicking something into gear." If you are the one kicking, you are delivering a physical or emotional blow. If someone in a dream kicks you, perhaps you are paying the price for getting your "kicks." See *Attack, Football,* or *Karate*.

Kickstand Dreams of a kickstand symbolize your need for something or someone to lean on. See *Crutch*.

Kidnap Dreams of being kidnapped or abducted symbolize control issues and your fears of being negatively influenced or overpowered by an external force. They are also about transformation and metamorphosis from victimhood to empowerment. If you are the one doing the kidnapping, you may be forcing your will onto someone else, or forcing yourself to do something that you know deep down is not good for you. See *Goddess* (Persephone).

Kidney If you dream of a problem with your kidney, then you have fears of growing up or a fear of being criticized. You also may be processing criticism you've recently received.

Kidney Stone Dreams of a kidney stone symbolize righteous resentment and an unwillingness to forgive. You are under the false impression that holding on to anger will keep you safe or morally superior.

Killing Dreams of killing someone symbolize a desire to get rid of an unacceptable aspect of self, extreme self-denial, perfectionism, suppressed anger, rage, destruction, fear, or defensiveness, and an expression of your fight for survival. Consider who is being killed and by whom, and this will help you to receive the gift of the dream. For example, if you dream of killing a male, then you are attempting to kill off your masculine energy; if you are killing a female, then you are attempting to kill your female energy, etc. Also, a dream of killing may denote your desire to eliminate a destructive habit. See *Shadow*. See also *Integration Dreams,* page 10, and *Venting Dreams,* page 8.

Kiln Dreams of a kiln symbolize commitment, transformation, creativity, turning up the heat, raising the stakes, and intensity of a commitment, relationship, or business venture that transforms creative ideas into manifestation. See *Fire*.

King Dreams of a king symbolize masculine power, the father archetype, God, higher knowledge, vision, and ambition. You are rising above the masses in terms of status and wealth because you are connecting to your higher purpose. If you are a man dreaming of a king, you are dealing with authority issues, either your own or those of someone you work with. If you are a woman dreaming of a king, then you may be looking to be rescued.

Kinko's Dreams of Kinko's are about copying someone or someone copying you. They may be a sign to get organized, and down to brass tacks, and to duplicate your power, work, and productivity. They may also be warning you to save or make copies of important documents. See *Xerox*.

Kiosk Dreams of a kiosk symbolize self-sufficiency and a desire to take life into your own hands. See *ATM*.

Kiss A kiss in a dream is a sign of love, affinity, acceptance, and camaraderie. A dream of kissing may be about the embrace of opposite aspects of yourself. Consider who is being kissed. See *Integration Dreams,* page 10, or *Wish Fulfillment Dreams,* page 18.

Kitchen A space of creation, a kitchen is symbolic of nurturing, feeding your soul, having an appetite for success, love, creative ideas, and solutions.

Kite Dreams of a kite signify that your soul is taking flight and that you are riding the winds of change as you joyously and playfully explore higher levels of consciousness. You are turning your life over to the winds of fate and destiny.

Kitten Dreams of a kitten symbolize the youthful feminine archetype within you, your connection to your feline nature and with the fragile, precious, vulnerable, warm, and tender aspect of yourself.

Kleptomaniac Dreams of a kleptomaniac signify that you are grappling with a distorted sense of justice, feelings of lack, insatiability, and the need to take what isn't yours out of a fear that you will be left empty-handed or with the short end of the stick. They reflect extreme opportunism.

Knapsack Dreams of a knapsack signify that you are prepared and resourceful.

Kneading Dreams of kneading mean that you are mulling something over, contemplating a decision, sorting through your thoughts, and attempting to make sense of a circumstance. Perhaps you are coming to realize that the power to fulfill your needs is within your own hands.

Knee Dreams of a knee symbolize flexibility and the ability to bend. If you dream that you have knee problems or discomfort, the dream may be giving you the message that you've been either too rigid, prideful, and egotistical, or the opposite, too wishy-washy, in your stance.

Kneeling Dreams of kneeling signify that you are abdicating your power and respect, and/or are offering yourself in service to someone or something greater than yourself.

Knife Dreams of a knife symbolize the use of force or violence to end a destructive pattern, or to eliminate a person from your sphere of influence. If a knife is being used against you, beware of nonsupportive energy in your life. Knives can also symbolize the male genitalia—powerful, strong, and erect.

Knight Dreams of a knight denote the desire for a hero or the desire to be a hero.

Knitting Dreams of knitting are symbolic of making plans and networking by bringing elements and people together. They also signify that you are weaving your skills together, and integrating aspects of yourself into unison, creating something out of nothing, and discovering that your ability to manifest and mend a problem is in your own hands. See *Weaving*.

Knob Dreams of a knob signify that you have access to opportunity because of your will and desire, as in the fact that you can be led to the right door but you must turn the knob. See *Door*.

Knock Dreams of a knock signify that an opportunity is forthcoming. Identify who or what is knocking at the door; this will inform you as to the opportunity that is coming into your life.

Knot Dreams of a knot symbolize confusion. Perhaps there are too many opposing forces pulling at you at once, representing your own conflicting needs and emotional entanglements. Dreaming of a knot may be giving you the message to take time to unwind. A knot can also represent a commitment, or that you are wanting to say "No, *not* now."

Knuckle Dreams of a knuckle signify that you are clutching or holding tightly on to a person, ideal, or point of view. Perhaps you are grasping at something or someone to hold on to. See *Fist*.

Koran Dreams of this holy book represent your thirst for spiritual guidance and higher wisdom. See *Bible*.

Krishna Dreaming of this enlightened deity signifies your own inner wisdom and that you are evoking the best of yourself. Krishna also represents your ability to access the divine and realize that you are in this world but not of it.

Kundalini Dreams of kundalini symbolize sacred sexuality, your ability to harness your power and channel it in healthy and empowering ways. You are experiencing energy that is helping you to elevate your thoughts and empower your creativity. See *Chakra* (1st), *Kama Sutra,* and *Snake*.

Kwanzaa Dreaming of this traditional African celebration symbolizes harvest, family values, community responsibility, commerce, and self-improvement.

L

Label Identifying the type of a label in a dream will tell you a great deal about how you are limiting yourself or setting yourself free. See *Judge*.

Laboratory Dreams of a laboratory reflect your desire or ability to experiment in your life, to make mistakes within the context of learning, growing, and improving. You are realizing that if nothing is ventured nothing is gained.

Labyrinth Dreams of a labyrinth indicate an initiation, test, or challenge. A significant aspect of a dream of a labyrinth is the way you feel as you make your way through the maze or rite of passage.

Lace Dreams of lace are symbolic of extravagance, beauty, and sexiness.

Ladder Dreams of a ladder reflect your ambition to climb and advance to higher ground in your life, to reach, strive, and climb upward on the ladder of success. Alternatively, if you are climbing downward, then this symbolizes that you are coming down to earth from a loftier place, exploring the depth of your being, or feeling discouraged or demoted. Consider the feeling tone. If a ladder is being used to rescue a person or animal, then this represents heroism and that you are rising above your egoic needs for a greater good.

Ladle Dreams of this serving utensil are about the nurturing and nourishment of your body, mind, or spirit and/or that aspect of those around you. If you are feeding others, then you are feeding people your ideas and philosophies. If you are being fed, then consider the content of what you are taking in.

Lake Dreams of this calm body of water are symbolic of your connection to the feminine, your innermost feelings, fantasies, intuition, and the mystery of life. Also, a lake represents the element of water, which is about emotional depth and self-awareness. See *Ocean.*

Lamaze Dreams of Lamaze signify that you are breathing your way through the birth of a new project or creation, finding grace as you move through the final pushes of this process. Perhaps it is time to give yourself a break and take a breather. See *Air* and *Breath.*

Lamb Dreams of a lamb signify that you are connecting with your childlike essence, that you feel dependent, vulnerable, and/or sheepish. Or you may be venting feelings of being a sacrificial lamb. See *Christ* and *Virgin.*

Lamp Dreams of a lamp signify that your bright spirit is helping you to remain inspired and to be illuminated and hopeful in the midst of a challenge. Or you are awakening to the divine light within you and you are feeling turned on and passionate. See *Flashlight* and *Light*.

Land Dreams of land are symbolic of your becoming grounded, pragmatic, grown up, and/or territorial. If you own land, then you are taking a stance and holding your ground. Undeveloped land represents potential for growth. If land is developed, then this is about taking pride in your accomplishments and seeing how much you've grown. A dream of land could also be a message that it is time to come down to earth.

Landslide See *Earthquake* and *Mud Slide*. See also *Breakdown/Breakthrough Dreams,* page 12.

Language If you dream of speaking a language you are learning, then your learning is becoming expedited. If you dream of speaking a Romance language that is foreign to you, it may represent your desire for more passion or romance in your life. Also, if you dream of speaking the language of a field of study that is foreign to you, such as physics, rocket science, or Windows XP, then this demonstrates the intelligence and wisdom of your mind, and that you are realizing that you are connected to the one mind. Consider your association with the language. If the language is foreign to you, see *Foreign*.

Lantern Dreams of a lantern signify that you are attempting to find your way through a dark time, or you are recapturing a memory or aspect of yourself from the past. See *Light*.

Lap Dreams of a lap represent being grounded, connected to the earth, to your mother, to a familial affiliation and life force. If you dream of sitting on someone's lap, then you are playing the role of child. If someone is sitting on your lap, then you are playing the adult. See *Chakra* (2nd).

Lap Dance If you dream that you are the one receiving the lap dance, then this denotes power, money, sex, and control. If you dream that you are the one giving the lap dance, then this is about getting and wanting power and control in a sexual way. See *Prostitute*.

Laptop Dreams of a laptop computer signify that you are attached at the hip to your work. Laptops can represent an extension of yourself, your power and ability to communicate. See *Computer.*

Laser Dreams of a laser signify that you have intense concentration, focus, and awareness, as well as the ability to see beyond the surface.

Lasex Dreams of Lasex, laser eye surgery, symbolize your willingness to see beyond the surface of things, to see what has been right in front of you all along.

Las Vegas Dreams of Las Vegas signify that you are taking a gamble on yourself, taking chances. They may be a warning to not lose your shirt, and to remember that all that sparkles isn't gold. Also, don't be fooled by impersonators. See *Gambling.*

Latch Dreams of a latch signify that you are hooking onto someone and you are dealing with your attachments and issues of dependence. If a latch is open, then opportunity is available. If a latch is closed, then you have closed yourself off to a potential opportunity, perhaps because you are feeling defensive and protective. See *Codependence.*

Latchkey Child Dreams of a latchkey child symbolize resourcefulness, street smarts, and abandonment issues. Dreaming of a latchkey child may mean you are processing and healing the wounds of your inner child, perhaps from having had to grow up too fast.

Late A dream of being late is a venting dream where you are releasing feelings of inadequacy. Being late in a dream also signifies that you are releasing your fear of getting into trouble or being punished for being unprepared and a step behind.

Latin Dreams of someone Latin, Latino, or Hispanic symbolize passion, expressiveness, love, emotions, and sensuality.

Laughter Dreams of laughter reflect genius, happiness, joy, frivolity, and the ability to have a good time and take yourself lightly. You are tickled by life.

Laundromat/Laundry Dreams of a Laundromat symbolize that an aspect of your life is being cleaned up, perhaps a conflict is being ironed out, nonsupportive habits are being hung out to dry, forgiveness is taking place, gossip is ending, and amends are being made. Also, they represent your public image or persona. So if your laundry is dirty, then this means your image or reputation has been soiled. And if you are cleaning your clothes, then you are in the process of improving your image. You are coming to peace with aspects of your past that used to haunt you. See *Clothes.*

Lava Dreams of lava symbolize the melting down of your ego walls. You are dealing with intense passionate feelings that are bubbling up to the surface, and you are allowing suppressed emotions to erupt. See *Breakdown/Breakthrough Dreams,* page 12.

Lavender Dreams of lavender symbolize peacefulness and loyalty. See *Flowers.*

Law Dreams of law symbolize your personal moral code and fixed beliefs that have been a part of your consciousness for as long as you can remember. They may be showing that it is time to reevaluate any rigid ideologies that no longer support your expanding consciousness.

Lawn If you dream of your front lawn, then it represents your outer appearance, ego, or image that you try to keep up so that your neighbors will have a particular opinion of you. If the lawn is well groomed and clean-cut, then you are presenting yourself as a polished, upstanding individual. If your lawn is unruly, and rough around the edges, then so is your self-image. See *Grass.*

Lawn Mower Dreams of a lawn mower signify that you are mowing down obstacles that are in the way of your happiness, joy, and success. You are trimming and manicuring your outward appearance. Sometimes when the outside is well groomed, the inside feels better, and vice versa.

Lawsuit Dreams of a lawsuit signify that you are sorting through feelings of blame and shame. You are shadowboxing with yourself as you try to sort out feelings of guilt and innocence. See *Integration Dreams,* page 10.

Lawyer Depending upon the context and feeling tone, a dream of a lawyer can symbolize the part of you that operates either on your behalf by seeing your innocence, or against you by prosecuting you as guilty. It can also reflect your need for justice and fairness.

Laxative Dreams of a laxative reflect a need for release from negative and toxic thoughts and feelings. They are about your desire to be rid of all that weighs you down.

Lazy Dreams of being lazy represent a coverup for shock, hopeless-ness, despair, and depression, and/or that you are thwarting your desires. Keep in mind that a dream of being lazy may also be a vent-ing dream helping you to release your resistance to taking a break so that you can rejuvenate your passion.

Lead If you dream of the mineral lead, you are asking heavy ques-tions of your higher self regarding the new direction in your life. You may be feeling the weight of the world and feeling pressure to have all the answers. You may be bringing a group of people to-gether, creating a strong bond and the awareness and advancement of the higher vision and goals of yourself and your group.

Leader Dreams of a leader signify confidence and boldness, that you are taking responsibility for your actions, managing your power, and holding a position of influence in your life. If you are following a leader, then this is about your issues with authority figures. You are standing up and taking center stage of your life and are coming into your power.

Leak Dreams of a leak represent a waste, loss, or drain of your en-ergy, and a hole in your power circle. A leak is usually where there is an unhealed wound or shock, and you are realizing that if you don't contain your energy responsibly, then you will become needy of the energy of the people around you. These dreams are a message to take responsibility for your power and greatness.

Learning Dreams of learning are great blessings and lessons. They denote openness, willingness, humility, and desire to grow. To learn in a dream is the whole point of dream interpretation and being on a path of enlightenment. See *School*. See also *Prophetic Dreams,* page 17.

Leather Dreams of leather signify instinctive and primitive feelings, and that you are bringing out your untamed inner animal. If you are wearing leather, then this represents connection to your wild side and that you are feeling sexy, tough, and strong.

Leaves Dreams of leaves symbolize the graceful, vulnerable, and flowing part of you that demonstrates your dance with the winds of change. Leaves also signify abundance and money, and that you feel you are taken care of and protected, shaded from the sun and rain.

Leaves are an outer expression of inner work. If leaves are brown, falling from a tree, or on the ground, then this represents the completion of a cycle, death, and endings. A dream of leaves could also signify a desire to"leave" a relationship or your job.

LED Dreams of LED, light-emitting diodes, represent the future, high-tech energy that knows how to be soft yet powerful. See *Light.*

Leech Dreams of a leech symbolize one-sided relationships, feeling needy or used.

Left Dreams of your left side represent your feminine side, feeling connected to your right brain, which is creative, receptive, intuitive, and also connected with your inner child, your most honest self. The left also symbolizes compassion, democracy, liberal politics, and creative solutions.

Leftovers Dreams of leftover food represent conservation of energy, having a "waste not, want not" mentality. If you are saving something because you are afraid of running out of what you need, then a dream of leftovers is helping you release scarcity consciousness.

Leg Dreams of a leg signify mobility, strength, confidence, motivation, and groundedness, and that you have a support system. Legs represent your ability to stand up for yourself, or walk away from a situation that is harmful to you. If someone is pulling your leg, then that person is lying to you. If you dream that you don't have legs, then the dream reflects that you don't have a leg to stand on, that you are releasing your feelings of powerlessness and insecurity. See *Body.*

Lemon Dreams of a lemon symbolize beauty and bounty. A lemon can also represent bitterness, jealousy, envy, and the pain of not being recognized or of being skipped over. In addition, a lemon can also signify that you are processing a deal that has gone awry or a situation that has failed to fulfill your expectations. See *Fruit* and *Yellow.*

Lemonade Dreams of lemonade symbolize optimism and your ability to look on the bright side of life. You are able to turn lemons into lemonade, or challenges/heartbreaks/disappointments into something sweet and wonderful. You will be successful because of your great attitude. See *Gratitude.*

Lemonade Stand Dreams of a lemonade stand are symbolic of entrepreneurial instincts. They reflect your childlike ability to turn tragedy into triumph.

Lens Dreams of a lens reflect your point of view. If lenses are rose-colored, you are being unrealistically optimistic. If lenses have a crack in them, then you are seeing a distorted perspective. If you have no lenses and are used to wearing them, then you may be blind to what is taking place right in front of you. If you have X-ray lenses, then you are seeing beyond appearances.

Leo Dreams of the astrological sign Leo symbolize your connection to leadership, royalty, passion, heroism, loyalty, narcissism, and a desire for respect. Perhaps it is time to work on being more diplomatic and sensitive to other people's feelings. See *Fire, Lion,* and *Sun.*

Leopard Dreams of a leopard symbolize a protective, defensive, ruthless mothering instinct. A leopard's spots represent eyes, and that you are being vigilant and watchful. See *Cat.*

Leotard Dreams of a leotard signify flexibility, expression, mobility, and freedom, and perhaps that you are feeling exposed. See *Dancing* and *Naked.*

Leprechaun Dreams of a leprechaun signify that you are connected to your magical, childlike essence. You are tapping into the awareness that all things are possible and luck is on your side.

Leprosy Dreams of leprosy represent fear of being abandoned, rejected, and/or made an outcast. You are allowing denial, self-rejection, self-doubt, and self-loathing to eat at you.

Letter Dreams of writing a letter symbolize the expression of your true feelings. If you dream of a venting letter, see *Venting Dreams,* page 8.

Lettuce Dreams of lettuce symbolize money earned in a healthy way. You are learning how to grow money and to become resourceful.

Levitating Dreams of levitating symbolize self-mastery, joy, and an unburdened lightness of being. You are connecting with your soul's essence and your ability to rise above your circumstances to see a higher point of view. See *Flying.*

Libra Dreams of the astrological sign Libra signify that you are connecting with being idealistic and speaking out on behalf of your convictions. This may be giving you the message to cultivate self-confidence and to be cautious of being overly critical and/or indecisive. Embrace mistakes as part of the learning curve of life, and consider the consequences of your actions. Perhaps this is a message for you to weigh and balance the pros and cons of a situation before making a decision.

Library Dreams of a library signify that you are learning, growing, and expanding. A library also represents the power of the written word, stories, and your wealth of inner wisdom and resources. Perhaps you have a desire for knowledge, research, and understanding, and you are realizing that it is accessible to you. See *Book, Internet,* and *World Wide Web.*

Lice Dreams of lice signify that you are picking up mental negativity and letting it fester in your mind. See *Ants* and *Itch.* See also *Venting Dreams,* page 8.

License Dreams of a license signify self-recognition of your status, validation of your worthiness, and that you are giving yourself permission to have authority over your life.

Lid Dreams of a lid symbolize protection, hiding, rigid belief systems, limitation, and preservation. A lid could represent that which keeps you from experiencing your infinite nature and freedom.

Lie To tell a lie in a dream reveals low self-esteem, and that you are attempting to preserve your self-image regarding something you did of which you are ashamed. A dream of a lie could be showing you that someone in your life is lying to you, or that you are lying to yourself.

Lie Detector Dreams of a lie detector represent cynicism, doubt, and distrust. What you are looking for you are looking with, so if you are preoccupied with looking for lies to prove someone else's guilt, you are exposing your own guilt and self-judgment. Alternatively, a dream of a lie detector may indicate that you are using your powers of discernment to read between the lines and lies. Consider the feeling tone of the dream to discern the significance.

Life Coach Dreams of a life coach symbolize your connection with your higher wisdom, authority, objectivity, and empowered viewpoint. It would be wise to follow the guidance that is revealed in these dreams.

Lifeguard Dreams of a lifeguard symbolize heroism, self-sacrifice, and possibly codependence. A lifeguard in a dream also represents your awareness that you are protected by a higher being. See *Angel* and *Hero/Heroine*.

Life Insurance Dreams of life insurance symbolize a fear of death and change. You may be attempting to avoid the inevitable. Also, dreams of life insurance can signify your willingness to take responsibility for your life, for your legacy, and the well-being of your family, and that you are coming to terms with your mortality.

Life Raft Dreams of a life raft symbolize your awareness that you have a helping hand when you need it most, a support system to get you through rocky times. Perhaps you are looking for a sense of safety in the midst of change and tumultuousness. See *Raft*.

Life Support Dreams of life support represent attachment to a form whose time has gone. They symbolize an inability to let go and trust in the life/death/life cycle. Perhaps you are attempting to hold onto or preserve a memory, an identity from the past, or maybe you are incubating while you transform into a new incarnation of yourself. See *I.V.*

Light Dreams of light represent solution, hope, faith, grace, intuition, awakening, confidence, and connection to your higher power. They are reminding you that the divine spark within you will lead you through whatever challenging situations you face.

Lightbulb Dreams of a lightbulb signify that you are coming into an awakened "aha" consciousness, and becoming receptive to the solutions you have been seeking.

Lighter Dreams of a lighter represent a catalyst. You are igniting, initiating, and evoking energy and power into your life. You are deliberately activating and accelerating spirit energy.

Lighthouse Dreams of a lighthouse signify inspiration, and that you are being reminded of who you really are and why you are here. They are also a warning to use the light of your awareness to circumvent challenging circumstances.

Lightning Dreams of lightning, or of a lightning bolt, symbolize masculine virility, a sudden realization, a great idea, or change, as well as a reminder that you are connected with the divine.

Lightning Rod Dreams of a lightning rod signify that you are becoming masterful in your abilities to direct energy and power into manifestation. You are becoming a more powerful vessel.

Limb Dreams of a limb signify an extension of yourself. You are reaching for your goals, for connection/intimacy in your relationships, or support and partnership in your business. You are going out on a limb, taking chances and risks. See *Arm* and *Gambling*.

Limousine Dreams of a limousine signify that you are driving through life in style, stretching out in the lap of luxury, feeling deserving of wealth and extravagance. You are allowing yourself to be driven, trusting that you will end up where you need to go. See *Car*. See also *Wish Fulfillment Dreams,* page 18.

Line If you are waiting in a line, then the dream is about your feelings about having to wait for what you want in life. Perhaps you are developing patience as you deal with feelings of deservability, status, and rank. If you step out of line or cut into line, then this represents disrespect of the rules and/or a desire to rebel and have your own way. If there is a straight line, then this signifies that you have an organized strategy to manifest a certain outcome.

Linen Dreams of linen symbolize elegance, good taste, and a desire to be nurtured. See *Clothes*.

Lingerie Dreams of lingerie signify sensuality and seduction, and that you are accentuating and embellishing your feminine power, appeal, and allure. Because lingerie is mostly hidden from view, it signifies that you are hiding a sexy secret and/or manipulating someone with your sensuality.

Link Dreams of a link symbolize connection, networking, interdependence, and integration. They may be showing you that you are an important, vital, irreplaceable link in the chain of humanity. If you dream of clicking on a link that takes you to a Web site, you are exploring new terrain, and opening a new portal and dimension of yourself.

Lion Dreams of a lion signify the king or queen of the jungle, leadership, an alpha, dominant personality, and that you are brave and courageous. Perhaps you are feeling protective of your mate and children. See *Animal* and *Leo.*

Liposuction Dreams of liposuction represent perfectionism, a desire to trim the fat from your life and eliminate excess, and all that weighs you down. If you dream of having liposuction, then you are willing to take drastic measures to have a pattern changed in your life. See *Cosmetic Surgery.*

Lips Dreams of lips represent kissing, talking, speaking, communication, connection, and intimacy. If the lips of someone are appealing to you, then this can represent that you like what the person has to say. If the lips are unappealing, then you are not in resonance with the person. See *Kiss.*

Lipstick Dreams of lipstick signify a desire to be noticed, and that you may be embellishing the stories you tell. See *Cosmetics.*

Litter If you dream of a litter of kittens, puppies, or other infant animals, then this represents the abundant wisdom of your most vulnerable, animal aspect and instinct. If you dream of garbage being littered, then this is about carelessness, disregard for others, and procrastination. See *Garbage.*

Lizard Dreams of a lizard, or any reptile, signify that you are in touch with your primitive survival instincts, and your ability to change and shed your skin in order to stay alive. In some cultures, especially in West Africa, mythology speaks of reptiles taking, fetching, or stealing fire from the sun, which means that you might feel that your energy is being drained or disempowered by a person or situation in your life. See *Chakra* (1st and 2nd) and *Snake.*

Load Dreams of a load symbolize that you are feeling burdened, pressured, and overwhelmed with responsibility. A dream of a load is giving you the message that it is time for you to share your burden. See *Codependence.*

Loaf Dreaming of a loaf of bread is about abundance and sustenance, and that you are being spiritually and emotionally fed. The dream can also be showing you where you feel that you are loafing, being lazy, unproductive, and procrastinating.

Lobster Dreams of a lobster's large claws signify that you are feeling the need for protection. Dreaming of eating a lobster for a meal signifies that you have rich taste. See *Wish Fulfillment Dreams,* page 18.

Lock Dreams of a lock, a locked box, a locker, a locked door, or a locked treasure chest symbolize both virginity and a real or imagined need for secrecy and privacy. A lock could also represent the need for a solution. See *Drawer* and *Key.*

Locket Dreams of a locket symbolize a secret that empowers you, as in a secret love or an admirer. Because a locket is worn around the neck, it is associated with your fifth chakra, your throat center, which could represent telepathic communication between you and the person pictured in a locket. See *Keepsake* and *Throat.*

Lockjaw Dreams of lockjaw signify anger or stress clamping your jaw shut, or that you are not trusting your true expression. Your subconscious mind is giving you permission to ask for what you want or need.

Locust A dream of a locust symbolizes the fear of having things taken from you, fear of wasting time, or fear of losing an opportunity. This venting dream is helping you to release negative self-judgments that are eating away at you and diminishing your progress. It is reassuring you that there is no such thing as wasted time.

Log Dreams of burning a log represent a slow-burning passion that sustains over time. Building with logs denotes that you are creating a solid relationship or a venture that can support your dreams and desires.

Lost Dreams of feeling lost signify that you are venting out feelings of insecurity and powerlessness while you are in the midst of a transition or transformation. Keep in mind that it is typical and healthy to feel unfamiliar, awkward, or out of your element as you integrate into your next level of evolution. Or perhaps you are lost because you've not taken the high road. Dreams of feeling lost may be a message to rethink your steps, and travel mindfully from this point forward. See *Abandonment.*

Lotion Dreams of lotion represent the need to lubricate a situation and soften the rough edges. You are realizing you need to moisten, smooth over, or heal hard feelings.

Lottery Dreams of the lottery symbolize good luck. If you dream of lottery numbers, it would be wise to write them down and take your chances. Dreams of winning the lottery signify great abundance and/or love coming into your life. See *Gambling*. See also *Wish Fulfillment Dreams,* page 18.

Lotus Flower Dreams of a lotus flower symbolize transformation; from the mud of your deepest existential pain grow the most beautiful insights. The lotus flower is also the throne of many eastern deities, such as Ganesh, Kwan Yin, and the Buddha, which signifies that enlightenment comes from walking through our greatest heartaches and challenges. See *Flowers* and *Phoenix*.

Loud If a sound or a voice is particularly loud in a dream, then an important message is being conveyed. Consider what the sound represents. If a sound is dissonant, then a dream of it is helping to amplify that which is no longer working for you so that it can be addressed and corrected. If a sound is melodious, then the dream is amplifying that which is already working in your life.

Loudspeaker Dreams of an announcement coming over a loudspeaker mean an important message is being broadcast for you. Consider what the message is and who is delivering it.

Love Feelings of love in a dream represent connection, integration, understanding, healing, and forgiveness. If you are dreaming of falling in love, feeling a familial bond, or simply having fond feelings for someone, you are recognizing an aspect of yourself in the mirror of another person's soul that you appreciate and value in yourself. Experiencing the sensation of love in a dream is always auspicious and a forecast of wonderful things to come, and that your heart is opening.

Lover Dreams about a lover symbolize feelings of desire, passion, sex, and romance. Your best self is reflected in your lover.

Love Seat Dreams of a love seat symbolize flirtation and romance. Sitting in close proximity to someone is an indication of intimacy, either emotional, physical, or both.

Low-class Dreams of someone or something being what you would label as "low-class" reflect low self-esteem, or a defeatist attitude. Keep in mind that there is a seed of greatness within you and everyone, and this may be your wake-up call to reconnect to your passion, purpose, and magnificence.

Lower Back Dreams of a lower back symbolize support and financial issues. If you dream of a strong, muscular back, then this signifies a healthy financial situation. If you dream of a back that is decrepit or in pain, then this signifies financial insecurity.

Low Tide Dreams of low tide symbolize a recession of energy, as in the inevitability of an inhale after an exhale. In a dream of low tide, you are experiencing the temporary feeling of emptiness and releasing so that you can later become full. Perhaps you are grappling with a relationship, job, or financial situation that is receding. Keep in mind that this stage is not permanent. A low tide experience can actually be joyous if it is embraced in its proper context.

Lozenges Dreams of lozenges symbolize aid and support in your expression. You are clearing the way to express your true feelings.

LSD Dreams of LSD signify that you are exploring different realms of consciousness and getting to know the universal you, love, and the feeling of being interconnected with all of life. Your subconscious mind is making you aware that addiction to spiritual practices is healthy for you, and the source never runs out, and the high just keeps getting better. See *Drugs*.

Lucid Dreams Being conscious during the dream state represents a high level of mastery. You are realizing an ability to powerfully orchestrate your life that will help you achieve clarity and empowerment.

Luck To feel lucky or to receive a lucky break in a dream is a symbol of being in the flow of serendipity in your life. To feel fortunate and charmed is a sign that you are in sync with the bounty of this universe and that you are on track and aligned with your highest destiny.

Luggage Dreams of luggage symbolize memories, heartaches, unresolved feelings, attachments to the past, and incomplete communications that you are carrying with you. The heavier the baggage, the more unresolved the emotional business you have. Consider the contents of the luggage. Your subconscious mind is giving you the message to resolve your issues so that your load can be light and your karmic debt can be resolved.

Lumber Dreams of lumber symbolize your resources and uncultivated raw materials/talent within you.

Lunch Food of any kind symbolizes the intake of energy, information, power. Lunch can particularly symbolize a social occasion or a business gathering. Consider what and with whom you are eating. See *Food*.

Luxury Dreams of luxury, wealth, and extravagance can be a statement of your current life circumstances or a desire for a more lavish lifestyle. See *Wish Fulfillment Dreams,* page 18.

M

Mace Dreams of mace signify protection and fear of being in and around adverse circumstances, and that you are on the defensive. You are feeling that you have a secret weapon up your sleeve, a dream of mace is cautioning you to use your power discriminately.

Machine See *Robot*.

Madonna If a dream is of the Material Girl pop star, then you are tapping into your rebellious creativity and transforming/reinventing yourself. If a dream is of the Virgin Mary, then this signifies your connection to the divine mother, your feminine power, and the purest and most powerful aspect of your maternal instincts. See *Goddess*.

Mafia A dream of the mafia symbolizes your willingness to resort to force and intimidation to get what you want or need. Perhaps you are experiencing feelings of loyalty, betrayal, or the need for retribution for a family member.

Magazine Dreams of a magazine signify education, voyeurism, sensationalism, and that you may be putting someone on a pedestal. If you dream of seeing your picture in a magazine, then this forecasts status and success. If it is a tabloid magazine, then you are identifying with the drama of celebrities and the archetypes they represent. Consider whom you are reading about. See *Celebrity* and *Newspaper*.

Magician Dreams of a magician signify that you are becoming aware of your mystical potential and your ability to manifest results out of thin air. They are about out-of-the-box thinking, and your untapped potential to create the circumstances in your life that you desire. See *Miracle*.

Magnet Dreams of a magnet symbolize attraction, seduction, influence, and an ability to draw people, places, and opportunities to you. Or they may be showing you that you've been magnetized by someone's charm.

Magnifying Glass Dreams of seeing things through a magnifying glass signify your ability to really know what is going on in your life, and that you desire to see the microscopic truth. Alternatively, they may be showing you that you are overanalyzing and/or blowing things out of proportion.

Maid Dreams of a maid denote that you have connected with helpful energy to assist you in cleaning out your inner house, as in your body, and body of affairs. Also, they may be telling you to clean up your act and get your affairs in order.

Mail Dreams of letters or packages symbolize hopes about receiving a desirable communication, unexpected surprises, unexpressed feelings and emotions. Take note of the feeling tone of the dream. If you feel energized and delighted at the mail or package, this means you are hopeful about news of fortuitous events. If you are disappointed or anxious, then you are apprehensive about a decision. See *E-mail* or *Letter*.

Mailman Dreaming of a mailman signifies that someone in your life will be delivering news to you, or you will be the one making the delivery.

Makeover Dreams of a makeover symbolize transformation, an opportunity to begin anew. You desire to be better and stronger. These dreams display your willingness to put your best foot forward and to make the most of what you've been given.

Makeup See *Cosmetics*.

Mall Dreams of a mall symbolize either a "have" or a "have not" consciousness. Because a mall has all that you desire and could materially wish for, dreams of a mall signify that you are shopping for ideas about what kind of life/relationship/job you want to have. See *Shopping* and *Spending*.

Malt Dreams of a malt denote your just desserts, a treat, reward, or compliment.

Man In general, dreams of a man symbolize masculine energy, power, force, initiation, strength, manifesting, decisiveness, and the focus to make things happen in the world. They can also represent the masculine energy within a man or woman. If you dream of a man you know, then consider the qualities he represents and what he means to you. See *Brother, Father, Husband,* and *King*.

Mandala Dreams of a mandala signify that things are coming full circle for you, that you are coming into balance and into your power. See *Circle* and *Medicine Wheel*.

Mannequin Dreams of a mannequin symbolize the desire for an unattainable ideal, superficiality, a desire for outer beauty at the expense of an inner life or a connection to your soul. See *Model*.

Manners Dreams of manners signify constraint and respect, and that you are grappling with your authentic expression versus what is socially or politically correct.

Mansion Dreams of a mansion signify wealth and prosperity, and that you are entering greater levels of your potential, power, creativity, and spiritual authority. See *Wish Fulfillment Dreams,* page 18.

Manufacturing Dreams of manufacturing symbolize creation and manifestation. You are realizing that the power to make your dreams come true is in your own hands.

Manure Dreams of manure signify your connection to the cycles of life, and that you are realizing that your challenges are giving rise to new growth, wisdom, and power. See *Feces* and *Fertilizer*.

Manuscript Dreams of a manuscript denote your awareness that you are the author of the story of your life. If you don't like the direction it is going in, you can right/write it. You are realizing that the power to have the life of your dreams is in your hands.

Map Dreams of a map signify that you are getting your bearings and a sense of where you are and where you are going in life. They show you that you desire certainty, direction, and guidance.

Marathon Dreams of a marathon denote a great accomplishment, achievement, or goal. You are putting yourself to the test and going the distance to prove yourself worthy.

Marble Dreams of marble represent lucidity and total recall of your dreams. You may be delving into previously unused aspects of yourself and actualizing your desires. If you dream of playing with marbles, then this signifies that you have a playful nature and are willing to take a risk. If you dream of collecting marbles, then you are aware of the inner resources that you've acquired. If you dream of losing your marbles, then you are feeling that you are losing touch with your past.

March If you dream of marching in a line or a squad, then you are supporting the whole, being a team player, making music with a community which may be a sacrifice to your individuality. If you dream of the month of March, then you are planting seeds of intentions for your future. See *Drum*.

Mardi Gras Dreams of Mardi Gras represent a desire to sow your wild oats. Perhaps you've been indulging in a decadent lifestyle and your subconscious mind is bringing your attention to your need for balance. However, if your life tips too far to the conservative edge, then a dream of a Mardi Gras may be suggesting that it may do you good to live on the wild side for a moment. See *Las Vegas*.

Margarita Dreams of this alcoholic beverage symbolize fun and festivities. See *Alcohol*.

Marijuana Dreams of marijuana represent a desire for an escape from reality, for an exploration of other dimensions of yourself, to feel high, and perhaps to find the humor in life. See *Drugs*.

Marriage Dreams of marriage symbolize integration and the embrace of opposites, such as the masculine and feminine aspects of yourself. If you are married, then dreaming of marriage may be a processing dream about the current circumstances you and your spouse are grappling with. If you are not married, then a dream of marriage may represent your desires and hopes for what your idealized marriage would look and/or feel like. See *Commitment, Vows,* and *Weddings*. See also *Wish Fulfillment Dreams,* page 18, and *Integration Dreams,* page 10.

Mars Dreaming of the planet Mars represents impetuousness, machismo, and immaturity. Mars was the god of war, so a dream of Mars signifies that you are dealing with feelings of hostility with regards to your convictions, beliefs, and passions. Also, if you are feeling at odds with your mate, the dream might be referencing the saying "Men are from Mars, women are from Venus," representing that your differences are also the very qualities that magnetize you together.

Marshmallow Dreams of a marshmallow represent that which is soft, sugary, sweet, and feminine. You are feeling deserving of a treat and/or reward. See *Pillow.*

Martha Stewart Dreams of Martha Stewart can represent resourcefulness, creativity, and a desire for the illusion of domestic perfection. Also, they could be about making sure that your insides match your outsides. See *Goddess* (Hestia).

Martyr Dreams of a martyr symbolize sacrifice, injustice, righteousness, selflessness, heroism, worthiness, and victimhood. See *Victim.*

Mascara Because your eyes are the windows of your soul, dreams of mascara signify that you are calling attention to your eyes, and to your point of view.

Mask Dreams of a mask represent a desire to be uninhibited. A mask can represent shame about your authentic self, fear that you are not good enough, powerful enough, or strong enough, and that you are unwilling to be authentic and naked. Keep in mind that sometimes the wearing of a mask is a necessary step of evolution until your ego has integrated the power the mask symbolizes, at which point the mask is no longer necessary. Masks also represent ancient symbols of power, evoking the medicine (qualities) of the gods/goddesses they represent.

Masquerade Dreams of a masquerade signify secrets, mystery, tricks and manipulation and that you are exploring different dimensions of your being and are playing a role. See *Halloween, Mardi Gras,* and *Mask.*

Massage/Masseur Dreams of a massage are about recuperation, revitalization, or working something out in your mind. Dreams of a masseur symbolize healing. They may be a signal for you to release tension and stress in your life and to take action to find your balance and natural rhythm.

Mass Production Dreams of mass production symbolize wealth, success, efficiency, and organization. See *Manufacturing*.

Master Dreams of a master signify that you've been cultivating your natural genius and are coming into your power and influence. They can also help you to vent out power struggles you have within yourself, in a relationship, or with someone at work. Consider the possibility that you are dealing with issues of having "power over" someone, or perhaps someone is lording his or her power over you.

MasterCard See *Credit Card*.

Masturbation Dreams of masturbation signify that you are embracing the beauty of your own sexuality, and realizing that the key to self-pleasure lies in your own hands. Alternatively, you may be processing conflicting issues of guilt and desire. Consider the feeling tone of the dream.

Match.com Dreams of Match.com symbolize your desire to meet someone special and to expand your circle of possibilities. They also signify your awareness that you are connected to a much larger playing field than your normal day-to-day reality. You are looking for love, feeling lucky, and hopeful that love is on the way. See *Online*. See also *Wish Fulfillment Dreams,* page 18.

Matches If you dream of playing with matches, you are playing with fire and taking chances where the risks are great. Perhaps you realize that you could get burned with your risky behavior. Alternatively, dreaming of matches suggests a desire for partnership and to meet your match.

Math Dreams of math represent order, logic, reasoning, and your attempt to make sense of your current situation and find resolution. You are coming upon the solution to what used to be a problem. See *Number*.

Matrix Dreams of a matrix are about your awareness of the conditioning that binds you to the system you live in, whether it is your financial system, family system, or the belief system of the collective consciousness. To become aware of a matrix represents objectivity and lucidity; the ability to disidentify with your circumstances; to be in this world, but not of it.

May The month of May is synonymous with flowers, Mother's Day, and your celebration of the feminine within you. See *Mother* and *Spring*.

Mayonnaise Dreams of mayonnaise signify that you are spreading it on thick, adding texture and substance to a situation or story, and/or embellishing the truth for a desired effect.

Mayor Dreams of a mayor symbolize your relationship with a role of responsibility, respect, and of decision maker. They may be telling you that it is time to take charge of your life because major changes will come as a result of your willingness to take responsibility for your life.

Maze Dreams of a maze signify a course of initiation, and that you are testing your ability to put your problem-solving abilities to the test. They may also be telling you that it is time to exit from a career, relationship, or habit pattern that is getting you nowhere. Consider the feeling tone.

McDonald's Dreams of McDonald's are about a quick fix to satiate your hunger (physical or emotional) that if indulged in too often could be harmful to your health. For many people, McDonald's symbolizes nostalgia for an age of innocence, a place where you can order a "Happy Meal" and make all your worries go away.

Meadow Dreams of a meadow signify that you are connecting with your inner sanctuary, where you can replenish your energy, seek solace, and find your answers. They are revealing an expansive place of beauty that resides within you, and that you are connecting with your soul.

Mean If someone is mean in a dream, it is your shadow expressing itself, the part of you that is critical about any negative belief you hold about yourself. The dream is an attempt to integrate your inner victim with your inner critic or judge. See *Witch*. See also *Integration Dreams,* page 10.

Measles Dreams of measles signify that you are venting out fears, anxieties, overwhelm, and victimhood. You are itching for a solution to a current dilemma.

Measuring Dreams of measuring denote comparison and competition. You are checking your progress, weighing and evaluating yourself against a preconceived standard. See *Critic* and *Jealousy.*

Meat Dreams of meat, if you are not a vegetarian, symbolize your desire and ability to nurture and provide for your well-being. If you are a vegetarian, then dreaming of eating meat signifies a desire to fulfill a neglected longing, or it could be venting out guilt or shame. Also meat denotes substance and a desire to get to the meat of the situation. See *Food* and *Protein.*

Mechanic If your car is your vehicle through life, then dreams of a mechanic symbolize energy that can help you to get through life more powerfully and repair problems regarding your forward momentum along your life's path. They may be a sign for you to check your fluids and consider whether you are drinking and eating properly. Consider the thoughts with which you are fueling yourself. It may be time for an overhaul of your thought system. See *Car.*

Medal Dreams of a medal signify honor, esteem, and courage, and that you are excelling and becoming worthy of recognition. A victory is in your midst.

Media Dreams of the media represent public aggrandizement. If it is good press, then you are aggrandizing and projecting larger-than-life qualities upon yourself or someone else. If it is bad press, then this is a blown-up version of gossip. A dream of the media may be a projection of your own future success. See *Wish Fulfillment Dreams,* page 18.

Mediation Dreams of mediation represent your attempt at integrating opposite aspects of yourself that have conflicting needs. See *Integration Dreams,* page 10.

Medicine Dreams of medicine are about a solution, a remedy, and your ability to solve or fix a current problem/challenge.

Medicine Wheel A Native American medicine wheel is a very powerful ceremonial symbol that represents a container of all the elements (air, fire, water, and earth). If you dream of being in the middle of a medicine wheel, then this signifies protection, balance, and blessings, and that you are connecting with the mystical in the midst of the mundane. See *North, South, East,* and *West.*

Meditation Dreaming of meditating represents objectivity, clarity, lucidity, and a desire to become awake and conscious in the dream state. You are in an advanced level of self-awareness, and are connecting with your infinite source of guidance, support, direction, and solutions.

Meeting If you are meeting someone in a dream, then this is about integrating one aspect of yourself with another. Consider the feeling tone. See *Integration Dreams,* page 10.

Megaphone A dream of a megaphone signifies that you are wanting to make an announcement and share your spirit, wanting to cheer so all the world can hear. Consider the message of the dream and if it is a message for you to heed.

Melon Dreams of a melon can symbolize a woman's full breasts, great opulence, delicious abundance, sensuality, and sexuality. See *Fruit.*

Melting Dreams of melting represent empathy and compassion. You are releasing preconceived ideas, limited thoughts, and obstructions to happiness. Your ego walls are dissolving in the midst of passion or the heat of transformation. See *Alchemist/Alchemy.* See also *Breakdown/Breakthrough Dreams,* page 12.

Men A dream of a club or pack of men symbolizes power and strength in numbers, force, and manifestation. You are realizing the power of persuasion. See *Man* and *Secret Society.*

Mending Dreams of mending signify that you are repairing a relationship, healing a wound, or remedying a situation. You are realizing the power of forgiveness. See *Sewing.*

Menopause Dreams of menopause symbolize the completion of a cycle. You are grappling with issues of desirability. This breakdown/breakthrough dream is about releasing attachment to youth, fears of aging, and no longer being sexy. You are in the midst of a transformative chapter of your life, and are discovering the wisdom that comes from age and perspective. See *Crone.*

Menstruation Dreams of menstruation denote clarity, sensitivity, and intuition, and that you are in a powerful and sensitive time in your life, feeling full and fertile with regard to your projects and relationships. You are feeling connected to your source and to your life blood, releasing negative thoughts, beliefs, and physical or emotional toxins that stand in the way of your healthiest expression. You are in the flow of life, fully experiencing the ebbs and flows, and highs and lows. See *Blood* and *PMS*.

Menu Dreams of a menu symbolize the choices you have in life with regard to a situation you are in. Your subconscious mind is giving you the suggestion to make decisions that feed and nourish your mind, body, and soul. Consider what is on the menu, and the item(s) you choose.

Mercury Dreams of the planet Mercury signify that you are swiftly adapting to changes in your life. Also, a message is being sent to you, and you would be wise to pay attention. If you dream of Mercury in retrograde, then this is a message for you to slow down and take time for introspection; there may be a challenge in your midst or a change in the air. If you dream of the metal mercury, then this represents that you are adapting and integrating your internal drives and external desires. The dream may be showing you that you have a whimsical nature that is quick, changeable, volatile, indecisive, and impetuous.

Mermaid Dreams of a mermaid symbolize your divine feminine essence, the aspect of you that is an aficionado of the deep end of your emotions and unconscious feelings and desires. They may be telling you to embrace your emotions and/or to dive into the uncertain waters of a romantic relationship.

Message Messages in dreams come in a myriad of forms. Whether your dreamtime message comes via bottle, telephone, answering machine, voice mail, FedEx, UPS, or a singing telegram, pay close attention to the literal and figurative aspects of it. Consider what the message is and who is sending it. See *Mail* and *Mailman*.

Metal Dreams of this conductor of energy symbolize heaviness, strength, rigid beliefs, and an unbending will. They are also about the transmission of information, electricity, and the amplification of energy. If something is testing your *mettle,* you are being challenged to see how strong, committed, and smart you really are.

Metal Detector Dreams of a metal detector symbolize that you are looking for either treasure or for fault. You may be feeling cynical as you look for a hidden agenda and/or you may be feeling on the defensive, wanting to see with X-ray eyes. Perhaps you are testing your mettle to detect how solid you really are.

Metro-sexual A dream of a male who is man enough to care for his appearance is about the balance of masculine and feminine energy. It is allowing the masculine part of you out into the light of day to get primped and primed, and sanding off the rough edges of your rugged masculine exterior and interior. Or it may be showing you that you are spending too much time caring for your exterior, and not enough time caring for your most essential, interior self.

Mexican/Mexico Dreams of a Mexican or of Mexico symbolize passion, music, devotion to family values and Catholicism, and an easy, relaxed lifestyle that includes a daily "siesta." They may be giving you the message to live for today, and to stop putting quality time with friends and family on a layaway plan.

Microphone Dreams of a microphone denote that you are finding your voice, your desire to be heard, and the passion to express yourself publicly. They also represent confidence, and the fact that you are ready to present yourself to the world. See *Loud*.

Microscope Dreams of a microscope signify that you have a critical eye, and that you are fascinated with the details of your life. Alternatively, they might reflect that you are micromanaging your life and it would benefit you to step back and get a glimpse of the big picture so as to not sweat the small stuff.

Microwave Oven Dreams of a microwave oven signify that things are heating up from the inside out in a relationship or business venture. They may be drawing your attention to your desire for instant gratification that could sacrifice the quality of what you are doing.

Middle Dreams of being in the middle of a situation signify focus and attention, and that you hold an important position in life. Dreams of being in the middle represent connectivity, a bridge between two polarities, and/or your being a translator. If you feel torn because you are in the middle of a situation that is pulling at you, a dream of being in the middle is showing you where there is a need for emotional and psychological integration of your extremes as well as your boundaries. See *Center*.

Middle Age Dreams of middle age symbolize wisdom, power, authority, and the capability to be in this world yet not of it. See *Crone*.

Middle Class Dreams of the middle class signify that you are either connecting with or rebelling against the collective consciousness and the status quo.

Middle East Dreams of the Middle East represent turbulence, unrest, soulfulness, spirit, passion, survival issues, and strong opinions. They are revealing that you have the ego strength to defend your opinions and grapple with tribal issues such as loyalty, customs, religion, and history.

Midnight Dreams of the bewitching hour signify that you are feeling between worlds as you transform from one phase of your life to the next. At midnight, the veil between worlds is thin, as well as the veil between your conscious mind and unconscious mind. See *Twelve*.

Midol Dreaming of this menstrual cramp pain reliever is about coping with the pain of releasing attachments to old forms and shedding old beliefs. It is helping you to release your resistance to being in the flow. See *Band-Aid, Menstruation,* or *PMS*.

Midwife Dreams of a midwife signify that you have support to assist you through the birthing process of a new chapter of your life, a new creative project, a new relationship, or a new incarnation of yourself. This is a message for you to handle change in a natural, organic, and feminine way. See *Angel, Birth,* and *Infant*.

Migraine Dreams of a migraine signify imbalance, a distrust of the organic flow of your life and fear of the future outcome of your current choices, and that you are feeling pressured to figure it all out logically. They are revealing that you are experiencing too much mental stress, and that the answers you seek will come when your mind is relaxed.

Mile Dreams of a mile symbolize the distance you have to travel to have compassion for another's plight; you have to walk a mile in someone else's shoes to understand that person. You are nearly at your destination.

Military Dreams of the military denote strict, rigid discipline and self-criticism. They signify that you are feeling defensive and under verbal or physical attack.

Milk Dreams of milk represent feminine nurturing of the heart, mind, body, and soul. They are showing you that you have the sustenance to make it through life. Dreaming of milk might also signify incomplete issues with your mother, that you are perhaps feeling as though you did not get enough nurturing when you needed it and your dream may be assisting you in filling this need. Consider the feeling tone of the dream to discern the significance. See *Mother*.

Milking Dreams of milking a cow or of milking a situation signify that you are taking advantage of the resources available to you. You are getting fed and filled up by the resources of another. These dreams may be giving you the message to find your own source.

If you dream of breast feeding, see *Breast Feeding* and *Milk*.

Mill Dreams of a mill signify that you are processing feelings and thoughts. You are coming to realize that adversity becomes a blessing in disguise when you funnel your experience toward your path of learning, as in grist for the mill.

Millennium Dreams of the millennium signify that you are at a turning point, a crossroads, and a threshold of transformation. See *Time*.

Mine Dreams of a mine signify that you are looking for answers and solutions, and are bringing the riches of your unconscious to the level of your consciousness. You are plumbing the depth of the treasures, wisdom, and potential of your being, and are exploring your rich spiritual inheritance.

Mineral Dreams of a mineral symbolize the substance of your being. You are getting down to basics and taking care of your most essential self. Dreaming of a mineral is giving you the message to treat yourself as if you were precious.

Minister Dreams of a minister symbolize your higher self. Perhaps you are connecting with your spiritual identity and authority, and are becoming aware of your spiritual beliefs. Or perhaps you are venting or processing your feelings and associations with religious leadership.

Mink Dreams of mink symbolize luxury, sexiness, extravagance, and the sacrifices one must make in order to have a lavish lifestyle.

Miracle This prophetic dream represents your ability to perceive beyond the confines of your five senses. You are realizing your ability to connect with divine guidance, angelic assistance, and to have the faith that all is well. See *Prophetic Dreams,* page 17, or *Wish Fulfillment Dreams,* page 18.

Mirror Dreams of a mirror suggest self-analysis, awareness, self-consciousness, and a preoccupation with how others see you. They are a reality check about your public image, a lucid moment filled with insight about your patterns of behavior.

Miser Dreams of a miser signify that you are venting out your fears of loss, lack, greed, deceit, limitation, and victimization. They are helping you to release the negative attachments and associations you have with and about money and support. See *Venting Dreams,* page 8.

Mist Dreams of mist denote an unwillingness and/or inability to see what is right in front of your face. Perhaps you have a fear of seeing the truth, which produces mental confusion. The feeling of a light mist also represents that you are connected to the mystical, magical, mysterious realm of enchantment within your own being. Consider the feeling tone.

Mistake Dreams of making a mistake signify that you are grappling with your own self-judgments, criticisms, and issues of perfectionism and forgiveness for having made a mistake, or of having been "wronged." They may be reassuring you that there is really no such thing as a mistake as long as you learn from what you do and keep moving forward.

Mistletoe Dreams of the Christmas tradition of kissing under the mistletoe symbolize romance, love, and passion. Don't be surprised if someone unexpected is coming your way to bring you a gift.

MLM Dreams of MLM, a multilevel marketing organization, signify opportunistic thinking, strategy, team building, sales, and that the success of one person means the success of everyone. They may be helping you to process fears of being seduced and manipulated, or of your own opportunistic tendencies.

Moat Dreams of a moat denote withdrawal, self-imposed isolation, and protection. They could also be exposing that you've been rejecting of yourself and others because of your unhealed emotional wounds.

Mob Dreams of a mob symbolize dissonance within yourself among all your many sub-personalities. Also, they may be cautioning you to be alert to the brainwashing that takes place when you are in a large group of people, and to be willing to maintain your sense of self. See *Group*.

Mobile Dreams of a mobile symbolize balance, harmony, and synergy. A mobile can also represent a tribe, family, group of people in your life, or energies within yourself that are interdependent yet intrinsically connected to one another. A mobile may be showing you that as one element moves, the rest of the mobile must shift and adjust to regain balance and mobility.

Model Dreams of a fashion model symbolize motivation and inspiration and an ideal to aspire toward. They may also be showing you that you are overreaching, and thus finding yourself discontent with what you have or who you are. Dreaming of a model home, building, or car represents the focal point you need to manifest your heart's desires. See *Mannequin*. See also *Wish Fulfillment Dreams*, page 18.

Molasses Dreams of molasses signify that you are feeling stuck and are consumed with fear that paralyzes your progress and growth. You are grappling with old patterns, sticky relationships, and gooey attachments that make it difficult to move forward. However, sometimes taking your time and enjoying the process of every rich moment can be sweet. See *Quicksand*.

Mold Dreams of mold symbolize old, rotted beliefs and ideologies. If you are breaking the mold, you are creating your own, unique path through life. If you are creating a mold, then you are connecting with your unique creative genius.

Money Dreams of money symbolize energy, power, and resources and the fact that success and prosperity is within your reach. You are feeling confident, potent, lovable, and valuable, worthy of respect, status, esteem, and success in the material world. To dream of losing money signifies that you are dealing with financial challenges and setbacks. To dream of stealing money signifies that you are feeling desperate and are in survival mode. To dream of having lots of money signifies a consciousness of wealth, and that you are preparing for great prosperity. If you dream of not having enough money, then you are venting out poverty consciousness.

Monk Dreams of a monk symbolize spiritual devotion, connection to spirit, and the aspect of you that is service oriented, altruistic, selfless, and generous, detached from the confines of your ego.

Monkey Dreams of a monkey represent playfulness, mischief, and freedom. The Hindu god Hanuman is said to be immortal and the link between humans and God. Dreams of a monkey as well can symbolize the freedom that leads to divine vision. A monkey can also represent frivolity, impulsivity, monkey business, goofing around, and that you are not taking life seriously.

Moon Dreaming of the moon evokes the ancient symbol of the stages of the feminine—maiden, maid, and crone. The moon symbolizes your connection to your intuition, mystery, passion, and soul. If a moon is new (a crescent), then this represents a time of new beginnings, and therefore a good time to set intentions for your life. If a moon is full, then this represents a time to celebrate what you have already accomplished and to acknowledge how far you've come. A full moon can also represent heightened feelings, even *luna*cy. See *Ocean* or *Water*.

Morning Dreams of the morning signify a new beginning, that you have a clean slate, a fresh perspective. Morning also represents your connection to youth, virginity, and inspiration.

Morph When someone or something in a dream starts one way and ends up another, this is about revealing a deeper significance or a layered meaning.

Mortgage Dreams of a mortgage denote that you are building up personal equity, status, self-esteem, confidence, strength, territory, and that you are acquiring energetic property, or owning your power. They could also be about feeling burdened by your obligations.

Mosquito Dreams of a mosquito signify that someone or something is subtly draining your energy without you knowing it. See *Vampire*.

Moss Dreams of moss signify that you are riding on the coattails of someone else's glory, clinging on, attaching yourself to a project or a relationship where you may or may not be welcome. Also, they may be telling you to watch out for hangers-on.

Moth Dreams of a moth signify that you have been hopelessly drawn to passionate flings and/or dangerous situations like a moth to a flame, and are being burned by your compulsive desires. You are looking for light, love, and inspiration.

Mother Dreaming of a mother varies in its interpretation depending upon your relationship with your mother, your view of motherhood, and whether your separation from your mother was graceful or traumatic. In general, dreams of a mother, or of your mother, are about unconditional love, spirit, life, protection, nurturing or the lack thereof. Consider if you feel that your most tender feelings are being taken care of and nurtured adequately. A dream of a mother may signify that it is time for you to cultivate your own inner mothering skills. See *Goddess* (Demeter).

Mother-in-law Dreams of a mother-in-law reflect your issues of worthiness.

Motorcycle Dreams of a motorcycle signify freedom, adventure, machismo, rebellion, independence, sexuality, youthful vigor, a passionate drive, and that you are throwing care to the wind. You embody the motto If You're Not Living on the Edge, You're Taking Up Too Much Room.

Mountain If you dream of climbing a mountain, then you are traversing challenges in your life, surmounting a goal or challenge. If you are at the top of a mountain, then you have achieved your goal. If you are at the base of a mountain, you are just beginning to take on a new challenge.

Mouse Dreaming of a mouse may be showing you that you are being nitpicky, scrutinizing every detail, or that perhaps you have been careless with dotting i's and crossing t's. It is showing you the importance in being detail oriented, organized, and focused. You may be feeling small and insecure. Consider the feeling tone.

Mousetrap Dreams of a mousetrap signify that you are being set up, or that you are setting a trap for someone else to get caught. You are feeling cautious, suspicious, and unsafe.

Mouth Dreams of a mouth signify expression and that you have something to say. A mouth can also represent physical and emotional hunger; perhaps you have been starving for affection. Your mouth is an avenue of communication, expression, passion, kissing, pleasure, and manifestation; consider what it is you are hungry for. An open mouth represents receptivity or a desire to express. A closed mouth represents secrecy or a fear of expression and exposure. See *Lips, Teeth,* and *Throat.*

Movie Dreaming that you are in a movie or witnessing a movie signifies that you are gaining objectivity about your life, the script, and the roles you play. It can also represent a desire for glamour and recognition. Consider the feeling tone. See *Camcorder.*

Moving Dreams about moving represent major changes in your life, and that you are expanding into a whole new awareness of who you are. See *Breakdown/Breakthrough Dreams,* page 12.

MTV Dreams of MTV, or of music videos and VH1, symbolize your connection to mainstream pop culture, fashion, sexuality, dancing, and cutting-edge creative expression.

Mud Dreams of mud signify hopelessness and despair, and that you are stuck in old, outworn habits. Keep in mind that in the darkest mud the lotus flower, which symbolizes the wisdom, compassion, and transformation gained through facing your deepest and darkest fears, is formed. If mud is being thrown, then you fear being discredited. In the mud is not a place to live but a phase to pass through as you integrate your shadows into your light. See *Dirt* and *Quicksand.*

Mud Slide Dreams of a mud slide symbolize an emotional meltdown, a loss of a mental construct that used to make you feel safe and grounded. You are going through major changes and transformation and you are feeling that your life structures are in an upheaval. See *Breakdown* and *Earthquake.*

Mud Wrestling Dreams of mud wrestling signify that you are fighting with your shadow or grappling with your fears. They could reflect that you have been wallowing in your darkness, and indulging in negativity, pessimism, and sloth. See *Mud.*

Muffler Dreams of a muffler are a message to quiet down, to prac-

tice discernment when expressing your point of view, and to think
before you act.

Mullet If you dream of a mullet you may be associating yourself
with the social implications of having that hairstyle, as in trailer
parks, six-packs of beer, and NASCAR. A dream of a mullet may be
about issues of self-worth and feeling in a low position in the social
strata. See *Hair* and *Hippie.*

Multiplex Dreaming of a multiplex cinema or shopping mall is
about your multidimensional self, reminding you of how many
opinions are always available to you. Your subconscious mind is
telling you to get out of your rut and expand your possibilities in
this infinite and abundant universe.

Mummy Dreams of a mummy symbolize a fear of change, your
feelings about death, and your attachments to old ways of being.
You are attempting to preserve dead, unworkable, dysfunctional aspects of yourself out of habit or a lack of faith that there is something better out there for you.

Mumps Dreams of the mumps denote negative, toxic thoughts taking over your belief system. You may be feeling so suppressed that
your creativity has imploded.

Murder See *Killing.* See also *Venting Dreams,* page 8.

Muscle Dreams of muscle symbolize force, machismo, potency,
bravado, health, strength, confidence, adequacy, and masculinity.
You are becoming masterful in a particular area.

Museum Dreams of a museum signify a desire to preserve great moments of your past. Perhaps you are paying homage to how far
you've come. Also, you are connecting with precious relics of your
soul that you want to cherish.

Mushroom Dreams of a mushroom symbolize gossip and how
quickly news travels. Perhaps you are feeling uncertainty about
whether or not a relationship or career opportunity is poisonous or
healthy for you. If you dream of a magic mushroom, see *Drugs* or
Hallucinogenics/Hallucinations.

Music If you dream of music or hear a song in a dream, then this
forecasts prosperity, harmony, and joy. Music heals the soul and it

also uplifts you emotionally and connects you to your most essential self. Consider the music. See *Singing* and *Song*.

Musical Instrument To see or hear musical instruments in a dream denotes pleasure and expectations of fun and frivolity. Someone may be playing your heartstrings or you may be allowing your soul to be in harmony with your higher source. See *Music*.

Mustache Dreams of a mustache signify a mask, something to hide behind, and that you have a desire to conceal your vulnerability or insecurity with machismo and bravado.

Mustard Dreams of mustard denote trust in a positive outcome, your belief and connection to a higher power. They are giving you the message that if you have faith the size of a mustard seed you can move mountains. See *Condiment* and *Yellow*.

Mute Dreams of being mute signify that you are suppressing your feelings. Perhaps you are especially aware of the power of words, and you are feeling trepidation about what would happen if you expressed yourself. Alternatively, dreams of being mute can be showing you that a lack of frivolous chatter makes for great introspection and depth, and that sometimes silence is golden.

Mystery Dreams of a mystery are integration dreams that reveal your relationship with the unknown, with your unconscious, and with your shadow. See *Integration Dreams,* page 10.

Mystic If you dream of a mystic, you are tapping into your innate ability to see beyond appearances to the gold that is always beneath the surface; you are accessing higher guidance.

Mythology If you dream of Greek or Roman mythology, then you are seeing beneath the myths that surround your life. Your subconscious may be prompting you to become more conscious of your personal mythology that has been running your life.

N

Nail Dreams of a nail signify that you are attempting to hold something together or to bond with something or someone. Perhaps they are telling you that you are right in your assessment of your current situation, and that you have hit the nail on the head. See *Fingernails*.

Naked Dreams of being naked or seeing someone naked represent a desire for honesty and intimacy. They can also represent the fear of others knowing your private thoughts and feelings. If you are comfortable being naked, then you feel you have nothing to hide in intimacy. If you are uncomfortable, ashamed, or embarrassed, then a dream of being naked is telling you to do some ego integration work, and begin the process of releasing your own judgments and criticisms.

Name Dreaming of someone's name can be an obvious reference to someone you know or it could be wordplay. For example, the name *Matt* could be a doormat, or the name *Mary* could be referencing marriage and commitment issues. If you call someone you know by a different name, then consider the quality of or your association with that name.

Napkin Dreams of a napkin are a message to make amends, forgive, and forget.

Narrow A dream of a narrow space can represent rigidity, limitations, restrictions, inaccurate presumptions, insecurity, and righteousness. It could also be suggesting that you need extreme focus and discipline to accomplish a task, blocking out anything that would interfere with your perspective or goals.

Native American Dreaming of a Native American symbolizes your connection with wisdom, authenticity, honesty, and your natural self. It could also be suggesting that family and home issues need some attention.

Nativity A dream about the Nativity is calling attention to major changes that are in process. You are giving birth to your spiritual essence and your highest potential. You are supported and shepherded by people and angels you may not even know. Your inner gifts are now accessed and ready to be shared. See *Christmas* and *Jesus.*

Nature A dream of being in nature is about renewal, freedom, and reconnecting with what enlivens and inspires you.

Nausea A dream in which there is a feeling of nausea is drawing attention to an imbalance, rejection, opposition, or resistance in your life. See *Vomiting.*

Navy Dreaming of the navy symbolizes a distrust of your sexuality and a fear of the unknown. You are going into the deep feminine with armor on. Also, it might include some wordplay, for example, for *seamen,* signifying fertility and promiscuity. See *Military, Ocean,* and *Water.*

Nearsighted A dream about being nearsighted is drawing attention to a lack of objectivity and compassion in your life. Alternatively, it could also be suggesting that you focus on what is right in front of you and not get lost in the big picture. Consider the feeling tone. See *Eyes.*

Neat A dream about being neat or being in a neat environment symbolizes order and mental clarity. It can also be drawing your attention to rigid or controlling behavior that could be stifling your creativity.

Neck Dreaming of a neck symbolizes flexibility and the ability to see different sides of a situation with fairness and equality. A neck is also a place of vulnerability, so if you stick your neck out, you are taking your chances and making a sacrifice. If you dream of having neck problems or a stiff neck, then this represents stubbornness and rigidity. See *Body.*

Necklace A dream of an adornment on the neck is about either the amplification of your expression, or the need to release your inhibited self-expression. See *Jewelry* and *Neck.*

Nectar Dreams of nectar signify that you are allowing into you that which nurtures and feeds your soul, heart, mind, and body. See *Fruit.*

Need Dreams of needing something or someone indicate issues of self-worth. Perhaps it is time to differentiate your "needs" from your "wants." Keep in mind that the infinite divine source is ever available.

Needle Dreams of needles can represent the fear of being invaded, hurt, or emotionally punctured. If you are threading a needle, then the dream suggests that there is a situation or relationship that needs mending. Needles are also phallic symbols. Consider the feeling tone.

Neighbor Dreams of a neighbor, or neighbors, are about your relationships with other people and your issues with boundaries.

Neptune A dream of Neptune is bringing your subconscious to the surface. You are dealing with issues that revolve around your use of your intuition.

Nest A dream about a nest symbolizes feelings and attitudes about home, interdependence, and dependence. An empty nest can represent the fear of abandonment or the desire for autonomy. A nest also is a symbol of female sexuality. Consider the feeling tone. See *Bird* and *Goddess* (Hestia).

Net Dreaming of a net can be a wish fulfillment dream or a venting dream depending upon whether you are being chased, rescued, or caught. A net in a dream can also represent an abundant future. See *Web*.

Netflix Dreams of this mail-order DVD service are about fantasy, escapism, and portals to other realities. Consider the title of the movie(s). See *Blockbuster Video* and *DVD*.

Networking A dream about networking reflects opportunistic tendencies and is showing you how all the aspects of life are interconnected. Also, you are dealing with communication issues.

New A dream about new things is about inspiration and your relationship with change and commitment.

News Dreaming of seeing or hearing news symbolizes the future. Pay attention, this may be very important. Alternatively, it could be helping you to vent out any negativity that you saw on the news recently. Consider the subject matter and the feeling tone to discern the significance of the dream. See *Prophetic Dreams,* page 17, and *Venting Dreams,* page 8.

Newspaper A dream about reading the newspaper is about seeking knowledge that is relevant to your current situation and about receiving information from your unconscious. Pay attention, the headlines are important to your present situation and to your future. See *Sign.* See also *Prophetic Dreams,* page 17.

New Year's A dream of a New Year's celebration represents a desire for a clean slate. It is suggesting that it is time to set your intentions and start anew.

New York A dream of New York represents your drive to realize your goals. If you can make it there, you can make it anywhere! Pay attention to the feeling tone of the dream and consider your associations with the city that never sleeps. See *City* and *September 11.*

Night If you dream of nighttime, then your unconscious desires and the shadow aspects of your life are expressing and revealing themselves. In terms of the stages of life, nighttime represents the end of life, wisdom, and old age. If this is a dark night of the soul, this is a time when light/solutions/hope/God feel distant, and clarity is waning. This period is usually followed by an extreme breakthrough. See *Breakdown* and *Dark.*

Nine The number 9 in a dream represents the end of a cycle. It is also related to compassion and generosity. See *Number.*

No A dream of your saying no or having someone saying no to you is about boundaries. It can be suggesting that you set boundaries or that you need to open up and be more receptive. If someone is telling you no, then a dream is trying to get your attention to be aware of the boundaries other people are setting that you may have been ignoring. See *Boundary.*

Nobel Peace Prize A dream about the Nobel Peace Prize symbolizes your commitment and desire for peace in your relationships and in your world. See *Award.*

Noise Often, the sounds that you hear in a dream take their cues from actual sounds happening around you (e.g., sirens, helicopters, etc.). If this is not the case, look up the symbol that the sound could have come from (CD player, hammer, etc.). Noise can reveal a great deal about the context and subtext of a dream. Consider the feeling tone.

Noodles Dreaming of eating and/or cooking noodles signifies a fortuitous event in the near future. A happy accident awaits. See *Food.*

Noose A dream of a noose around your neck symbolizes self-defeating actions that you may be engaged in. If the noose is around someone else's neck, then it represents your feelings about a relationship that is ending. See *Rope* and *Suicide.*

North If you are aware of facing north or traveling north in a dream, then this represents completion of a cycle of your life. North represents wisdom, winter, and the guidance of your elders. See *Directions* and *Medicine Wheel.*

North Star A dream about the North Star symbolizes consistency and direction. The North Star is telling you all is well, that you are moving in the right direction.

Nose Dreams of a nose represent your ability to use your instincts and intuition and to sniff out a situation. Consider if something smells funny, bad, or good to you. Your nose knows. The answers you seek are as plain as the nose on your face. See *Body*.

Notary Public A dream about a notary public is calling you to give your stamp of approval, or to acknowledge a relationship as valid and official. See *Commitment*.

Note Dreams of a note are a reminder or a message for you to pay attention to something. Consider the content and the purpose of the note.

Notebook To dream of writing in a notebook symbolizes your connection to details, organization, and your personal feelings. See *Diary*.

November Dreams of November are about harvesting the seeds you have planted, and being grateful as you reap the benefits of your hard work. See *Autumn, Eleven,* and *Thanksgiving*.

Nuclear Bomb A dream of a nuclear bomb represents fear of the future and insecurity. You are moving into a time of major transformation and this may be causing anxiety and anger. See *Apocalypse*. See also *Venting Dreams,* page 8.

Numbness Dreams of numbness signify that you are having difficulty coping with a shock; you are processing through frozen feelings.

Number Dreams of a number represent order, logic, and a desire to figure things out, solve a problem, assign a value, classify, and/or organize. Each number has its own significance; look up the number in this dictionary. If the number in a dream is more than a single digit, then add the digits together to get a single digit. For example, 196 would be 7 (1+9+6=16, 1+6=7). See *Eleven, Math, 24/7,* and *Twenty-one*.

Numerology Dreaming of numerology symbolizes your quest to know the deeper truth about yourself and others. Consider the numbers that show up in a dream and your personal association with them. See *Number*.

Nun Dreams of a nun signify your connection to God, martyrdom, and/or deprivation of natural sexual feelings and desires. Nuns also represent extreme sacrifice, the ability to renounce human wants, needs, and desires for a higher goal. Perhaps you've been too strict with yourself, allowing yourself to have *nun* of the good things in life. Consider the feeling tone of the dream.

Nurse To dream of being a nurse reveals a compassionate nature, maternal instincts, sacrifice, and generosity. To see a nurse in a dream means you have a desire to be taken care of and possibly to have your health concerns dealt with. See *Angel* and *Doctor.*

Nuts A dream about nuts is foretelling good fortune and abundance. An empty shell is suggesting that you take precautionary measures to protect yourself in an existing financial matter. See *Acorn.*

Nymphomaniac Dreams of a nymphomaniac symbolize not only your animal nature and sexual expression but also issues with not having boundaries. Having intercourse with a nymphomaniac represents your desire to be free from social constraints. See *Boundary* and *Sex.*

O

Oak An oak tree signifies strength, and that you can adapt to any situation. You are tapping into your divine potential. See *Tree.*

Oar To dream of using or seeing an oar symbolizes your desire to control and direct a situation in your life. Your ability to maneuver through your ocean of emotions is being tested. If you have only one oar, you might be spinning in circles without realizing it. See *Boat* and *Water.*

Oasis Dreams of an oasis represent your inner paradise that replenishes, soothes, nurtures, and feeds your soul. They represent your desire for rest and relaxation.

Oath A dream of taking an oath signifies that you are dealing with your relationship obligations and commitments, and the need to walk your talk. Consider the feeling tone. See *Marriage* and *Vows.*

Obedience To dream of being obedient or having someone obey you is about your power struggles. Perhaps you are realizing that when someone submits to the will of someone else, then it is inevitable that that person will eventually rebel or act out passive-aggressively. However, if you dream of obeying a higher calling, then your path is filled with grace.

Obesity Dreams of obesity signify extreme emotional pain comforted and shielded by layers and layers of protection. They are showing you the consequence of indulging in unhealthy patterns. See *Boundary* and *Fat.*

Obituary Dreams of an obituary symbolize your feelings about death. You are at the end of a cycle, relationship, or pattern. If you dream of reading your own obituary, then you are gaining a wise and objective perspective of your own existence, dying to your former egoic self, and making a quantum leap in your spiritual growth. See *Death.*

Obscene Dreaming about what you consider obscene is an integration dream where you are attempting to embrace your shadow, dueling with your inner demons, facing, embracing, erasing, and replacing them with energy that supports you.

Observatory Dreams of an observatory symbolize an objective look at your life, self-reflection, and an awareness of your infinite nature and starlike qualities. See *Star.*

Obstacle Dreams of an obstacle signify that you are dealing with resistance to getting what you want in life. If you dream of an obstacle course, then you are testing your strength, smarts, and resourcefulness. Keep in mind that a person doesn't realize his or her inner hero or shero unless he or she has been challenged. See *Breakdown/Breakthrough Dreams,* page 12.

OC Dreams of OC, or Orange County, represent your desire for an upscale, carefree, upper-class lifestyle, and the illusion of perfection. See *Wish Fulfillment Dreams,* page 18.

Ocean Because the depths of an ocean are deep and mysterious and the waves are cyclical, dreams of an ocean symbolize sex, sensuality, your unconscious desires, and emotional issues. You are being exposed to a strange and foreign area of life. An ocean also represents your vastness, passion, and spirituality. See *Moon* and *Water.*

October Dreams of October represent Halloween, masks, a time when the veil between worlds is thin and you are connecting to your spirit guides and ancestors. Also, you may be seeing the fruit of your labor. See *Halloween.*

Octopus Dreams of an octopus signify that you are multitasking and attempting to fulfill your various needs, wants, and desires. An octopus can also signify that you have been needy, clingy, desperate, and forgetting the truth that all that you need is within you. See *Eight.*

Office Dreams of an office are usually processing dreams about organizing the data that you have accumulated during your nine-to-five experience. They can also represent work, efficiency, industriousness, productivity, diligence, and a dedication to your work. You may also be processing or venting out your hostility and frustrations about your job. See *Processing Dreams,* page 7.

Off-ramp Dreams of an off-ramp symbolize the desire for an exit, a departure from the course you are on, or perhaps simply the need for a break. See *Breaking.*

Oil Well Dreams of an oil well signify that you are connecting with an old form of energy and inspiration, and may be telling you to look to a higher source that will never run out. Alternatively, a dream of an oil well may be a sign that you are striking it rich because you have tapped your inner source of creativity and love.

Old Age Dreams of old age reflect your attitudes and feelings toward aging, ways of the past, tradition, and nostalgia. In some instances, something old can become an antique; the older it is, the higher its value. See *Antiques.*

Olive Dreams of an olive signify nurturing and that you are taking good care of your health.

Olive Branch Dreams of an olive branch symbolize peace, truce, and a desire for harmony.

Om Dreams of this sacred sound and chant that represents the sound of the earth mean that you are in harmony with the earth, with your mother or the feminine presence, with the universe, and the whole of life.

One If you dream of the number 1, then this represents unity, synergy, wholeness, individualist desires, independence, and the need for personal attainment. You may be connecting with your talent for leadership, and of being a creative role model.

Onion Dreams of an onion symbolize your spiral journey of awakening, growth, development, and unfolding. Making progress, and getting closer and closer to the center/end, like peeling away the layers of an onion, may seem slow, painstaking, tearful, and repetitive. If you dream of eating onions, then you are wanting to be left alone.

Online Dreams about being online symbolize your inherent connection with the world, the masses, and quantum consciousness. If you dream of online dating, then this signifies your openness to endless possibilities in love, and that your mental, emotional, spiritual, and geographical boundaries are expanded beyond your familiar sphere of possibilities. See *World Wide Web*.

Open Dreams of an open door or window signify receptivity, willingness to allow something new to come in, and that you are saying a yes to new opportunities.

Opera Dreams of an opera signify high drama in your life, extreme passion, and that you are hitting the high notes of tragedy with a theatrical flair. See *Drama Queen/Drama King, Music,* and *Play.*

Operation Dreams of an operation indicate that you are undergoing major healing, transformation, and repair, that you are healing emotional wounds and mending deep emotional/relationship issues. Consider which part of the body is being operated on. See *Body.* See also *Breakdown/Breakthrough Dreams,* page 12.

Oprah Winfrey A dream of Oprah Winfrey signifies altruism and inspiration, and that you are exalting your gifts for the benefit of all. Synonymous with Oprah is *"Remember your spirit"*—becoming all that you can be, materially, physically, and spiritually.

Orange Dreams of an orange symbolize health, creativity, confidence, happiness, vitality, and immunity against negativity. An orange also represents femininity, feminine genitalia, as well as female reproductive organs. See *Chakra* (3rd), *Color,* and *Fruit.*

Orchard Dreams of an orchard symbolize abundance, plenty, results, fruitfulness, fertility, and the fact that you reap what you sow. See *Flowers.*

Orchestra If you dream that an orchestra is playing harmoniously, then this represents integration of all the many aspects of yourself.

If an orchestra is playing disharmoniously, then this represents disharmony within yourself and that you have unresolved conflicting needs. See *Music*. See also *Integration Dreams,* page 10.

Orgasm Dreams of an orgasm, or ejaculation, are about release, relief, inner harmony, enjoyment of your sexuality, and a desire for more sexual expression in your life. These highly pleasurable dreams are a result of the lack of inhibitions during the dream state, which is a healthy and natural occurrence. See *Sex*.

Orgy A dream of an orgy symbolizes sexual expression, oneness, and a complete melting of all ego boundaries. It may be an integration dream where you are exploring, expressing, and making love to all aspects of yourself.

Orient Dreams of the Orient signify that you have an emotionally cool exterior, restricted expression, and disciplined behavior. They might also be bringing your attention to the philosophy of Eastern religions. See *Buddha, China,* and *Krishna*.

Orphan Dreams of an orphan signify that you are feeling alone, lonely, cast out, uprooted, ungrounded, unloved, and maybe even victimized. You are in the midst of transformation, walking through the phase where you feel cast out from your former comfort zone, and you are having to find your own strength. During this challenging time, between the old and the new, don't give up, keep moving as you do some soul-searching that will lead you to the home that is within you. See *Latchkey Child*. See also *Breakdown/Breakthrough Dreams,* page 12.

Oscar Dreams of an Oscar, or an Academy Award, signify that you are preparing for greatness and the recognition of your accomplishments and success. See *Wish Fulfillment Dreams,* page 18.

Ostrich Dreams of an ostrich's neck that is in the sand symbolize embarrassment, shame, avoiding confrontation, or dealing with awkward moments in life. If an ostrich's head is raised high, then this represents that you are confident, bold, and willing to stick your neck out and take a risk.

Ouija Board Dreams of a Ouija board symbolize connection to your spirit guides, your desire for answers and solutions from your higher self. Consider the feeling tone and the message you receive. See *Precognitive Dreams,* page 15.

Outcast Dreams of an outcast are about your issues of rejection, feelings of loneliness, and alienation. You may be afraid of exposing your true feelings for fear of being rejected. Keep in mind that the only approval you really need is your own.

Outer Space Dreams of outer space symbolize your awareness of the infinite nature of the world, solar system, and universe. They are expanding the parameters of your normal, everyday thinking, and offering you solutions, inspiration, and a higher vision.

Oval Dreams of an oval signify imperfectly perfect mother love and a womb, and that the winding road you've been on is coming full circle. They may also be processing your thoughts and feelings about the government, as in the Oval Office. See *Circle.*

Ovaries Dreams of ovaries represent female reproduction, fertility, creativity, femininity, motherhood, and the possibility of new life. You are being given a fresh start and a new beginning. See *Egg, Spring,* and *Vagina.*

Owl Dreams of this nocturnal bird symbolize wisdom, patience, and intuition. An owl is also the symbol of Athena, goddess of wisdom, discernment, competition, success, and leadership. Because of its excellent night vision, an owl reflects the aspect of you that sees things in the dark that go unnoticed by your day-to-day consciousness. In Shamanism, an owl represents a creature that travels between worlds, between life and death, the underworld and the outer world. As well, an owl is a wise adviser or guide.

Oxygen A dream of oxygen may be a message to appreciate the people and things in your life that are the most crucial, that you may have taken for granted. Also, it may be telling you that you are in need of a break, and that it is time for a breather. See *Air.*

Oxygen Bar Dreams of an oxygen bar are about the need for clarity, breath, space, and an inner and outer cleansing of your social life, perhaps the desire to socialize with people that give you space to breathe.

Oyster Dreams of an oyster symbolize a tough shell to protect your vulnerability, or an aphrodisiac, and your sexual thoughts and feelings. Keep in mind that a pearl is formed by a grain of sand that irritates the oyster, which reflects that our most painful moments are what yield our greatest life lessons and wisdom. Consider the feeling tone of the dream to discern its meaning for you.

P

Pacifier Dreams of a pacifier symbolize a need for reassurance, comfort, and relaxation, and the awareness that all will be well.

Package A dream of a package is a message that a mysterious offering will be coming your way. Consider the feeling tone of the dream to discern its meaning for you. See *Gift, Letter,* and *Mail.*

Packing Dreams of packing symbolize your attitudes and feelings about change, transition, and attachment to form. You are at the end of a cycle, or you are preparing for a new experience, and are taking what you want and leaving the rest behind.

Paddle See *Oar.*

Pagan Depending upon your associations, dreams of a pagan reflect your reverence for and connection to the elements, the seasons, the natural world, and to the magical and mystical side of life.

Page Dreams of a page of a book symbolize a moment in time that is a significant piece of your story, albeit one with a narrow perspective. Keep in mind that once you turn the page the story changes. If a page is blank that means the story has not yet been written. A dream of a page may be giving you the message to keep an open mind.

Pain A dream of pain is an indicator gauge telling you when to stop, when too much is enough, or that you are out of balance. Pain can also represent suppressed emotions, feelings of unworthiness, shame, guilt, self-judgment, and a lack of feeling safe. Consider the area of your body or life where you are experiencing the pain.

Paint Dreams of paint reflect a refreshed perspective. You are renewing, reviving, and expressing your creativity on the canvas of your life, coloring your life a new shade. Alternatively, paint can signify that you are covering up or hiding an unsightly aspect of yourself.

Consider the feeling tone. See *Color.* See also *Integration Dreams,* page 10.

Paintbrush Dreams of a paintbrush denote your awareness that the power to create and manifest is in your hands. They may be a message to be careful not to brush over the facts or ignore your true feelings.

Pajamas Dreams of wearing your pajamas in a social situation suggest that you are revealing a secret and personal aspect of yourself, or that you are afraid of exposure. Alternatively, they could represent that you are comfortable, intimate, and well integrated in your current life circumstance. Consider the feeling tone. See *Lingerie* and *Naked.*

Pale Dreams of a pale color signify that a commitment has lost its passion and is washed out, or that there are lukewarm feelings about a particular relationship or project.

Pallbearer Dreams of a pallbearer signify your feelings about death and change, and that you are participating honorably in the completion of a project or relationship or period of your life.

Palm Reading/Palm Reader Dreams of a palm reading represent your desire to get a handle on your future. If you dream of a palm reader, then you are connecting with a future hope or desire as you realize that your future lies in your own hands. See *Precognitive Dreams,* page 15.

Pan Dreams of a pan signify that you are cooking up ideas and creatively cooking. Take note of what is in the pan and what you are creating. See *Pot.*

Pancakes Dreams of pancakes symbolize a treat or reward. Perhaps you are acknowledging the stack of all the good and sweet things you've done recently. You are taking good care of your inner child.

Pandora's Box This integration and/or venting dream is about coming to terms with your secrets, mystery, supressed feelings, and shadow side. The dream is showing you that you ultimately must take the contents of your Pandora's box and face them, embrace them, erase them, and replace them. Keep in mind what you resist persists. See *Integration Dreams,* page 10.

Panic This venting dream is assisting you to release and let go of your attachments to that which scares you or negatively impacts your life. Perhaps you've been running from your problems, feeling overwhelmed or overshadowed by their power. Dreaming of panic is helping you to come to terms with your shadow. See *Fear*. See also *Venting Dreams,* page 8.

Panther Dreams of a panther signify that you are embracing the unknown and mysterious aspects of your being and exploring the power of your unconscious. They also signify that you have the courage to be yourself, to face your shadow, and delve into the places within you that need healing. See *Animal* and *Cat*.

Panties Dreams of panties are about a flimsy cover for your intimate sexual feelings, attractions, and impulses. Panties represent girlishness, innocence, virginal attributes, and/or seduction.

Pants Dreams of wearing a pair of pants are about being in control, and being in your powerful, masculine energy. See *Clothes*.

Paper Dreams of a blank paper symbolize a blank slate in front of you, your ability to begin anew, and your desire to express yourself creatively. A dream of a stack of papers signifies clutter, pressure, and overwhelm at all the things you have to do. A paper doll symbolizes an ego that is fragile, insecure, vulnerable, and paper-thin. See *Page*.

Parachute Dreams of a parachute symbolize a desire to be saved or rescued from a dangerous situation. They could also be cautioning you to have a backup plan, something to cushion yourself should you fall.

Paradise See *Heaven*. See also *Prophetic Dreams,* page 17, and *Wish Fulfillment Dreams,* page 18.

Paralysis Dreams of feeling frozen signify that you are processing shock from a traumatic experience or loss of connection to your spirit. You are venting out the feelings of being out of control. See *Frozen* and *Shock*.

Parasite Dreams of parasites signify that you are letting little things eat at you. They also may be showing you that something or someone in your waking state is draining your energy, eating away at your self-esteem. See *Vampire*.

Parents Dreams of your parents often symbolize the way you see God. Your parents in your dreams, and in real life, reveal to you your best and worst characteristics. Also, dreams of your parents can be exposing your feelings and attitudes toward parenthood. See *Father* and *Mother*.

Paris Dreams of Paris symbolize romance, passion, fashion, decadence, love, and adventure.

Park A dream of a park where children play signifies freedom and joy, and that you are reconnecting to your childlike essence. You are allowing yourself permission to let go, be messy, loud, and wild, as you are realizing the value and necessity of having fun. If you dream of a park in nature, then this represents that you are connecting with your soul, your essence, and true nature. If you dream of parking your car, then it means that you are in a holding pattern, waiting to reengage with life. See *Parking Lot*.

Parking Attendant Dreams of a parking attendant reflect your leaving your physical and emotional well-being in the hands of someone you barely know and abdicating responsibility to someone else. The I Ching calls "the keeper of keys" (the valet) a person that has possessions in great measure. See *Valet*.

Parking Lot Dreams of a parking lot signify that you are taking a break, stopping in your tracks, and checking out. They may be showing you that you've been too sedentary, that you may have given up your drive, and that it is time for you to get back into gear and take a chance again.

Parrot Dreams of any winged animal symbolize spirit or a closeness to the heavens. In a dream, a parrot repeating and copying what it hears is a symbol of your mimicking someone else, not allowing your originality to shine through. A dream of a parrot may be giving you the message to be mindful about the temptation to gossip or run your mouth unconsciously.

Party Dreams of a party represent your feelings and attitudes toward groups and/or family gatherings, your public persona, and your people/social skills. They might symbolize that you are walking through a rite of passage. Whether the party is joyous or uncomfortable, it reflects your level of self-integration, your relationships, and the level of harmony in your life. See *Celebration*. See also *Integration Dreams,* page 10.

Passenger If you dream of being a passenger, then the dream is revealing that you are passive in your life, and allowing someone else to drive you or dictate your direction in life. See *Cab*.

Passport Dreams of a passport signify that you are in transition, traveling back and forth between where you are familiar and where you want to go. If you dream of having your passport in your possession, then you feel empowered to do what you need to do, and to come and go as you please. If you dream of not having your passport and are looking for it, then you are struggling with issues of self-empowerment regarding your ability to do what you want/ need in life. See *Foreign*.

Password Dreaming of having the correct password signifies that you have access and permission to get what you want and need in life. You are in on the secret and in control. Consider the numbers and/or letters to decode the deeper significance of this symbol. See *Number*.

Patch Dreams of a patch symbolize a desire to conceal an emotional wound or undesirable aspect of yourself. You may be trying to hide the truth from others or yourself, or you may be in the process of healing. Consider the feeling tone. See *Band-Aid*.

Patent Dreams of a patent represent your desire to take credit where credit is due, to honor and take ownership and responsibility for your contributions and creativity.

Paving Dreams of a paved road signify foresight. You are contemplating your legacy and the path you are paving for others to follow.

Pawnshop Dreams of a pawnshop signify that you are willing to lower your standards and trade yourself for less than you know you are worth in a job situation or in a relationship.

PDA Dreams of a PDA, an electronic or personal data assistant, are about efficiency, organization, control, and being on top of the details of your life. You are realizing that you have the whole world in your hands. See *BlackBerry*.

Pea Dreaming of peas in a pod represents your affinity and connection to someone or a group/tribe of people. Because a pea is diminutive in size, it can also represent feelings of insignificance, or wordplay expressing that you need to *pee*.

Peach Dreams of a peach are symbolic of the female genitalia. You are connecting with your sweetness and your virginal innocence and essence.

Peacock Dreams of a peacock, with its lavish display of tail feathers, symbolize pride, vanity, and a desire to be noticed, praised, adored, and respected. A peacock can also represent a macho male ego. Alternatively, it can represent the immortality of your soul because of its ability to lose its feathers and grow them back again.

Peak Dreams of a peak signify that you have either reached your goal, or you are well on your way. They are giving you the message to keep your eyes on the prize, remain focused and confident, and you will attain success and fulfillment.

Pearl Dreams of a pearl symbolize well-earned wisdom, inner beauty, and knowledge that have come from hardship. They are showing you that your life lessons and pearls of wisdom are priceless, but not to cast your pearls before swine. See *Jewelry.*

Pebble Dreams of a pebble are a message telling you to pay attention to the little things in life and that there is no such thing as a neutral action. They are showing you that every action you take is like a pebble tossed into a lake that causes a ripple effect of change. See *Rock.*

Pedal Dreams of a pedal symbolize self-empowerment and your ability to move forward in life via your own efforts. If you dream of a gas pedal, then your forward motion is being accelerated. If you dream of being unable to reach the pedal, then you are venting out your frustration at feeling incapable of accessing your own energy.

Pedestal Dreams of a pedestal signify that you are grappling with "better than/less than" issues. Perhaps your subconscious mind is giving you the message that your unrealistic delusions of grandeur that you project on others or yourself are destined to fail, because we are all equally magnificent, lovable, and worthy of success. Alternatively, if you dream of someone who is on a pedestal, then that person might be helping you to aspire toward a goal or vision. See *Celebrity.*

Pelican Dreams of a pelican denote that your eyes are bigger than your stomach. Perhaps you've been overly ambitious and overzealous, biting off more than you can chew. Dreaming of sleeping while standing up denotes that you are attempting to be lucid while you sleep. See *Bird.*

Pen Dreams of a pen symbolize your ability to "write" your wrongs, and be the writer/creator of your destiny. A pen also signifies a tool for freedom as well as a desire to communicate and be creatively expressed.

Pencil Dreams of a pencil signify that you are in the process of editing your expression, and that you are aware that it is safe to make a mistake.

Pendulum Dreams of a pendulum signify that you are seeing things in black and white, good and bad, and right and wrong. They may be showing you that it is OK to go to extremes before you find your balance, but that, ultimately, the middle road is the road of wisdom. If you dream of using the pendulum to communicate with a spirit guide, then this is about your desire for higher direction.

Penguin Dreams of a penguin symbolize loyalty, formality, and extreme coping skills to be able to function and survive in a relatively chilly emotional climate.

Penis Dreams of a penis represent masculine power. Dreams of an erect penis represent virility, potency, sexuality, strength, and a feeling of being competent in the world and capable of producing and manifesting your creative ventures. If a penis is limp, then this represents feelings of powerlessness and emasculation.

Penny Dreams of a penny signify good luck, and that blessings from unknown sources are coming to you like pennies from heaven. Alternatively, a penny can represent poverty-consciousness. Consider the feeling tone of the dream to discern its meaning for you.

Pension Dreams of a pension symbolize money, resources, and energy that is constant and reliable. You are receiving the benefits of your hard work, labor, and good karma that you accrued in the past.

Penthouse Dreams of a penthouse symbolize ambition and your desire for the best. You are reaching for the stars and gaining a higher perspective on life.

People Dreams of people reveal your role in relationships, your social skills, survival skills, and attitudes and feelings about the people in your life. If you dream of a specific person that you know, then identify the qualities that he or she represents to you (e.g., friendliness, fearfulness, inspiration, etc.), and realize that these are a reflection of aspects of yourself. See *Integration Dreams,* page 10.

People Pleaser Dreams of a people pleaser reveal your disease to please. They may be giving you the message to begin to cultivate a feeling of deservedness for your own wishes and point of view. See *Boundary* and *Codependence.*

Pepper Dreams of pepper reflect that you are spicing up your life. Things are beginning to heat up for you as you connect with your wild nature.

Peppermint Dreams of peppermint symbolize refreshing thoughts, maybe an "aha" moment, and a crisp new point of view. Perhaps someone or something in your life is stimulating your senses.

Perfume Dreams of perfume symbolize the sweet smell of success. Often a fragrance will connect you with memories and associations from the past. If you dream of something that smells good, then this is a sign that something fortuitous is happening.

Personal Assistant Dreams of a personal assistant are about your issues of authority, support, and your ability to handle the details of life. If you dream of being a personal assistant, then you are connecting with the part of you that is supportive of your dreams and goals. If you dream of having a personal assistant, then this reflects that you allow other people to support you.

Personal Shopper Dreaming of a personal shopper signifies that you are allowing support and guidance into your life in the area of your outer appearance and the impression you make. If you identify with the role of personal shopper, then this is about your desire to meet the needs of other people perhaps at the cost of neglecting your own.

Personal Trainer Dreams of a personal trainer signify your higher self and that you are seeking discipline to stay on track with your physical, emotional, and spiritual fitness goals. See *Life Coach.*

Pet Dreams of a pet reflect an adored, lovable, and innocent aspect of yourself. Perhaps you are feeling that you have domesticated your animal nature. Also, these dreams can represent your attitudes and feelings about responsibility, caring, and protecting, and the sacrifices you make in order to care for the vulnerable yet wild aspect of yourself. See *Bird, Cat, Dog,* and *Fish.*

Peter Pan Dreams of Peter Pan signify the aspect of you that is immature yet magical, and that you may be avoiding adult responsibility and allowing others to take care of you. They may be a message for you to stop flying around in make-believe, let your feet touch planet Earth, and bring some of your magic into adulthood.

Phat Dreams of referring to something as phat symbolize your desire to be on the cutting edge of cool with regards to fashion, trends, style, and pop culture.

Phoenix Dreams of a phoenix signify transformation and that your greatest challenges can become your greatest source of strength and wisdom. You are rising from the ashes of a difficult time into a new beginning. See *Breakdown/Breakthrough Dreams,* page 12.

Phone Dreams of a phone symbolize telepathy and a desire to be in communication and/or to be intimate with the people in your life. See *Phone Number.*

Phone Number Dreams that feature your phone number are about a desire for intimacy and connection. See *Number.*

Photograph Dreams of a photograph symbolize a significant memory or person from your past, or your desire to remember an important occurrence or life lesson. Consider who and what are in the photograph.

Phreaking Dreams of hacking into phone systems for free calls is about wanting a personal connection without paying the price. You are considering the repercussions of stealing, manipulating, and misusing your power. See *Thief.*

Piano Dreams of the black and white keys of a piano represent your light and dark side harmoniously embracing. See *Music* and *Musical Instrument.* See also *Integration Dreams,* page 10.

Pickle Dreams of a pickle denote that you are in a bind. They may be bringing your awareness to the fact that you have been inundated with information and other people's influence, and you need a break to get back to your own conditioning field.

Pickpocket Dreams of a pickpocket signify that you are stealing or wanting what is not yours. They are showing you that you are preoccupied with coveting what other people have while neglecting the process of actualizing your own talent and potential. See *Karma* and *Thief.*

Picnic Dreams of a picnic signify that you are enjoying the abundance and deliciousness of your life. They are giving you the message to not allow the ants to put a damper on your joy; don't sweat the small stuff.

Pie Dreams of a pie represent your just desserts, your ability to revel in your well-earned success. When you are dividing a pie, consider how much of a piece you give yourself. The size of your slice symbolizes your feelings of deservedness and generosity, and reflects your sense of fairness in life.

Pier Dreams of being on a pier signify that you are overlooking the ocean of your emotions from a safe distance. You may be peering out over the edge to get a more objective look in an attempt to understand the ups and downs of your emotional waves. If you dream of being beneath a pier, then you may be venting out your feelings of inadequacy, of being beneath your "peers."

Pierce If you dream of receiving a piercing, then you are allowing someone to impress you and leave his or her mark on you. Or you are wanting to hold on to a touchstone of a significant memory from your past. If you dream of piercing someone else, then this signifies your desire to make an indelible impression or to leave your mark. Consider which part of the body is pierced. See *Body* and *Tattoo.*

Pig Dreams of a pig signify that you've been greedy, selfish, and slothful, and are realizing your seemingly insatiable appetite for love, success, attention, or food. Perhaps you've been taking too much credit or taking more than your share. Dreaming of a pig may be giving you the message that the only way you will ever be satiated is if you give yourself the love you have been craving.

Pigeon Dreams of a pigeon signify that someone is trying to send you a message, or that an important communication may be flying right over your head.

Pilates Dreams of Pilates represent your desire to become stronger in your core, in your second chakra, which gives you the ability to walk with confidence, with a tall spine, as well as an ability to become more flexible and go with the flow of life. See *Exercise* and *Yoga*.

Pill Dreams of a pill are about the desire for a quick fix, and making your physical or emotional pain go away. If you are swallowing a bitter pill, then you are making sacrifices in your life, or facing the hard facts. If a pill is a recreational drug, see *Drugs*. If this pill is medication, see *Band-Aid* or *Medicine*.

Pillar Dreams of a pillar signify that you are identifying your role model, leader, hero, belief systems, or self-concepts that uphold the temple of your life. Also, they represent someone or something in your life that is strong, sturdy, and dependable.

Pillow Dreams of a pillow symbolize comfort, support, security, and reassurance that all is well. You are realizing that you always have a soft place to land during challenging times.

Pilot Dreams of a pilot signify that you are taking charge of your success, and claiming responsibility for where you want to go in life. You are reaching for the stars of your greatest achievement. Regardless of the turbulence in life, you are rising from glory to greater glory. See *Airplane*.

Pimples Dreams of pimples mean that you have been feeling a lack of self-love and acceptance. Your negative feelings are coming to a head in order to be released. Consider the exact place on your body where the pimples are. See *Venting Dreams,* page 8.

Pin Dreams of a pin signify that you are dealing with identifying your sharp edges and self-criticism. You may be feeling cautious and awkward, as though you were walking on pins and needles. See *Needle*.

PIN Dreams of your PIN, your personal identification number, represent access to your heart and soul. Your PIN number is symbolic of your self-image or your interior life. See *Password* and/or *Phone Number*.

Piñata Dreams of a piñata symbolize a celebration. Because breaking a piñata involves being blindfolded, these dreams can symbolize that perhaps your desire is blind and that you are lashing out to obtain something that you aren't even sure you want or need. They could also mean that there are always goodies awaiting you, even if you can't see them. See *Blindfold.*

Pineapple Dreams of a pineapple represent a juicy and delicious reward that comes after arduous labor, as is symbolized by its prickly exterior and its delicious interior. A pineapple can also represent your protective mechanism that surrounds your most sensitive and vulnerable feelings.

Pink Dreams of the color pink are symbolic of innocence, naïveté, an open heart, and youthful femininity. See *Color.*

Pioneer If you dream of a pioneer, then you have an adventurous spirit and are embarking upon a brave new you in a brave new experience.

Pipe Dreams of a pipe symbolize fertility, impregnation, and sexuality. The stem of a pipe (the male) enters the bowl of the pipe (the vagina), symbolizing the seeding of life. The joining of the masculine and feminine in combination with the prayer to the Great Spirit represents sacred sexuality, a divine joining. If you dream of a peace pipe, then you are clearing the smoke to a harmonious resolution. If you dream of a pipe used for drugs, then this is a vehicle for an escape from reality. If a pipe carries water or electricity from one place to another, then you are realizing that you are a conduit of energy, a messenger. See *Integration Dreams,* page 10.

Pirate Dreams of a pirate are about rebellion, breaking the rules, anarchy, seeking a treasure that is buried or out of reach of your egoic desires. A skull and crossbones is a symbol of an ancient brotherhood that stood for wealth and power through dominance. Dreaming of a pirate may be showing you where you are blinded by your desires and perhaps ruthlessly willing to pursue what you want at any cost.

Pisces Dreams of the astrological sign Pisces signify that you are connected to your spiritual essence and your sensual/sexual aquatic nature. You may be feeling emotional or idealistic. These dreams are giving you the message to stay true to your dreams and aspirations. See *Fish.*

Pit If you dream of biting into a pit in the middle of a delicious piece of fruit, then you've gotten carried away with the sweetness of the moment and this is a reminder to keep your head about you. If you dream of a pit, a hole, then you may be going through a depression, feeling that your life is the pits. See *Mud* and *Quicksand*.

Pitcher If you dream of serving beverages with a pitcher, you desire to share your feelings and creative ideas with others. Dreaming that there is a crack or leak in a pitcher signifies a wound that needs to heal so that you can properly hold your feelings and emotions. If a pitcher is big and strong, then this represents your capacity to contain the fullness of your emotions.

Dreams of a baseball pitcher symbolize initiation, getting the play or interaction started. Perhaps you are playing hardball in your negotiations or business dealings, asking tough questions and being confrontational and/or combative. If you are throwing a curveball, then you are being tricky and manipulative and trying to throw others off balance so that they strike out. If you lob a ball, then you are attempting to make it easy to hit, even abdicating your power to the player at bat. If you are at bat, dealing with a pitcher, then you are feeling on the defensive. See *Baseball*.

Pitchfork Dreams of a pitchfork signify that you are using force in taking what you want or in getting rid of what you don't want. You are cultivating your strength, power, and willfulness.

Placenta Dreams of a placenta signify that you are nurturing your innocence and are being taken care of from the inside out. They could also represent your feelings of dependence upon someone or something in a way that infantilizes you. Your subconscious mind might be giving you the message to take what you want and leave the rest behind.

Planet Dreams of a planet symbolize your belief system: the habitual orbit of thoughts within which you are gravitationally pulled, and which you magnetically resonate with. You also may be connecting with a higher and greater consciousness and intelligence from other planets. Consider which planet you dream of as well as its particular attributes. See *Astrologer/Astrology, Earth, Mars, Mercury, Moon, Neptune, Pluto, Saturn, Sun, Uranus,* and *Venus*.

Plank Dreams of walking the plank signify the fear of death, punishment, and/or that you are hovering just over the deep end of your unconscious, contemplating taking a plunge into the unknown. They might also signify that you are extending yourself and building up a support system.

Plant Dreaming of a plant is a message to become grounded, grow roots, and stand firm in your convictions while developing mastery in your area of expertise. If you dream of a manufacturing plant, then it is about efficiency, and mass production of your ideas, visions, and plans. See *Flowers* and *Garden*.

Plaster Dreams of plaster mean that you are molding and creating life to your liking. See *Mold*.

Plastic Dreams of plastic signify that something or someone in your life is fake or pretending to be someone other than who he or she says. Alternatively, plastic also symbolizes durability and resilience.

Plate Dreams of an empty plate signify that you are open to receiving a new helping of nutrition and nourishment. Or possibly you are feeling needy and hungry for a new life experience. Dreams of a full plate signify that you have an active life and a busy social calendar.

Platinum Dreams of platinum symbolize success, high-quality work, and durability. Also, platinum signifies that you are focused on being number one, being the best at what you are doing, and/or winning an award or getting recognition. See *Color* and *Silver*.

Platter Dreams of a platter denote your feelings and attitudes about being served or about being of service. If you dream of being served something on a platter, then this reflects a desire to be spoiled, pampered, and/or treated like royalty. If you are the one carrying a platter, then this reflects your feelings and associations with being in the humble position of a supportive role.

Play Dreams of a theatrical play symbolize your desire to present yourself to the world, to take your thoughts and feelings from behind the scenes of your mind and heart and display them in the spotlight of center stage. If you dream of acting in a play or watching a theatrical production, then this represents objectivity in your ability to witness the roles you play in life. The dream may be reminding you that you are the writer, director, and star of the show, so if you don't like the direction in which the play is headed, then you have the power to change it. If you dream of playing, as in a child at a park, then this represents that you are in touch with your creativity, freedom, and unique expression. If someone is playing a game, such as chess or checkers, then you are becoming aware of the aspect of you that can be strategic and manipulative in your desire to win. Consider the feeling tone of the dream. See *Script* and *Stage*.

Plaza Dreams of a plaza symbolize your feelings and attitudes toward social and communal situations. They could mean that an important event or rite of passage is about to take place.

Plow Dreams of a plow signify that you are turning over the soil of your mind as you contemplate all options regarding an important decision. Perhaps you are preparing for a new beginning in your life and are preparing yourself mentally and energetically to plant new seeds and create new thoughts that will support you.

Plug Dreaming that a plug is in an electrical socket means that you are energetically plugged into or committed to a job, project, or relationship. Consider the feeling tone of the dream to discern whether the outlet is one that energizes or drains you. See *Electricity*.

Plumbing/Plumber Dreams of plumbing or of a plumber signify that you are unclogging old, unworkable systems and releasing emotional blockages or breakages. They can also be a commentary on the energy, blood, and fluids that flow through parts of your physical body, such as your kidneys, intestines, bladder, or colon. Perhaps these dreams are giving you the message that you are releasing blocks to being in the flow of affluence, clarity, and vitality.

Pluto Dreams of the planet Pluto, the grandmother of the zodiac, because it is the farthest planet from Earth, could be showing you that you are being cool, aloof, and distant. This dream could also be revealing a deeper truth about you.

Plywood Dreams of plywood symbolize support, flexibility, and strength. They are showing you that you have the resources and the inner substance to build your life the way you want it to be.

PMS Dreams of PMS signify extreme sensitivity and connection to your intuition, and that you are coming into your authority, and powerfully (P) manifesting (M) the sacred (S). See *Blood*.

Pocket Because the contents of a pocket are hidden from view, dreams of a pocket represent your innermost thoughts, feelings, and secrets.

Podcasting Dreams of podcasting symbolize telepathy and desire for connection with the people in your life, as well as a pull to be on the leading edge of information, technology, intelligence, and current affairs. Consider the content of the podcast.

Poem Dreams of a poem symbolize your creative expression, love, devotion, wisdom, profound feelings, and the celebration and honoring of something or someone with whom you have a deep connection. See *Song*.

Poison Dreams of poison reflect negative, nonsupportive feelings, thoughts, beliefs, habits, or relationships that your subconscious mind is assisting you in releasing.

Police Dreams of the police signify protection and security, and that you are reinforcing your sense of justice and morality. They can also reflect your inner critic and that you are releasing feelings of guilt for having done something wrong. See *Critic* and *Judge*.

Polishing Dreams of polishing symbolize your desire to perfect your skills or to master your talent.

Politician If you dream of being a politician, then you are campaigning for approval, looking for validation and positive reinforcement about who you are and what you stand for. The dream may be giving you the message to practice discernment and read between the lines and lies.

Poll Dreams of a poll signify that you are attempting to measure your success and effectiveness with your current choices. They may be giving you the message "to thine own self be true." Keep in mind that your vote is the one that counts the most in your life.

Pollen Dreams of pollen symbolize success and fertility with your projects and creative ventures. They could also forecast pregnancy, sensuality, procreation, and that you will be financially and creatively prospering with a cocreative group of people. See *Bees*.

Pollution Dreams of pollution denote that you've been careless with your resources. They are a message for you to take personal responsibility and make some major changes in your lifestyle.

Pomegranate Dreams of a pomegranate symbolize fertility, ovaries, and transformation. See *Goddess* (Persephone).

Pond Dreams of a pond symbolize inner reflection. You are taking time to ponder the looking glass of your unconscious mind as you connect with your intuition and inner guidance. See *Water*.

Pony Dreams of a young horse symbolize unbridled enthusiasm. They may be giving you permission to horse around, get carried away, and have some fun. See *Horse*.

Ponytail Dreams of a ponytail symbolize innocence, naïveté, and simple enthusiasm. See *Hair*.

Pool Dreams of a pool represent your depth; your inner pool of wisdom. If a pool is shallow, then this denotes that you have been focused on the mundane, superficial aspects of life. If a pool is deep, then you have taken the time to understand and explore the vastness of your being and to swim in the deeper regions of your subconscious mind. If you are taking a swim in a pool, then you are allowing yourself to be immersed in your fantasy world, intuition, and spiritual and sensual essences. See *Ocean, Pond, Swimming,* and *Water*.

Poor Dreams of being poor signify that you are processing and venting out identification with lack, victimhood, finite resources, humility, and simplicity. Alternatively, they could be showing you to have compassion for those who have less than you, and to be grateful for what you have.

Popcorn Dreams of popcorn signify creative stimulation and that as your inspiration heats up, everything else will open up for you.

Pope Dreams of the pope are prophetic dreams helping you to enlighten your consciousness and to recognize a higher level of awareness. Consider the spiritual message he is trying to impart to you via the feeling of the dream. See *Catholicism*. See also *Prophetic Dreams,* page 17.

Poppy Dreams of a poppy symbolize eternal love and transformation. If you dream of a tall poppy, then this is also a symbol of being confident and secure enough to be your most authentic, natural, extravagant, and fully expressed self. See *Goddess* (Demeter).

Pop-ups Dreams of pop-ups express your frustration at being interrupted, intruded upon, and having your space invaded and disrespected. Also, they could be a message for you to be more mindful and sensitive about other people's feelings.

Porcelain Dreams of porcelain symbolize a desire for elegance and unblemished perfection. Porcelain can also represent your extremely fragile, vulnerable, and breakable ego.

Porch Dreams of a porch represent the need for a breather from the intensity of your life. Your subconscious mind may be giving you the message to step outside your circumstances to glimpse a broader, more objective perspective.

Porcupine Dreams of a porcupine symbolize your egoic defense mechanisms kicking in to protect the aspects of you that feel the most vulnerable, weak, or fragile. They may be giving you the message that just because a relationship feels prickly, it doesn't mean it is time to walk away. It might be an opportune time for growth, transformation, and healing of all your sharp edges.

Pornography Consider the feeling tone of a dream of pornography to discern its meaning for you. If the dream is pleasurable, then it denotes a healthy fantasy life and feelings of sensuality, sexuality, and a celebration of your body. If the feeling tone is negative, the dream could be a venting dream helping you to release shame, guilt, objectification, and victimhood from past sexual experiences. See *Sex*.

Portfolio Dreams of a portfolio symbolize pride in your accomplishments, confidence, and self-respect. Alternatively, they could be giving you the message that you are *not* your work or your accomplishments.

Portrait Dreams of a portrait represent a desire to glorify one's self-image. They denote your ability to see a person as his or her highest and best self. See *Paint* and *Photograph*.

Postcard Dreams of a postcard symbolize long-distance connection, telepathy, and a desire to be in touch and in communication with those you love. Consider the picture on the postcard; it tells a thousand words.

Poster Dreams of a poster signify that a larger-than-life message is being sent to you. A poster can also signify aggrandizement and idolization, and that you've put someone on a pedestal. See *Billboard*.

Post Office Dreams of a post office denote your interest and willingness to do the work involved in keeping relationships alive, staying in touch, sorting out issues, organizing and filing important information. Alternatively, they could denote your frustration at your job and feeling "postal," as well as helping you to release your aggression. Consider the feeling tone.

Postpartum Depression If you dream of postpartum depression, then you are venting out and processing the physiological and psychological changes of having a baby or of giving birth to a creative project. You are growing through a challenging time in your life, and a dream of this may be giving you the message to seek support. See *Breakdown/Breakthrough Dreams,* page 12.

Posture In real life and in dreams, your posture reflects your feelings of confidence and self-esteem. If your posture is erect, then you are feeling proud and self-composed. If your posture is hunched, then this represents shame or insecurity.

Pot Dreams of a pot signify that you are being held or contained as you grow and change. In India, a pot is a symbol of feminine energy, and the water in it a symbol of the very stuff of manifestation. In Africa, a pot symbolizes the womb, a space to hold you during a process of transformation. An empty pot reflects receptivity, or, alternatively, could be a symbol of neediness and emptiness. See *Cook/Cooking.*

If a dream is about marijuana, then it is revealing that you have distracting tendencies that are a smoke screen to your effectiveness and lucidity. See *Drugs* or *Marijuana.*

Potato Dreams of a potato symbolize sustenance and creative fuel that is found underground, in the more "earthy" aspects of your nature. See *Food* and *Starch.*

Pot Holder Dreams of a pot holder symbolize your need to proceed with protection and caution in a spicy, passionate situation that is heating up. They are a message to handle the relationship or situation with care so as to not get burned.

Pottery Dreams of pottery signify that you are realizing that the power to manifest the life of your dreams lies in your hands. Also, they may be giving you the message that with a little bit of creativity, you can turn your trauma into triumph. See *Mud.*

Poverty Dreams of poverty are venting dreams that are helping you release scarcity consciousness, inadequacy, victimhood, and insecurity. They are giving you the message to rise up from your negativity, struggle, and victimhood and realize the richness of your being. See *Venting Dreams,* page 8.

Powder Dreams of powder are a message to soften your touch or smooth out your approach to life. If you dream of face powder, see *Makeup.*

If you dream of explosive powder, see *Gun.*

Power Dreams of power symbolize your desires, attitudes, and opinions about power, abuse, victimhood, or denial. If they connect you with your power, then you are in resonance with your source, energized, in touch with your spirit, inner strength, confidence, genius, talent, and purpose in life. If you feel disconnected from your power, then these dreams are showing you where you have work to do to release resistance to that which is naturally yours.

PowerPoint Presentation Dreams of a PowerPoint presentation represent a desire to get your point across and to *project* your ideas and thoughts upon the screen of life.

Prayer Dreams of prayer reflect your awareness of your direct connection with spirit. They denote that you are awakening to your higher self, connecting with a divine perspective and a state of grace. See *Prophetic Dreams,* page 17.

Pregnant Dreams of being pregnant signify that you are pregnant with possibilities, ripe with desire and ideas, and that your creativity is unfolding and blossoming into manifestation in your life. They may reflect that a new development is about to be birthed and that your dreams are taking form. A dream of being pregnant may also be a literal prediction about a pregnancy or a desire to be pregnant.

Prescription A dream of a prescription denotes a desire to fix what is broken, heal what is sick, or soothe what is ailing you. You are on the hunt for a solution to a current challenge. See *Processing Dreams,* page 7.

President Dreams of a president signify that you are stepping into leadership, standing in your authority, and taking responsibility for your life. They could also reflect your issues and feelings about the government. Consider the feeling tone.

Priest Dreams of a priest symbolize spiritual authority, devotion, dedication, and sacrifice. Perhaps they reflect that you are putting your spiritual growth ahead of your material goals. Alternatively, dreaming of a priest might be a message to find a healthy expression for your sexual feelings or any desire you have that you deem less than holy. See *Integration Dreams*, page 10.

Priestess Dreams of a priestess symbolize your connection to your feminine essence, your introspective energy, and spiritual power.

Prince Dreaming of a prince is often about a romantic ideal, chivalry, honor, respect, and treating people nobly. If you are a woman, then the dream reflects your animus, the best part of the masculine energy within you. If you are a man, then the prince represents intense focus and concentration with regards to accomplishing your worthy goals. You are evoking your inner hero.

Princess If you are a male, then dreams of a princess represent your anima, the best part of your feminine energy. If you are a woman, then you are connecting with your preciousness, your value, and royal self-esteem.

Principal Dreams of a principal symbolize your issues with authority. If you dream that you are a principal, then the dream reflects the way you handle your power and responsibility. If you dream of being in a weaker position beneath a principal, then the dream is about how you struggle for power, rebel, or learn from someone in a higher position. A dream of a principal could be wordplay, giving you the message to connect with your higher *principles.*

Printing/Printer Dreams of printing represent legitimacy, validity, and power. If you dream of printing, as opposed to cursive writing, then this symbolizes your need and/or desire for control over your life. Consider what is being printed.

Printing Press Dreams of a printing press symbolize creation, manifestation, and a desire to broadcast your creativity, message, theology, belief system, passion, and voice to the masses.

Prison Dreams of prison symbolize your self-imposed restrictions, borders, definitions, belief systems, and identities. You are venting out feeling suppressed and restrained by your job, a relationship, health, or finances. Also, dreaming of prison signifies your awareness of karma, and that you are grappling with issues of punishment, blame, shame, regret, and atonement. The dream could also be giving you the message to recognize that you've locked up your talent and self-expression and it is time to set yourself free. After all, you are the jail, the jailer, the prisoner, and ultimately the only one who can post bail, declare your innocence, and set you free.

Prize See *Award, Gift,* and *Reward.* See also *Wish Fulfillment Dreams,* page 18.

Probation Dreams of probation denote that you are feeling under scrutiny, needing to prove yourself and be on your best behavior. They are giving you the message that if you continue to make amends and practice forgiveness, you will succeed in finding your freedom.

Promotion Dreams of a promotion signify that you will be receiving recognition and advancement, and that you are supported as you move in the direction of your dreams. See *Raise.* See also *Wish Fulfillment Dreams,* page 18.

Prop Dreams of a prop denote that you are lifting someone else's spirits, and taking a secondary, supportive role as you help someone realize his or her vision. If you're feeling as though you're just a prop, you are venting your feelings of being unessential, which, of course, you're not. See *Accessories.*

Prosecuting A dream of prosecuting someone is an integration dream reflecting your desire to prove another's guilt to exalt your own position. The qualities you are "prosecuting," which you find so offensive, are disowned aspects of yourself. See *Critic* and *Judge.* See also *Integration Dreams,* page 10.

Prostitute Dreams of a prostitute are a message to be cautious of selling yourself out, misusing your sexual power to get what you want or need, and compromising your integrity.

Protein Dreams of protein symbolize slow-burning energy, as in a long-enduring romance, stable job, or reliable friendship, that sustains, stabilizes, and nurtures you. See *Low Carbs* and *Meat.*

Prozac Dreams of Prozac denote your desire to be in control of your feelings and emotions, to become grounded, and to get back in balance.

Psychiatrist If you dream of a psychiatrist, then this represents your desire for self-understanding and a desire to discover the solution to your challenges. You are tapping into your own compassion and ability to discover the solutions you seek. Perhaps a dream of a psychiatrist is showing you that the labels you put on people or on yourself are either empowering or disempowering. Consider the feeling tone. See *Life Coach*. See also *Processing Dreams,* page 7.

Puberty See *Adolescence*. See also *Breakdown/Breakthrough Dreams,* page 12.

Publicist Dreams of a publicist symbolize your inner advocate and champion. They are revealing your healthy self-esteem and belief in yourself, which make up the winning formula to true success. See *Cheerleader*.

Publicity Dreams of publicity symbolize a need for attention, recognition, acknowledgment, and a desire to draw attention to yourself and your projects. Keep in mind that the person you most need to impress is you. Alternatively, dreams of publicity denote confidence and boldness.

Publishing Dreams of publishing denote influence, change, transformation, and mutation of human consciousness. You desire to make your mark on the world. See *Printing Press*.

Puddle Dreams of a puddle symbolize trapped emotions, slippery topics that you prefer to skirt in the midst of a difficult emotional terrain. Consider the feeling tone.

Pulitzer Prize Dreams of this literary accomplishment signify that you are realizing the power of your words, whether written, spoken, or contained within your own mind. See *Award* and *Play*.

Pulpit Dreams of a pulpit symbolize your desire to express yourself and your spiritual convictions. Perhaps they are giving you the message to follow your higher calling. See *Priest*.

Pump Dreams of a pump signify that you desire to increase your self-esteem, profits, and energy level.

Puppet Dreams of a puppet signify that you've been abdicating your power, or that you have been abusing it. If you are feeling powerless, manipulated, or used, then these dreams are a message to cut the strings that bind you and take back your authority. If you are a puppeteer, you are realizing your powers of manipulation.

Puppy Dreams of a puppy symbolize your most innocent, cute, cuddly, and playful self. You are realizing how lovable you are, and perhaps you are discovering how lovable someone else is. Dreaming of a puppy could signify puppy love, and that you have a crush on someone.

Purple Dreams of the color purple symbolize spirit, wisdom, and intuition. See *Indigo*.

Purse Dreams of your purse represent important aspects of yourself, your soul, your identity, and *purse*onal power. If you dream that you lose your purse, then you are going through an ego-identity transformation.

Puzzle Dreams of a puzzle symbolize your attempts at solving life's mystery. You are recognizing the order in the midst of the seeming randomness of the people, places, and events of your life. Things are beginning to make sense to you. See *Processing Dreams,* page 7.

Pyramid If you dream of a pyramid, then you are connecting to ancient wisdom and mystical secrets. Dreams of a pyramid denote your connection to ancient days of Egyptians, Mayans, and Toltecs. If you are building a pyramid in a dream, then you might be feeling overwhelmed by a Herculean task in front of you. If you are climbing a pyramid, this signifies that you are engaged on a very noble and spiritual path. Dreams of a pyramid may be warning you about a pyramid marketing/"get rich quick" scheme.

Q

QT Dreams of being on the QT denote that you are unfolding the mystery of your life in a secretive way, and perhaps your intentions are incognito. Perhaps you are hiding from yourself. See *Detective*.

Quack Dreams of a quack signify that you are grappling with issues of trust and authenticity, or that you are venting out your fear of being found out as not who you claim to be.

Quarantine Dreams of being quarantined denote feelings of isolation, loneliness, and the misconception that you are inherently flawed, unloved, and unlovable. They may also be telling you to take some alone time to get in touch with your spiritual source and energy that support you while you release that which no longer serves you.

Quarry Dreams of a quarry signify that you are finding the blessing in disguise in the midst of a current life challenge, and that you are extracting your spirit from the rubble of your ego. See *Stone.*

Quartet Dreams of a quartet denote that you are harmonizing your sub-personalities, aligning your body, mind, spirit, and soul. See *Four.*

Quartz Dreams of quartz crystal represent preciousness, and the ability to make a positive impact on people. Also, they signify that healing is taking place and that your life's purpose is being amplified.

Queen Dreams of a queen signify noble stature and authority, and that you are in touch with your earthly power, confidence, and purpose. They also reflect your relationship with powerful women, your mother or grandmother.

Quesadilla Dreams of a quesadilla symbolize circular patterns with regards to the way you nurture yourself. See *Food* and *Mexico.*

Quest Dreams of a quest are a sign that it is time for you to courageously engage upon your mission and connect with your higher vision. Perhaps you've already begun courting your higher attributes and fulfilling your most noble destiny.

Questionnaire Dreams of a questionnaire represent your inquisitive nature. If you feel confident about a questionnaire, then you are sure of yourself and feel that there is nothing to hide. If you feel uneasy about a questionnaire, then this denotes secrecy, uncertainty, and/or insecurity.

Quicksand Dreams of quicksand symbolize seduction, gluttony, and entropy. You are getting seduced into a belief system that you inherently know isn't good or healthy for you. Dreaming of quicksand is giving you the message to get out before it envelops you.

Quilt Dreams of a quilt symbolize the random aspects of your personality and life experiences weaving together. You are sewing together fragmented pieces of your past experiences and future visions into a context that provides warmth for your soul. See *Blanket.* See also *Integration Dreams,* page 10.

QVC See *Home Shopping Network, Retail Therapy,* and *Shopping.*

R

Rabbi Dreams of a rabbi symbolize your connection to your higher self and spiritual values. If you are Jewish, then the dream may be telling you to deepen your commitment to your spiritual path.

Rabbit Dreams of a rabbit signify abundance and luck, and that good things are multiplying for you. Alternatively, they can symbolize a fearful state of mind. Consider the feeling tone.

Raccoon Dreams of a raccoon reflect that you are feeling like a protector of the underdog. Perhaps you've been providing for those less fortunate than you and wearing a mask to protect your identity while you are performing random acts of kindness and senseless acts of beauty. Dreaming of a raccoon is telling you that your benevolence will come full circle for you.

Race Dreams of a race symbolize competition, comparison, winning, and losing. Your competitive edge may be inspiring you to become your personal best, pushing you to cross the finish line toward victory and a successful life. A dream of a race is giving you the message to do your best every day, and to compete only with the person you were yesterday. See *Sports.*

Racetrack Dreams of a racetrack symbolize competition, and habitual, addictive behavior getting the best of you. They are giving you the message that you've become caught up in circular tendencies that are getting you nowhere quickly. See *Gambling, Horse,* and *Race.*

Rack Dreams of a rack reflect a desire to display your accomplishments, to show off, and to expose your best and an "if you've got it, flaunt it" mentality.

Racket Dreams of a tennis racket signify that you are on the defensive, feeling the need to either protect yourself or to serve up a competitive banter in a relationship. Also, dreaming of a racket may be giving you the message to be discerning in your relationships so as to not get tricked into anyone's racket or scheme.

Radar Dreams of radar denote your own inner guidance system and intuition that is beckoning you to pay attention to the signals and insights that flash across the screen of your mind.

Radio Dreams of a radio symbolize your mind's ability to transmit thoughts, ideas, and information beyond your five senses. They could be giving you a sense of the wavelength of thought, feeling, and vibration on which you've been resonating. Consider the message or music that you hear from the radio. See *Music* or *Talk Radio*.

Raffle Dreams of a raffle signify that you are taking your chances in life, perhaps feeling that your good luck is a matter of chance. They are giving you the message to recognize that you are already a winner. See *Gambling*.

Raft Dreams of a raft denote that you are enjoying your feelings and emotions and observing them with objectivity and detached wisdom. See *Life Raft*.

Rags Dreams of rags signify completion and death, and that you are holding on to the past, perhaps because of a fear of letting go. See *Homelessness* or *Poverty*.

Railing Dreams of a railing signify support and reassurance, and that you are wanting something or someone to hold on to to help you to get a grip on reality.

Railroad Tracks A dream of railroad tracks symbolizes your life choices. If you are on track with your highest purpose, then the dream will be pleasant and you will feel as though everything is going your way. If you feel that you have gotten off track, then the dream is giving you the message to engineer your way back in the direction of your dreams. Dreaming of railroad tracks may also be giving you the message to move from the wrong side of the tracks to the side that is most supportive of you, and that perhaps it is time to switch your career or relationship track. See *Conductor* and *Train*.

Rain Dreams of rain, like crying, mean that you are clearing, cleansing, transforming, purifying, releasing, and being made new.

Rainbow Dreams of a rainbow represent your journey from heaven to earth and from earth back to heaven. You are growing in your spiritual awareness, perhaps because you have just undergone an emotional rainstorm.

Raise Dreaming of a raise in your salary denotes improvements to your life and forecasts an increase in your social status, income, and self-esteem. See *Promotion.*

Raisin Dreams of a raisin symbolize too much exposure to intense energy in your life. They are giving you the message to take a break to prevent your energy from shriveling.

Rake A dream of a rake signifies that you are cleaning up your life. It may be a precognitive dream showing you that if you clear out the space, soon you will be raking in the dough.

Ram Dreams of a ram mean that you are being pushy, headstrong, dominating, and rebellious. A ram is also associated with the astrological sign Aries, which represents leadership, fertility, masculinity, and a strong sex drive. See *Aries.*

Ranch Dreams of a ranch symbolize your life and the upkeep required to have all parts of your life operating in balance. They also reflect that you are in sync with your animal nature, your connection to the seasons and cycles of life, and your most natural, authentic self. See *Corral.*

Ransom Dreams of a ransom signify that you are in a power play, dealing with issues of manipulation and opportunism. They may be calling your attention to realize that the more attached you are to a person or situation in your life, then the more easily you can be manipulated. See *Kidnap.*

Rape Dreams of rape signify that you are grappling with victim/perpetrator issues. Perhaps you have taken what is not yours, or you have allowed someone to take advantage of you. See *Boundary.*

Rapid Dating Dreams of rapid dating represent discernment, abundance, and intuition with regards to intimacy. Also, they represent a desire to find "the one," to meet an intimate partner, to play the field, and/or to get "out there" in the dating pool. See *Match.com.*

Rap Music Dreaming of rap music represents a desire to turn your feelings of injustice against oppression into creativity, success, and empowerment. You may be coping with the challenges in your life by using your street smarts. See *MTV* and *Hip-hop music.*

Rash Dreams of a rash signify that something is rubbing you the wrong way, and that you are going against the grain of your intuition and rhythm. They may also be showing you that you are embarrassed about the public revealing of something personal to you.

Rat Dreams of a rat represent dishonest, disloyal, corrupt energy in your life. Someone or something is unhealthy for you and is gnawing at your self-worth and power.

Rattle Dreams of a rattle, whether of a snake rattle or a baby rattle, signify that you should proceed with caution. Your spirit guides may be trying to get you to pay attention.

Raw Foods Dreams of raw foods denote extreme attention to your intake of energy and your ability to make the most of a situation, and garner that which supports your vitality. Perhaps you are feeling naked, unabashed, authentic, and connected to your spirit and pure essence. Alternatively, you may also be feeling raw and vulnerable, and desirous of a more juicy and passionate life.

Razor Dreams of a razor symbolize a sharp wit. They may be giving you the message to clean up your act and to shave away your ego barriers so that you may be more naked, intimate, authentic, and exposed. Also, your spiritual journey is a razor's edge, so stay alert and awake. See *Knife*.

Reading Dreams of reading denote understanding, realization, and learning. Consider the content of what you are reading.

Real Estate Dreams of buying or selling real estate symbolize a change and/or advancement in your financial situation, prosperity, and expansion. They represent real, solid, three-dimensional expression of your worth and value.

Reality TV Dreams of a reality TV show signify the glorification of real life and proof that art imitates life, and that your real life is as fascinating as anything that could be televised.

Realtor Depending upon the feeling tone of the dream, dreams of a realtor can represent either opportunism or that you are connecting with the aspect of yourself that is grounded and giving you a "reality" check. Perhaps you are realizing all that you've been buying into, and you are dealing with issues of responsibility and ownership, territory, and power. See *Salesperson*.

Rebellion Dreams of rebellion reflect a desire to assert your individuality and face the anarchy within you as you resist your own controlling behavior. You are undergoing great change and transformation as you are grappling with your own conflicting needs.

Receipt Dreams of a receipt reflect monitoring and keeping track of where you spend your energy. You are taking into account what has been expressed and received and what remains in the balance. Perhaps you are dealing with issues of self-worth and financial concerns. See *Money*.

Reception Dreams of a reception or a reception line mean that your ideas, your contribution, and/or your talents will be received favorably. You are preparing for great success.

Record Dreams of a record symbolize a desire to remember something, to deeply etch an experience into the grooves of your mind. If you dream of a broken record, see *Recurring Dreams,* page 13.

Record Player Dreams of a record player signify that you are replaying the same old memories and stories in your mind over and over, relating to yourself from a historical, nostalgic viewpoint. Keep in mind that the past can't hold a candle to what you are capable of now. Perhaps it's time to trade in your old records for stories that empower who you are becoming. See *Music*.

Recycling Dreams of recycling reflect that you are maximizing your energy and resources. You are connecting to the cycles of life, as in the life/death/life process. Alternatively, these dreams might be showing you that you have been recycling and rehashing disempowering thoughts about yourself and that perhaps it is time to throw them out for good. Consider the feeling tone. See *Garbage*.

Red Dreams of the color red symbolize alarm, passion, rage, sexuality, blood, and volatility. Red can also represent a desire to stop or end a situation in your life. See *Chakra* (2nd) and *Color*.

Red Light Dreams of a red light are messages to "stop, do not proceed." A red light can also be a sign of prostitution, and a message to beware of the temptation to sell yourself without regard to your talents, gifts, and/or resources. See *Prostitute*.

Refinancing Dreams of refinancing signify that you are taking stock in your personal assets, reframing your value, worth, power, and equity. Perhaps you are rearranging your belief systems around money, abundance, and self-worth.

Reflection Dreams of a reflection denote your identity, your self-awareness, and your present self-image. You are able to see yourself objectively, and view what is normally in your blind spot.

Refrigerator A dream of a refrigerator symbolizes plenty, abundance, and preservation. Consider the contents of a refrigerator for a more precise understanding of the dream. It could signify that you are maintaining friendships and alliances that are supportive to your growth and well-being. Or it could signify that you have a chilly disposition, displaying cool and aloof feelings because you feel a real or perceived need to protect yourself. Perhaps the dream is giving you the message that a relationship is cooling off.

Register If you dream of registering to vote or of signing up for something, then this represents a willingness to allow that which you've signed up for to influence your life. Consider what you are registering for so that you can understand what you are subconsciously saying yes to. If you dream of a cash register, see *Cashier.*

Rehab Dreams of rehab symbolize transformation, and that you need to take time to clean out, purify, and release your addiction to an unhealthy substance, person, or way of life. Keep in mind that downtime is essential to detox from your former identity and cultivate new empowering habits. Keep in mind too that if real change is to take place, it takes time, persistence, and an ongoing structure of support. See *AA* and *12-step Program.*

Reincarnation A dream of reincarnation symbolizes your realization of the timelessness of your soul. The details of the dream are symbolic of your unfinished business.

Reindeer If you dream of a reindeer, as in the song "Rudolph the Red-Nosed Reindeer," then you are realizing that your unique and "strange" qualities are your greatest gifts to your community and to the world.

Relationship Any relationship dream is always symbolic of your relationship with yourself and your higher power, as well as an attempt to process or sort out current relationship issues, challenges, and desires. If you are not in an intimate relationship, then you may be preparing yourself for one, fantasizing about an ideal, or sorting through the challenges that are in your way of having one.

Religion Dreams of religion signify that you are receiving a spiritual message, exploring your spiritual beliefs and roots. Perhaps you are grappling with what you authentically believe and feel passionately about versus what you were raised to believe. See *Prayer*. See also *Prophetic Dreams,* page 17.

Relish Dreams of relish signify that you should take time and relish and savor this delicious time in your life. Something wonderful is happening to you and your subconscious mind is giving you the message to enjoy it fully. See *Condiment*.

Remote Control Dreams of a remote control represent your desire to control and have power over people or situations. If you dream of looking for a remote control, this represents your struggle to get control over your life and influence of people. If you have a remote control in your possession, then it is time for you to recognize the power you've already attained.

Rent Dreams of renting symbolize the price you are willing to pay for what you need, want, and use. Perhaps you are processing your feelings about whether or not the price you pay is worth what you are getting in terms of where you live, a relationship, or your job. If you dream that you are collecting rent, then this is about your attitudes about receiving what is due you. If you dream that you are paying rent, then you are processing feelings of stress about being able to afford your lifestyle. See *Borrowing*.

Repair A dream of making a repair is a message to correct a broken agreement, make amends, or forgive someone or yourself, and get your life back on track.

Report A dream of a report denotes objectivity, clarity, certainty, and a "just the facts, ma'am" point of view. The dream may be about your attempts to gain clarity as you assess what you've learned, lost, and gained. Consider what the report is about and for whom it is meant.

Rescue A dream of being rescued is a cry for help. It is a sign that you are looking for a hero or are looking to be a hero. The dream could also represent the gratitude you feel toward someone who helped you during a vulnerable time. Consider the feeling tone. See *Codependence* and *Hero/Heroine*.

Reservoir Dreams of a reservoir symbolize your resources, talents, wealth, abundance, and storehouse of good karma you have accumulated over this lifetime. They could be showing you that you've been hoarding for fear of being left empty. Consider the feeling tone. See *Warehouse*.

Restaurant Dreams of a restaurant represent the need to feed your soul, to be refueled and energized. Because a restaurant serves you, the dream denotes a desire to receive. Dreams of a restaurant also carry the message that you have choice with the menu of your life with regards to the information you want to take in and the kinds of relationships you want to be in. Consider what type of restaurant it is, what kind of food is being served, and how it makes you feel. See *Menu*.

Resurrection A dream of a resurrection denotes a new beginning in your life. You are realizing that what didn't kill you makes you stronger. This breakdown/breakthrough dream is preparing you for your next stage of growth and development in the eternal life/death/life cycle. See *Butterfly*.

Resuscitation Dreams of resuscitation reflect that you are breathing new life into an old relationship or project that you thought was dead. They might denote an unhealthy attachment, an unwillingness to let go, or a commitment that is strong enough to fend off death. Consider the feeling tone. See *Recycling* and *Resurrection*.

Retail Therapy Dreams of retail therapy signify insatiability and that you are buying into the idea that there is an external fix to an internal problem. They are revealing that you have fallen prey to the belief that there is something "out there" that will make you sexier, wealthier, prettier, skinnier, smarter, or better. Alternatively, they could be showing you the abundance of resources that is at your disposal to improve your life. Consider the feeling tone. See *Bling Bling* and *Shopping*.

Retreat Dreams of a retreat symbolize the need for alone time, introspection, clarity, and focus on your inner life and spirit. See *Dugout* and *Hermit*.

Revenge If you dream of seeking revenge, you are processing through your anger and feelings of victimhood. The dream is showing you that what you do to another you do to yourself. See *Karma*. See also *Venting Dreams,* page 8.

Revolution If you dream about a revolution, then it is time for a drastic change in your life or for things to come full circle for you. Energy that you've suppressed can no longer be contained. See *Breakdown/Breakthrough Dreams,* page 12.

Reward Dreams of receiving an honor or reward forecast recognition and admiration, and that you will be applauded for your unique contribution to life. See *Award*. See also *Wish Fulfillment Dreams,* page 18.

Rewinding Dreams of rewinding a tape or a clock signify that you are going backward out of a fear of moving forward in your life. Or perhaps you are feeling the need to introspectively review your life to reclaim old terrain and retrieve an aspect of your past that you've denied. See *Backward*.

Rhinestones Dreams of rhinestones symbolize superficial sparkle, glamour, love, and success. Dreams of these counterfeit diamonds are giving you the message to not settle for the imitation if you want the real thing. See *Bling Bling* and *Diamond*.

Rhinoceros A dream of a rhinoceros is a message that you have the power to move mountains. The dream may be alerting you to make sure that you are channeling your power in the direction of what you really want to manifest.

Rib Dreams of a rib or rib cage denote the need for protection for your heart, feelings, and emotions. Also, they may be showing you where you are using humor to keep people at bay as a defense to avoid pain and the possibility of rejection. See *Adam and Eve*.

Ribbon Dreams of a ribbon symbolize a prize. Perhaps you are in the process of winning something or achieving a degree of success. If you dream of a hair ribbon, then you have a desire to stand out and be recognized as the prize that you are. See *Bow, Hair* and *Reward*.

Rice Dreams of rice are fortuitous, forecasting abundance, plenty, and wealth. See *Carbs/Low Carbs*.

Rich If you dream of being rich, then you are coming into your natural inheritance, your true abundance and infinite, expansive nature. You are in the process of preparing for material and spiritual success in your life. See *Wish Fulfillment Dreams,* page 18.

Riddle Dreaming of a riddle signifies transformation, that you are going through a rite of passage, initiation, or challenge. See *Joke.*

Ride Dreams of taking a ride signify that you are in a state of allowing, surrendering, entrusting, and abdicating responsibility to someone else. They may be making you aware that you have allowed someone other than you to be in the driver's seat of your life, and that that person may be taking you for a ride. Perhaps it is time to reclaim your power.

Right The right side of something represents that which is aligned with God and has divine authority. Dreams of the right side of the body denote power, dominance, and confidence. If you dream of a right arm, then you are dealing with an issue that is crucial, important, and invaluable. If you dream of a right hand, then this signifies superiority, and that you have a handle on things, as in a "right-hand man" is a man who gets things done. If you dream of the right wing of the government, then this dream is expressing either your devotion to or your dissatisfaction with conservatism. If you dream of having the right to do something, then you desire to be worthy and allowed to be a part of an important club, or relationship. Consider the feeling tone of the dream to discern the meaning for you. A dream may be showing you the *right* way of doing something, or that you are acting *righteously.*

Ring A dream of a ring or rings symbolizes permanence, partnership, strength, unity, and wholeness within one's self. Also, a ring denotes successful negotiations and continuance. Two gold rings represent commitment to a beloved. See *Circle* and *Goddess* (Hera).

Ring Tone Dreams of a ring tone signify your self-image, and that you are realizing that you have creative control over your life and personal expression. As in the sound of a ring, they may be a call for you to pay attention to an important message that is being broadcast to you; it is up to you to see what rings true. Consider the sound of the ring tone as an important aspect of the message of the dream.

Rising Dreams of rising denote that you are moving up in the world, rising to new heights, and upleveling your consciousness.

Rite of Passage Dreams of a rite of passage signify that you are progressing, growing, changing, and developing in an honorable way. You may be in the midst of a transition, in which case the dream may be giving you the message to deepen your connection to your spirit so that you may continue your positive momentum. See *Ceremony* and *Ritual.*

Ritual Dreams of a ritual are auspicious and fortuitous and signify that you are evoking the sacred within yourself, acknowledging the power of the mystical and magical that is inherent within ordinary moments. They are giving you the message to take care of yourself as you emerge into the next phase of your life. See *Ceremony, Medicine Wheel,* and *Rite of Passage.*

Rival Dreams of a rival are venting dreams that are assisting you in grappling with issues of competition and of being better than or less than. Consider that a rival is also an angel in that he or she is challenging you to become your best. See *Enemy* and *Sports.*

River A dream of a river represents fluidity, change, and the feminine principal of the path of least resistance. You are going with the flow and connecting with your sensuality. If you dream that a river is flowing gracefully, then you are in sync with your emotions and instincts. If you dream that you are going against the current, then you are resisting your instincts, intuition, and deeper feelings. If a river is raging, then you are having an emotional catharsis, dealing with strong emotional currents. If you dream that you are crossing a river, then you are taking great risks and making courageous changes in your life. See *Ocean* or *Water.*

Road Dreams of a road symbolize your life's path. If you dream of an untraveled path, then you are on a very unique life path. If you dream that you are on the road to nowhere, then the dream is giving you the message to pull over, check your map, and reconnect with your inner compass. If there is construction or there are detours on a road, then you are dealing with obstacles that are in your way. If you dream of a road stretched out before you, then this represents your future. And if you dream of a road that runs behind you, then the road signifies your past. Dreaming of a road may be affirming that you are on the right track, and that you are aligned with your highest destiny. Consider the feeling tone and keep in mind that all paths are sacred.

Roar Dreams of a roar symbolize desire, passion, deep longing, existential pain, and a release and eruption of previously suppressed emotions. See *Lion*.

Roast A dream of a roast represents your ability to make fun of yourself. The dream is helping you to realize that when you can see the humor in your attributes, as well as in your shortcomings, it is a sign of enlightenment and self-mastery. If you dream of roast beef, then you have a desire to nurture yourself in a hearty way. If you are a vegetarian that dreams of roast beef, then you are venting out your feelings of victimization and compassion for those less fortunate than you. If you dream of roasting food, see *Cook/Cooking*.

Robe Dreams of a robe symbolize a subtle cover for your naked vulnerability and authenticity. Perhaps they are revealing your modesty and fear of being exposed. If you dream of a robe that is a costume or ceremonial, this means that it is intended to evoke a sense of superiority, secrecy, power, and status.

Robot Dreams of a robot signify efficiency and that you have lost touch with your deeper feelings and intuitions. Perhaps you have become comfortably numb by overvaluing your logical thought process and operating on autopilot in your relationships or going through the motions in your job. If this is the case, dreaming of a robot is giving you the message to deprogram yourself of conventional paradigms and reconnect with your emotions and the feelings of your soul.

Rock Dreams of a rock symbolize strength, groundedness, stability, and ancient wisdom. Perhaps you have become stubborn and rigid in your judgments. Consider the feeling tone. See *Earth*.

Rock and Roll Dreams of rock and roll signify that you are connecting to the longings and yearnings of your soul and that you are resonating with primal feelings of love, loss, and passion for life.

You have a desire to express your passion and creative ideas, and to be wild and free. See *Music.*

Rocket Dreams of a rocket signify that you are blasting off in your career, or that your love life is taking off. They also signify that you are in touch with your masculine energy, or that your sex life will soon be exalted to new heights.

Rocking A dream of rocking signifies the rhythm of love, that you are cared for and nurtured in a maternal way. Allow the dream to reassure you that all is well.

Role Dreams of playing a role reflect that you are gaining objectivity over the roles you play in life. For example, you may be too attached to your role as a mother, student, teacher, or provider and ignoring and squelching other important roles within you. See *Play.*

Roll Whether it is of food or something with wheels, a dream of a roll signifies that you are rolling with the punches of life, going with the flow, and relinquishing your hard edges of resistance. The dream may be giving you the message to assert yourself so that others won't roll over you. Perhaps this is wordplay for the *role* that you are playing. See *Role.*

Rollerblades If you dream of being on Rollerblades, then you are on the fast track of life. If the dream feels exhilarating, then you are enjoying moving through life with velocity. If, however, you feel scared in it, then this denotes that a relationship or your career is taking off too quickly, and you are feeling unstable, ungrounded, and insecure.

Roller Coaster Dreams of a roller coaster symbolize mood swings, feelings of being out of control, and your attitudes about the ups and downs of the cycles of life. If you are enjoying the tumultuousness of the ride, then you are handling uncertainty with an adventurous spirit.

Roof Dreams of a roof symbolize your concept of life, your philosophy, belief systems, limitations, and/or survival skills. They can also represent safety, constraints, or a lid upon your awareness. If you dream that a roof is leaking or caving in, then the dream is giving you the message to take time to review your belief systems and make some repairs. If you are standing on a roof, then this can either represent aloofness or a quest for higher consciousness. Consider the feeling tone. See *Cover* or *Lid.*

Room Dreams of a room symbolize support for a particular function, a womb to cradle, nurture, or hold a space for your development. Consider the room that you dream of and its particular feeling tone and energy. See *Bathroom, Bedroom, Dining Room, Hallway,* and *Kitchen.*

Rooster Dreams of a rooster are an alarm reminding you that you have something important to do. If you have been sleepwalking, then it is time for you to wake up, rise and shine, suit up, and show up. A rooster or cock also symbolizes your masculine energy which will allow you to aggressively take on the world. A rooster is a phallic symbol that represents potency, fertility, and sexuality. Dreaming of a rooster may be teaching you to not be so cocky, boastful, arrogant, and chauvinistic.

Root Dreams of a root represent your connection to your physical reality, body, family, culture, and tribal customs. You're tapping your core, the heart of the matter. If you dream of your root chakras, then they are showing you that you are supported.

Rope Dreams of a rope signify that you are learning and exploring a new dimension of your being and learning the ropes. A rope symbolizes a strong connection between you and someone else. If you dream of being tied up by a rope, then you are feeling confined and stuck, and are holding back your true feelings. Also, consider the condition of a rope, which reflects the strength of your connection. If you are walking on a tightrope, then your partnership is in a very precarious condition. See *Tightrope.*

Rosary Dreams of rosary beads symbolize prayer, meditation, connection with spirit, and a desire for divine assistance.

Rose Dreams of a rose represent love. A particular color of rose symbolizes a specific aspect of love: *Pink*—happiness; *White*—charm and innocence; *Red*—desire (a single red rose = "I love you"); *Burgundy*—unconscious love; *White* and *red*—unity; *Orange*—passion; *Yellow*—joy and gladness.

Rosebud Dreams of a rosebud symbolize beauty, youth, and virginity.

Rosebush Dreams of a rosebush are about passion, great love, joy, expression, and manifestation of your heart's desires.

Rotten Dreams of something that has become rotten signify a pattern, habit, or relationship that has gone sour and needs to be thrown out. They are giving you the message that holding on to relationships, jobs, or life situations past their expiration can be hazardous to your health.

Roulette If you dream of playing roulette, then you are playing with your life, taking your chances, and betting on yourself. See *Gambling* and *Wheel of Fortune.*

Rowboat A dream of a rowboat symbolizes vulnerability in the sea of intimacy. It shows that you are courageous and willing to participate in working through your intimacy issues. If you are in a rowboat alone, then you may be feeling that you are struggling all alone. If you are sharing the rowboat with someone else, then you are working through your relationship challenges.

Rubber Dreams of rubber symbolize your willingness to allow emotional upsets to bounce right off you. Perhaps they are showing you that you will bounce back quickly from an upset and become buoyant and flexible. See *Condom.*

Ruby Dreams of a ruby are about romantic love, passion, and romance. They are giving you the message that you are rising from martyrdom to the level of love, nobility, wealth, and respect. See *Jewelry.*

Rug Dreaming of a rug means that you are in need of comfort, protection, and support. It may be making you aware that you have been sweeping your true feelings under the rug, avoiding unpleasant issues. Or, perhaps it is giving you the message that you are in for a surprise that will pull the rug out from under you. See *Carpet* and *Doormat.*

Rugby If you dream of playing rugby, then you are working out your aggression in a healthy way, channeling your angst and frustration toward a particular goal. See *Sports.*

Ruins Dreams of ruins reflect the buried treasures of your heart and soul. If you dream of discovering ruins, as in a shamanic soul retrieval, then this signifies reunification of lost pieces of your soul that allows you to feel connected and unified to your wisdom and spiritual bounty. Alternatively, dreaming of ruins could signify old and worn out aspects of your self that no longer serve you. Consider the feeling tone. See *Antiques.*

Rules A dream of rules symbolizes a right and wrong mentality, as well as your own moral code. If the dream feels stressful, then you may be attempting to understand or second-guess your own guidelines.

Rum Dreams of rum symbolize warmth, reassurance, and perhaps false security. See *Alcohol.*

Run If you dream of running away from someone or something, then you are afraid, procrastinating, and/or are dealing with feelings of guilt. You are avoiding an important confrontation because of your insecurity or feelings of inadequacy. If you are running toward someone or something, then you are motivated, inspired, passionate, and excited for the challenge/opportunity at hand. Consider the feeling tone.

Rupture Dreams of a rupture signify an emotional wound that needs to be healed. You have recently experienced a shock or interruption to your sense of well-being, and you need help patching yourself back together and coping with this trauma. See *Breaking* and *Patch.*

Rust Dreams of rust denote feelings and attitudes about aging. They may be showing you that you have been neglecting something or someone important in your life. Perhaps you are feeling that you have allowed your talents, skills, and attributes to go to waste. Dreaming of rust is giving you the message to take better custodianship of your talents, gifts, and important relationships.

RV Dreams of an RV, a recreational vehicle, signify that you are carrying home and a sense of belonging with you wherever you go. You are feeling stable, grounded, and a sense of permanence in the midst of all the change in your life.

S

Saccharine Dreams of this overly sweet, artificial sugar signify that you or someone in your life is being disingenuous. They are giving you the message that flattery will ultimately get you nowhere. And when you are courageous enough to see through appearances, though it might be a bitter pill to swallow, the truth will set you free.

Sacrifice Dreams of sacrifice denote either maturity or a disdain for an aspect of self. Also, consider that *sacrifice* has the some root as *sacred: sacr-*. Perhaps you are realizing that in order to improve your life, and make it sacred, you need to give something up of lesser value that is no longer serving you. Perhaps dreaming of sacrifice is reflecting your willingness to bypass short-term gratification for a long-term reward. See *Integration Dreams,* page 10.

Saddle Dreams of a saddle symbolize control, mastery, or influence. If you are seated in a saddle, then you are using your will and are in the seat of your power.

Safari Dreams of a safari represent your willingness to explore your inner jungle, connect with your animal instincts, and face and embrace your dark side. You are learning to master your inner jungle, which increases your personal power. See *Animal.* See also *Integration Dreams,* page 10.

Safe Dreams of a safe signify that you are hiding, protecting, and keeping secret your greatest assets and gifts, perhaps for fear of not knowing how to handle the attention they would garner. Your subconscious mind is making you aware of the difference between feeling safe and feeling alive.

Sage Dreams of a sage symbolize your connection to your own guidance of your higher self. If you dream of burning sage, then you are going through a spiritual cleansing. See *Prophetic Dreams,* page 17.

Sagittarius Dreams of the astrological sign Sagittarius are a sign of your independence and deep feelings. They are giving you the message to use discernment before allowing others into your private world. See *Goddess* (Artemis).

Sailing Dreaming of sailing signifies that you are in rhythm with the ebb and flow of life. It also denotes that you are enjoying a relaxing life and that you are feeling free to express your creativity. Because sailing is a water sport, the dream symbolizes your connection to your emotions, your unconscious, and your deeper feelings, longings, and desires.

Sailor Dreams of a sailor symbolize the seaworthiness of your emotions. A sailor can also represent promiscuity. See *Captain.*

Saint Dreams of a saint symbolize your connection to your own wisdom, unconditional love, and spirituality. Consider the feeling tone and the message of the dream. See *Prophetic Dreams,* page 17.

Salad A dream of eating a salad signifies that you are ingesting healthy choices. Perhaps the dream is forecasting salad days to come, a time of joy, lightness, healthy vitality, and happiness. Dreaming of salad can also forecast that an abundance of money is coming your way, perhaps as a reward for maintaining your health and well-being.

Salad Dressing Dreams of salad dressing symbolize your need to spice up and add flavor, zest, and joy to your life.

Salary Dreams of a salary signify that compensation for your energy is forthcoming. You will be recognized for your services, talents, and good works to the degree that you recognize yourself. See *Money.*

Salesperson Depending upon the feeling tone of the dream and the circumstances surrounding the salesperson, dreaming about a salesperson can be either about your desire for self-promotion and expression, or your desire to be wary of your own opportunistic tendencies.

Salmon Dreams of salmon signify that you trust your gut instinct and inner knowing, even if they are against all odds and against the tide of conventional paradigms. Alternatively, they might be giving you the message to go back to your roots, back to the beginning, to understand how you arrived at this place in your life. If you dream of the silver on the salmon, then this represents that wealth and riches are within your grasp. See *Fish.*

Salt A dream of salt is a message that good luck is forthcoming, and to remain grounded, as in being the salt of the earth. You have the ability to turn a bland situation into something zesty and alive.

Sample Dreams of a fluid sample denote a desire to be analyzed and understood. If you dream of a sample of clothing or of food, then it is about all the choices that are available to you, and that you are advised to take your time making up your mind.

Sanctuary Dreams of a sanctuary signify your inner calm and peacefulness, and that your connection with your spirit provides you with sanctuary wherever you are and no matter whom you are with. See *Church.*

Sand Dreams of sand may be giving you the message to appreciate the little things in life that you have been taking for granted. Sand is also a symbol of abundance and prosperity in that there are more grains of sand on a stretch of beach than can conceivably be counted. As well, sand represents the passage of time, as in sand through an hourglass; or it can be an irritant, as sand in an oyster, that brings about your greatest pearls of wisdom. Consider the feeling tone.

Sand Trap Dreams of a sand trap reflect the way you handle adversity. Perhaps you are feeling stressed and frustrated because you have lost sight of your goals. Dreaming of a sand trap is showing you that it is up to you to dig your way out. See *Quicksand.*

Santa Claus Dreams of Santa Claus symbolize generosity, abundance, and joy. They may be showing you that because you have been good, you should prepare to reap the rewards. You are realizing that from the one to whom much is given much is expected. See *Gift* and *Karma.*

Sapphire Dreams of sapphire signify prosperity, and that you have the ability to sustain the gift of healing. The color sapphire is normally associated with the throat chakra, which signifies expression and communication, and that you are clearing out the blocks to expressing your true self in this world. See *Chakra* (5th) and *Jewelry.*

Saran Wrap Dreams of Saran Wrap represent a desire to preserve or sustain a relationship, a thought, a habit, or a belief. Or perhaps you have a desire to keep an idea fresh. See *Transparent.*

Sardines Dreams of sardines reflect the need for space, solitude, and alone time.

Sash Dreams of a sash symbolize honor, rank, nobility, and pride. If you dream of wearing a sash, then this denotes a desire to be seen and appreciated for your accomplishments.

Satellite Dreams of a satellite represent telepathy. Consider the message that you are sending or receiving.

Satellite Dish Dreams of a satellite dish symbolize your receptivity to streams of information beyond your five senses. They also represent your openness to receive wisdom, awareness, knowledge, compassion, and telepathy.

Saturn Dreams of the planet Saturn denote that which rings true for you. They are revealing to you the rules that you live by as well as your belief systems that keep you feeling safe as you orbit through life. Alternatively, dreaming of Saturn may be revealing that you are going in circles, and that it may be time to break a non-supportive pattern. See *Ring*.

Sausage Dreams of a sausage signify a phallic symbol, and perhaps that you are hungry for intimacy or that you have a strong sexual appetite. See *Meat* and *Penis*.

Savings Account Dreams of a savings account signify a desire for security, and that you are taking action to honor your future needs, wants, and desires. Alternatively, a savings account can signify talent, desires, and potential that you have yet to express. If this is so, then a dream of a savings account is giving you the message to live for today. See *Investment*.

Saw Dreams of a saw represent destruction that leads to creation. They are giving you the message that sometimes your life structures need to be torn down before they can be re-created. See *Knife*. See also *Breakdown/Breakthrough Dreams,* page 12.

Sawdust Dreams of sawdust symbolize the remnants of your former belief systems and identities. You are in the midst of a great transformation as you release your relationships and habits back to the dust from whence they came. See *Ashes* and *Dust*.

Scaffolding If you dream of scaffolding, then you are under construction. You are tearing down the old ways of being and creating new structures that are large enough and strong enough to contain this next re-creation of yourself. Keep in mind that although things may not look pretty right now, soon you will be grateful you made the improvements. See *Breakdown/Breakthrough Dreams,* page 12.

Scale Dreams of a scale indicate a desire for justice, balance, and equanimity. Also, they can reveal that you are weighing the pros and cons of a situation in which you must make a decision. A dream of a scale may be giving you the message to become more balanced as you weigh your logic against your feelings and instincts. If you dream of weighing yourself, then you are assigning value to yourself based upon your physical standards.

Scalp Dreams of this cover for your crown symbolize protection for your deepest, innermost thoughts, spirit, and highest wisdom. If you dream of being scalped, you are afraid of losing your mind or of being negatively influenced. Be mindful of with whom and where you share your insights. See *Head*.

Scandal If you dream of a scandal, then the dream is helping you to grapple with your innermost feelings versus your ego and the reputation of your public persona. See *Gossip*.

Scar Dreams of a scar are about memories of emotional and physical trauma from your past. They are giving you the message to learn from your mistakes so that you don't repeat them.

Scarecrow Dreams of a scarecrow symbolize animosity toward people who have trespassed over your emotional boundaries, or anger at yourself for having allowed this. They are giving you the message to protect what is most sacred and precious and to feel reassured that it is OK to fend off unwanted influence. Alternatively, this dream may be revealing that your ego barriers are keeping love, intimacy, or opportunities at bay. See *Boundary*.

Scavenger Hunt Dreaming of a scavenger hunt signifies that you are on a hunt for clues, trying to figure out the mystery of a pattern in a relationship or business.

Schedule Dreams of a schedule represent a desire for organization and to prioritize your commitments based upon your higher life vision. See *Processing Dreams,* page 7.

Schizophrenia A dream of schizophrenia is an integration dream showing you aspects of yourself with which you've denied association. It is giving you an opportunity to integrate your polarities—shadow/light, masculine/feminine—and conflicting needs. The message of the dream is to release judgments, shame, and blame about any aspect of yourself as you embrace the full-spectrum, multidimensional being that you are. See *Integration Dreams,* page 10.

School Dreams of school are symbolic of your life lessons. They may be helping you to see that every challenge you face helps you to become more resourceful and solution oriented than before. They could also denote a hunger for knowledge, or a thirst to share your wisdom. Dreaming of a school is a reflection of your learning process and it may be revealing the way that you deal with issues of authority, rebellion, heartaches, victories, and issues from your school-age years. See *Homeschooling, Student,* and *Teacher.*

Scientist Dreams of a scientist signify that you are exploring and experimenting in life. They may be assisting you to release your fears of making a mistake so that you can feel free to discover a breakthrough for yourself. See *Laboratory.*

Scissors Dreams of scissors signify that you are undergoing a change and transformation. Consider the feeling tone to discern whether or not you are attempting to cut someone or something out of your life. See *Knife.* See also *Integration Dreams,* page 10.

Scorpio Dreams of the astrological sign Scorpio denote that you are using your charms and resourcefulness to get what you want and need. Or perhaps you are feeling defensive and are blaming someone or something because you didn't get what you needed. These dreams are giving you the message to stop being so hard on yourself when you make a mistake. See *Astrologer/Astrology* and *Scorpion.*

Scorpion Dreams of a scorpion signify feelings of revenge and that you should tread with awareness lest you get stung. They are giving you the message to release your resentments, otherwise your poisonous thoughts will prevent you from attracting that which you desire.

Scrabble Dreams of Scrabble indicate that you are playing word games and giving mixed messages. Perhaps you are trying to say the right thing to score points and win someone's favor. See *Spell.*

Scrapbook Dreams of a scrapbook signify that you are celebrating the joy and beauty of your history. You are preserving your soul lessons and referring to precious moments from the past that remind you of how rich you truly are. Consider the memory and life lesson that is being revealed to you. See *Keepsake.*

Scratching Dreams of scratching an itch represent your desire to quench your own thirst and fulfill your own desires. Consider what you are scratching.

Screen Saver Dreams of a screen saver reflect your default self-image, the "you" that the world sees when you are checked out or shut down, as in when the lights are on but no one's home.

Screwing Dreams of screwing something together represent a desire for compatibility, having sex, or perhaps that someone is manipulating you. They could also be showing you where you have made a mistake or *screwed* up.

Script If you dream of a script, then your subconscious mind is helping you to realize that you are the writer of the play/movie called your life, and that the power to change your life script is always in your hands. See *Play* and *Writing.*

Scroll Dreams of a scroll signify that official, important information is being imparted to you. Consider the content, and recognize this is an important announcement for you.

Sculptor/Sculpture Dreams of a sculptor or sculpture represent your realization that you can create the life you desire, and that you have the power to manifest your dreams and/or visions into reality.

Seafood Dreams of ingesting food from the sea are about your receiving the mystery of the feminine, the awareness of your unconscious depths, and a deeper love.

Seal Dreams of a seal signify that you are learning your life lessons through joy and laughter. They could also be showing you that you are easily trainable and suggestible to what others want you to do or be. Also, you may be giving yourself or someone else your seal of approval, or you are looking for validation from others. Consider the feeling tone.

Seam Dreams of a seam signify that you are sewing random pieces of your life together, and are making connections between the seemingly unrelated aspects of yourself. See *Integration Dreams,* page 10.

Seamstress Dreams of a seamstress symbolize your connection to the aspect of you that knows how to weave and sew your dreams into manifestation. You are realizing your ability to repair rips and tears to your self-worth and re-create yourself as good as new.

Séance A dream of a séance is about your connection with deceased loved ones, revealing that you are capable of communicating with spirits in other realms. Consider the message you receive from the dream. See *Prophetic Dreams,* page 17.

Search Bar Dreams of a search bar signify receptivity and curiosity, and that you are seeking something important. Consider the word you typed into the search bar to be a clue toward what your subconscious mind is wanting you to discover. See *Keyword* and *Searching.*

Search Engine Dreams of a search engine denote that you are wanting to find or be found, noticed, or recognized. You are strategically networking. See *Search Bar* and *Searching.*

Searching Dreams of searching signify that there is an aspect of your life in which you feel incomplete, unhealed, or less than whole. Your subconscious mind is giving you the message that when you are ready, that which you seek will appear right before your eyes.

Sea Serpent Dreams of a sea serpent symbolize the fear that unlocking your sexual desires will be unsafe, dangerous, or painful. They are a message for you to irrigate the murky waters of your unexpressed desires so you can find a healthy expression for your deeper longings.

Seashell A dream of a seashell symbolizes femininity and the female genitalia. A seashell also signifies your ego defensiveness to protect your vulnerability. Dreaming of a seashell is also a sign that you are evoking Aphrodite, goddess of love, passion, creativity, and sensuality. See *Goddess* (Aphrodite).

Seasons Dreams of the seasons denote cycles, lessons, and wisdom learned and earned. You are realizing patience as you discover that everything is unfolding in perfect timing. Each season has a message for you about the stages of your life. See *Spring, Summer, Fall, Winter,* and *Holiday.*

Seat Dreams of being seated signify that you are in the seat of your power, owning your energy and influence, sitting back to gain perspective about your life. They can be showing you where you have become complacent and sedentary, or that you are waiting or taking a pause before engaging more actively in your life. Consider the feeling tone. See *Throne.*

Seaweed Dreams of seaweed symbolize tangled emotions and difficulty expressing what you truly feel. Perhaps they are showing you that you are too wrapped up in the drama of your life.

Second Dreams of being second or of playing second fiddle reflect competitive feelings and frustration at not being first. They may be a message to focus on being the best that you can be and to stop comparing yourself with others. If you dream of seconds flying by, then you are deeply enjoying whomever you are with and whatever you are doing. If you dream of having seconds, as in second helpings of food, then this denotes a hunger for life and insatiability.

Second Hand Dreams of a second hand of a clock mean that you are anticipating an important occurrence.

Secondhand Dreams of secondhand things or hand-me-downs are about feelings of deservedness and of using that which is not originally yours. They may be permission for you to express your originality. Alternatively, secondhand items can be a message for you to be more resourceful.

Secret Dreams of a secret symbolize distrust, caution, and fear. Secrets can represent either that which is sacred or that which is based on shame and fear. A dream of a secret may be giving you the message that people are as sick as their secrets, and to consider sharing your most shameful secrets with a qualified therapist or trusted friend. See *Integration Dreams,* page 10.

Secret Society Dreams of a secret society signify power and mystery, and that you are being initiated into deeper realms of your infinite nature. They may be cautioning you to be mindful of how you use your personal power. Also, you are being cautioned to be responsible for your part in a collective power that is generated when you participate with a zealous group of individuals. See *Ceremony.*

Seducer/Seductress Dreams of a seducer or seductress symbolize sexual desires, manipulation, and immature ego tricks to gain power. They may be an opportunity for you to vent out your struggle with what you want versus what you know is good for you. See *Spider* and *Vampire.*

Seeds Dreams of seeds symbolize thoughts, ideas, beliefs, plans, goals, and visions. Also seeds can represent sperm, pregnancy, and fertility. See *Sperm.*

Seesaw Dreams of a seesaw signify that you are teetering back and forth on an issue that you are weighing and balancing. Or perhaps they are giving you the message to find balance in your life amidst your career, family, and your spiritual practice.

Selling Dreams of selling something are about an exchange of energy, ideology, finances, or resources. Consider what belief system you are *buying* into or what belief system you are wanting other people to *buy* into and for what reason. See *Salesperson*.

Separate If you dream of being separated from someone or of being left out, then you are processing through your feelings and attitudes about loss, rejection, loneliness, abandonment, autonomy, and freedom. See *Abandonment* or *Breakup*.

September Dreams of September are synonymous with going back to school, back to work, and back to the drawing board. They may be giving you the message that your vacation is over and it is time to get back to work. See *Autumn* or *September 11*.

September 11 Dreams of September 11 and the destruction of the World Trade Center are venting dreams that are helping you to release your shock and devastation over terrorists, war, bombing, and destruction. Keep in mind that the darkest hour is always just before the dawn, and that you may be at that turning point. See *Breakdown/Breakthrough Dreams,* page 12.

Serenade If you dream of a serenade, then the dream is giving you the message that if you are not already experiencing love and romance, you soon will be. See *Music*.

Servant Dreams of a servant signify humility and service, and that you are putting the needs of others ahead of your own. Dreaming of a servant also denotes altruism, martyrdom, and victimhood, as well as your attitudes and feelings about master/slave relationships.

Seven Dreams of the number 7 symbolize luck, peace, and affection. Also, the number 7 denotes that you are identified with your intellect, and need facts to substantiate your theories. To dream of the mystical number 7 signifies that you are realizing spiritual wisdom as you gain awareness of the power of the cycles of your life.

Sewer Dreams of a sewer reflect toxic emotions and negative thoughts that you are flushing out of your system. See *Venting Dreams,* page 8.

Sewing To dream of sewing signifies that you are mending the past, forgiving someone, making amends for transgressions, as well as stitching together relationships that have become frayed. Also, dreams of sewing denote your ability to manifest the things in life that you desire and require. You are realizing that you reap what you "sew." See *Seamstress.*

Sex Dreams of sex symbolize your desire, creativity, and passion. Erotic dreams are also helping you to balance out your unsatisfied or secret physical attractions, longings, and desires. You are feeling alive within your body temple, attractive or attracted to someone, and in touch with your body's need for expression, attention, and celebration. Dreams of intercourse represent connection, acceptance, affinity, love, and the embracing and melding of the qualities of the person or people involved in the act. If you dream of having sex with a particular person, then you are connecting to that person and/or what he or she represents to you. See *Integration Dreams,* page 10.

Shade Dreams of shade signify that you are connecting with your shadow, your inner mystery, and aspects of yourself that are edgy, shady, and socially unacceptable. They are attempting to assist you to become more assimilated with the light of your being so that you may emerge into more of your power. See *Shadow.* See also *Integration Dreams,* page 10.

Shadow Dreams of a shadow symbolize your dark side, that which you fear or resist, and that which is unintegrated, rejected, or perceived as unaccepted and suppressed. Keep in mind that it is your dark side in the shadow only until you've embraced it in the light of your awareness. See *Integration Dreams,* page 10.

Shakespeare Dreams of Shakespeare, or of Shakespearian language, represent poetry, romance, tragedy, or comedy. They are giving you the message that "all the world's a stage," which means to remember that whether you are sleeping or awake, you are in a dream theater and you are the director, actor, and writer of your play. See *Play.*

Shaking Hands As is true in real life, shaking hands with someone in a dream symbolizes that you are uniting, making an agreement, declaring a truce, or aligning on a promise.

Shaman Dreaming about a wise, interdimensional healer/medicine man represents your desire to evoke more of your own innate healing wisdom. You are connecting with your own inner spiritual source and infinite wellspring of talent, power, and passion. See *Prophetic Dreams,* page 17.

Shampoo Dreams of shampoo signify a desire to wash a person or situation out of your hair, and out of your memory. See *Hair* and *Washing.*

Shark Dreams of a shark symbolize a fear of death, of being destroyed, overpowered, and devoured. Sharks represent the aspect of you that is merciless. Dreaming of a shark may be warning you of untrustworthy people in your business life.

Shave Dreams of shaving represent your desire to be socially accessible, to have a clean slate, and to prepare for intimacy. Dreams of being clean shaven signify courage, boldness, fearlessness, nakedness, and forthrightness.

Shawl Dreams of a shawl symbolize emotional warmth and the need for protection from the chill of rejection or withheld feelings. They also signify your ability to comfort yourself and create your own cocoon of nurturing.

Shed Dreams of a shed symbolize resourcefulness. You are realizing that you have accumulated many tools for life as well as strategies and coping mechanisms to handle the challenges life throws at you. See *Tools.*

Sheep Dreams of sheep signify that you are following a leader, and being influenced. They may be telling you to think for yourself and stop being so sheepish. See *Lamb.*

Sheet Music Dreams of sheet music signify that you are seeking instruction regarding the expression of your sensuality and creativity and self-expression. See *Music* and *Singing.*

Sheets If you dream of sheets on a bed, then this represents unconscious behavior or a veil to cover your unconscious and intimate feelings. If you dream about sheets blowing in the wind, then you are being cautioned about overindulging in drunkenness. See *Bed* and *Page*.

Shelf If you dream of something being displayed on a shelf, then it represents honor, status, pride, a desire for recognition. However, if you dream of a relic on a shelf collecting dust, it represents an aspect of your desires, talent, or creativity that has been ignored.

Shelter Dreams of shelter symbolize protection and hiding. Perhaps you are feeling unsafe, defensive, in need of support, or you have a desire to be mothered. Consider the feeling tone. See *Goddess* (Hestia) and *Sanctuary*.

Shepherd Dreams of a shepherd symbolize leadership and responsibility for your flock, for your energy, for your projects, and/or for the people whom you influence. You are becoming aware of your benevolent power and influence.

Shield Dreams of a shield signify protection, defensiveness, the ego, and that you are in the midst of conquering your deepest fears. Consider the image(s) depicted on the shield as well as its strength. See *Goddess* (Athena) and *Vest*.

Ship Dreams of a ship indicate your ability to ride your emotional highs and lows, and steady yourself during turbulent moments in a relationship on the high seas of intima*sea*. See *Boat*.

Shirt Dreams of a shirt reflect the image you want to show to the world, your public persona, and self-image. Consider the type of shirt you are wearing and how it makes you feel. See *Clothes*.

Shock If you dream of going into shock or of being electrically shocked, then this represents an initiation, trauma, or an instant awareness. Also, you may be venting out feelings of overwhelm, helplessness, and/or victimization. Consider the feeling tone.

Shoe Dreams of a shoe or a pair of shoes symbolize your position or place in life, your status, self-perception, or life circumstances. If you dream of removing your shoes, then you are attempting to be more grounded or you are leaving an old role behind. If you dream of wearing someone else's shoes, then you are having compassion for that person, and learning what it would feel like to walk a mile in his or her shoes. Consider the type of shoes and the feeling tone of this dream.

Shooting Star Dreams of a shooting star denote a message from the heavens. They might be an affirmation that you are in the right place at the right time, telling you to make a wish because you have the power to make it come true.

Shopping Dreams of shopping signify that you are buying into a particular belief system or ideology. Dreaming of shopping is a message from your subconscious mind to take your time and shop around before deciding upon a relationship or perspective that you will eventually buy into. See *Retail Therapy.*

Shore Dreams of being on the shore signify that you are remaining grounded as you contemplate your intuition, and the mystery of your deeper feelings and emotions. See *Beach.*

Short If you dream that someone or something is short, then it represents something having little importance or a shrinking value to you. A diminutive adult in a dream might also represent connection with your inner child, and that you are feeling vulnerable. If you dream of being short and of someone else being tall, then you are processing feelings of inferiority, powerlessness, and intimidation. If, however, you dream that you are tall and someone else is short, then the dream expresses your feelings of superiority, power, and domination. Consider the feeling tone. See *Dwarf.*

Shot Glass Dreams of a shot glass signify that you are attempting to be in control of your indulgences in behaviors that could get you into trouble. See *Alcohol.*

Shoulders Dreams of broad shoulders represent strength and confidence. Dreams of shoulders that are slumped represent insecurity or shame. Dreams of shoulders that are rolled back reflect confidence, self-esteem, and self-assertion. Dreaming of shoulders could also be revealing to you that you need a shoulder to cry on, or that you are carrying the weight of the world. See *Codependence.*

Shovel Dreams of a shovel symbolize your ability to dig your way out of a hole. If you are digging your own grave, then you have been indulging in negativity. Also, dreaming of a shovel can represent introspection and your willingness to dig deep within yourself for answers. You are realizing your ability to uncover, discover, and discard aspects of your past that no longer support you.

Show Dreams of a show or a play signify that you are putting on an act and perhaps behaving with inauthenticity for an effect. Also, they demonstrate that you have a desire for exposure of your true feelings, to perform and share your talents with the public. See *Play* and *Stage*.

Shower Dreams of a shower are a message of cleansing, releasing, and healing, and that you are washing down the drain that which no longer serves you. They can also denote that abundance and affluence is showering down upon you. See *Rain* and *Water*.

Shrinking If you dream of a problem shrinking, then you are rising above your challenges. If you dream of shrinking in the face of an increasing problem, then this denotes a challenge to self-esteem. Dreaming of shrinking is giving you the message that no one can make you feel small without your permission. See *Short*.

Shuttle Dreams of a shuttle signify that you are in transition, moving from one phase of your life to the next. Or they might be showing you that you are getting carried away and you need to come back down to earth. Consider the feeling tone of this dream to discern the meaning for you.

Sick If you dream of being sick, then you are venting out an undesirable experience from your system. The dream might also be a message for you to take time to integrate new information that has been coming to you. Also, dreaming of being sick might signify a blockage, a storehouse of unexpressed feelings, or an imbalance of energy. Consider the area of the body affected by the illness.

Side Dreams of the right side symbolize strength, power, and the energy to manifest. Dreams of the left side symbolize receiving and allowing flowing energy. If you dream of taking sides, then you are integrating and grappling with your own conflicting needs. If you dream of standing be*side* someone, then you are supporting that person, and adding your strength to his or her position.

Sidewalk Dreams of a sidewalk symbolize your life path. If the sidewalk is straight, then it represents a straight and narrow road. If you dream of walking on the sidewalk, then this represents safety in the midst of a hectic life, and that you are paving the way to your success. See *Road*.

Sign Dreams of a sign are a direct message, a burning bush with guidance and direction. For example, a No Smoking sign, if you are a smoker, is a sign for you to stop smoking. If you aren't a smoker, this could be a sign to cool your heels in a relationship or job so that you don't burn out. If you dream of a street sign, this is a landmark informing you of where you are or where you should be heading.

Signature Dreaming of your signature signifies a desire to do things your way, with your unique style and flair. If you dream of signing a document, then this means you've given your consent, commitment, agreement, and seal of approval. See *Autograph*.

Silk Dreams of silk signify that you are feeling fluid, easygoing, sexy, wealthy, extravagant, lavish, and classy.

Silver Dreams of silver signify good luck and that you are in touch with your higher power. See *Color* and *Platinum*.

Singing Dreams of singing symbolize a desire for joyous self-expression, and a need to voice your true feelings. They also denote the expression of creativity, and that you are in harmony with the uni*verse* and with your soul. Consider the song that you are singing.

Single If you dream of being single, then the dream represents either freedom or loneliness. If you dream of a single red rose, then it is about romance. If you dream of being singled out, then you are either feeling special or on the spot. Consider the feeling tone. See *One*.

Sink Dreams of a sink signify that you are purifying, cleansing, and washing away undesirable energy. Consider that the dream may be wordplay for being in *sync* with life, with your lover, business partner, or with desirable events in your life. If you dream of something that sinks to the bottom of the ocean, then the dream is showing you where you are giving up and giving in. See *Drain* and *Drown*.

Siren Dreams of a siren are a sign to pay attention; there is a red-alert emergency for you to tend to. In Greek mythology, the sirens were beautiful female creatures who would lure sailors to destruction by their singing, so a dream of a siren could be a warning to stay alert and be aware of the temptation to be seduced into something that could have harmful consequences. See *Seducer/Seductress*.

Sister If you dream of your sister, then it can literally be about her, the aspect of you that she represents, or the qualities that you project upon her. If you don't have a sister, then the dream reflects someone with whom you share a kinship, a sisterly bond, where your secrets are safe and you feel nurtured. For some, a sister represents rivalry or competition. Consider the feeling tone.

Six Dreams of the number 6 signify prominence and a strong sense of responsibility, and that you are feeling idealistic. They could be reflecting that you are a role model, aloof, distant, and wise in your ability to attune to higher realms. Also, dreams of the number 6 signify symmetry of mind, body, spirit, and your sixth sense, which means that they could be giving you permission to follow your intuition. Consider that six could also be wordplay for *sex*.

Skateboard Dreams of riding a skateboard suggest that you may be taking a ride on someone else's energy, or that someone is riding on your coattails. Perhaps you are gaining downhill momentum, and expressing your adventurous, carefree spirit.

Skating Dreams of skating signify that you are moving gracefully through life with velocity, gliding and striding by, sidestepping adverse circumstances with balance and ease. Alternatively, they can signify that you have been skating through life, getting by on your laurels with a hope and a prayer. Consider the feeling tone of the dream to discern the meaning for you.

Skeleton Dreams of a skeleton symbolize your feelings about death, impermanence, and your shadow. They could be giving you the message to embrace feelings or aspects of yourself you have denied, suppressed, or deemed unlovable, unappealing, or socially unacceptable. Also, a skeleton can reflect the foundational structure of your business, relationships, or your life in general. If the bones are strong and healthy, then so is your foundation. If the bones in your dream are weak or brittle, then this is a message for you to strengthen your foundation from the inside out. See *Bone* and *Shadow*.

Skiing Dreams of skiing signify freedom, adventure, joy, and becoming unified with nature, and that you are moving boldly with velocity and mastery through the ups and downs of your life. They also signify skillfulness in coping with frozen emotions.

Skin Dreams of skin can reflect a superficial covering of your deepest feelings. Skin can also represent the ego, in its ability to be shallow and only skin-deep. Dreaming of skin might also be helping you to get in touch with your feelings, and to get a sense of self. Consider that your skin is how you make personal contact with the world, so the dream can express your desire for intimacy or sex.

Skull Dreams of a skull signify mindlessness and that you are venting out your fear of losing your mind by opening up to another person's point of view. You might also be opening to your ability to read other people's minds. See *Pirate* and *Skeleton*.

Sky Dreams of the sky symbolize your connection to spirit, God, heaven, and higher consciousness. You are tapping into your greatest potential and opening to solutions for your current challenges.

Skydiving Dreams of skydiving symbolize a desire for extreme adventure. If you feel excited, then you have a positive expectation about falling in love and taking risks in your business. If you are terrified, then you are venting out your fear of coming down to earth, and losing your sense of self. Alternatively, dreaming of skydiving could signify that you are bringing your spiritual awareness down to earth. Consider the feeling tone of the dream. See *Falling* and *Flying*.

Skyscraper Dreams of a skyscraper signify that you are reaching for the stars, stretching beyond your comfort zone, and realizing that the sky is the limit. They are giving you the message to remain grounded on the earth with your attention in the heavens, to be in this world but not of it.

Slaughterhouse Dreams of a slaughterhouse are venting dreams attempting to assist you in releasing your self-cruelty and disdain for your most vulnerable, animal aspects of self. See *Integration Dreams,* page 10, and *Venting Dreams,* page 8.

Slave Dreams of a slave signify that you are grappling with your power, abdicating your authority, and venting out victim/perpetrator master/servant karma. You have a desire for freedom from negative influence, including your own thoughts, habits, and addictions. If you dream of treating someone like a slave, then this represents your own disrespect of self.

Sleep If you dream of being asleep, then this signifies apathy, depression, and a desire to check out. Dreams of sleeping also signify vulnerability and a feeling of being out of control and disengaged.

Sleigh Dreams of a sleigh are a message that gifts, joy, and abundance are on the way to you. You are reaping the benefits of your hard work and are celebrating the completion of a cycle. See *Winter.*

Slide If you dream of sliding or going down a slide, then this signifies that you are experiencing a loss of control in your life. If the context of a dream is an atmosphere of play, then you are enjoying losing control and finding ecstasy in reckless abandon. See *Slip.*

Slip If you dream of a slip that is worn under a dress, then this denotes sensuality, a desire for intimacy, and perhaps a wish to protect yourself or to be slightly veiled and mysterious. See *Lingerie.* If you dream of giving someone the slip, then you are running from yourself, or the aspect represented by the person who is chasing you. If you slip on a banana peel, then this denotes that you are venting your fear of losing control, of being reckless and careless. Dreaming of slipping may be giving you the message to avoid slippery situations, to wake up, and get a grip on your life because when you fall, you not only get hurt, but you take others down with you.

Slippers Dreams of slippers symbolize warmth, nurturing, and support. Because you wear slippers at home or before retiring to sleep, slippers symbolize that you feel grounded, comfortable, and at home with yourself. See *Cinderella, Feet,* or *Slip.*

Smell Dreams of a fragrance or aroma signify whether or not something is healthy for you. If a smell is pleasing, then consider that the dream is giving you a green light to proceed with the relationship, career opportunity, or creative project you are considering. If a smell is offensive, then consider this to be a message to stop and take a step back to sniff out what is really going on. Also, dreams of a particular fragrance or scent can reconnect you with a *scent*sational memory, or a nostalgic and powerful aspect of yourself. See *Nose.*

Smile As is true in "real life," in dreams a smile signifies a gesture of friendship, acceptance, goodwill, warmth, civility, affinity, and happiness.

Smog Dreams of smog signify overwhelm, negativity, mental clutter, and/or a smoke screen to mask what is really going on in your life. They may be giving you the message that you are in need of an emotional rainstorm, a good cry to cleanse the pollution in your mind and heart.

Smoke Dreams of smoke are indicators of fire, passion, or danger. Smoke is also a symbol of a veil, mystery, or mist to hide a secret, as in "smoke and mirrors." Rings of smoke represent a signal for help. Also, Native Americans consider smoke to be a visual demonstration of prayer and communion with the Great Spirit. Consider the feeling tone.

Smoking If you dream that you are smoking a cigarette, then this represents self-sabotage and that you are allowing yourself to ingest negative energy that is toxic, unhealthy, and dangerous for you. Smoking in a dream also represents a deeper need for a healthy way to relax and unwind, and to step out from behind the smoke screen and start anew.

Smooth If you dream of a surface that is smooth, then this represents that you have an integrated ego, and thus are easygoing and able to go with the flow. You have done the spiritual work to sand down your rough edges, and good things in life are coming to you easily and without resistance.

Smoothie Dreams of drinking a smoothie signify that you are ingesting positive energy and are taking the action necessary for your life to operate as smoothly as possible. Also, because smoothies are blended health drinks, this represents ego integration and the synergy of all aspects of yourself.

SMS Dreams about an SMS, a satellite messaging service, are about your need for constant communication in your relationships. You are realizing your interconnectivity and ease of access to all those in your intimate circle of friends. See *BlackBerry, Cell Phone,* or *Text Message.*

Snail Dreams of a snail signify that you are taking your time and practicing patience. They may be giving you the message to stop being in such a rush, and to trust that even if your progress appears to be slow, you are making deliberate and distinct strides forward and are leaving a legacy trailing behind you. Dreaming of a snail may also be revealing your feelings of vulnerability, and that you are attempting to protect yourself from being hurt.

Snake Dreams of a snake signify wisdom and intuition, and that you are connecting with your unconscious, mystery, and untamed power. A snake is also a phallic symbol that could represent either sexual healing or sexual trauma. A snake, because it sheds its skin, denotes your ability to release old incarnations, attachments, and identities and reinvent yourself. Many religious teachings depict a snake as evil, offering temptation as in the Garden of Eden, and even as the devil. However, the Hermetic traditions taught that a snake represented the wisdom that is earned in facing and embracing your shadow. Consider the feeling tone. See *Goddess* (Persephone) and *Kundalini*. See also *Breakdown/Breakthrough Dreams,* page 12.

Snorkel Dreams of a snorkel are about your bringing consciousness to your unconsciousness and integrating both realms of your being. You are becoming aware of the places you used to be unaware of, accessing regions of your power and psychic abilities.

Snow Depending upon the feeling tone, snow can symbolize emotional frigidity, distance, aloofness, and shock. Or snow can symbolize purity, as in "fresh as fallen snow," virginity, innocence, and joy. See *Winter.*

Snowboard Dreams of a snowboard symbolize skill and agility as you traverse chilly emotional terrain. Or perhaps a dream of a snowboard is showing you that you are able to keep your wits about you even in a financial snowstorm and that you are finding adventure even in adverse circumstances. See *Skateboard.*

Snowflake Dreams of snowflakes signify that you are realizing the miracle of your one-of-a-kind, unrepeatable essence. They are giving you permission to be authentic and to celebrate the diversity of the many unique people with whom you interact.

Soap Dreams of soap signify that you are cleaning, purifying, and releasing old thoughts, habits, and ways of being. Perhaps you are coming clean about a secret you have to tell or amends you have to make. Dreaming of soap may be telling you to clean up your past by forgiving those who have harmed you and by seeking forgiveness for those you have harmed.

Soap Opera Dreams of a soap opera signify that you are being a drama queen or drama king, glorifying and glamorizing your emotional mood swings from hope to pain and back on this roller coaster called life. If you dream of a particular soap opera or star, then you are either relating to the story line or fantasizing that this was your life. A dream of a soap opera reflects that you have been participating in revenge, glamour, lust, fantasy, betrayal, and victimhood. See *Drama Queen/Drama King*.

Sober Dreams of being sober signify maturity, and that you are growing up, taking control of your life, and becoming lucid. See *AA*.

Socialite Dreams of a socialite symbolize your feelings and attitudes about image, status, prestige, and your public persona. They may be giving you the message to delve a bit deeper to connect with the richness and authenticity that lie beneath social masks. See *Celebrity*.

Socket If you dream of an empty socket, then this signifies that you are feeling unplugged and are in need of guidance regarding your direction and purpose in life. If you dream that a socket is being used, then you are plugged into your purpose in life. If you are feeling drained, then you may be plugging your energy into circuits that are not supporting you, and/or you are allowing people to drain your energy. If this is the case, then you are advised to unplug from one-sided relationships.

Socks Dreams of socks signify that you are nurturing yourself and giving yourself the reassurance that all is well. Perhaps you are getting up the courage to confront your challenges, make a commitment, and thaw out your cold feet. See *Slippers*.

Software Dreams of software symbolize your attention to and connection with new information. You are on the cutting edge of thought, your learning curve is sky-high, and you are downloading a whole new belief system and/or paradigm. See *Computer*.

Solar Power Dreams of solar power represent that you are maximizing your personal resources and tapping into your infinite spiritual source that will never run out.

Soldier Dreams of a soldier symbolize sacrifice and your connection to the hero archetype. Perhaps you are contemplating putting your life on the line and standing for a cause. You may be grappling with issues of life and death. See *Hero/Heroine, Military,* and *War.*

Son If you dream of your actual son, then you may be processing your feelings about him and grappling with feelings of protection, nurturing, support, and/or tough love. A dream of a son might also represent the "young boy/man" archetype within you, vulnerability, bravado, and an "I don't care" attitude that masks insecurity. See *Knight* and *Prince.*

Song Dreams of a song reflect creativity, joy, love, devotion, and deep, soul feelings that words alone cannot convey. Consider the lyrics and the melody of the song. See *Music* and *Singing.*

Soot Dreams of soot symbolize negative belief systems and the residue from past hurts, shock, and pain from the fire of a relationship. See *Dirt.*

Soul Dreams of your soul signify lucidity and that you are awakening to your higher self, connecting with your internal guidance system, intuition, and unconditional love that connects you with all people and all of life. See *Prophetic Dreams,* page 17.

Soup A dream of eating soup signifies that you are allowing yourself to be nurtured, comforted, and loved. You are integrating and blending together all aspects of yourself into unity. See *Food.* See also *Integration Dreams,* page 10.

South Dreams of the direction south are symbolic of fire, passion, and sexuality, and your inner teenager. You are either enjoying sensuous expression or you are allowing yourself to express your creativity with joyous abandon as you manifest your heart's desires. See *Fire, Summer,* and *Teenager.*

Space Dreams of space away from those you love are about objectivity and the necessity to take a step back in order to gain objectivity. See *Outer Space.*

Spaceship Dreams of a spaceship signify that you are exploring higher consciousness, and that you are curious about quantum evolution.

Spade Dreams of a spade signify that you are brutally honest, telling the truth, and are calling a spade a spade, realizing that sometimes the truth cuts like a knife. Dreams of this digging instrument with a sharp point symbolize focus and cutting through the density of uncertainty. Perhaps you are feeling defensive and the need to attack and protect your vulnerability from adverse forces.

Spam A dream of spam represents a lack of boundaries and that you are being inundated with energy that you don't want from people whom you don't enjoy. If this is the case, then the dream is giving you the message to set clear boundaries with people in your life. If you dream of being the one who is sending the spam, then this could be a message for you to reestablish integrity in your communication and be more respectful of other people's boundaries. See *Pop-ups*.

Spanking Dreams of spanking someone symbolize a desire to punish, and assert control, over a naughty, unruly aspect of yourself. The adult part of you is reprimanding the child in you for acting or behaving in a way your ego deems inappropriate.

Sparrow Dreams of a sparrow signify gossip and that you are having difficulty keeping a secret. You are realizing that you have been acting flighty. Also, a sparrow is often used as a code word for something else. Consider the feeling tone of the dream to discern its meaning. See *Bird*.

Speak Dreams of speaking signify that you have a desire to get a message across. Consider the words you speak and to whom you are speaking them. If you are wanting to speak in a dream but are unable to, then the dream is trying to show you that your life circumstances are inhibiting you or you are being blocked or edited by your own inner critic. See *Phone*.

Speech If you dream of giving a speech, then this reflects your public self/persona's expressing what you are passionate about. You are identifying your personal message to the world or you are working out your fears of public speaking. Dreaming of giving a speech may be a preparation for an upcoming presentation, helping you to see yourself as confident, eloquent, and prepared. Also, dreams of a lecture can represent a one-sided point of view, opinions, and passionate feelings about a particular topic.

Speed Dreams of speed signify that you are moving swiftly through life, that you are on the fast track and are making great strides. Also, they may be showing you that you are moving too quickly, in an attempt to outrun feeling pain. Consider the feeling tone of the dream and what is motivating you to move so quickly. See *Fast Lane*.

Speedometer Dreams of a speedometer denote that you are becoming aware of your progress in life and the rate of speed at which you are going. Perhaps you are getting a reality check to make sure you are not getting ahead of yourself.

Spell Dreams of casting a magic spell represent the power of your words, and your desire to create and manifest what you want in this life. They may be showing you where you are being willful and attempting to manipulate people and circumstances for your short-term gain. See *Witch*.

If you dream of spelling out a word, then it signifies your desire to deliver a clear message. Consider the word that you are spelling. See *Letter*.

Spending Dreams of spending money reflect your feelings and attitudes about abundance and financial flow. If you feel stressed out about spending money, then you are venting out a lack mentality, and the illusion that there is a limited supply of money, love, health, creativity, solutions, ideas, and good things for you here in this world. If you are joyous as you spend money, then you are resonating with prosperity-consciousness, aware that more is constantly being added unto you.

Sperm Dreams of sperm symbolize masculine energy, a drive to succeed, conquer, create, and make your dreams come true. Also, dreams of sperm denote fertility, potency, and perhaps even pregnancy. See *Seeds*.

Sphinx Dreams of this creature with the body of a lion, wings, and a woman's head symbolize the intersection of your spirituality, humanity, and animal nature, the embrace of all aspects of yourself. You are in the midst of an important and life-changing initiation/rite of passage into your power. See *Riddle*. See also *Integration Dreams,* page 10.

Spice Dreams of spice reflect feelings of passion and sensuality. Perhaps they are giving you the message to add some flavor and spice things up in your love life, career, or any area of your life that has become stagnant and status quo.

Spider Dreams of a spider signify that you are weaving your dreams into reality, and using your wisdom to seduce and entice people into your web of life. You are becoming aware of your feminine charm, allure, patience, craftsmanship, creativity, and ability to weave a universe of possibility. Alternatively, you may be tangled in a particular pattern or belief system as you attempt to meet your survival needs. See *Goddess* (Athena) and *Web*.

Spilling Dreams of spilling signify that you are clumsily revealing your true feelings. If you are spilling the beans, then this denotes your desire for honesty and the relief that comes when you have nothing to hide. A dream of spilling could be forewarning you to discover a tactful, graceful way to express yourself that is not injurious to anyone. See *Accident*.

Spine Dreams of a spine are a message for you to hold your head up high, to face your challenges, and rise to the occasion of your current growth opportunity. If you dream of a curvature of the spine, then this signifies that you are ashamed of something and are attempting to hide. If you dream of an erect spine, then this denotes confidence, fearlessness, and a readiness to take on the world. See *Back* and *Posture*.

Spinning Dreams of spinning, as in a cycling class, signify that you are working hard but you are spinning your wheels. They are giving you the message to reevaluate where you allocate your energy and plug it into that which will actually move you forward in life. See *Bicycle*.

Spiral Dreams of a spiral symbolize the process of your evolution and growth. If you dream of a spiral staircase, then the dream is giving you the message to continue onward and upward even if you think you aren't making progress.

Spirit Dreams of your spirit, a spirit, or the Spirit, signify that you are awakening to God consciousness and to the truth of the love and light that you truly are. See *Soul*.

Spitting As is true in "real life," spitting at someone or something in a dream is a sign of disrespect, disgrace, dishonor, disdain, and rejection. See *Integration Dreams,* page 10.

Spleen Dreaming of your spleen signifies that you are grappling with issues of well-being and physical survival. Also, a dream of your spleen is giving you permission to follow your intuition and to realize that your first thought is usually the most accurate one.

Splinter Dreams of a splinter are symbolic of an emotional injury that you have been carrying around, unaware. You are dealing with a minor annoyance that causes you to be defensive and reactive. See *Thorn.*

Split Dreams of a split represent discord, polarization, and conflicting needs within you. See *Integration Dreams,* page 10.

Spokes Dreams of spokes of a wheel symbolize issues of autonomy, independence, and interdependence as you relate to a system or tribe of people. They are about your sub-personalities coming together and connecting to the hub that is your center. A dream of spokes can also be wordplay about words that you've *spoken.*

Sponge A dream of a sponge signifies that you are receptive to, allowing of, and suggestible to the energy that is around you. You might be coming to terms with how you feel about others sponging off of you. Or the dream might be showing you where you must become more self-reliant and considerate of the boundaries set by others. Also, dreaming of a sponge reflects your resilience, in that your life circumstances can squeeze you dry but you quickly expand back to your natural way of being. Consider the feeling tone of the dream. See *Drinking.*

Spool Dreams of a spool reflect how tightly wound you are. If you are tightly wound, then the dream is telling you to let loose and relax. If you are too loosely wound, then the dream is telling you to pull your act together and to tie up your loose ends.

Spoon Dreams of a spoon symbolize your ability to nurture and feed yourself with the support you need to survive and thrive. If a spoon is silver, then this signifies that you will be coming into wealth and privilege.

Sports Dreams of sports are about your attitude toward teamwork, competition, and sportsmanship, winning and losing. They also denote your desire to come out ahead in your current life challenge. Consider whether or not you are handling your circumstance with fairness and sportsmanlike conduct.

Spot Dreams of a spot symbolize a mistake, blemish, failing, or sign of imperfection. Consider the feeling tone of the dream, because it can also indicate that you are in the right place at the right time, as in "an X marks the spot." See *Stain*.

Spotlight Dreams of a spotlight forecast success, attention, validation, and that you are preparing yourself for a fortuitous opportunity. However, if the feeling tone of the dream is stressful, then you are feeling interrogated. See *Stage*.

Spring Dreams of spring represent new life, young love, starting over, a beginner's mind, and innocence. You are feeling inspired as you are realizing that you have a new lease on life.

Spur Dreams of a spur signify that something or someone is a thorn in your side, an irritant that keeps you moving, growing, expanding, and evolving on your learning edge. You are realizing that your challenges are a great learning experience.

Spy Dreams of a spy denote that you are suspicious, discerning, skeptical, and looking for fault in the people with whom you work or with whom you are in relationships. If you dream that someone is spying on you, then you are grappling with your own feelings of shame and guilt. See *Stalking*.

Square A dream of a square is a sign to develop more balance, equanimity, order, and organization in your lifestyle. Alternatively, it could be giving you the message to think outside of the box, and to stop being so square. Consider the feeling tone of the dream. See *Box*.

Squirrel If you dream of a squirrel, then this indicates that you should plan for the future, become more industrious, and honor yourself by being prepared for changes to come. Alternatively, if you are feeling nutty, then a dream of a squirrel could be telling you to let go, sit still, and trust that you will be taken care of. Consider the feeling tone of the dream.

Stable Dreams of a stable symbolize responsibility for self and are a sign for you to stabilize your animal instincts, harness your power, and rope in your energy. See *Corral*. See also *Integration Dreams,* page 10.

Stadium Dreams of a stadium signify that you are grappling with feelings of competition and a desire to win in a current project, relationship, or challenge. If you are on the field, then you are pushing yourself to go beyond your personal best regarding your goals and aspirations. If you are watching a game from the bleachers, then the dream is giving you the message to join the game.

Staff If you dream of a staff of people, then this signifies either that you are supported or that you are wanting to be supported by the power of a group. If you dream of a staff made of wood, then this signifies that you are coming into your authority, power, and respect, and that you are shepherding lost members of your flock—your inner sub-personalities. See *Integration Dreams,* page 10.

Stag Dreams of a stag, or deer, symbolize fertility and renewal. A stag is also associated with Artemis, goddess of the hunt and independence. A stag was also believed to guide good souls to the Elysian Fields, where they enjoyed eternal happiness after their life on earth, which means that you are being guided to a happy and successful time in your life. See *Goddess* (Artemis).

Stage If you dream of speaking or performing on a stage, then you have a desire to express yourself, take a stand for something, display your talents, and be noticed and appreciated for your unique contribution to life. Also, dreams of a stage symbolize your awareness of the roles you play and the particular scene that you are acting out in the drama of your life, or that you are willing to express yourself publicly. See *Play*.

Stain Dreams of a stain reflect unhealed wounds, lingering trauma, and your fear of being found out for being less than perfect. They are giving you the message to make amends for past transgressions and forgive those who have hurt you, including yourself. See *Scar* and *Spot*.

Staircase If you dream of ascending a staircase, then you are moving up in the world, and discovering higher and loftier aspects of yourself. If you dream of descending a staircase, then you are either giving in to negativity and depression or you are exploring deeper regions of yourself. Consider the feeling tone of the dream to discern the meaning for you. In general, a staircase signifies that you are taking a step-by-step approach to progress in life. See *Elevator* and *Ladder*.

Stalking If you dream of being stalked, then you are venting out feelings of victimhood and are running from your shadow. The dream is giving you the message to face and embrace this shadow aspect of your being so that you can live in peace. If you dream of stalking yourself, as in Native American shamanic teachings, this represents a high level of mastery as you are seeking to become aware of what you are unaware of, to make your unconscious conscious, and to become free from fear. If you dream of being a stalker, then this represents that you are giving your power over to someone whom you have put on a pedestal, and your dream is cautioning you to bring your power back. See *Pedestal*.

Stall If you dream of a horse stall, or even if you dream of a stalled car, perhaps you are allowing your fears to paralyze you. The dream may be giving you the message to take a break, reconnect with your higher purpose, and then come out fighting. See *Dugout*.

Stallion Dreams of a stallion mean that you are coming into your power, taking charge of your life, and tapping into your virility and stamina. See *Horse*.

Stammer Dreams of a stammer indicate nervousness and stress, and that you are venting out and releasing feelings of self-criticism and a fear of saying what you really want to say. See *Throat*.

Stamp Dreams of a stamp symbolize your opinions and judgments. Consider the scene in the dream and whether or not you are approving or rejecting, giving a thumbs-up or thumbs-down.

Star Dreams of a star signify divine direction, and that you are on track with your life, connecting with your soul and the light of your intuition. They also signify leadership, luminosity, and that you are being guided toward success, power, and influence. See *Movie Star* or *North Star*.

Starbucks Dreams of Starbucks represent a tribal ritual and a desire for community. They could also be a symbol of creative stimulation and a desire to percolate your productivity and get a buzz on the day.

Starch Dreams of starch mean that you are in a sticky situation, bonding, and/or are feeling stuck. Dreams of starchy foods symbolize a desire for a burst of energy and inspiration that burns quickly. See *Bread, Carbs/Low Carbs,* and *Potato.*

Starvation Dreams of starvation signify that you have been depriving yourself and neglecting your needs, and that you are lacking self-nurturing. Also, they could represent that you are literally hungry, and that your blood sugar has dropped. A dream of starvation is giving you the message to get back into balance and honor the natural urges of your body temple and the promptings of your soul.

State Dreams of a state symbolize your awareness of your limits and boundaries, or that perhaps you are gaining objectivity over your belief system, your mental, emotional, and spiritual states. Consider which state it is and your association with it. See *Boundary.*

Station Dreams of a train station indicate that you need a rest, that it is time to stop and refuel, recharge, reconnect, reorganize, and reassess your game plan before heading out toward your next destination.

Statue Dreams of a statue signify stillness and coldness, and that you are memorializing someone and putting that person on a pedestal, or honoring a precious moment that is frozen in time. Alternatively, they could be showing you that you have distanced yourself from your feelings and are feeling aloof. It is time to gently let your defenses melt and realize that you cannot heal what you cannot feel. See *Mannequin* or *Robot.*

Steam Dreams of steam signify that you are venting pressure, anger, anxiety, and frustration. It may be time for a break to let off some steam and get a higher perspective.

Steamroller Dreams of a steamroller mean that you are either feeling flattened out by someone's overbearing behavior, or that you have been taking over a situation and are rolling over people's feelings, leaving them flat and depleted. Consider the feeling tone to discern the significance for you. See *Bulldozer.*

Steel Dreams of steel symbolize a rigid, stubborn, unyielding will.

They are revealing your strength as well as where you may be behaving inflexibly. See *Iron/Ironing*.

Steep If you dream of a steep hill or mountain, this forecasts challenges ahead. Keep in mind that if you are determined, you will rise to this occasion and surmount the obstacle one step at a time.

Steer If you dream of steering a vehicle, then you are responsible, in control, and in the driver's seat of your life. You are taking your life in your own hands.

Step Dreams of a step symbolize progress toward a dream, plan, or goal. Consider if you are taking a step forward or a step backward. Keep in mind that sometimes you have to step backward in order to take two steps forward. See *Staircase*.

Step Aerobics A dream of step aerobics signifies that you are making step-by-step progress toward your goals. Your subconscious mind is giving you the message to engage more actively in the process of making physical improvements in your life or else the dream is acknowledging that you are already well on your way. Also, because step aerobics usually involves high energy as well as music, dreaming of it might be revealing that you will make more progress toward your goals if you amplify your energy and make what you are doing fun and joyous. See *Aerobics*.

Stepford Wife Dreams of being a Stepford wife represent your attempts to live up to an impossible ideal of the perfect woman, wife, and mother. You are realizing the price you pay when you strive for the outer appearance of perfection while ignoring the richness of your soul. Perhaps you have a dream of a Stepford wife to remind you that you are already perfect.

Stepmother/Stepfather If you dream of being a stepmother or stepfather, then the dream is about your feelings of not fitting in, being seen as an intruder or an unwelcome interloper. If you dream of dealing with a stepmother or stepfather, consider your role, and feelings, toward her or him. A dream of a stepparent reveals your feelings and attitudes about unwelcome and disruptive energy at home. Alternatively, it can signify a desire for more mother love/father love in your life.

Stepsister/Stepbrother Dreams of a stepsister or stepbrother signify competition for mother love/father love, attention, and affection. They are venting dreams where you are releasing your fear of scarcity, a lack of love, energy, attentiveness, and attractiveness.

Stereo Dreams of a stereo represent harmony and synergy, and that you are working in concert with a relationship partner. See *Music*.

Sterilizing Dreams of sterilizing symbolize a desire to come clean about information you have been withholding. Perhaps your subconscious mind is giving you the message to clean up your act and clear the wreckage of your past by making amends for your transgressions and forgiving yourself and those who have hurt you. A dream of sterilizing is helping you to have a clean start. See *Cleaning*.

Stethoscope Dreams of a stethoscope symbolize a desire to deeply hear what a person has to say, or a desire to be listened to beyond the surface, to have the contents of your heart truly understood.

Stick Dreams of a stick can represent anger and a desire to protect yourself against a real or imagined threat. A stick also signifies intimidation, and that perhaps you are being overly forceful in your negotiations. As well, a stick can be a phallic symbol, which represents aggressive sexual feelings. Consider the feeling tone of the dream to determine its significance for you.

Stillborn Dreams of a stillborn baby are rarely ever a premonition. They are symbolic of incomplete endeavors, thwarted intentions, unfulfilled desires, unfinished business, and that you are grieving about ideas or projects that never got to fully live.

Stilts Dreams of wearing stilts reflect a desire for heightened responsibility, and an elevated stature, or they are a message letting you know that you are bigger and more powerful than you realize. Stilts also signify a desire to stand out in a crowd, to stand above, and that you will be receiving a raise, and gaining status that will allow you to move up in the world.

Sting Dreams of a bee or insect sting signify that you are processing hurt feelings made by an injurious comment, remark, or criticism. Also, they can represent pregnancy and fertility. If you dream of a sting operation, then you are venting out your fear of having a secret discovered. See *Splinter*.

Stockings Because stockings are worn on your legs, dreams of wearing stockings signify that you are gathering your strength and support as you prepare to take a stand for yourself and move forward in life. If you dream of fancy or sexy stockings, then you have a desire for attention and validation of your sexiness and feminine appeal. If you dream of stockings that are hung by a chimney, then this represents receptivity, deservedness, and the expectation of gifts, blessings, and good tidings to come.

Stock Market Dreams of the stock market, depending upon the feeling tone, can mean that you are coming into great wealth or that you are afraid of losing your wealth. Consider them to be a message to seek guidance with regards to whom and what you choose to invest your time, money, and energy. Dreams of the stock market could also be a message from your subconscious mind to begin putting stock in what is valuable to you, as in spending quality time with your family or doing what you really love to do. It is time for a leap of faith, or at least a calculated risk, with regards to love or a creative project. See *Gambling*.

Stockpot Dreams of a stockpot signify that you are marinating in a particular culture, feeling tone, and/or belief system. They are helping you to gain objectivity regarding the ideas and energy you are absorbing from your current environment. See *Cook/Cooking* and *Pot*.

Stomach Dreams of a stomach are about your personal needs, hunger, and gut instincts. They are showing you that you have the courage and the guts to follow your intuition. Dreaming of a stomach also reflects how well you are assimilating or stomaching a new situation or perhaps digesting a new relationship. It is asking you to contemplate what you are truly hungry for. See *Abdomen*.

Stone A dream of a stone symbolizes cold, hard, hurt feelings. Perhaps someone has verbally cast a stone at you and this has caused your heart to turn to stone. If this is the case, then the dream is helping you to remember that sticks and stones may break your bones but names will never hurt you. Also, if you are the one casting the stones, consider that what you do to another you do to yourself. If you dream of getting stoned with marijuana, see *Marijuana*.

Store Dreams of a store symbolize materialism, options, opportunity, and abundance. They may be giving you the message to be mindful of what belief systems you are buying into. See *Grocery Store, Mall,* and *Shopping*.

Stork Dreams of a stork signify that good news is being delivered to you, that you are being rewarded for sticking your neck out, and of course, they could be a sign that a new baby is on the way. See *Bird*.

Storm Dreams of a storm denote that a change is in the air and transformation is afoot. They may be helping you to vent your feelings of overwhelm, and to release feelings of shock regarding your life structures being blown to bits. Keep in mind that if you find your center in the midst of a storm, you will have a sense of exhilaration in the midst of the changing times. See *Venting Dreams,* page 8, and *Breakdown/Breakthrough Dreams,* page 12.

Stove Dreams of a stove signify that something new is cooking up in your life. A romance, a creative endeavor, an idea, or a new opportunity is heating up for you. See *Cook/Cooking*.

Straight Dreams of a straight line, straight hair, or a straight and narrow path reflect simplicity, directness, and honesty.

Straitjacket Dreaming of a straitjacket is a venting dream reflecting a lack of self-trust and your desire to restrain your wild, untamed, crazy, out-of-control feelings. You are wanting to get your emotions under wraps, committing to getting ahold of yourself, and remembering that feelings are not facts.

Stranger Dreaming of a stranger symbolizes an aspect of yourself you haven't met yet. That which is foreign can be judged at first as a threat, bad, or wrong (as in "stranger danger"). Perhaps dreaming of a stranger is a message to keep an open mind in order to learn something from someone new. See *Integration Dreams,* page 10.

Strangle Dreams of being strangled signify inner disharmony, that fear is choking off your ability to express, speak, or communicate your true feelings. Consider what aspect of you is being choked, and what it is that you are resisting expressing.

Straw If you dream of drinking through a straw, then the dream is showing you that you are sucking energy from a particular source to get nourished, quenched, and filled up. Consider what it is that you are drinking and how it makes you feel. If you dream of drawing straws, then you are grappling with the fear of coming up short, or fearing that if you win someone else will come up short. Dreams of a house made of straw mean you have flimsy structures of support in your life that could be huffed and puffed and blown over. In general, straw symbolizes warmth and wealth that is not yet manifested.

Strawberry Dreams of a strawberry represent romance, passion, delicious, juicy love. A strawberry is also symbolic of the vagina, sexuality, fertility, and sexual pleasure. See *Fruit*.

Stream A dream of a stream symbolizes creative flow. If the water in a stream is flowing, then so is your creativity. If the water is stopped or dammed up, then so is your life force. Consider what is blocking you and allow the dream to be a sign for you to begin the process of removing the blocks to your life force so that you can go with the flow. Also, dreaming of a stream may be giving you permission to trust your stream of consciousness, creativity, and artistic expression.

Stretcher Dreams of a stretcher signify that your wounds are being tended to as you move from the scene of the injury toward healing. You are being handled with care as you are carried through a difficult time.

Stretching Dreams of stretching reflect that you are growing and expanding beyond your comfort zone and into your next greatest version of yourself. They can also be giving you the message that you have been stretching yourself too thin, and perhaps it is time for you to set some boundaries. See *Boundary*.

String A dream of string is a message that you are barely holding on to a particular relationship, job, role, or way of seeing yourself. The plot is unraveling, and you may be tying up loose ends, and/or mending what has been torn apart. Perhaps you feel that you are being controlled or manipulated, like a puppet on a string. Consider the feeling tone of the dream to understand its meaning for you. See *Bait, Rope,* or *Sewing*.

Stripe Dreams of a stripe symbolize beauty and style via contrast. You are realizing the magic that happens when opposites attract to make something unique and potentially more interesting than either part would be alone. If you dream of a stripe on the back of a credit card, you are dealing with issues of validity and magnetism. Stripes on an officer's jacket signify that you are dealing with issues of rank, prestige, and respect.

Stuck If you dream of being stuck, then the dream is revealing that you've been stagnant, resigned, and perhaps paralyzed by fear. Also, the dream may be helping you to release your attachments to old ways of being, a relationship, a job, a habit, or your fear of the unknown. See *Quicksand.*

Student If you dream of being a student, then you are open to life's lessons and either you are going through a growth spurt, or you are venting out the stress and pressure of being in a learning environment. The dream may be giving you the message that you can be taught only that which you already know, and that "beginner's mind," according to Buddhists, is a state of enlightenment. See *School* and *Teacher.*

Stump Dreams of a stump symbolize emasculation. Perhaps you've recently been cut down to size and you are feeling lifeless. A dream of a stump is giving you the message that it is time to get into a nurturing environment as you allow yourself to recover.

Submarine Dreams of a submarine symbolize wisdom and mastery in the waters of your deepest, most vulnerable feelings. You are on the defensive and may be preparing for an emotional attack.

Substitute Dreams of a substitute reflect your level of flexibility as it relates to change and transformation. Perhaps you are grappling with feeling second best, an imposter, or you are attempting to fill a void. Dreaming of a substitute may be giving you the message to be patient because in time sometimes a substitute or replacement, upon acceptance, can turn out to be a blessing in disguise and maybe even better than the original.

Subtitle If you dream of a subtitle, then you are grappling with issues of communication and the attempt at understanding another person's language, or you are wanting to be understood. Perhaps you are attempting to read between the lines and grasp the deeper motives and subtext that underlie a person's words.

Suburb A dream of a suburb symbolizes your feelings and attitudes about "the American Dream," settling down, family, home, and kids. Depending upon the feeling tone of the dream, you could be venting out your feelings of disillusionment with the "white-picket fence" ideal. Consider whether it feels like a dream come true or a nightmare.

Subway Dreams of a subway reflect your ability to move in and out of your own underworld, your ability to connect with your shadow and your depths and reemerge into light. See *Goddess* (Persephone). See also *Integration Dreams,* page 10.

Sucking Dreams of sucking signify that you are hungering for emotional, physical, or spiritual sustenance. They may be showing you where you are needy and overly dependent, and that it is time for you to grow up and take responsibility for fulfilling your own needs. See *Vampire.*

Sugar Dreams of sugar signify that you are connecting with the sweetness of life, that you are enjoying the rewards of your labor, or that you are in the process of creating and manifesting something wonderful. Also, they may indicate that you are sweet on someone and love is in the air.

Suicide As is true in "real life," suicide in dreams is about self-loathing, defeat, helplessness, and giving in to negativity. A dream of suicide may be helping you to vent and release self-criticism or is revealing to you the importance of integrating neglected aspects of self. Keep in mind that the darkest hour is just before the dawn, so don't give up five minutes before the miracle. See *Venting Dreams,* page 8, and *Integration Dreams,* page 10.

Suit Dreams of wearing a suit represent formality, a desire to put your best foot forward and be your best. Your subconscious mind is preparing you for a prestigious and successful event. See *Clothes.*

Suitcase Dreams of a suitcase signify that you will be traveling, or that you are transitioning from one level of consciousness to another. Consider the contents of a suitcase as well as the feeling tone, and whether you are carrying your victories or your heartaches into your future. A dream of a suitcase might be helping you to realize that you can begin to release emotional baggage that you have been carrying around that has been weighing you down. See *Luggage* and *Purse.*

Summer Dreams that take place in the summer mean that you are in touch with your your passion, sexuality, and creativity. Also, for many, dreams of the summer indicate a need for rest, relaxation, fun, and a reward for their hard work all year long. See *Goddess* (Aphrodite) and *Sun.*

Summit Dreams of a summit signify that you are accessing your peak potential, your higher self, and your most successful expression. Your goal is in sight and/or you are realizing the solution to your challenge.

Sun Dreams of the sun reflect that you are connecting with your inner light, essence, and charisma. You are coming into a new level of radiance, spirituality, and power.

Sundae Dreams of an ice cream sundae symbolize a treat, reward, pleasure, and satisfaction with your life.

Sunday Dreaming of Sunday represents a desire for a reprieve from business and obligations, to connect with your spiritual practice, and have a meditative reverie as you bask in your inner sunshine. See *Sun.*

Sunflower Dreams of a sunflower denote that you are expressing the sunshine of your spirit. See *Flowers* and *Sun.*

Sunglasses Dreams of wearing sunglasses reflect mystery and secrecy, and that you are being blinded by the light of spiritual realization, or that you may be keeping love and light at bay while you are wearing a cool, aloof mask of protection. Your stylish appearance may be hiding self-doubt and insecurity. Also, a dream of sunglasses could be forecasting that your future will be so bright you will need sunglasses. Consider the feeling tone.

Sunrise A dream of a sunrise indicates a new beginning and infinite opportunity, and that new ideas are beginning to dawn upon you. See *Light* and *Sun.*

Sunset A dream of a sunset symbolizes a successful completion. Also, a sunset forecasts romance or affirms that love and magic are in the air.

Sunshine If it is sunny in a dream, this symbolizes optimism, a positive outlook, an agreeable attitude, and that fortuitous events are on the horizon. Sunshine in a dream is also a sign of higher guidance and good luck, and that things are looking sunny-side up for you. See *Summer.*

Supersizing Dreams of "supersizing it" represent overindulgence and decadence, and that you may be numbing out your feelings while filling up on distractions that don't feed your soul. Consider what it is that you are "supersizing." See *Drive-Through.*

Surfing Dreams of surfing ocean waves can represent oneness with nature and your ability to ride the ebbs and flows of life with mastery and grace. Dreams of Web surfing represent exploration and a desire for information, answers, solutions, and mental stimulation. Channel surfing can be an expression of insatiability. See *Ocean* and *World Wide Web.*

Surgery See *Operation.* See also *Breakdown/Breakthrough Dreams,* page 12.

Swamp Dreams of a swamp signify stagnation and procrastination, and that you have been holding on to old unworkable patterns in your life, relationships, and/or career that are in need of change, movement, and transformation. See *Stuck.*

Swan Dreams of a swan symbolize elegance, grace, and beauty. The soft down of a swan represents all things sensual. A swan represents the perfect joining of masculine and feminine energy within you. See *Goddess* (Aphrodite).

Sweat Dreams of sweat mean either that you have too many blankets on while you sleep, or that you are working out tough issues in your dreams, pushing yourself to the limit as you are working toward results. Also, they may be giving you the message to stop sweating the small stuff.

Swimming Dreams of swimming symbolize an ability to meet your emotional needs and your unconscious desires. You are navigating through your feelings, exploring your soulful depths, reveling in your sexuality, and/or daring to understand the mysteries of your feminine side. See *Ocean, Pool,* and *Water.*

Swing Dreams of a swing signify that you are going back and forth, unable to make up your mind. They can also signify that you are joyously experiencing your own sacred rhythm, and perhaps getting into the swing of things. Consider the feeling tone. See *Pendulum.*

Switch Dreams of a switch signify that you are recognizing that it is your prerogative to change your mind. If you dream of knowing where a switch is, then this indicates control, and self-understanding. If you dream that you cannot find a switch, then you are venting out feelings of powerlessness.

Synchronicity If you experience synchronicity in your dreams, then this denotes a high level of lucidity and genius. Consider the events and details. See *Prophetic Dreams,* page 17.

Syringe Dreams of a syringe mean that you are tying off your power, helping to focus your attention as you search for meaning in your life. Consider the feeling tone of this dream to discern the meaning for you. See *Blood* and *Drugs.*

Syrup Dreams of syrup symbolize sentimentality and nostalgia. Alternatively, they may mean that you are laying flattery on thick and being disingenuous in order to get something.

T

Tabernacle Dreams of a tabernacle symbolize your deep commitment to your higher purpose, to God, and to your mission in life. See *Church.*

Table If you dream of something being on top of a table, then it is something that you are dealing with honestly, clearly, and directly. If you dream of something being under a table, then the dream is revealing that you are being secretive and mysterious, and that there is a hidden agenda. Consider what is on or under the table.

Tack Dreams of a tack reflect awareness of your sharp edges. They could also be a message to consider being more tactful so that your criticism doesn't injure someone. Consider the use of a tack. Also this can be wordplay for your judgments about something or someone in your life being tacky, or having tacky behavior.

Tail Dreams of a tail signify that you are following the leader, allowing someone else to guide you, influence you, or take precedence over your needs.

Tailor Dreams of a tailor symbolize your ability to alter a situation to meet your needs, to make the best out of the raw materials you have been given. See *Clothes* and *Seamstress*.

Talisman Dreams of a talisman symbolize your connection to a time in your past when you felt confident and powerful. They are assisting you to reconnect with an important event or aspect of yourself, an exalted state of consciousness, or a peak experience.

Talk If you talk in your dreams, then this expresses a desire for communication, connection, and to be understood. If you dream of having a difficult time talking, then it is a venting dream helping you to release the fears that keep you from expressing yourself freely. Consider what words you are saying, and to whom, as well as the feeling tone of the dream.

Talking Stick If you dream of a talking stick, then you are becoming aware of the power and impact of your words, or perhaps you are finding your authority along with the desire to express how you really feel. Dreaming of a talking stick might also be a message to you to be respectful of the people with whom you are speaking. You may be realizing that it is as important to listen as it is to speak. See *Wand*.

Talk Radio/Talk Show If your dream features a particular host, DJ, or TV or radio show, then you are identifying with the show's point of view, either idealizing or opposing its opinion. If you dream of being a guest on a radio program or of calling in to one, then this signifies your desire to expose and make public your opinions, passion, and feelings. If you dream of a TV talk show, then this signifies that you are becoming an expert or expressing the area of expertise that you have mastered or that you will master. Consider the topic that is being discussed and the feeling tone of the dream. See *News*, *Oprah Winfrey*, or *Radio*.

Tambourine Dreams of a tambourine symbolize joy, playfulness, and celebration. See *Musical Instrument*.

Taming If you dream of taming an animal, then you are attempting to harness your animal instincts, and manage your true, natural, and authentic feelings in order to be more socially acceptable, to fit in, or to get a desired result. Consider that many health issues are a result of suppression and constraint of natural urges and desires.

Tan Dreams of a tan represent radiance, health, and vitality. If you dream of being too tan, then this represents burnout and insecurity that results in overcompensating. You've been working too hard to achieve an outer appearance.

Tank Dreams of a military tank signify power and defensiveness, and that you may be struggling with an internal war. Your emotions may be tanked up, suppressed, and withheld. If you don't find a healthy expression, there will be an explosion.

If you dream of a water tank that is clean and fresh, then it represents your inner state of being, your vitality, aliveness, health, and well-being. If a tank is dirty, then this represents ill health, and that you are due for a cleansing of your negative thoughts and feelings that may be poisoning your mind, body, and spirit.

Tantric Sex Dreams of tantric sex symbolize your awareness of the sacred in the sexual and the sensual/sexuality of your spiritual devotion. They may also be reflecting the value of being able to properly channel your sexual desires and urges in the direction of your higher aspirations.

Tantrum A dream of a tantrum is a venting dream assisting you to release pent-up rage. Your subconscious mind is suggesting that you find a healthy expression for your anger so that it doesn't bottle up, then explode. See *Anger*.

Tape Dreams of tape signifiy that you are holding things together, perhaps making an effort to remain bonded to a relationship, project, or job. If you dream of recording tape, then this is about holding on to the past, memories, evidence, and proof, and about your ability to preserve your thoughts, feelings, and creations.

Tapestry Dreams of a tapestry reflect your feelings about your life, your past, your experience, your family history, patterns, and habits that you have sewn together over time. Tapestries also signify wealth, luxuriousness, and prosperity that come from life experiences that you have woven together. See *Art/Artist*.

Tar A dream of tar signifies your being stuck or that you have allowed yourself to be pulled into an unworkable pattern.

Target Dreams of a target signify that you are goal oriented, focused on achievement, and preparing to hit your mark. If you dream of hitting a target, then this is an affirmation that you are right where you are supposed to be, prepared, and on track. If you stray far from your target, then you have allowed yourself to be distracted and this is a sign that it is time to get back on track with your goals, life visions, and aspirations.

If you dream of Target, the store, then you are focused on what beliefs you are buying into and looking for a good deal.

Tarot Dreaming about the tarot deck signifies your desire for self-understanding and a peek into your future, and that you are realizing the power of cycles of your life and the roles/archetypes you represent. Perhaps you are seeking direction from an outside source, and the dream is giving you the message that your answers lie within. Consider the card(s) you pull.

Taste Dreams of a particular taste reflect your instincts, intuition, preferences, likes, dislikes, standards, and values. If something tastes good to you, then this is a sign to move forward and proceed in that direction. If something tastes bad, you know it is not for you, or perhaps it will become an acquired taste. Consider what it is you are tasting. See *Mouth*.

Tattoo Dreams of a tattoo signify that you are leaving an indelible mark on someone or on yourself, etching a memory into your soul. They also signify a desire to wear your soul on your sleeve, to make a commitment, and to leave your mark on the world. Dreaming of a tattoo as well can symbolize affiliation or association with a particular tribe or group consciousness. Consider the type of tattoo as well as its place on the body. See *Body* and *Talisman*.

Taurus Dreams of the astrological sign Taurus signify that you are feeling powerful, solid, blunt, stubborn, and perhaps bullheaded and critical. They are giving you the message to beware of taking on too much responsibility and of taking too long to make decisions. Seek to find balance through play, and curb your bluntness. Also, a dream of Taurus could be telling you that it is OK to apologize for making a mistake. See *Bull*.

Tax Dreams of being taxed usually signify that you are venting out feelings and attitudes about being punished or having something taken from you against your will. They also reflect your attitudes about sharing resources, about what you owe, and/or what is due you.

Taxi See *Cab*.

Tea Dreams of tea reflect a desire for a state of relaxation and calm, being soothed and nourished.

Teacher To dream of being a teacher is about attitudes and feelings about authority, a projection of status on someone else, mastery and authority of a particular school of thought. If you dream of being a teacher, consider whether or not you feel adequate for the job, frustrated, or joyous. If you dream that the teacher is someone other than you, then you are projecting what you already know onto that person, and/or projecting your power outside of self. See *School*.

Team Dreams of a team reflect your level of integration among the various aspects of yourself. If you are operating with synergy, then the dream signifies that you are powerfully unified within yourself and you can accomplish whatever you set your mind to. If a team is operating in disharmony, then the dream is a message for you to organize your various sub-personalities into a singular focus so that you can win this game called life.

Teasing Dreams of teasing symbolize flirtation, playfulness, camaraderie, trust, and rapport. You are connecting and engaging with the childlike essence within you and the person you are playing with.

Teddy Bear Dreams of a teddy bear symbolize security, protection, self-love, and comfort for your inner child. They are reassuring you that all is well. See *Bear*.

Teeth Because teeth are located in the mouth, dreams of teeth have a great deal to do with issues of communication and your ability to process, or "chew on," data that you have acquired throughout the day. If you dream of losing your teeth, then you are venting your feelings of insecurity, powerlessness, financial stress, or about the loss or death of a family member. If you dream of false teeth, then you are processing your feelings about lies, broken promises, and falsities. If your teeth are strong and white, you feel bold, confident, and powerful. If you dream that someone is showing you his or her teeth, then this is a sign of aggressiveness and intimidation. If you dream of flossing or brushing your teeth, then you are polishing up your verbal skills, your presentation, and your communication skills in order to make a good impression. Or this could be a sign to clean up a communication that went awry and has left a bad taste in your mouth. Consider the feeling tone of the dream to discern the meaning for you.

Telephone Number Dreams of a telephone number symbolize the importance of making contact or getting your message through to a particular person. If you are unable to dial the numbers or unable to establish a connection, this symbolizes a challenge/breakdown in communication with the person. Consider the numbers you dial and whether or not you are able to get through. If you do make contact, then this can signify your ability to telepathically communicate with the person. See *Number* and *Phone*.

Telephone Operator Dreams of a telephone operator signify your receptivity to assistance, support, and help regarding your communication issues.

Teleprompter Dreams of a teleprompter symbolize inauthenticity, in that you have been relying too heavily on the intelligence and opinions of others and not trusting your own intuition or wisdom.

Telescope Dreams of a telescope symbolize your desire for truth and clarity. You are tapping into your ability to see beyond the scope of your normal, mundane vision into a more vast and far-reaching, intuitive higher vision.

Teleseminar Dreams of a teleseminar indicate that you are learning, teaching, and/or sharing information in a quick and efficient manner. They can also represent the unification among different parts of you: the teacher, students, telephone, and the material that is being taught. See *Conference Call, School, Student,* and *Teacher.*

Television If you dream of watching television, then this is about the wisdom that comes from being able to look at life objectively. Consider the television show, the characters, and the scenario that you are watching. The dream could be a message for you to stop being content to live vicariously through other people and to engage more fully in your own life. If you dream of being on television, then this signifies prominence, success, and recognition. Perhaps you are preparing to become more public with your work, mission, or life's purpose. See *Actor/Actress* and *Celebrity.*

Temple Dreams of a temple signify that you are connecting with the place within you where heaven and earth align. You are recognizing the inherent sacredness of your body. See *Church.*

Ten If you dream of the number 10, this represents perfection, and your attempt to achieve an ideal.

Ten Commandments Dreams of the Ten Commandments signify your attitudes and beliefs about the rules that govern your life versus your authentic feelings. They can also signify your moral code, rules, and standards that you impose upon others or that you rebel against.

Tennis Dreams of tennis signify that you are giving and receiving, and participating in the back-and-forth of love and a relationship. They can also represent feelings of a competitive banter, that you are keeping score, trying to get your point across, and making sure that your message makes it over the net.

Tennis Court Dreams of a tennis court indicate your rules and parameters with regards to love. If you are on a tennis court, then you are actually engaged in a relationship or you are willing to play the game.

Tent Dreams of a tent signify adventure, that you are living on the edge, and perhaps desiring a temporary shelter and reprieve from life as you know it.

Terminal Dreams of an airport terminal symbolize the beginning or completion of a journey. You are in the midst of a transition. If you dream of a terminal illness, then the dream reflects your feelings and attitudes about death, dying, and attachment to the people, places, and things that are important to you in life.

Terrorist A dream of a terrorist symbolizes fear of death, or of your unintegrated shadow. Because every person in a dream reflects an aspect of you, the dream could be an integration dream helping you to embrace and bring to balance your extreme feelings of right and wrong, righteousness, and fierce attachment to your belief system. A nightmare about a terrorist attack is a venting dream allowing you to release and process through your fears of being violated and invaded, and feelings about world events. See *Venting Dreams,* page 8.

Test To be tested in a dream indicates that you are going through a rite of passage. If you dream of passing a test, then you are ready to move on to the next level of advancement in your life. If you don't pass a test, then you are more aware of what it is that you need to focus on and learn in order to pass, or you are venting out your fears of failing. If you feel that you are being put to the test during a challenging time in your life, then the dream is helping you to rise to the occasion. See *Labyrinth* and *Sphinx.*

Testes Dreams of testes symbolize masculine strength, will, virility, force, power, and potency. If you've got balls, you have the gall to put yourself out there. You are feeling audacious, courageous, and sexual.

Testosterone Dreams about testosterone symbolize your feelings and attitudes about male virility, masculine strength, empowerment, heroism, and/or abuse. Consider your feelings and associations and whether or not they empower you. See *Ego* and *Hero/ Heroine.*

Text Message Dreams of a text message signify telepathy and a desire to connect and to stay in touch with someone from afar. You have a desire to get to the point, and to spell out what it is you want to communicate.

Thanksgiving Thanksgiving represents a state of grace. If you dream of Thanksgiving your attitude of gratitude is aligning you with grace and the resonance of miracles, magic, and abundance. A cornucopia of blessings is forthcoming.

Thank You Dreams of someone saying, "Thank you," signify that you are embracing an attitude of gratitude. Dreams of giving thanks or of someone saying thank you to you are indicating that you will soon be acknowledged and that you are allowing yourself to be recognized as you are becoming more aware of all the things in your life that are worthy of your gratitude.

Thawing Dreams of thawing something that has been frozen reflect a desire to break the ice in a relationship or with a colleague at work. You may be warming up emotionally, mentally, and sexually, allowing your fears to melt, and your ego walls to dissolve.

Theater Dreams of a theater symbolize a desire for exposure, expression, and recognition. Perhaps you are wanting some attention and validation, or you are becoming aware of the masks you wear in life. You may be observing the thoughts, feelings, and attitudes you present to the world, and perhaps you are beginning to recognize that all of life is a play. See *Drama Queen/Drama King* and *Stage.*

Therapist Dreams of a therapist signify that you are connecting with your higher self, your own inner wisdom and objectivity that have all the answers you need. You would be wise to take your own advice. See *Life Coach.* See also *Prophetic Dreams,* page 17.

Thermometer If you dream of a thermometer, then your body might be literally too hot or too cold. Also, a dream of a thermometer could signify degrees of separation between you and someone you love. It might be showing you where you've gotten out of balance, and where it might be appropriate for you to heat things up in your life, or to take time to chill out. See *Cold.*

Thermos Dreams of a thermos signify that you are attempting to control and/or maintain your energy level. If you are attempting to keep something hot or warm, you are wanting to keep the passion alive. If you are trying to keep something chilled, you are trying to keep things cool and calm.

Thief Dreams of a thief symbolize a shadow aspect of you that feels disenfranchised and thinks that it can be satisfied only by using and taking advantage of others. Your fear-based thoughts and behaviors are robbing you blind. Also, these dreams can be showing you that you have allowed your power and energy to be stolen.

Thigh Dreams of a thigh signify the strength to stand up for yourself, and that you have the will to support and honor yourself. They signify your power and ability to walk away from what you don't want and/or to walk toward your heart's desires. If thighs are open, then you are receptive to a person or situation in your life. If thighs are closed, then you instinctively are resisting someone that wants to interact with you.

Thimble Dreams of a thimble signify that you desire protection from the jabs and pokes of negativity from your inner critic.

Thin If you dream of a thin person or animal, then this signifies a frail and vulnerable aspect of yourself. Depending upon the context of a dream, thin can signify a lack of significance, as opposed to something that is heavy being important and weighty. However, if you are weight-conscious, then you might believe that thinner is the winner. So a dream of being thin might be a wish fulfillment dream for you. Or perhaps, it could be giving you the message to release an obsession about your body.

Third Eye Dreams of a third eye represent wisdom and telepathy, and that you can see beyond the mundane into the fourth dimension and create and/or deepen a spiritual context for your life.

Thirst If you are thirsty in a dream, this could represent literally that your throat is dry, and in need of refreshment. However, it may very well mean that you are thirsty for knowledge, information, love, security, and spiritual connection. It could be telling you that there is a drought in your life that needs to be tended to immediately. See *Drinking*.

Thirteen Dreams of being thirteen years old symbolize rebellion and awkwardness as you move through a changing and transforming time of your life. Also, they may be assisting you in releasing your fears of the illusion of bad luck.

Thorn To dream of a thorn signifies an annoyance, an unhealed emotional wound, or a place of extreme pain and sensitivity in your life. Dreaming of a thorn, you are revealing your defense mechanisms and rough ego edges that protect your vulnerability and truest self. See *Splinter*.

Thread If you dream that a thread in a garment is coming loose, you are in the process of unraveling a particular issue, structure, or role that you wear. If you dream that you are sewing, then you are creating something new or repairing a communication that has gone awry. A dream of thread could also be showing you that your relationship is hanging by a thread, and that it is time to either cut it loose or sew it back together. See *Sewing*.

Three Dreams of the number 3 represent a triad, successful alliances, a trinity, mind/body/spirit, or mother/father/child. They are giving you the message to explore your creative expression, in public speaking, acting, or writing. Alternatively, they may indicate that you feel that three is a crowd, and that you are the third wheel. See *Triangle*.

Threshold If you dream of a threshold, then you are on the verge of change, transformation, expansion, adventure, and growth from one level to another.

Thrift Shop Dreams of a thrift shop symbolize opportunism, thriftiness, and being a penny-pincher. You may be grappling with issues of lack and limitation, and feeling undeserving of something new. See *Antiques* and *Hand-me-downs*.

Throat Dreams of a throat symbolize communication, expression, creation, and manifestation. You are realizing that words have power, and what you say has the potential to create and change things. Dreaming of a throat might be a message for you to speak up for yourself, or to realize that sometimes silence is golden. A throat in a dream also represents your vulnerability or your issues with betrayal, as in someone "going for the throat" or being a "cut-throat." Consider the feeling tone of the dream to discern the meaning for you.

Throne Dreams of a throne signify that you are in your seat of power and connecting with your divine stature. A throne in a dream represents a place of authority, confidence, belief in your abilities, and the awareness that you need not chase after opportunities; they will find you.

Throwing If you dream of throwing a ball, then you are aware that you get what you give in the reciprocal nature of life. Also throwing signifies that you are releasing or eliminating something or someone.

Thumb Dreams of a thumb symbolize your ability to judge, rate, and have an opinion on what is happening in your life, as in thumbs up, or thumbs down. If you have a dream that you are under someone's thumb, then the dream may be waking you up to your ability to change your current circumstances and claim your power. A thumb in a dream can also represent something that is important yet taken for granted. Consider trying to pick something up without using your thumb.

Thunder Dreams of thunder symbolize power and your acceptance or resistance to it. Thunder can also represent anger or rage that brings about change and transformation.

Tiara Dreams of a tiara signify that you are connecting with your royal essence, your higher faculties, and most illuminated wisdom. See *Chakra* (7th) and *Crown*.

Tick Dreams of a ticking sound signify that you are aware that the clock is ticking and that you are afraid that time is running out. Or you may be realizing that which makes you tick, your passion and bliss, and that which gets your heart racing. If a dream is about a bloodsucker, see *Leech*, *Parasite*, or *Vampire*.

Ticket If you dream of getting a ticket for doing something wrong or breaking the law, then this signifies your inner critic or judge punishing you for breaking your own moral code. If you dream of a ticket to a theatrical event, then this signifies that you have paid the price for what you want in life, and you are feeling valid, deserving, and entitled.

Tidal Wave Dreams of a tidal wave symbolize emotional overwhelm, as in extreme sadness or as in falling in love. They are reflecting that you are undergoing great transformation and the message for you is to dive down into the deep end of your emotional ocean where the waters are still, calm, and peaceful. Or, if you prefer, allow yourself the space to cry and release any energy that has been held back.

Tides Dreams of the ocean tides symbolize your awareness of the cycles of life, endings and beginnings, giving and receiving, and fullness and emptiness. Perhaps you are coming to trust the patterns of life. See *Cycle*, *High Tide*, *Low Tide*, and *Moon*.

Tiger Dreams of a tiger reflect your realization of your untamed, animal instincts, your passion, sexuality, and power. See *Animal*.

Tight Dreams of tightly fitting clothing symbolize constriction, and a lack of freedom and mobility. If you are feeling tight inside, then you may be venting out your fear of expressing yourself. Perhaps a dream of feeling tight is showing you that in a close bond you share with someone perhaps there has become too much dependency or codependence. If this is the case, the dream may be giving you the message to allow yourself some space. See *Codependence*.

If a dream is about being drunk, see *Drunk*.

Tightrope A dream of a tightrope signifies that you are living on your cutting edge. It could signify either adventure and courage or a feeling of vulnerability, frailty, and insecurity. Consider the feeling tone of the dream and whether or not there is a safety net to catch you if you fall.

Tile If you dream of decorative tile, then this represents your ego, or protective devices to cover up, hide, and defend your true essence or your perceived flaws.

Timber Dreams of timber symbolize your passion and that which ignites warmth within you. If you dream of someone yelling, "Timber!" then the dream is giving you the message to get out of your own way, because the relationship or life situation you are in just may come crashing down upon you. See *Wood*.

Time Dreams of time reflect your attitudes and feelings regarding time, punctuality, deadlines, order, and structure. They are a reflection of how you operate within the ego world. Dreaming of wanting to know the time signifies a desire for a reality check, as in "What's really going on here?" You may be coming to your senses and venting out your fear of being late. See *Clock* and *Watch*.

Time-out Dreams of a time-out can signify that you are being punished by your inner critic for being naughty, or they may be telling you that you need to pause to reflect, to become centered and refocused so that you can reemerge powerful and operating as your best. See *Dugout*.

Tire Tracks Dreams of tire tracks signify that you are going somewhere with your life, and you are on track to leave proof of your existence and to make your mark. If you see tire tracks in front of you, then you may be feeling that you have been left or abandoned. If you see tire tracks behind you, then you are leaving a situation, perhaps a job or a relationship, behind.

Tissue Dreams of a tissue reflect that you are nurturing, taking care of, and cleaning yourself up, perhaps allowing yourself to cry or to have an emotional release.

TiVo Dreams of TiVo represent your desire for control and power over the programming of your mind and life. They are showing you that you are attempting to keep track of your favorite memories, and/or that you are holding on to the past.

Toaster Dreams of a toaster signify that you are warming up emotionally in or to a project or a relationship. They might also be giving you the message that you are plugged into your purpose for being alive and that is why you feel warm, fuzzy, and toasty.

Toastmasters A dream of Toastmasters signifies that you are preparing for a public presentation of the thoughts, feelings, expertise, and unique gifts you have to share with the world. If the dream feels stressful, then you are venting out and moving through your fears of public speaking, and you are building up your confidence to express yourself more effectively. See *Speech*.

Tobacco According to certain Native American traditions, dreams of tobacco are considered to be a sacred offering and a blessing. If you dream of smoking tobacco, then this could symbolize a prayer or petition to God or to the Great Spirit. Alternatively, tobacco can signify that you have a dirty habit that is an attempt at masking your hurt and pain and keeps you blind to what's really going on. See *Pipe* and *Smoking*.

Toes Dreams of toes signify that you are paying attention to the details, and honoring the little things in life that make all the difference. You are getting a grip on your life and finding your balance.

Toilet Dreams of a toilet signify that you are releasing and letting go of negativity as you flush your troubles down the drain and become willing to start anew.

Toilet Paper Dreams of toilet paper denote that you are wiping away your troubles, cleansing and clearing negativity from your life, and releasing energetic residue you might have from unhealthy relationships or old disempowering life circumstances.

Tomato Dreams of a ripe tomato symbolize passion and healthy sexuality in full swing. If you dream of a green or an unripe tomato, then this signifies that your passion and romantic feelings are budding or just beginning to unfold and they require patience, and tender loving care. If you dream of a tomato being thrown at you, then you are venting your fears of being publicly humiliated or embarrassed. See *Fruit* and *Red.*

Tomb Dreams of a tomb reflect your feelings and attitudes toward death and dying. See *Cemetery, Death,* and *Goddess* (Persephone).

Tomboy Dreaming of a tomboy signifies that you are getting in touch with and celebrating your young boy energy. Perhaps the dream is giving you the message to give yourself the freedom to take some risks, to be wild and adventurous, and to remember that it is OK to make a mistake and skin your knees. See *Boy.*

Tongue Dreams of a tongue symbolize expression, speech, taste, your preferences, likes, and dislikes. They also represent your feelings about expressing yourself. See *French Kiss, Talk,* and *Taste.*

Tools A dream of tools symbolizes your street smarts and coping mechanisms for life, your resources, and formula for handling challenges. If tools are in good shape, then you are prepared to take on your life challenges. If tools are broken or ineffective, the dream is telling you that it's time to acquire some new coping strategies. Keep in mind that every challenge you face affords you a new opportunity to discover a new tool. See *Drill, Hammer,* or *Shed*

Toothbrush Dreams of a toothbrush signify that you are cleaning up a communication that perhaps went awry, polishing and editing your ability to express yourself. They may be giving you the message to think before you speak, to be impeccable with your words, and to say what you mean and mean what you say. See *Mouth* and *Teeth.*

Toothpick Dreams of a toothpick are a message for you to pick your words carefully and edit your words mindfully. See *Teeth.*

Torch Dreams of a torch signify that you have hope, faith, and the ability to see beyond human limitations. They are also about your connection to your spiritual source, your triumph over your challenges, and your confidence in your ability to confront your shadows.

Totem Pole Dreams of a totem pole symbolize a sacred marker to remind you of your power and of who you really are. They can also represent rank, status, and power. Consider whether you are high or low on a totem pole. As well, a totem pole is a phallic symbol, perhaps representing your desire for sacred sexuality.

Toupee If dreams of hair represent your power, then dreams of a toupee denote a desire for power, sexuality, youthful virility, and strength. If you dream of wearing a toupee, then you are unwilling to be naked and honest about yourself in your relationships or in your life, perhaps because you are ashamed of exposing your true thoughts. See *Hair* and *Wig*.

Tourist Dreams of being a tourist signify your attitudes and feelings of being out of your element. To dream of being a tourist means that you will either be traveling soon, or that you are going through major changes in your life. See *Foreign*.

Towel Dreams of a towel reflect that you are feeling comforted as you are cleaning up your life and getting yourself together. Dreaming of a towel means that you have assistance that will help you through the transitions of your life.

Tower Dreams of a tower are about power. If you are towering over someone, you are overpowering or intimidating that person. In the fairy tale the princess gets locked in a tower, representing prison, isolation, emotional distance, aloofness from the rest of the world, and victimhood, longing, yearning, captivity, and unjust punishment. According to the tarot, dreams of a tower signify that your foundation has been rocked and that you are reexamining your foundational beliefs.

Tow Truck Dreams of a tow truck signify that you are either in need of assistance, or that you are realizing how helpful and crucial your talents and gifts are to the well-being of those who need you. Perhaps you are stuck and are in need of being pulled out of your comfort zone or places of difficulty in your life.

Toy Dreams of a toy signify that you are having frivolous fun, taking life playfully, and connecting to your childhood essence. They might also be revealing your childish attitudes toward life, and immaturity. See *Teddy Bear*.

Track If you dream of being on a racetrack, then you are participating in the human race, in the game of life, and are on track with your goals. If you dream of being off the track, then the dream is showing you that you have become distracted or you have lost your way, and it is giving you the message that you must use your instincts and read the signs to find your way back. If you dream of being on the wrong side of the tracks, then the dream is showing you that you have gone against your instincts, and that it is time to get back on track to your highest destiny.

Tractor Dreams of a tractor signify that you are upleveling your life, unearthing your foundation, and undergoing major transformation. Perhaps you are feeling disheveled in the midst of this life makeover or because you are digging up old memories that connect you to aspects of your past that you had forgotten about. See *Breakdown/Breakthrough Dreams,* page 12.

Trade Dreams of a trade denote that you are sharing and offering an exchange of energy. Consider the feeling tone, what is being traded, and to whom. See *Stock Exchange.*

Trader Joe's Dreams of Trader Joe's signify that you are accepting the many deliciously diverse aspects of yourself. You are realizing the beauty and richness of the people you interact with in your life and as you do your soul is being fed a feast. See *Grocery Store.*

Traffic Dreams of traffic mean that you are feeling mentally backed up, emotionally congested, or sexually frustrated, stuck in a gridlock of your unprocessed feelings and unexpressed ideas. They are giving you the message that you need to process, vent, and release your stress, anxiety, guilt, and shame. See *Constipation.*

Trailer Dreams of a trailer signify that you are riding on the coattails of someone else's energy, getting hitched, and/or realizing that if you hook up with the right person, you can go places. Perhaps they are showing you that you have been relying too heavily upon someone else, and it is time for you to take the wheel of your own life, and own it with full responsibility. See *Parasite.*

Train Dreams of a train indicate that you have drive and momentum, and that you are moving boldly through life by making connections with other people. They are a message either that you are already on track with your goals and desires or, if you are not, to get on track with them. Consider the feeling tone of the dream. See *Conductor, Railroad Tracks,* and *Track.*

Transformation If you dream of going through a transformation, then you are making great progress in your own evolution. You are realizing that sometimes what might appear to be the worst thing that could ever happen to you turns out to be a blessing in disguise, and that something bigger, greater, and more expansive is always in store for you. See *Butterfly.*

Transition Dreams of a transition signify that you are making changes, progress, and improvements, and that you are evolving along your enlightenment path. Your life is under construction; and though the process might be messy, it can be healthy for you to die daily and be reborn with each breath you take. See *Breakdown/Breakthrough Dreams,* page 12.

Transparent If in a dream something is transparent, then this could signify either a lack of importance, or that your true feelings are being exposed and you are wearing your heart on your sleeve with nothing to hide. See *Fishbowl.*

Transsexual A dream of a transsexual is about sexual expansion or confusion. Consider the feeling tone of the dream to discern its meaning for you. You are either embracing your opposite and/or dismissing or disowning your own sex. Dreaming of a transsexual can also be about the celebration of your opposite nature, feminine or masculine.

Trap If you dream of being caught in a trap, then you are venting your feelings of victimhood and releasing your fear of intimacy and commitment, and of losing your freedom. If you dream of setting a trap, then the dream is revealing that you have been operating with ulterior motives and perhaps you are releasing your guilt, shame, and/or fears of being caught. See *Quicksand* and *Tar.*

Trapeze Dreams of being on a trapeze signify freedom and skill, and that you have the ability to masterfully swing to your spiritual heights. See *Tightrope.*

Trauma Dreams of a trauma are assisting you to vent out your fear, overwhelm, and feelings of victimization. See *Breakdown/ Breakthrough Dreams,* page 12, and *Venting Dreams,* page 8.

Traveling See *Journey.*

Tray Dreams of a tray symbolize service. You are either wanting to serve or to be of service to someone else. See *Platter.*

Treadmill Dreams of a treadmill represent frustration with the circular nature of your life, repetition, and feeling that you are getting nowhere quickly. They may be giving you the message to stop what you are doing, break the pattern, and await clarity and divine direction before reengaging your energy.

Treasure Dreams of treasure signify your spirit and that you are connected to your authentic self. Also, they forecast wealth, prominence, richness, and success. If a treasure is buried, then you are grappling with your finances and issues of abundance, and the illusion that your wealth is out of reach. Also, a dream of treasure may be giving you the message that you need not seek riches because your greatest resources and treasures are in your own backyard.

Tree Dreams of a tree mean that you are solidly rooted, deeply grounded, and yet exalted in your stature and connection with spirit. Also, they might be giving you the message to branch out and connect with your family tree. See *Branches.*

Trenches Dreams of being in the trenches signify that you are in the thick of a life-altering situation. You may be feeling as if your life is a war zone, and you are realizing that it is your responsibility to create a peaceful resolution. See *War.*

Trespassing Dreams of trespassing indicate that you have or someone else has crossed your moral boundaries and/or someone has invaded your space. They may be giving you the message to forgive those who have trespassed against you, or to make amends to those whom you have crossed. See *Boundary.*

Trial Dreams of a trial signify that you are assessing your innocence or guilt or that of someone who has hurt you. You are integrating and grappling with your inner critic and judge, passing a verdict about an important situation that has just occurred in your life. See *Guilty, Innocent, Judge,* and *Jury.*

Triangle Dreams of a triangle symbolize a sacred trinity. They may be giving you the message that you are integrating your mind, body, and spirit, or father, mother, and child, aspects of yourself. You may be feeling the power or the tension of being between two important people in your life. See *Three*.

Trick Dreams of playing a trick on someone symbolize your connection to the shamanistic way of learning, growing, and transforming. If you dream of playing tricks on someone, then the dream is revealing your ego games, manipulation, and avoidance techniques to mask unhealed wounds. If you dream of magic tricks, see *Magician*.

Trinity Dreaming of a trinity represents your desire for balance of your body, mind, and spirit, and your alignment with the Father, Son, and the Holy Ghost. See *Triangle*.

Triplets If you dream of triplets, then you are integrating three distinct and important aspects of yourself. Consider the feeling tone of each of the triplets and the feeling of the dream. See *Three*. See also *Integration Dreams,* page 10.

Triumph Dreams of a triumph are an affirmation that you will overcome the challenges you face. Also, you may be realizing that the difficulties in your life offer you an opportunity to realize how heroic and wise you are capable of being.

Trophy If you dream of winning a trophy, then you are acknowledging yourself for your hard work and accomplishments. Your subconscious mind is giving you the message that you have just reached a milestone. The dream is helping you to prepare shelf space in your heart and mind for a forthcoming win, victory, and success.

Truck Dreams of a truck signify that you are powerfully driving through life with ambition, force, and the willpower to go where you want to go. Also, they signify that you have the strength to carry other people along with you. See *Car*.

True North If you dream of the North Star or a compass pointing at true north, then this represents that you are on track with your goals and your highest destiny, and you are connected to your inner guidance system. See *Compass*.

Trump Card Dreams of a trump card signify that you are feeling confident, successful, bold, and powerful because you have an ace up your sleeve and a secret weapon to help you to master your circumstance and manifest your heart's desires. See *Donald Trump*.

Trumpet Dreams of a trumpet signify tooting your own horn or singing the praises of someone you are proud of. They are giving you the message to take pride in your accomplishments and to relish your victories. See *Musical Instrument*.

Trust Fund Dreams of a trust fund reflect your awareness of being abundantly supported by the universe. You are free, taken care of, and trusting that all is well. See *Inheritance*.

Tsunami Dreams of a tsunami represent an enormous emotional catharsis. You are undergoing a massive, radical, and quantum change, physically, mentally, and spiritually. See *Ocean, Tidal Wave,* and *Water*. See also *Venting Dreams,* page 8, and *Breakdown/Breakthrough Dreams,* page 12.

Tummy Tuck Dreams of a tummy tuck can represent a desire for a more svelte shape and to be more physically appealing. They could also be a message to release all that blocks you from being able to connect with your gut instinct. See *Stomach*.

Tumor Dreams of a tumor are about negativity and disempowering beliefs that have become stuck within you. They are a wake-up call to heal past traumas and shocks to your body, mind, and soul. Keep in mind that you cannot heal what you cannot feel.

Tunnel If you dream of a tunnel, then you are exploring and moving through the deeper regions of your psyche, bringing awareness to your unconscious thought patterns and beliefs. If you are moving through a challenging time, as in a "dark night of the soul," then the dream is giving you the message that the darkest hour is before the dawn. See *Integration Dreams,* page 10.

Tunnel Vision Dreams of tunnel vision are giving you the message to focus on the accomplishment of the task at hand. Alternatively, they could be giving you the message that you have become rigid and stubborn, and that perhaps you should look on the bright side and broaden your perspective.

Tupperware Dreams of Tupperware reflect that you are preserving and saving your energy, ideas, resources, and potential for a later date. See *Ziplock Bag*.

Turkey Dreams of turkey signify that you are connecting to the martyr archetype, becoming saintly and virtuous in your willingness to sacrifice yourself so that others may live and have a better life. If you dream of a turkey dinner, then this represents that you are feasting on an attitude of gratitude and abundance. See *Bird* and *Thanksgiving*.

Turquoise Dreaming of turquoise represents balance between your masculine and feminine aspects of self, your human and divine nature, your light and your dark. You are learning to creatively express and manifest your intuitive guidance into reality.

Turtle Dreams of a turtle are a message for you to sit still, be patient, and go slow. Once you find your center and go at a slower pace, you just might find that you will win the race. Dreams of a turtle are also a message for you to honor your creative source, to maintain your groundedness and connection with your mother, or perhaps mother earth. Because a turtle's shell is hard, these dreams can be revealing your defense strategies and your tough outer shell that protects and defends your vulnerability, and might be keeping you at arm's length from the intimacy you desire. Consider the feeling tone.

Tweezers Dreams of tweezers signify that you are plucking from your life experience the thoughts, feelings, and people that do not support you. You are realizing your ability to choose what empowers you and eliminating that which does not.

Twelve Dreams of the number 12 signify completion. Perhaps you have come full circle in a project, a relationship, or an issue. Because there are twelve months in a year and twelve astrological signs in the zodiac, perhaps dreaming of the number 12 is telling you to wait a year, or a full cycle, before you make a decision. Consider that numerologically a twelve becomes a three (1+2=3). See *Three* and *12-step Program*.

12-step Program Dreams of a 12-step program represent a light at the end of the tunnel. You are coming to believe in a higher power, and becoming willing to turn your life and will over to the care of that higher power in order to get you through a drastic and powerful time of change. You are becoming honest about what is no longer working for you, and willing to take responsibility for your life. If you have not yet started on this path, a dream about it may be a sign for you to begin. See *Breakdown/Breakthrough Dreams,* page 12.

Twenty-one Because the age of twenty-one in North America represents adulthood, dreaming of it can signify your feelings and attitudes about adulthood, freedom, responsibility, rebellion, or maturity.

If a dream is about the card game, see *Cards* and *Gambling.*

Twins Dreams of twins signify the twin aspects of you, which may be your opposing sub-personalities, and dualistic thinking. See *Two.*

Two If you dream of the number 2, then this signifies partnership, relationship, intimacy, duality, polarity, completion, and fulfillment. The two in the I Ching represents receptivity, sensitivity, and femininity. So a dream of the number 2 is suggesting that you are open and receptive to a fulfilling partnership.

Tylenol Dreams of Tylenol symbolize a desire for relief from physical, emotional, or psychological pain, or a quick fix. Keep in mind that you can't heal what you can't feel.

Typewriter If you dream of a typewriter, then you are romantic, idealistic, and even nostalgic for days gone by. The dream can also be showing you that your communication style is rigid, old-fashioned, and outmoded. Consider that the dream may be telling you that it is time for you to learn a new way of expressing yourself.

U

Udder Dreaming of a cow's udder is about motherhood, nurturing, sacrifice, and that you are being fed and nurtured by what is essential in life.

UFO Dreams of a UFO reflect your attitudes, feelings, and opinions about people, ethnicities, customs, and traditions that are foreign to you. Because of the changes in your life, these dreams may be helping you to process the fact that everything seems different and strange to you. They may be a message for you to connect to the vastness of life, to expand your consciousness to behold greater understanding and intelligence beyond your normal scope. See *Integration Dreams,* page 10.

Ugg Boots Dreams of Ugg boots signify that you are standing up for your childlike essence. You are willing to accommodate your innocence and your desire for coziness, nurturing, and warmth in order to help you feel grounded. And your cold feet are thawing out so that you can step into commitment.

Ugly Dreams of an ugly person or object signify that you are grappling with your shadow. They are helping you to come to terms with and embrace all aspects of yourself, especially those aspects that you deem unflattering, unlovable, and unappealing. See *Shadow.* See also *Integration Dreams,* page 10.

U-Haul A dream of U-Haul means that you are in transition between one space in your life and another. It also indicates that perhaps you need support during this time of your life, or that it is time to be more self-sufficient. Consider the feeling tone to determine the message for you.

Ulcer A dream of an ulcer signifies that there is something eating at you. You have been holding back your feelings and the dream is giving you the message to express yourself and to stop procrastinating regarding making amends to or forgiving someone that has wronged you.

Umbilical Cord Dreams of an umbilical chord represent your connection to your mother. They are revealing that your most vulnerable, infantile self needs to feel connected to a nurturing, higher, and loving source. Or they are showing you that you have become dependent on a source outside of yourself.

Umbrella Dreams of an umbrella reflect your coping strategies, the way you handle challenges, confrontations, change, or unpredictable circumstances. They can also represent the real or perceived need to protect your thoughts from negative influences.

Uncle A dream of an uncle can be a sign to surrender, to release and let go. Consider the qualities you would use to describe this male role model and the feeling tone of the dream.

Unconscious Dreams of your unconscious mind signify that you are dealing with an issue that is in your blind spot, something that you can't quite put your finger on. Or perhaps you are bringing awareness to the places in your life in which you have been sleep-walking and were unaware.

Under A dream of feeling under the thumb, under the control, under the scrutiny, or under someone's authority is telling you that you have allowed yourself to be in a weak position. Also, the dream can be showing you that you are searching for the esoteric truth that lies beneath the surface. Alternatively, something under, as in the ground under your feet, can represent support and even unconditional love. Consider the feeling tone of the dream to discern its message for you.

Underground Dreams of being underground symbolize your awareness of your deeper feelings, creativity, and intuition. They can also reveal your need to take a break, hide out, and heal. If something takes place underground, such as an "underground operation," then this signifies secretive feelings and motives that you are ashamed of, or that have yet to be embraced by the light of your being. See *Goddess* (Persephone) and *Subway*.

Understanding Dreams where you have compassion and/or you deeply understand another person who heretofore you judged as inadequate, inferior, or unlovable can be deeply healing and transforming. When you dream of having compassion for how another person feels or thinks, you can then transfer that understanding into your waking state, and experience enormous breakthroughs in your relationships and in your life in general. See *Integration Dreams*, page 10.

Undertaker Dreams of an undertaker symbolize the aspect of your consciousness that can escort you between the realm of life and death. You are opening your eyes to the reality of change and are embracing life's passages. See *Goddess* (Persephone).

Undertow Dreams of an undertow signify that you are feeling overwhelmed and out of control with emotions and passion. You may be venting out your fear of being seduced or unable to stand your ground in the face of a persuasive person.

Underwater Dreams of being underwater signify that you are allowing yourself to be immersed in a relationship, a belief system, or your feminine nature, and you are exploring the deep end of your mysterious nature, sexuality, and depth.

Underwear Dreams of underwear represent what is "behind the scenes" of your life, your true, intimate feelings and sexual longings or fantasies.

Undressing A dream of undressing reflects a desire for intimacy, sexuality, and exposure. Consider the feeling tone of the dream. If you feel good, then you are enjoying being honest, truthful, and naked. If you are uncomfortable, then you may not be quite ready for intimacy and revealing your true feelings. Also, if you are uncomfortable, the dream can be helping you to vent and release shame and negativity about your body and sexuality. See *Naked.*

Unemployed Employment is symbolic of value, power, purpose, and being plugged into your purpose for being alive. A dream of being unemployed may reflect that you are temporarily disconnected from your source, and that you have taken a detour from your life's path. The dream may also be helping you to release your attachments to what you do for a living as being a statement about who you are.

Unfaithful Dreams of being unfaithful signify that you are grappling with your ability to trust yourself or not. You are coming to terms with your opportunistic tendencies, and fears of intimacy and/or commitment. You may be venting out and releasing feelings of grief, guilt, and shame about past transgressions.

Unicorn Dreams of a unicorn signify that you are connected to magic, miracles, innocence, enchantment, and the fact that dreams do come true.

Uniform If you dream of wearing a uniform, then you are processing your feelings about conforming to the norm, and identifying with a particular role, custom, or tribe. Perhaps the dream is showing you that you have been hiding your uniqueness and suppressing your individuality. Consider the feeling tone of the dream.

Universe Dreams of the universe represent your awareness of your connection to the whole of life, the big picture, your higher purpose, and your connection to all people and all things everywhere.

University If you dream of a university, then you are in a phase of great learning, growing, and expanding. You are developing and cultivating your gifts, talents, and potential with an openness to receive the lessons the universe is trying to teach you. See *School, Student,* and *Teacher.*

Unraveling Dreams of a string or fabric unraveling signify that the fabric of a relationship, or your ideas and foundational beliefs about life are falling apart at the seams. They are revealing your attitudes and opinions about death, life after death, and attachments.

Unwrapping Dreaming of unwrapping a gift reflects your wanting to reveal the true essence of yourself, your intimate relationship beliefs, and the true nature of life. You are looking for honesty and wanting to remove the layers and veils that keep it hidden. See *Undressing.*

Up Dreams of turning something up signify an amplification of energy, heightened power, and optimism. They may be showing you that you are moving up in the world, feeling above your worries, and knowing that great opportunities are on the horizon.

Uphill If you are walking or driving uphill, then you are surmounting your challenges a step at a time, and doing what it takes to make progress in your life. You may be venting out or releasing your frustration, stress, and resistance to life being more difficult than you bargained for, or for things taking longer than you expected. See *Mountain.*

Upholstery Dreams of upholstery signify a desire for a kind word, a gentle touch, or a nurturing embrace to take the edge off a challenging situation, or just to make your life more comfortable. Perhaps these dreams are showing you that you have a soft place to land should you fall. Alternatively, they may show that you are resisting someone's compliments because you feel that they are all fluff and that that person is disingenuous.

Upper Back Dreams of your upper back reflect your issues with giving and receiving support. Perhaps you feel that you are carrying the weight of the world, or that you are in need of a pat on the back from the people in your life. See *Back* and *Codependence.*

UPS A dream of UPS forecasts that an important message is being quickly delivered to your doorstep. The dream is sending you the message to be alert and to receive that which is coming to you. See *Mail* or *Message.*

Upstairs Dreams of walking upstairs signify that you are moving up in the world, that you are elevating your consciousness and seeking a higher perspective. Dreams of upstairs also are a message to use your mind, logic, reasoning, and mental processes.

Upstream Dreams of swimming upstream denote that you are following your instincts and boldly asserting your beliefs regardless of the flow of the rest of the world. Consider whether or not your struggle is worth the price you pay. Alternatively, these dreams may reflect that you are being rebellious just for the sake of it. See *Salmon.*

Uranus Dreams of the planet Uranus may be forecasting a major life change, and/or that you will be making the most of your unusual talents and gifts.

Urgent Dreams of an urgent matter are helping you to vent out your stress about being caught in the illusion of time. Alternatively, they may be giving you the message that it is time for you to take action and to stop procrastinating. See *Processing Dreams,* page 7.

Urine Dreams of urine signify that you are releasing negativity, nonsupportive energy, so that *your in*stincts and *your in*tuition may flow more easily in your life. See *Laundromat/Laundry.*

Urn Dreams of an urn reflect your feelings and attitudes about death and dying. Perhaps you are hanging on to a relationship, clinging to the past, or wanting to salvage your memories. An urn is also a symbol of the human body, so a dream of one means that you are realizing your eternal connection with your family, and remembering that your experience here on earth is temporal, but the love you share is eternal.

Used Car Salesman Dreams of a used car salesman symbolize underhanded motives and opportunism. Perhaps you are dealing with trust issues and feeling taken advantage of or you are grappling with the aspect of you that just wants to make a buck. You are dealing with issues of integrity and realizing that what goes around comes around.

Usher If you dream of being an usher, then you are assisting others in their evolution. If you dream of being ushered, then you are realizing that you are divinely supported as you move through your life. See *Threshold*.

Uterus Dreams of a uterus symbolize your feelings and attitudes about pregnancy, motherhood, nurturing, and creativity. Perhaps you are pregnant with a great idea or you are in the beginning stages of a new chapter of your life. See *Vagina* and *Womb*.

V

Vacation Dreams of a vacation signify the need for a break from your daily routine. They may be giving you the message that you would be more effective in your job and in your relationships if you stepped away to gain some objectivity. See *Holiday* and *Traveling*. See also *Wish Fulfillment Dreams,* page 18.

Vaccination Dreams of a vaccination reflect a desire for protection and boundaries against undesirable influence and negativity.

Vacuum Cleaner Dreams of a vacuum cleaner symbolize your subconscious's attempt to clean up a mess. They may be telling you to make an apology or to forgive someone who has hurt you. Or they may reflect that someone in your life is having a "vacuum cleaner effect" on you, sucking your time and energy and leaving you feeling empty.

Vagina Dreams of a vagina signify your connection to your femininity, to the mother archetype, and to the Goddess. A vagina is also a symbol for openness, receptivity, sensuality, sexuality, the mystery of life, and fertility. See *Goddess* and *Uterus*.

Valedictorian Dreams of a valedictorian symbolize the perfectionistic aspect of you that is competitive, driven to make the grade and to be the best. See *A* and *Goddess* (Athena).

Valentine Dreams of a valentine represent true love, chivalry, and romance. You are in the honeymoon stage of love, feeling passion, desire, and sexuality. See *Goddess* (Aphrodite) and *Letter*.

Valet A dream of a valet signifies the aspect of self that is task-oriented, supportive, and helpful. Consider the feeling tone of the dream. If you dream of being the valet for someone else, then you may be venting out feelings of victimhood and of taking better care of others than you do of yourself. See *Parking Attendant*.

Valium Dreams of Valium reflect a desire for peacefulness and to escape and/or avoid pain. They may be showing you that you have detached yourself from your feelings and disassociated yourself from all the drama going on around you. See *Drugs*.

Valley Dreams of a valley symbolize stagnant feelings and desires that have not yet been expressed. You may be in a lull and moving through a depression. If you feel that you are moving through the valley of the shadow of death, having a "dark night of the soul," keep in mind that you are protected, guided, and cared for. See *Low Tide, Quicksand,* and *Swamp*.

Valve Dreams of a valve are about your ability to control, manipulate, and/or regulate the flow of abundance, joy, and creative energy in your life. If you dream that a valve is shut off, then you are realizing that you are at choice regarding turning it on.

Vampire Dreams of a vampire signify that you have either been abusing your power or been allowing someone else to suck your life force from you. They are a message for you to set healthy boundaries with needy people, to monitor your dependence upon the people in your life, and to tap into your unlimited source and supply that allow for a win-win situation for all involved.

Van Dreams of a van indicate that you are moving through life carrying a lot of cargo. You are capable of carrying people along with you, and you have a lot of resources and power. Consider the contents of the van. See *Car* and *Truck*.

Vanilla Dreams of vanilla signify that you are coming into a very sweet time in your life, or depending upon the association, they might also signify that you are playing it safe and taking a "middle of the road" approach to life.

Varnish Dreams of varnish signify that you are adding the final touch, the extra TLC, to refine and bring luster and beauty to a relationship or current project.

Vase Dreams of a vase symbolize your body, a container for beauty, and an ability to display your talents and beauty as they flower into form. See *Flowers.*

Vatican Dreams of this beautiful and grandiose church headquarters symbolize your feelings and opinions about the Catholic faith. The Vatican also symbolizes your body temple, a sanctuary where the human and the divine intersect. A dream of it may be a message to uplevel your spiritual practice and make it more of a central theme of your life. See *Catholicism, Church,* and *Pope.*

Vault Dreams of a vault signify your secret feelings and resources, and that perhaps you don't want people to know how powerful you truly are. Also they may be showing you that you have a great deal of untapped potential, uncultivated talent, and unrealized wisdom. Consider the contents of the vault. See *Treasure* and *Warehouse.*

Vegan/Vegetarian Dreams of a vegan or vegetarian indicate that you are paying close attention to the energy you are taking in and ingesting. You are in touch with your natural drives and instincts, and taking responsibility for the care of your animal instincts and of those that need your care. See *Vegetables.*

Vegetables Dreams of vegetables represent self-love, strength, and good health, and that you are taking care of your body's basic needs and well-being. See *Food.*

Veil Dreams of a veil reflect an element of mystery, surprise, secrecy, lack of disclosure, and intimacy. See *Mask.*

Vein Dreams of a vein signify that you are reaching out to connect with your family bloodline and ancestry, or that perhaps you are feeling the pride of your lineage or tribal roots. Also you may be trying to branch out and find your autonomy within the confines of your family's mythology and belief systems. Vein could also be wordplay for *vain,* as in *you're so vain!* See *Blood.*

Velvet Dreams of velvet symbolize luxury, wealth, extravagance, status, and elegance.

Venereal Disease Dreams of a venereal disease signify sexual guilt, blame, and shame, and that you are out of touch with your innocence and sexual beauty.

Venetian Blinds Dreams of venetian blinds represent a desire/need for privacy, intimacy, secrecy, and alone time away from the world for introspection, rest, and reflection.

Venom Dreams of venom signify that you are processing through and venting out fear-based words or actions that have injured you. You are realizing that when you harbor vengeful feelings or thoughts toward someone, you are the one who is poisoned. See *Snake*.

Vent Dreams of a vent signify the need for an emotional and/or psychological release. They may be telling you to let yourself cry and to find a supportive person to express your feelings to. See *Venting Dreams*, page 8.

Ventriloquist If you dream of being a ventriloquist, then you desire to have power over someone or to take control of a conversation. If you feel like the puppet that is being overpowered by a ventriloquist, then the dream is giving you the message to take your power back and reevaluate your beliefs and conditioning.

Vest Dreaming of a vest represents modesty, protection, and defensiveness around your heart and emotions. See *Goddess* (Athena or Hestia).

Veterinarian Dreams of a veterinarian signify that you are caring and have compassion for the innocent, helpless, sweet, and vulnerable parts of yourself. You are tending to and caring for your animal instincts.

Veto Dreams of a veto reflect your instinct and negative feelings about a situation. They are reminding you that you always have the right to say no. See *Boundary*.

Viagra Dreams of this passion-enhancing drug represent a desire for more potency, effectiveness, aliveness, and an upleveling of your virility, stamina, and sexiness. Perhaps you have a desire to res*erect* your passion for life or to rise to the occasion of a situation you are being called to handle.

Victim A dream of being a victim represents that you are resisting stepping into your power, claiming your greatness, and setting energetic boundaries. It is a venting dream in which you are releasing feeling powerless and small while everyone else seems big and powerful. The dream is giving you the message to heal your wounds and step into your power, even if it is a subtle, graceful power.

Victory Dreams of a victory reflect that you are successfully overcoming the obstacles that are in your life. They are giving you the message to celebrate and acknowledge your achievements.

Videotape Dreams of a videotape symbolize a desire to record events, hold on to the past, and reclaim your soul. See *Blockbuster Video, Movie,* and *Photograph.*

Village Dreams of a village reflect your feelings about family and community, as well as your level of integration with the various aspects of yourself. They might be an expression of your desire for support, belonging, and the power of synergizing resources with people who have a common goal.

Vine Dreams of a vine represent your connection with your family tree, ancestors, and friends. They might be showing you that you are being too clingy and attached to an identity, role, or to someone's love and support. It would be wise to find a sense of autonomy. See *Vein, Wine,* and *Web.*

Vinegar Dreams of vinegar forecast that you will be rewarded for dealing with an unpleasant person or bitter circumstance.

Vineyard Dreams of a vineyard signify that your hard work is paying off and you are coming into the fruition of your heart's desires. You are ripe with possibilities as you are harvesting your strengths and natural genius. A dream of a vineyard may be a message to be patient and know there will be no wine before its time.

Violence Dreams of violence are venting dreams that assist you in releasing hostility and destructive patterns. See *Knife.* See also *Venting Dreams,* page 8.

Viral Marketing Dreams of viral marketing represent your interconnectivity to all people, that you are never alone, and that we are all one. Also, they can reflect your participation in gossip or your desire to be in the know. See *Blog.*

Virginity Dreams of virginity reflect your connection to your innocence, naïveté, and trusting childlike essence. They are giving you the message to operate from the place of purity within, for this is where your wisdom resides. See *Goddess* (Artemis, Athena, and Hestia).

Virgin Mary If you dream of the Virgin Mary, then you are connecting with unconditional mother love and the highest expression of your feminine divinity. Consider the message she is sending you. See *Goddess*. See also *Prophetic Dreams,* page 17.

Virgo Dreaming of the astrological sign Virgo is telling you to remain vulnerable and humble while maintaining your high standards.

Virus If you dream that you or your computer has a virus, then this reflects betrayal, violation, and your fear of being invaded by a negative influence. The dream is telling you to set clear boundaries with people in your life who are not watching out for your highest good and to take precautions to defend what is precious to you. The dream may be a warning to take precautions to protect your assets in a more secure way. See *Fire Wall* and *Sick.*

Vise Dreams of a vise signify that you are between a rock and a hard place, under a great deal of pressure, perhaps being pushed from both ends, as you deal with conflicting needs within yourself. See *Processing Dreams,* page 7, and *Venting Dreams,* page 8.

Vision If you dream of a favorable vision of the future, then you are aligning yourself with that which you desire to manifest. If you dream of a future vision that is foretelling a particular event, then you are perhaps predicting the future. If you dream that your vision is impaired, then your subconscious mind is giving you the message that you have been shortsighted, and that it is time to step back and see the big picture. If you dream of having better vision than you normally have, then the dream is showing you that your instincts and intuition are right on, that you are seeing the truth. See *Precognitive Dreams,* page 15, and *Wish Fulfillment Dreams,* page 18.

Visitor Dreaming of a visitor is being reacquainted with a foreign part of yourself that you are in the process of integrating. Consider the qualities of the visitor. If you dream of being a visitor, then you are courageously exploring new terrain and are curiously open to learning new ways of thinking and being. Alternatively, you may be feeling that your space is being invaded energetically, physically, or psychically. Consider the feeling tone of the dream to discern the significance.

Vitamins Dreams of vitamins are a message to take better care of your body, mind, and spirit. If you dream of a particular type of vitamin, then consider that this may be a message to you about what your body is needing or missing.

Vlog Dreams of a vlog represent your need to visually express yourself. Perhaps you are expressing your desire to see and be seen, and to understand and to be understood. See *Blog*.

Voice If you dream of hearing a voice, then you are attuning yourself to your intuition and your ability to communicate telepathically. For a more precise understanding of the dream, consider whose voice you hear, the tone, and the words that are spoken.

Volcano See *Venting Dreams,* page 8.

Vomiting If you dream of vomiting, then you are purging negativity, guilt, shame, and undesirable energy or programming. You are also releasing resistance to creativity, love, and abundance that you desire. A dream of vomiting could be a message to find a healthy way to express and communicate your true feelings. See *Venting Dreams,* page 8.

Voodoo A dream of voodoo is giving you the message to be mindful of your judgments, fears, resentments, or the desire to wish ill will upon someone, because what you send out will come back to you. The dream is also giving you the message to shield yourself with light or a violet flame if you feel that someone is projecting negativity onto you. Consider that your willingness to pray for your enemies is the fast track to your own enlightenment.

Voting Dreams of voting signify that you are using your personal power and influence in a responsible way. You are realizing that your feelings, thoughts, and actions make a difference and that you have the ability to have a say in the matters of your life. Consider what you are voting on and whether you give it a thumbs-up or a thumbs-down.

Vows Dreams of vows symbolize your commitment to a higher vision, faithfulness, and devotion. Consider the content of your vows and what you are promising to whom. These dreams can also reflect your own issues and feelings about commitment. See *Commitment.*

Voyage Dreams of a voyage signify that you are taking an excursion into the waters of your unconscious, uncharted, sacred, sexual, mysterious, intuitive feminine, and mystical nature. They may be an integration dream where you are attempting to bring light to your shadow and shadow into your light. See *Journey.*

Voyeur Dreams of a voyeur reflect curiosity, and observation of a pattern or habit. Consider if you are the Peeping Tom or if you are the one being watched. These dreams may be telling you that if you are spending an inordinate amount of time peeping into the lives of other people, then perhaps it is time to become interested in your own life. If you feel violated by other people's interest in your life, then it is your responsibility to set clear boundaries. See *Stalking.*

Vulgar If you dream of something that you find to be vulgar, then you are venting out that which does not support you, and/or you are integrating a wild side of your nature that you have been resisting. See *Integration Dreams,* page 10, and *Venting Dreams,* page 8.

Vulture Dreams of a vulture symbolize your associations with victim/perpetrator archetypes. They may be showing you that you have been taking advantage of and preying on those less fortunate than you, or helping you to release feeling vulnerable to the attacks of people who are in a greater position of power than you.

W

Wading To dream of wading in a shallow pool represents trepidation of diving into the deeper waters of commitment, love, or intimacy. You may be gently easing your way into an exploration of a friendship or your own subconscious mind.

Waffles Dreams of waffles symbolize a treat, reward, or forthcoming special occasion. See *Breakfast.*

Wagon Dreams of a wagon signify that you are caring for people, carrying the concerns or burdens of others, with empathy, compassion, and a desire to be of service. Because there is no engine, you may be attempting to pull the weight by yourself. These dreams may be telling you to hitch up with the divine source that never runs out.

Waif A dream of a waif signifies that you are identifying with the aspect of you that is vulnerable, flimsy, helpless, childlike, and insecure. Perhaps you have given your power away and the dream is helping you to realize that you need it back. See *Victim*.

Waiter Dreams of a waiter reflect your attitudes and beliefs about service-oriented roles. They can also signify that you have been waiting for someone to do for you what you must do for yourself to take responsibility for the success of your career, financial well-being, health, vitality, or spiritual growth. Also, a waiter represents the serving, nurturing, caretaking aspect of yourself. Consider the feeling tone of a dream to discern its meaning.

Waking Up If you dream of waking up, then this is an attempt at lucidity, awakening, and enlightened consciousness.

Walking Dreams of walking suggest progress and that you are applying your will in a particular direction. You are feeling confident, capable, and powerful as you take forward strides in your life.

Walkman Dreams of a Walkman signify that you are tuning the world out while you tune into the music of your soul and walk to the beat of your own drum. See *iPod* and *Music*.

Wall Dreaming about a wall represents strength, reliability, support, and the people and beliefs that uphold your life. A dream of a wall could be showing you that you have built walls as barriers to keep love and intimacy at bay; or, alternatively, that you need to set healthy boundaries with people who demand too much of you. Also, it may be reflecting that you feel that your back is against a wall. Consider the feeling tone of the dream to discern its message for you.

Wallet Dreams of a wallet symbolize your sense of self-worth, identity, and personal importance. If you dream of your wallet being lost or stolen, then you are going through a transition and grappling with a changing sense of identity and security. See *Money* and *Purse*.

Wallflower Dreams of being a wallflower reflect your feelings of invisibility and a lack of importance. They are giving you the message that you must recognize yourself, your talents, and beauty before anyone else will. Also, they may be telling you to take notice of the things in life that you typically overlook. See *Transparent*.

Wallpaper Dreams of wallpaper represent the soft, decorative style you use to camouflage your boundaries or ego walls. See *Wall.*

Wall Street Dreams of Wall Street symbolize your financial attitudes, issues, fears, and desires. You are gambling with the fluctuation and allocation of your money, energy, and resources, and perhaps you are realizing the effect that your actions have on the web of humanity. Also, Wall Street can be wordplay for feeling that your life path is pre-paved or that you are walled in to a particular way of life.

Wal-Mart Dreams of Wal-Mart signify that you are being frugal with your resources, time, energy, and money. Consider what you are buying because it reflects the beliefs and mythology you are buying into. Seeing that Wal-Mart is a big corporation, you might be processing your feelings and associations about how you handle/will handle the responsibility of your power. See *Costco* and *Shopping.*

Walrus Dreams of a walrus reflect your sweet and blubbering feelings of adoration and love. Or you may be releasing feelings of sluggishness, laziness, apathy, and sloth.

Wand Dreams of a wand represent power and magic, and that you are realizing your ability to manifest your desires.

Want Ads Dreams about the want ads symbolize that you are unfulfilled in your current work, a relationship, or life situation, and that you are willing to expand your horizons and explore other opportunities. They may be helping you to realize the options available to you. Alternatively, they may be revealing your insatiability, and that you have the "grass is greener" syndrome, in which case, you are realizing that you can run but you can't hide from yourself. See *Craigslist* and *Job.*

Wanted Poster If you dream of someone in a wanted poster, consider that that person represents something or someone by whom you are being seduced. Perhaps the love you feel for the person with whom you *want* to be in a relationship is criminal, or maybe you are venting out and exposing your guilty feelings about him or her.

Wanting To dream of wanting something may be revealing what the needs, drives, and desires of the true you are, as opposed to the needs, drives, and desires of your public persona.

War Dreams of a war signify chaos, endings, and death, and that you are tearing down old belief structures and are undergoing massive transformation with regards to internal conflicts within yourself. Also, dreaming of war can be a venting dream helping you to process and release the shock and trauma from hostile circumstances in your life and in the world. See *Fight.* See also *Venting Dreams,* page 8.

Warden Dreams of a warden reveal a fear-based aspect of you that feels it is its job to keep your talent and true expression locked up and every action monitored and scrutinized. See *Critic* and *Jail/Jailer.*

Warehouse If a warehouse is full, then a dream of one is about abundance of resources and/or unfulfilled potential. It also may be about unfulfilled dreams of the past, memories, and ambitions you've put in storage. If a warehouse is empty, then a dream is telling you to pay attention to your finances, and begin to invest your time, money, and energy in ways that will create spiritual and material security for yourself.

Warm Dreaming that something is warm, whether it is a person, a towel, or a bowl of soup, signifies tender feelings, pleasure, comfort, and well-being. You are feeling hopeful, optimistic, balanced, and just right.

Warrant Dreams of a warrant signify that you are punishing yourself for something you did or didn't do that is against your own moral code. They are giving you the message to pay back your karmic debt and face any unfinished business from which you have been running.

Warrior Dreams of a warrior represent your connection to your source and power. You are discovering your heroism in the face of your fears. You are realizing that in the face of your greatest challenges is where you find your strength. See *Hero/Heroine* and *Shaman.*

Wart Dreams of a wart signify that you are feeling unworthy, and unattractive, and that there is a mark against you. Also, you may be identifying with the power of the witch or crone archetype. See *Pimples* and *Witch*.

Washing Dreams of washing are about healing, detoxing, and releasing negativity so that you may start again, fresh, cleansed, and renewed. Also, they may be giving you the message that it is time to clean up your act. See *Crying*.

Washing Machine If you dream that a washing machine is plugged in and well functioning, then you have a healthy energetic laundry system. However, if a washing machine is unplugged or malfunctioning, then this is a message to seek help to process through recent traumatic or overwhelming events in your life.

Wasp Dreaming of a wasp is being forewarned about being stung, hurt, shocked, criticized, or devastated by someone in your life, or alerted to the fact that you may still be carrying around a stinger from the past. Or perhaps a dream of a wasp is telling you to be more mindful of the words you speak, and of the impact your actions have on people.

Waste Dreams of waste may be a message to you that you have been squandering your talents and resources, and perhaps not valuing the gifts you have been given. As well, they are a message that you are cleansing and releasing that which is no longer useful to you. Consider the feeling tone of the dream to discern its message for you. See *Garbage*. See also *Venting Dreams,* page 8.

Watch Dreams about a watch represent a reality check, and a need to know what is really going on. They reflect your desire to be in touch with the three-dimensional world and to have your feet firmly planted on the ground. See *Clock*.

Watching If you are watching the scene that is being played out in your dream, then this is revealing that you are getting an objective view of your life and perhaps getting clarity about a situation that you previously could not make sense of.

Water Dreams about water are associated with emotions, sexuality, cleansing, healing, and indicate that you are exploring the infinite depth of your unconscious mind. You are connecting with the essence of your being, and are going with the flow. Because water is associated with the cycles of the tides, it is also associated with your feminine energy. So if you dream of water spilled on the floor, then this represents that your feminine side, creativity, or emotions are feeling out of control. If water is contained in a glass or jar, then you may be feeling that your feminine side, emotions, or creativity are being suppressed. If water is flowing, as through a hose or river, then this signifies that your feminine side, emotions, or creativity are in full flow. Keep in mind that you are, after all, made up of 90 percent water. See *Moon* or *Ocean*.

Water Balloon   If you dream of throwing water balloons, then you are playing games with your emotions, and trying your hand at manipulation. Dreams of a water balloon signify compartmentalized feelings and that you are attempting to contain, restrain, understand, and/or make light of the mystery of life.

Waterfall   Dreams of a waterfall signify surrender and that you are cleansing, purifying, and having an emotional catharsis. They also signify that you will have a continuous stream of wealth and abundance.

Watermelon   Dreams of a watermelon symbolize pregnancy, feminine strength, and tenderness. You are feeling ripe, juicy, and sensually delicious. See *Fruit*.

Water Sports   If you dream of Jet Skiing, water skiing, surfing, or participating in any water sport, then you are attempting to master or get control over your emotions and your understanding of your subconscious mind. If you dream that you are excelling in a water sport, then you have a degree of mastery over your feelings and emotions. If you dream that you are not doing well in a water sport, then you are working toward emotional understanding. See *Surfing*.

Wave   If you dream of waves, you are becoming aware and perhaps accepting of the ups and downs, highs and lows, ebbs and flows of the life/death/life cycle of life. If you are riding and/or surfing waves competently, with your head above water, you have a level of mastery with the emotions and cycles of life. If you are drowning or having a hard time keeping your head above water, then perhaps it would be good for you to take a reprieve on dry land before going back into the deep end of intimacy. If you are waving hello, then you are making an attempt at pleasantries, keeping the peace, and perhaps saluting the divine or offering a sign of recognition.

Wax Dreams of wax symbolize wealth, riches, being polished and refined in a superficial way. If you dream of a house of wax or a wax museum, then this is giving you the message to stop being disingenuous, or alternatively to stop being gullible to the falsities with which people are trying to impress you.

Weak If you dream of feeling weak, then you are venting out fears of being powerless. If you are used to playing a dominant role in life, then the dream is helping you to find balance, integration, and compassion.

Wealth Dreams of wealth are a sign that your subconscious mind is preparing you to receive more abundance, good health, good luck, love, and happiness.

Weapon Dreams of weapons symbolize the desire for protection, defense, and perhaps to end old patterns, or to kill off a habit or belief that is no longer serving you. Also they represent the fight for survival, and the terror of feeling that your life is being threatened. See *Gun* and/or *Knife*. See also *Breakdown/Breakthrough Dreams,* page 12.

Weapons of Mass Destruction Nightmares about weapons of mass destruction represent that you are venting out your fear of death, destruction, ego obliteration, and grand-scale annihilation. See *War*. See also *Venting Dreams,* page 8.

Weaving Dreams of weaving reflect synergy integration of your subpersonalities, talents, desires, experiences, and your mind, body, and spirit. See *Goddess* (Athena). See also *Integration Dreams,* page 10.

Web Dreams of a web are synonymous with joining forces, networking, and weaving your higher wisdom into real life. A web can also represent seduction, getting caught, and being tangled in a mass of lies. Perhaps you are in a sticky situation from which you want to escape, or you are attempting to lure someone into your embrace. See *Spider*.

Web site If you dream of having a Web site, then this represents your desire to catch people's attention, to announce yourself to the world, and to go public with your thoughts, opinions, and products. See *Blog, Computer,* or *Internet*.

Wedding A dream of a wedding symbolizes the joining of the opposite aspects of you—the masculine and feminine, the intellectual and emotional, the logical and intuitive, child and elder, and the divine and human. If there is fear or anxiety in the dream, you are venting out and releasing your trepidation about your own wedding, marriage, or fear of commitment. You are preparing yourself for great happiness. See *Commitment, Husband, Marriage,* and *Wife.*

Wedding Dress Dreams of a wedding dress symbolize your connection to your goddess lineage and the divine feminine. A wedding dress also denotes spiritual alchemy in that it turns an ordinary woman into a Goddess. A dream of a wedding dress is revealing your feelings, hopes, and desires about your wedding and marriage. See *Goddess* (Hera).

Wedding Planner Dreams of a wedding planner signify the pragmatic, rational aspect of you. Perhaps you have had your head in the clouds and your dream is a message to come back to earth.

Wedding Veil Dreams of a wedding veil symbolize suspense, secrecy, and the magical mystery of your relationship. You are realizing that you will never really know all there is to know about your beloved as you embrace the element of surprise in your partnership.

Weed Dreams of a weed represent negative, fear-based thoughts and patterns that don't serve you. If you dream of plucking weeds, then you are releasing these thoughts from the garden of your life. Also, weeds represent something that appears to be useless, but contains a hidden beauty and value. See *Integration Dreams,* page 10.

Weekend Dreams of the weekend symbolize a break, the desire for a vacation, a breather, and some time alone. See *Vacation.*

Weighing If you dream of weighing something, then you are evaluating and judging the pros and cons to discern its value and worth, and to determine whether or not it is for you.

Weight If you dream of lifting weights, then you are building up your emotional and psychological strength to handle the challenges you face or to carry a burden that has been weighing heavily on you. If you dream of being overweight or underweight, then this could be a venting dream assisting you to release your concerns with being unable to take control of your life. Alternatively, if you dream of something or someone that is heavy, then this can also reflect effectiveness, power, and status, as in a "heavy hitter." And perhaps a dream of weight is a message for you to carry your own weight. See *Heavy, Light,* and *Weighing.*

Well Dreams of a well reveal your depth and perhaps your desire to explore intimacy and connect more deeply with people. A well also represents the sacred feminine, the womb, the vagina, and the depth of your wisdom, sexual longing, heart's desires, and personal power. If you dream that a well is dry, then this means that you need some alone time and introspection to empower your well-being and fill your well. If you dream that a well is full, then this signifies that you are balanced and abundant. If you dream of being stuck at the bottom of a well, then you have gotten stuck in your depths, darkness, and pessimism and you are in need of levity, joy, and playfulness to bring yourself back into the light and into balance. See *Goddess* (Persephone).

Wench Dreams of a wench symbolize sloppiness, debauchery, alcoholism, and a lack of respect for your feminine and masculine selves. See *Prostitute* and *Tool.*

Werewolf Dreams of a werewolf signify your connection and integration with your animal instincts, and that you have been perhaps overindulging in your base needs and desires. They might also be showing you that you have been predatory and/or that you have been taking without reciprocation. See *Animal* and *Vampire.*

West The direction of west represents a need for introspection, connection to your intuition and depth and to the element of water. You are moving toward the completion of a chapter in a relationship or project, or toward a wild adventure that will bring you fortune and fame. See *Autumn* and *Water.*

Wet Suit Because when a wet suit is worn, a person resembles marine life, a dream of it signifies your desire to connect with the ocean of your emotions or to go swimming in the deep end of inti-ma*sea.* Dreaming of a wet suit can also signify a false security to keep your ego warm, incubated, and safe from getting hurt in a relationship. See *Fish.*

Whale Dreams of a whale signify that you are in touch with your enormous, oceanic power, intuition, and reproductive drive. Grand-scale opportunities are flowing to you as you prepare for a whale of a time. This may be a message for you to use your power discriminately and take responsibility for your largesse.

Wheat Dreams of wheat symbolize your drive to provide physical and spiritual sustenance for your children and/or those who depend on you. You are coming into a time of great wealth and abundance. See *Goddess* (Demeter).

Wheel Dreams of a wheel symbolize wholeness, wisdom, integration of the whole of you, and your realization of the life/death/life cycle of life. They can also be about eternal life, everlasting love, and the infinity of your spirit. Consider the condition of a wheel and whether it is spinning in place, going somewhere, squeaking, rusty, or stagnant. If you are behind the wheel of a car, then you are in control and are taking responsibility for where your life is headed. See *Mandala* and *Medicine Wheel*.

Wheelchair Dreams of a wheelchair represent the need for support during a challenging time. You are grappling with a real or imagined handicap, perhaps physical, emotional, or spiritual. These dreams are a message that there is an aspect of your life that is in need of attention, healing, and nurturing.

Wheel of Fortune Dreams of a wheel of fortune signify that you are taking a gamble on life, hoping for a miracle, and that your luck is about to change. Your life has just taken a spin on the karmic wheel, and you may be feeling out of control or overwhelmed. A dream of a wheel of fortune is giving you the message to connect with your center of spiritual strength, that which is changeless and solid, and you will come through the changing times more powerful and wiser than ever.

Whip Dreams of a whip signify that you are exposing, venting, and releasing the punishment, judgment, and criticism of your inner critic that is disapproving of your actions and choices. They are revealing how your inner critic uses pain in a vain attempt to positively motivate your behavior. See *Sting* and *Wasp*.

Whirlwind A dream of a whirlwind is about feeling overwhelmed while you are in the midst of a major transformation. It is giving you the message to find your center, the eye of the storm, a solid place to stand, and a nonresistant attitude that will allow you to be unruffled by the winds of change. See *Wind.* See also *Breakdown/ Breakthrough Dreams,* page 12.

Whiskers Dreams of whiskers signify the need for protection, defensiveness in communication and intimacy, and that your animal instincts are feeling out a situation.

Whisper Dreams of a whisper indicate secrecy, mystery, caution, and that you are feeling the need to be discerning about with whom you share your thoughts and feelings.

Whistle Dreams of a whistle are a message from your subconscious mind telling you to pay attention and be alert because something important is being revealed.

White Dreams of the color white symbolize innocence, surrender, peace, and protection. See *Chakra* (7th) and *Color.*

Wholesale If you dream of purchasing something at a wholesale price, then you are hunting for a bargain, grappling with what you are willing to pay to get what you need, and considering whether or not it is worth the price. See *Retail Therapy* and *Shopping.*

Widow Dreams of a widow symbolize your feelings, attitudes, or beliefs about being alone or self-sufficient, losing your role as wife, loneliness, or being without the need for a man. Or perhaps you have killed off your inner masculine self, and disowned your power and effectiveness in the world. See *Crone* and *Witch.*

Wife A dream of a wife reflects your feelings and associations with marriage, and your projections about what a woman's role in a wedded partnership should be. Consider the feeling tone to discern its message for you. You are either feeling in need of the goddess archetype that stabilizes home and family, or you are grappling with resistance, rebellion, or feelings of betrayal toward this domestic archetype. See *Goddess* (Hera).

Wig Dreams of a wig symbolize false power, ideas, or thoughts. Also, they represent the desire to be in disguise or that you or someone in your life is being disingenuous. Consider the style and color of the wig, and how it makes you feel. See *Hair.*

Will A dream about a will reflects that you are coming to terms with your mortality and are contemplating the value you feel that your life has, your sense of self-worth, and the contribution/difference you feel that you have made with your gifts and talents to the people in your life. The dream could also be a literal message to put your affairs in order, to tie up your loose ends, and consider the legacy you will leave behind. If you dream of being the beneficiary in someone's will, see *Inheritance*.

Win To dream of winning a competition symbolizes an upcoming victory or accomplishment. See *Sports*. See also *Wish Fulfillment Dreams*, page 18.

Wind Dreams of wind are a symbol of divine will, change, mysterious blessings, and creative inspiration that is moving and influencing you. See *Hurricane* or *Whirlwind*.

Window Dreams of a window symbolize your ability to be psychic or to glimpse the truth of what is really going on in your life. They are a sign to do some introspection into your soul and deeper feelings and emotions. If you are on the inside looking out, then you are looking to gain a broader perspective, perhaps a more worldly view. If you are on the outside looking in, then you may be feeling like an outsider with a desire to be a part of the life happening inside. A dream of a window may also be a message that an unexpected opportunity will be coming to you, as in "when a door closes, a window opens."

Wine Dreams of wine signify that you are celebrating a victory and/or are drunk in love. Your ego walls are melting as you release your inhibitions and express how you really feel. Also, wine signifies your family and ancestral bloodlines. Consider that because alcohol lends itself to intoxication, you are opening up to mysterious realms of your being. Consider your associations with wine and the feeling tone of the dream.

Wine Cellar Dreams of a wine cellar signify that you are cultivating a secret that enriches your soul and becomes more valuable over time. You are learning patience as you recognize your reservoir of underground mysteries and magic. See *Wine*.

Wings Dreams of wings symbolize a desire for freedom, abandon, glory, self-expression, and to take flight from the confines of your earthbound life so that you may feel a closer connection to God/Goddess/Spirit. See *Bird* and *Flying*.

Wink Dreams of a wink signify that you are flirting or that you are in on the secret that life is a game and you have already won. Consider the feeling tone of the dream.

Winter Dreams of winter represent the completion of a cycle, death, and emotional/sexual coldness, and that you are embracing the wisdom that comes from hindsight.

Wire Dreams of a wire may signify that you are feeling electrically connected to someone, feeling the sparks and heat of your chemistry. Also, they signify your feelings, thoughts, and motivations that take place behind the scenes. Perhaps you are feeling a desire to connect with someone or to rewire your thoughts and feelings in a way that aligns you with a higher being.

Wireless If you dream of a wireless phone or a wireless connection, then this signifies that you feel connected with someone yet completely free, autonomous, and interdependent. See *BlackBerry, Cell Phone, Laptop,* and *Microphone*.

Wise Man/Wise Woman Dreams of a wise man or wise woman symbolize guidance, an enlightened message, and connection to your inner crone, witch, grandmother, grandfather, sorcerer, goddess, or guru. See *Prophetic Dreams,* page 17.

Wishbone Dreams of pulling apart a wishbone forecast good luck. If you end up with the long side of a wishbone, then you are realizing that your wish will come true and that your optimism will create miracles in your life. If you end up with the short side of a wishbone, then you are releasing your doubts about your dreams coming true. See *Wish Fulfillment Dreams,* page 18.

Wishing Well Dreams of a wishing well are a symbol of good luck, and that you are in the process of manifesting the reality of your desires. See *Wish Fulfillment Dreams,* page 18.

Witch If you feel empowered by a dream of a witch, this signifies your irreverent power and ability to create magic in your life. If you feel weakened or scared by the dream, then you are running from your power, and are afraid of the negative influence it could have. See *Crone*.

Wite-Out Dreams of Wite-out symbolize a desire to release and let go of past transgressions, correct your mistakes, make amends, and forgive and forget a hurtful word or deed.

Witness Dreams of a witness symbolize your objectivity, clarity, and lucidity over your current life situation. Also, they may be showing you where you disconnect or disassociate from challenging situations and emotions.

Wizard Dreams of a wizard symbolize enchantment, multidimensional power, lucidity, and your ability to cut through the limitation of the five senses and manifest magically. See *Magician* and *Shaman*. See also *Prophetic Dreams,* page 17.

Wolf Dreams of a wolf signify that you are finding your true path as you are connecting with your feelings of fidelity, loyalty, strength, psychic power, and protectiveness over your family and loved ones while maintaining your autonomy and individuality. These auspicious dreams signify that it is time to claim your authority, step into your power, and transition from student to teacher. Consider that in order to do this you may need to claim some alone time and reconnect with the cycles of the moon. See *Animal* and *Moon.*

Woman A dream of a woman is about your connection to the goddess, the feminine archetype, to cycles, intuition, softness, and sensitivity. If you are a man, then the dream may be a message for you to get in touch with your feminine side. If you are a woman, then it is about your feelings, attitudes, and acceptance of your femininity. Consider the feeling tone of the dream and the qualities you ascribe to the female. See *Daughter, Goddess, Grandmother, Mother,* and *Sister.*

Womb Dreams of a womb symbolize a desire for protection, unconditional love, nurturing, and a supportive space in which to grow, heal, and be taken care of. Perhaps you are giving birth to a new idea, project, relationship, or aspect of yourself. You may be craving connection with your mother or with the divine feminine. See *Goddess.*

Wood Dreams of wood signify your potential, raw talents, and inner resources to create, build, and manifest your visions into reality. Wood can also represent the absence of emotion, that you are shocked or trying to be invulnerable to pain or heartache. Consider the feeling tone of the dream to discern the meaning for you.

Woodpecker Dreams of a woodpecker signify that opportunity is knocking on your door. You are grappling with persistent challenges that are spurring you into growth. A dream of a woodpecker can also be wordplay for *penis,* male sexuality.

Wool Dreams of wool represent a desire for warmth, comfort, and nurturing. They may be giving you the message that you have been naive, allowing the wool to be pulled over your eyes.

Work Usually dreams about your work signify that your subconscious mind is attempting to give you solutions, answers, and clarity to help you work out your unfinished business of the day. See *Processing Dreams,* page 7.

Workaholic A dream of a workaholic is a sign from your subconscious mind that you might be more productive if you took a break. Perhaps you are working out and releasing your feelings of inadequacy, your misconceptions about not being enough, and the illusion that self-*worth* and self-*work* are one and the same.

World Dreams of the world, or of the globe, symbolize your universal awareness, feelings of unification, global concern, and compassion for people outside your day-to-day life. Perhaps you are expanding the sphere of your influence, awareness, mission, and/or vision. See *Earth* and *People.*

World Trade Center Dreams of the World Trade Center represent your financial structures. And though they may fall, your inner wealth and well-being cannot be shaken. Consider that the tower in the tarot represents destruction that precedes transformation and new beginnings. Twin towers can also represent that which holds up the temple of your being, the tension of opposites, and the integration of your polarities—the dark and light, the masculine and feminine, etc. See *Tower.*

World Wide Web Dreams of the World Wide Web represent your connectivity to global consciousness; you are searching for a portal of inspiration, connection, insight, opportunity, awareness, and expansiveness.

Worm Dreams of a worm symbolize sneakiness and a desire to be unnoticed as you inch through your life. You may be feeling insignificant and worthless because you have been feeding on negativity that keeps you feeling small.

Worship Dreams of worshipping someone reflect your ability to recognize the beauty, value, and magic in yourself and others. If you have put someone on a pedestal, then the dream may be a sign to remember that you are above and below no one. See *Pedestal*.

Wound Dreams of a physical or emotional wound denote your awareness of the aspect of yourself that is in need of attention, nurturing, and healing. Consider the location of the wound, and realize that you cannot heal what you cannot feel. Keep in mind that once you are healed in the area of your life where you've been the most wounded, this is where you develop your greatest wisdom, strength, creativity, compassion, and contribution to others. See *Breakdown/Breakthrough Dreams,* page 12.

Wreath The circular shape of a wreath represents the full circle of life, your wholeness, and connectivity to the universal oneness.

Wreck Dreams of a wreck signify a major life overhaul and a wake-up call. Consider what has been wrecked, and realize that transformation is taking place in that area. A dream of a wreck could also be a warning to become more attentive and present in your life. See *Breakdown/Breakthrough Dreams,* page 12.

Wrecking Ball A dream of a wrecking ball signifies that you are tearing down an old, outmoded system in order to build up a new structure that is better, stronger, and more powerful. The transformation you are in the midst of is a shock to your system, and the dream is giving you the message to be gentle with yourself as you move through this rite of passage. See *Wreck*. See also *Breakdown/ Breakthrough Dreams,* page 12.

Wrestle To dream of wrestling signifies that you are grappling with conflicting needs, feeling the tension of opposite aspects of yourself creating an inner conflict, and/or are engaged in the process of conquering your greatest fears.

Wrinkles Dreams of wrinkles denote your feelings and associations with aging and the value of wisdom and hindsight that comes from having been around the block. If you dream of a wrinkled article of clothing, then you are feeling unkempt, worn-out, and unpresentable. Consider the feeling tone of the dream to discern the message for you.

Wrist Dreams of a wrist represent flexibility, receptivity, and generosity. If you dream of having wrist pain, then this signifies rigidity and that you are moving through challenges regarding giving, receiving, and going with the flow of the universe.

Writing Dreams of writing signify that you may be "righting" a wrong, creating and manifesting your heart's and soul's desires, or you are realizing the power of the written word to manifest, correct, mutate, change, and/or create reality. Dreams of handwriting, as opposed to printed or typed words, represent emotions, feeling, expressiveness, and personal style. The most significant aspects of these dreams are the words you write as well as the pressure with which words are written. The heavier the pressure, the more impassioned the message. Consider the content of what you are writing as well as the feeling tone.

X

Xbox Dreams of playing with an Xbox signify a desire to win, and to become an expert in the art of strategy and game playing. You are activating your sense of courage, adventure, and heroism.

Xerox Dreams of a Xerox machine signify that you are grappling with issues of originality versus copying someone else's style. They may also be a message to back up your work, and release your concerns of being copied, because imitation is the greatest form of flattery. See *Kinko's*.

X-Files Dreams of *The X-Files* signify that you are willing to investigate beyond the surface of things, to look at what may at first be shocking to your belief system. You have the courage to discover who you truly are.

X-rated If you dream of pornography or sexually explicit material, then this represents unfulfilled sexual desire and perhaps repressed sexual feelings. Perhaps your dreams are sending you the message to find a healthy way of integrating your natural sexuality into your waking life. See *Sex*.

X-ray Dreams of an X-ray signify that you have a desire to know the microscopic truth, to read between the lines and see what is really going on in a relationship, in your job, and/or with regards to your physical health and vitality. You are realizing that the truth shall set you free.

Y

Yacht Dreams of a yacht symbolize your desire for luxury, abundance, freedom, and connection with the ocean of your emotions. See *Boat*.

Yard Dreams of a yard signify that you are measuring your personal growth; you are improving, stretching, and making strides toward your most successful expression. Also, these dreams could be a reminder to you that the treasures you seek are always in your own backyard. See *Garden*.

Yarmulke Dreams of a yarmulke signify that you are protecting your thoughts from adverse elements, holding tight to your belief systems, and honoring your connection to the divine as sacred. See *Hat*.

Yarn Dreams of yarn are a message to be careful not to get unraveled by life circumstances. Perhaps you are becoming aware of your fixed patterns and routines. Also, a dream of yarn might be giving you the message to be mindful that the stories you weave are ones that empower you and those around you.

Yawn Dreams of a yawn signify that you are disinterested, disenchanted, bored, and tired of your current circumstances. They may be telling you to stretch yourself beyond your comfort zone and try something new.

Year Dreams of a year signify the completion of a cycle of growth, a period of learning, a mark of advancement, and maturation. See *Anniversary* or *Birthday*.

Yeast Dreams of yeast represent that you are realizing that what you invest your energy in will rise, grow, and manifest. You have the ability to lift off, perk up, and rise above your circumstances.

Yelling Dreaming of yelling represents the expression of emotions that you normally suppress in waking life. A dream of yelling reflects your desire to be uninhibited, unabashed, and passionate, and that you are calling forth a change or manifestation in your life. Consider the feeling tone of the dream and whether it is an exclamation of anger, warning, joy, ecstasy, or help.

Yellow Dreams of yellow signify that you are scared, timid, and afraid. Yellow is also associated with the sun, which stands for power, illumination, summertime, lightness of being, optimism, and light. Consider the feeling tone. See *Color*.

Yes Dreams of saying yes signify a willing spirit, a courageous heart, and a trusting soul. You are receptive and open to the influence of the person or thing you are saying yes to. Identify if your "yes" comes from a true place within you, or is an obligatory social nicety.

Yin and Yang If you dream about the yin and yang symbol, then this reflects your inner balance of your masculine and feminine energies, centeredness, and wholeness.

Yoga Dreams of yoga represent a need or desire for balance of your body, mind, and spirit. They also represent your ability to be flexible, harmonious, and peaceful as you stretch beyond your comfort zone. You are gaining strength and wisdom from your ability to breathe through and overcome your life challenges.

Yolk Dreams of a yolk represent fertility in business, relationships, and/or your creative endeavors. They can also symbolize pregnancy, or a fertile time for creativity. See *Egg*.

Yourself When you dream of yourself, as if from another person's perspective, this reveals objectivity and lucidity. Consider the way you see yourself and what you observe regarding your true self or your public persona.

Yo-yo Dreams of a yo-yo signify that you have been emotionally erratic, and unable to make up your mind. They are your message to stop and drop into the silence and to allow your guidance to emerge from your centeredness. See *Yin and Yang*.

Z

Zealot Dreams of a zealot represent your passionate opinions and an intense need to express them. They may be warning you that your fanaticism is off-putting and to respect the validity of the opinions of others. See *Yelling*.

Zebra Dreams of a zebra symbolize the integration of your polarities, and the power you are capable of having when all aspects of you harmoniously synergize. See *Integration Dreams,* page 10.

Zenith Dreams of a zenith signify your ability to see the big picture, that you are having an "aha" moment, connecting with your intention for being alive, and are realizing who you really are.

Zero Dreams of a zero represent nothingness, emptiness, or that you are starting over. If there are a lot of zeros, then this forecasts wealth, abundance, and success. Zero also represents the full circle of life, the feminine symbol of space, the womb, secrets, mystery, hidden knowledge, a void, receptivity, wisdom, and the value of your intangible intuition, feelings, and mystery. Consider the feeling tone of the dream to discern its message for you.

Zip Line Dreams of a zip line represent that you are moving swiftly and joyously from one place in your life to another. Consider the feeling tone of the dream and whether or not you feel that you have a handle on these rapid moves and changes in your life.

Ziplock Bag Dreams of a Ziplock bag symbolize your desire to keep a secret sealed, or to preserve your true feelings. You might feel that you need to zip your lips until you feel it is safe to express yourself.

Zipper Dreams of a zipper signify that you are opening and closing yourself to intimacy. Perhaps you are feeling tentative about revealing your secrets and/or exposing your true feelings. Consider whether the zipper is opened or closed.

Zircon A dream of a zircon signifies that you are settling for second best. You desire true love and a magnificent life, and the dream is helping you to vent out feelings of unworthiness to have the quality of life that you desire.

Zone Dreams of being in the zone signify that you are resonating with your highest self, you are in your center, connecting with your source, and creating a powerful reference point of success, joy, and fulfillment for yourself. See *Wish Fulfillment Dreams,* page 18.

Zone Diet Dreams of the Zone Diet signify your desire for optimum health and youthful vitality. This dream reveals your willingness to trim the fat out of your life by eliminating all that no longer serves you while you amplify your passion and desire for living the life of your dreams. See *Diet.*

Zoo Dreams of a zoo symbolize your primal urges, sexual drives, and protective instincts in their multifaceted splendor. Alternatively, the fact that the animals are caged may be giving you the message to unleash your natural urges and let your true feelings roam free. See *Animal.* See also *Integration Dreams,* page 10.

Zucchini Dreams of zucchini represent a healthy sexual appetite, and the desire for good, clean, sensual pleasure. See *Vegetables.*

KELLY SULLIVAN WALDEN is a dream coach who specializes in empowering people so they can live the life of their dreams. As a certified clinical hypnotherapist, ordained interfaith minister, human design analyst, Goddess Queen Gathering facilitator, inspirational speaker, and popular media guest, Kelly blends the art of dream analysis into her holistic coaching style. Kelly's approach to dream analysis is old wine in new wineskins. With her classically Jungian style, she weaves Buddhism, Hinduism, Shamanism, Goddess archetypes, religious science, and her respect for the mystical core of all major religions into her dream symbols and interpretations. As a practical mystic and leader in the modern Goddess movement, Kelly offers a perspective that uplifts and empowers women and men to dream themselves awake. Kelly's grounded, accessible, and entertaining approach will inspire you to live the life of your dreams.

Kelly lives in the Hollywood Hills, California, with her husband, Dana, and dog, Woofie.

Kelly is the author of the following books and CDs (available at www.goddessqueen.com and www.goddessqueenmagazine.com): *Discover Your Inner Goddess Queen* (Goddess Queen Unlimited), *Goddess Queen Pearls of Wisdom Journal* (Goddess Queen Unlimited), *Goddess Queen Visioning Journeys* (Goddess Queen Unlimited), *Turn Your Drama into Phenomena* (Goddess Queen Unlimited).

Contact Kelly at www.ihadthestrangestdream.com